A History of
CHILDREN'S
BOOKS
IN 100 BOOKS

Roderick Cave and Sara Ayad

BRITISH LIBRARY

For Dawn, children's librarian, and wife, mother, grandmother
– without whom this book would not have been written.

Words in **bold type** are defined in the Glossary.

First published in 2017 by
The British Library
96 Euston Road
London NW1 2DB

Cataloguing in Publication Data
A catalogue record for this publication is available
from The British Library

ISBN 978 0 7123 5698 5

Designed and typeset by Briony Hartley, Goldust Design
Printed and bound in Hong Kong by Great Wall Printing Co. Ltd.

Half title: Richard Doyle, *In Fairy Land: A Series of Pictures from the*
Elf-World. With a Poem by William Allingham. London: Longmans,
Green, and Co., 1870. The British Library.
Frontispiece: Robert Michael Ballantyne, *The Coral Island ... With*
illustrations by the author. London: T. Nelson & Sons, 1858.
The British Library.

A History of
CHILDREN'S
BOOKS
IN 100 BOOKS

THE CORAL ISLAND

a Tale of the

PACIFIC

OCEAN

CONTENTS

INTRODUCTION

This book is a survey of the history of books read to, or by, children: for the most part, those from Britain or the former British Empire, but also including children's books from the United States, the continent of Europe, and a few from further afield as well.

The idea for this book came from a book in our own collection, *Robinson Crusoe in Words of One Syllable* by one 'Mary Godolphin' (the pseudonym of Lucy Aikin, 1781–1864), published by McLoughlin Brothers in New York in 1882. In looking at this volume, with its cheerful, brightly coloured and charmingly illustrated pasted-paper boards, it struck us that children's books have their own story to tell. Battered on all edges and missing much of its spine, foxed on the title page, its endpapers scribbled on, and even with one or two small inky fingerprints staining the pages here and there, it was clear this book had, as an object, a *forensic* interest to the cultural historian. Such books invite a different way of looking at them than adult literature might, to do with their life outside the printed page. Keen readers may never (we hope) grow out of the joy they learned as infants in discovering where books could take them, but as adults they seldom as fully *inhabit* their books as child readers do. Children's books in themselves are objects, to be perused for hours on end, or thrown rapidly aside; with unpleasant or scary pages to be skipped over; to be read aloud to them by a parent, or to be read to oneself, perhaps painstakingly slowly, following the text with a finger; and, for babies, there to be gazed at, patted, sucked or chewed. How many infants and even adolescents have coloured in pages, scribbled their own illustrations on the endpapers or

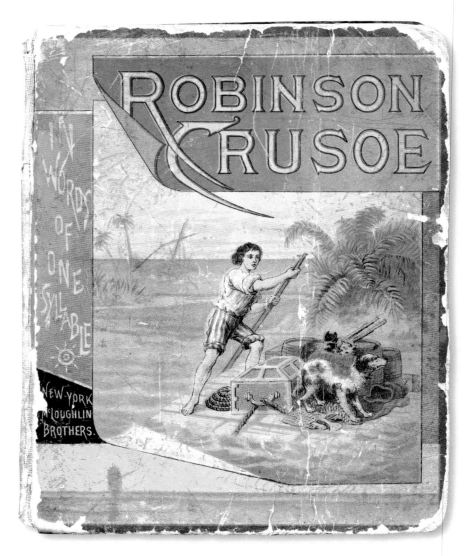

loudly crayonned their names upon them ['My Book']?

So, in writing about books intended for children, we necessarily have a different scope and content. Although there is evidence from the earliest times about the care and attention which has been given to educating children (and this book includes one tablet from Sumeria inscribed over 4,000 years

Mary Godolphin (pseud. of Lucy Aikin), *Robinson Crusoe in Words of One Syllable*. New York: McLoughlin Brothers, 1882.

Author's collection

ago), much of this was left to women, and much of this belongs to oral history: early educators and child carers left relatively few written records about their work. There is plenty of *anecdotal* evidence about how children were reared, clothed and fed, but very little about the thoughtful, deliberate production of books for child readers, until enterprising London publishers in the early 18th century saw a potential market. The market for very young, or pre-readers, that is, for **toy books** and such for the nursery, emerged later, in the 19th century.

In this book, we have concentrated on picture books and books read *to* or *by* children in the context of contemporary juvenile publishing, which is now a large, flourishing and highly competitive industry. Looking at those books which children have read in the past was important in our selection of the 'one hundred' books to include here. We have talked to many friends and acquaintances about the books they read as children. Some people had near-total recall of the importance of reading, for instance, *Robinson Crusoe* or *Anne of Green Gables*. Others said with complete honesty that they couldn't remember *any* of the books that were read to them: 'I know my mother did read to me, [but] I don't remember which ones I might have loved or asked to have read to me again and again.' One friend gave us a detailed list of books he read in Patagonia during the Second World War, and his list was remarkably similar to one of the present authors' memories of reading material available to him in wartime Britain. Another friend, from a tropical country, could recall only the excerpts of books included in her school **readers** (see Chapter 4).

In addition to our interviews with people from many different parts of the world, we studied and took note of recommended or loved books in many autobiographies and biographies; memoirs of governesses and

teachers, publishers' and collectors' catalogues, and many other sources too. But a lot of children's books have only a relatively short life in people's memories: apart from cultural historians, does anybody now read *The Wide Wide World* (1850) or *Queechy* (1852) by 'Elizabeth Wetherell', over which so many 19th-century girls reportedly wept?

The 'half-life' of children's books varies wildly. As one young novelist whom we contacted wrote, 'I wore out my copy of *The Secret Garden* [and] read and re-read all of the *Anne of Green Gables* books.' Her use of the verb to 're-read' is significant: for many children, the very repetition of passages in favourite stories provides much of the pleasure – and woe betide the tired or bored parent who tries to skip passages when re-reading *The Enormous Turnip* for the *nth* time. Although an individual child inevitably grows beyond the enjoyment of reading or re-reading a particular title, some books retain their half-lives for many years within a family, with the same story being passed down through the generations. In the same way, nursery (and playground) rhymes continue to be repeated, sometimes unconsciously changed and re-made anew.

Historically, such repetition was often disliked, or even feared, by those people who wanted to change and to direct the life (and ideas) of the child. The quotation attributed to the Jesuits, 'Give me a child for the first seven years, and you may do what you like with him afterwards', underpinned many beliefs about children's upbringing, and many educationalists and politicians (including Lenin) shared the same way of thinking. The ideas of John Locke in the late 17th century, and Jean-Jacques Rousseau some sixty years later, had an enormous effect on the books written specifically for children after juvenile publishing emerged as an important, and sometimes very profitable, branch of the book trade in the 18th century. Increasingly, women undertook a significant role. By the early 19th century, it was possible for women (however invisible, underpaid or exploited) to earn a living by illustrating or writing children's books.

Books for children, whether intended for education or for diversion, in the past seldom received much serious attention from scholars, or indeed book historians. People like Samuel Johnson (so Hester Thrale Piozzi reported in her *Anecdotes*, 1786) dismissed Newbery's books for children as:

> ... too trifling to engage their attention. 'Babies do not want (said he) to hear about babies; they like to be told of giants and castles, and of somewhat which can stretch and stimulate their little minds.' When in answer I would urge the numerous editions and quick sale of *Tommy Prudent* or *Goody Two Shoes*: 'Remember always (said he) that the parents buy the books, and that the children never read them.'

It was possibly a reasonable assumption by Johnson – but recent investigations into reading at Rugby School have shown that in fact schoolboys both bought, and read, *Goody Two Shoes*. Adult assumptions about children – and their reading – are often faulty.

The history of children's reading is full of mistakes, misunderstandings and misrepresentations. In her *Essay on Christian Education*, the formidable Sarah Trimmer proclaimed that 'There is not a species of books for Children and Youth which has not been made in some way or other an engine of mischief.' How, in our survey of children's books, could the authors select which of these 'engines of mischief' to include?

An attempt to identify these 100 books as 'classics' would surely be counter-productive, as according to André Brink, 'Any "Classic" which is forced upon one becomes a dead weight, like Bunyan's sanctimonious

verbiage'; or, in Julie Burchill's equally acid remark, 'calling a book a classic is the quickest way to put children off them at school'. Waterstones' survey, *The Test of Time: What Makes a Classic a Classic?* (1999), from which these quotations were taken, interestingly included hate lists of certain classics, with Richard Beswick's response to *The House at Pooh Corner* being perhaps the funniest of the lot: 'I agree with Dorothy Parker: "Tonstant Weader Fwowed Up".'

Such lists of dislikes are often very useful for helping readers understand why books might succeed or fail with child readers, although of course there is no single 'child reader'; their reading appetites and responses to books are as wide-ranging, eccentric and varied as adults'. When a writer of the stature of A. S. Byatt includes the stories of Beatrix Potter among those which influenced her in her decision to become a writer, it is illuminating. But then again, we needed no recommendation of Potter's books. When a friend in New Zealand was emphatic that we really *should* include Juan Ramón Jiménez's *Platero y Yo* (*Platero and I*), we had to think long and hard; Jiménez was highly regarded in Latin America and the Swedish judges had selected his work for the Nobel Prize for Literature. In the end lack of availability – British publishers have done little to introduce him in English editions – made us decide to leave *Platero* out. Other children's books very highly regarded in non-English-speaking countries, such as Jan Karafiát's Czech classic *Broučci* (*Fireflies*), or, more recently, books by the Belgian writer Kitty Crowther or the Argentinian Isol, have so far failed to appear in English editions.

Nowadays there are many deserving and good-quality books for children. Authors, publishers and others in the entertainment industries are well aware of the huge financial awards that may be accrued by a few authors like J. K. Rowling (for example), and hope to repeat her success. From the relative dearth of good books for children in early Victorian times, as Mrs Molesworth reported in her once-popular book *Carrots* (1876), nowadays informed critics emphasise the range of books available. The online journal *Books for Keeps* comments that 'for every book that makes a shortlist [for a book award], there will be others, just as good, that couldn't'.

Because children's tastes change as they grow older, their response to those books encountered too early or too late can be significant. Liz Attenborough, formerly of the National Literacy Trust, judged that 'books like *The Water Babies* or *Lorna Doone* are really not best suited to anyone at the start of their reading career', and almost every reader could name similar 'misses'.

A reader's age is not the only factor: in her perceptive account *Howard's End Is on the Landing: A Year of Reading from Home* (2009) Susan Hill wrote, 'One reason why some children's authors attain popularity among their young readers is, of course, because adults disapprove of them. It was one of the reasons we were all so devoted to Enid Blyton.' Hill thought adults disapproved of Roald Dahl 'because he believed life was a continuing war between them and children, and he was always and everywhere on the side of the latter'. Young readers quickly sense if they are being condescended to.

In this volume we mention briefly many other authors and books as well as the hundred we selected. Our one hundred books emphatically are *not* the 'classics', or the 'Best'; they include volumes because they are rather interestingly bad or objectionable, and many for which children today would not be grateful. We attempt to survey significant developments in book production and distribution over the past few hundred years, and so the books selected have been chosen for many different reasons – perhaps because they were typical of certain styles of writing, different commercial practices or changes in readers' tastes. The children's book industry is just that, a trade. Rather too few book historians, or those studying children's books, pay much attention to trade conditions; the significant roles played by designers and editors are also often ignored.

Every reader of our book will have their own preferred choices, and may be dismayed or incredulous that his or her favourite is not included. It seems that the majority of readers feel strongly about the books they read as children. In researching for this book, we heard the phrase 'You must!', again and again. Ours is a personal guide only, from our own perspective as early and mid-century British readers, and one which we hope covers a broad spectrum. In the 21st century, there are so many digitised versions available online that it is possible to read and explore the enchanting world of children's books in depth. And when one makes a study of an old children's book as an artefact, it's possible to realise still more fully the art, craft and hard work that was involved in making it.

Roderick Cave and Sara Ayad

CHAPTER 1

First Steps: Oral Traditions and Pre-Literacy

Some of the earliest books in a child's life are those used by parents to introduce their babies to the idea of reading.

In the 21st century, long before weaning, and before any serious introduction for babies to the idea of books and reading, many parents now introduce their children to aspects of the Information Age in a way quite inconceivable sixty or seventy years ago. Very small children, it seems, quickly learn to recognise pictures, and to relate to the content of images seen on a tablet or mobile phone screen. Before they reach two years of age, children have learned to recognise themselves and family members in 'selfies', and a young child may quickly become totally absorbed by a tablet showing a television or film version of *Teletubbies* or whatever other children's programme is currently popular for the very young.

Debate about this (rapidly changing) development, that is, children's early exposure to new media, is unending, yet the problems for those concerned about the effects of the Information Age are by no means new. How, or even *when*, children should be taught to read, and how to think, is an ongoing question. Should children be introduced to nonsense verse? How should very young children be introduced to frightening ideas or images (or should they be completely cushioned from them)? How can they be saved from undesirable information or ideas?

How can parents, concerned that their offspring should get a good start in life, save their children from repeating their own mistakes?

Parents have always sought advice or reassurance that their own instincts are sound, by turning to wise women, priests or medical advisers; in short, others they believe more knowledgeable than themselves about the best way to raise a child. In Britain in the 20th century, one revered 'expert' was Sir Truby King (1858–1938), a New Zealander who had a tremendous influence on ideas on child-rearing, in Britain and Canada as well in the South Pacific (though Australian paediatric specialists were less receptive). Almost *all* British children were taught (and 'taught' is the right word) to be potty-trained, to sleep through the night, to take their milk regularly, and generally to fit in with Truby King's beliefs. Well-meaning parents put themselves and their babies through a fairly demanding programme, which presumably had its effects on the children's emotional development.

Beliefs such as those advocated by Truby King seem to have been widely accepted in the United States, but some of the policies advocated by King and his followers were challenged by the American paediatrician Dr Benjamin Spock (1903–98), who used psychoanalysis to try to elucidate family

She is pleas'd that you look,
Into her little Book,
And like her Songs fo well
That her Figures you know,
Before you can goe,
And Sing them
Before you can fpell.

'Nurse Lovechild', *Tommy Thumb's Pretty Song Book for All Little Masters and Misses*. London: probably 1744, vol. 2, p. 63. This is the first known anthology of English-language nursery rhymes (closely followed by the *Nancy Cock Song-Book* (see p. 109), recently discovered, and advertised in May the same year as 'the Second Volume to that great and learned Work').

The British Library

Feeding and Care of Baby (1908) and his later paediatric books were, like Spock's, in no way intended as books *for* children, both Truby King and Spock had a profound effect on 20th-century views of the way to treat infants.

Even though there is usually a plenitude of advice from friends or family, there has always been a place for sensible advice from books, like the 1833 *Advice to Young Mothers on the Physical Education of Children* by 'A Grandmother' (Margaret Jane Moore, Countess Mount Cashell) – one of the largely forgotten authors who also sought ways to simplify parenthood. (Lady Mount Cashell was the author of several books, written in words of one syllable, for Harris's Cabinet of Amusement and Instruction, 1807, which included *Approved Novelties for the Nursery*.) There were many other competent, and often woefully underpaid, female writers, like Marian Fairman Cole, who as 'Mrs. Felix Summerly' wrote *The Mother's Primer: A little Child's first Steps in many Ways* (1844). Mrs Cole had been a governess before she married her cousin Henry Cole, and no doubt she had an active role in her husband's work for his series of children's illustrated story books, published from 1841 as the *Home Treasury*. It would be good if more was known about her.

Sarah Trimmer and later Charlotte M. Yonge were active in trying to guide children (and their guardians) into reading the 'right' books. In the middle of the 20th century, the New Zealander Dorothy Butler, who would have grown up under a Truby King regimen herself, offered her own suggestions. Like Spock, Butler (1925–2015) took a much more permissive approach in her *Babies Need Books*, and her influence on the children's book trade was both enormous and beneficial. Though certainly advocating the use of board books for use with young children, she recognised that children love the 'rustly, crinkly, delectable vulnerability' of 'real' books, noting that 'books are surprisingly durable, given

dynamics and children's needs. Dr Spock's *Common Sense Book of Baby and Child Care*, first published in New York in 1946, became immediately popular, and in its first fifty years, sold over 50 million copies. Second only to the Bible in sales in America, 'Spock', as it was often known, was to underpin the post-war policies and procedures in every English-speaking country. Spock took a much more permissive approach to child-rearing than Truby King ever had: though both King's

minimal adult supervision'. Her permissive approach was surely correct.

One can only speculate about how in the days before the invention of printing, mothers, nursemaids and governesses undertook to entertain and educate their young children. Much of it must surely have been through lap games. Though Caroline Martin's *Lap Games and Other Songs for Children* (published by the Whittington Press in 1989) is collected more as fine printing than as a book to be given to children, there can be little doubt that the lap games it describes often involved singing. It is entirely appropriate that the oldest surviving example of mother and child interaction of this type is a Sumerian lullaby, dating from about 2000 BCE (see p. 14).

Folk tales and stories of the supernatural were commonplace in the early 17th century, as John Aubrey averred: 'When I was a child (and so before the Civill Warres) the fashion was for old women and mayds to tell fabulous stories nighttimes, of Sprights and walking of Ghosts, &c.' Apart from these, the songs, rhymes and verses taught to little children seem to be the oldest. By the end of the 17th century, it was perceived that the way to make books alluring to the young was by printing the text in small books in an attractive way, using 'a fair and pleasant letter'. This came to be recognised as the best way to do it, but it was not fully realised until the publication in 1744 of *Tommy Thumb's Pretty Song Book for All Little Masters and Misses* by 'Nurse Lovechild' (see p. 16). Although 18th-century authors of children's books recognised the advantage of writing verses and songs, scholarly attention to them, as a literary form, really only started a century later. The value of such lullabies and songs was undoubted, as *Read's Weekly Journal* (29 August 1730) averred: 'When cutting Teeth, or ill plac'd Pin / Molest a tender Infant's Skin / Shrill Lullabies in Nurses Strain / Assuage the Peevish Bantling's Pain.'

As all parents know from experience, children's approach to books can be pretty

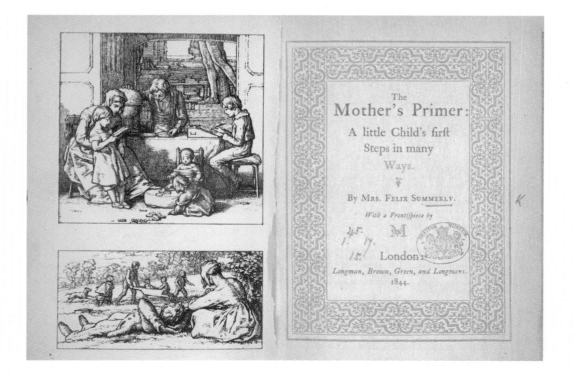

Mrs Felix Summerly [Marianne Fairman Cole], *The Mother's Primer: A little Child's first Steps in many Ways*. London: 1844. In its preface, Mrs Summerly suggests that 'learning to read may be a pleasant instead of a painful task', and that children may more happily and profitably learn to read by exposure to short sentences from the outset, rather than learning the alphabet and sounds by rote.

The British Library

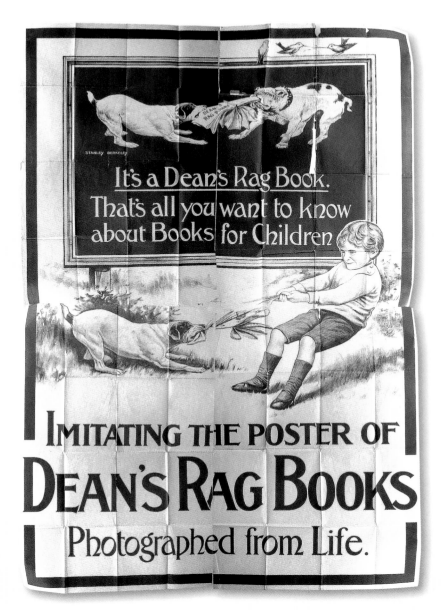

The production of 'object books' with only pictures and usually no text has been another minor branch of children's publishing which has been found in most countries. In Germany in particular, and for older children the teeming scenes of *Wimmelbilderbuch* (or *Wimmelbooks*) are popular, perhaps best known to English-speaking children through Martin Handford's *Where's Wally?* series. These present a different type of cognitive challenge from reading. The production of such object books shows a steady increase in the graphic sophistication used by their makers, some of which, like the Steichens' *First Picture Book*, have long been influential on publishing for the young (see pp. 20–21). If a publisher manages to hit the right approach, huge profits can be earned, and a clever approach can result in a style of production which will sell and sell. '**Touchy-feely**' books also have a continuing success with adults seeking an appropriate book to give a young baby (see pp. 22–3).

Similarly many early learning books are produced with increasing sophistication and the chance of huge rewards continues to encourage publishers and designers. To create books for the blind has been a problem which has interested many book publishers, though the technical difficulties (and limited market) have often proved too much of a deterrent. Modern computer-based publishing, however, seems to offer the possibility of making tactile books much more readily than was true in the past, and there has been some interesting experimentation on this theme (see pp. 26–7). Though no publisher or illustrator will ever make their fortune from these, there seems to be reason for optimism about the innovative way in which some tactile books are being produced nowadays.

An advertising poster for Dean's Rag Books, *c.*1910. The company logo, of a Jack Russell engaged in a rag-book tug-of-war with a British bulldog, was devised by Stanley Berkeley, R.A., a well-known military painter. A test of the **rag books**' avowed 'indestructibility' is clearly too much of a temptation for the 1930s child here.

Vectis Auctioneers Ltd, Stockton-on-Tees

destructive. The production of **hornbooks** and **battledores**, using hard materials with greater resilience than paper, showed some of the attempts to produce books which could survive. To print books on fabric (instead of paper) was one fairly obvious but surprisingly late development (see pp. 18–19), which comes and goes in fashion: the adults buying these cloth books seldom regard them as 'real' books, and the children grow through the stage of enjoying them relatively quickly.

Sumerian Songs

In almost every society, parents sing lullabies to their young babies to help them sleep. What lullabies were there in the ancient world?

Looking at cave paintings where we can see the handprints and other marks left by children, we often wonder what life was like for our earliest ancestors. It might have been nasty, brutish and short; but however primitive, mothers of young children have always wanted to protect and comfort their babies. They sang them lullabies, urging the child to sleep, making soothing sounds yet often also warning them about the dangers facing them if they misbehaved. It was the child's first exposure to literal or spoken imagery, holding the promise of nursery rhymes and fairy tales to come, at an age when he or she was still too young to read.

Almost all surviving lullabies are relatively recent, like this from 17th-century Aragon, threatening children with the Coco, a terrifying bogeyman:

> *Duérmete, niño, duérmete ya ...*
> *Que viene el Coco y te comerá.*
> *Sleep, child, sleep now ...*
> *Here comes the Coco and he will eat you.*

from *Auto de los desposorios de la Virgen*
by Juan Caxés, *c.*1610

Perhaps there were lullabies in ancient Egypt, but the oldest one known came not from Egypt, but from the Sumerian settlements along the Tigris and Euphrates (now southern Iraq) and dates from about 2,500 BCE. The Sumerians developed irrigation and started to plant crops and to utilise and domesticate animals (asses, cattle and sheep). Their ability to store an excess of food was the foundation of modern civilisation that allowed other

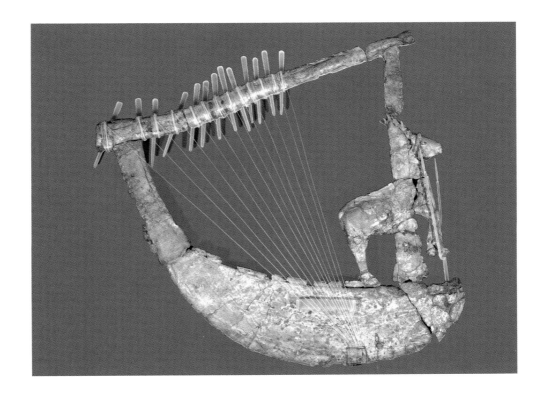

innovations to flourish: the population within their walled cities included tradesmen working in building, pottery, weaving and metalwork. They were also the first people to develop a system of writing, a cuneiform script incised into clay slabs with a stylus. A great many of these artefacts have survived to the present day, but only in the 19th and 20th centuries did scholars finally learn how to read them.

The skills of reading and writing were not uniformly spread amongst the general population, but nor were they limited to the priests. The bureaucratic nature of Sumerian society meant that many 'middle-class' boys learned to develop these skills in what were probably the earliest schools anywhere in the world, and many of their practice cuneiform slabs (the Sumerian equivalent of a school slate) give us a lot of information about their methods of teaching.

One early cuneiform piece made in about 2500 BCE contains a lullaby, in which a mother implores sleep to come to her ailing son:

U-a a-u-a
in my ururu [song] *may he grow big*
in my ururu *may he grow large ...*
Sleep will fill your lap with emmer [wheat],
I will make sweet for you the little cheeses
Those little cheeses that are the healers of man.

Elsewhere in her chant, the mother prays for the future health and happiness of her son, foreseeing him with a loving wife and healthy son of his own, and a loyal nursemaid to suckle the baby. In some ways this is so different from the world we live in today, but this lullaby, written over 4,000 years ago, still resonates with the hopes and concerns of all parents about their children. We have no idea what tune the mother hummed, but there is a lot of evidence of the Sumerians' interest in music, and we can be pretty certain that the mother sang while she nursed her child.

Song Books for All Little Masters and Misses

We assume that nurses and mothers used to tell nursery rhymes to infants, long before they were read out loud. But it took changes in the 18th-century book trade for printing children's books to become profitable.

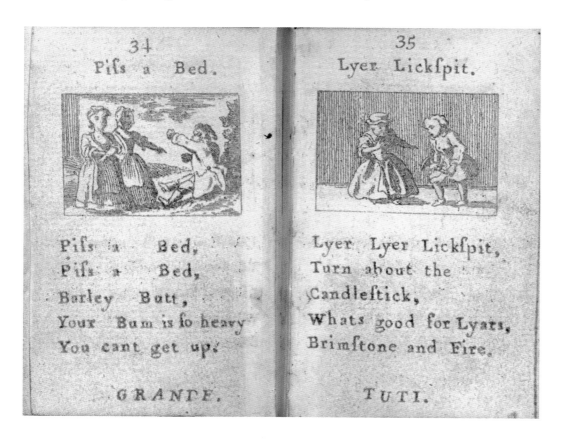

'Nurse Lovechild', *Tommy Thumb's Pretty Song Book for All Little Masters and Misses*. London: Printed according to Act of Parliament. Sold by M. Cooper, Paternoster Row, [March 1744], vol. 2, pp. 34–5. Only two copies of this rare second volume (and none of the first) are known. The child-sized book, designed to appeal to its young reader, includes thirty-nine rhymes such as the familiar 'Bah Bah, a Black Sheep' as well as the rather earthier verses shown here, their scatalogical humour doubtless appealing to young children. The engravings were by George Bickham Jr., a political caricaturist and seller of pornographic and seditious prints, who may have also produced the book.

The British Library

After Pieter Bruegel had painted his extraordinary *Kinderspiele* (*Children's Games*) in 1560, there could be little doubt that children's play involved rhyming songs and games, and possibly always had done so. There is evidence that nursery (or 'Mother Goose') rhymes were known in Shakespeare's time, but evidently they didn't start to be printed until well into the 18th century. The reasons were commercial and technological: there was a need for awareness that such productions could be profitable, that they could be distributed widely through the country (and in the colonies), and that they would be attractive to potential buyers and the children for whom the books would be purchased. Such books needed to be affordable, in small formats and with text large enough to be comfortable for new readers to enjoy.

As early as the 1670s the Czech educationalist Jan Amos Comenius showed the value of small formats (see pp. 78–9) and his book, *Orbis Sensualium Pictus*, was widely printed in England. John Locke's argument, that parents and teachers should teach children how to learn, and to enjoy learning, were also influential.

A little duodecimo book published by John Harris, *A Play-Book for Children, to Allure*

Them to Read as soon as they can speak plain (1694) was on the right lines; it was advertised as 'composed of small pages, on purpose not to tire children, and printed with a fair and pleasant letter' and priced at a modest 4d., but it had no real successors for nearly fifty years.

By 1740 English **type founding**, book design and illustration were showing that British book production was mature, self-assured and ready for new developments. *Tommy Thumb's Pretty Song Book for All Little Masters and Misses; to be Sung to Them by their Nurses 'till they can sing themselves* by 'Nurse Lovechild' was published in March 1744. This was published (together with 'A Letter from a Lady, on Nursing') without serious didactic intentions: the volume was intended for enjoyment only, and it is the first known book to contain nursery rhymes. (A letter to the *Boston Evening Transcript* in 1860 claimed, perhaps falsely, that an earlier collection, *Rhymes for the Nursery; or Lulla-Byes for*

Children, had been circulating in London in 1650, but no evidence has been found for such a book.) Recently a book of similar verse, *Nancy Cock Song-Book* (see p. 109), also purporting to be by Nurse Lovechild, was discovered, published the same year, with illustrations very similar to those of *Tommy Thumb*.

Tommy Thumb's Pretty Song Book gave the name of Mary Cooper as publisher on the title page. She was the widow of Thomas Cooper, whose books ranged from sermons and plays to business manuals, magazines and juvenilia, including *The History of England by Thomas Thumb Esq.*, a substantial book published in 1749 (and later praised by Peter Opie, see following paragraph); but seemingly children's books were not a major part of the Coopers' business. But books for children *were* in demand, and the song book for all little masters and misses was a great success, pirated and imitated by other printers and publishers in Britain; and influencing future publishing in America.

Many later artists such as Randolph Caldecott, Walter Crane, Mervyn Peake (alarmingly for infants) and, in our own age, Quentin Blake and Raymond Briggs, have produced volumes of nursery rhymes illustrated in their own style to divert children. But strangely, only in the Victorian period did scholars start to collect nursery rhymes in order to try to determine their provenance or argue about their meaning. A century later, Iona and Peter Opie devoted their lives to the study of nursery rhymes and the lore of children's games: to know that 'Hickory Dickory Dock' (included in *Tommy Thumb's Pretty Song Book*) was originally a counting game used as part of Westmoreland shepherds' numbering systems makes their *Oxford Dictionary of Nursery Rhymes* a delight to consult.

Another popular early compilation was *Mother Goose's Melody: or, Sonnets for the cradle: containing the most celebrated songs and lullabies of the old British Nurses*. London: 1817. The reference to 'old British nurses' suggests that such verses (some of them quite alarming like the 'Tell Tale Tit' here), had by then long been in circulation.

The British Library

14 Mother Goose's Melody.

Hush-a-by baby,
  On the tree top,
When the wind blows
  The cradle will rock;
When the bough breaks,
  The cradle will fall,
Down tumbles baby,
  Cradle and all.

Cross patch, draw the latch,
  Sit by the fire and spin;
Take a cup, and drink it up,
  Then call your neighbours in.

Mother Goose's Melody. 15

Tell tale tit,
  Your tongue shall be slit,
And all the dogs in our town
  Shall have a bit.

Little Tom Tucker
Sings for his supper;
What shall he eat?
White bread and butter:
How will he cut it,
Without e'er a knife?
How will he be married,
Without e'er a wife?

The Invisible Indestructibles

In the 19th century enterprising publishers started to market children's books which they boldly described as indestructible.

Producing books made of cloth is not a modern idea. In China, books were written on silk at least 2,000 years ago, before the Chinese invented the (much cheaper) substance, paper. In Europe, the normal writing surface used was parchment: too valuable to be thought suitable for children. The relative toughness of **hornbooks** made them a natural choice for teaching the alphabet to children, and these continued to be produced into the 19th century.

It is uncertain when publishers first printed children's books on fabric. Fabric printing was perfected in the English textile industry in the 18th century, and map publishers started to issue maps with paper panels mounted on linen which withstood rough handling. Eventually enterprising printers realised that printing small books on fabric would open up new marketing opportunities. One was a young Scottish immigrant to the United States, John McLoughlin, who in the 1840s was a partner in a New York printer and publishing house. By the 1850s the business was taken over by John McLoughlin Jr., and under his care the McLoughlin Bros. Company became the largest American publisher of children's books, remaining controlled by the family into the 1920s. In 1875 they advertised 'Aunt Louisa's Big Picture Books' mounted on linen; by 1880 they were advertising a linen ABC book, priced at 20 cents retail. By 1895, McLoughlins' catalogue listed four pages of linen books. Because the fabric frayed when cut in irregular shapes, some of their shaped or figural books (like their 1894 *Ten Little Niggers* and *Our Baby's ABC*) were printed

Will (William Graham) Kidd, *The Life of a Bold AB on his Ship in the Rolling C*. London: Dean & Son, 1903. The earliest of Dean's cloth books, first published 1902, with verses by T. A. Polson. Printed in a single colour on calico, Kidd's bold illustrations made this book hugely successful. Its first edition of 5,000 copies was followed by further printings, despite its rather expensive price of 6 shillings. The *Publisher's Circular* (1902) declared it to: 'not only be the greatest novelty in the market this year, but it is at the same time so thoroughly practical and such a splendid conception that we marvel that it has never been done before'. The British Library

Who Killed Cock Robin? Akron, Ohio: Saalfield Publishing Co., c.1900. Despite its supposed indestructibility, the front of this very early muslin edition has been torn in two and – by the young reader's mother, perhaps – discreetly stitched back together.

Wolfsonian-FIU Rare Books and Special Collections Library

on paper mounted on linen. Their catalogue also advertised a dozen German-language linen books. By the 1920s the McLoughlin company was in decline.

The demand for cloth books continued, with the Saalfield Publishing Company of Akron, Ohio (working from 1899 to 1977) as one of the USA's biggest publishers. Saalfield's technique was different, often using pinking blades for the edges of the pages, giving a serrated edge, and its books are also now highly collectable.

Cloth books *ought* to have been developed in England much earlier than by these American enterprises, as the technology for printing maps on linen was well known. In the early 19th century Dean & Son,

the London publishing firm, became famous for its innovative range of pop-up books (see pp. 64–5 and 68–9). Dean's foray into publishing fabric books came at the end of Victorian times, with **rag books** of high quality from their subsidiary the Dean's Rag Book Company (which patented 'books with cloth leaves' on 18 December 1903). This firm advertised widely; the firm's centenary history claimed that by 1904 'rag books were pouring off the presses in their tens of thousands'.

Dean's sales were not limited to Britain or the Empire: translations were issued through Hachette in Paris, and versions in Danish, Dutch, Hungarian and Swedish were being issued as late as 1916. As Hungary was then at war with Britain, these books' publication in Budapest was remarkable, even though during war years sales to allies and neutrals were permissible. These sorts of continental connections faded away by the 1920s.

It is hard to take in now that these books, advertised as 'quite indestructible', were so widespread then. Rag or cloth books were not really regarded as *books* and libraries seldom acquired or preserved them. Critics dismissed them as unhygienic and smelly. Archives for the two American companies are now preserved in the United States, but the records of the Dean's Rag Book Company have long been destroyed, like many of their books. Even in history, the indestructible books are now almost invisible.

Retailers' logo display model for Dean & Sons. Papier-mâché and painted wood, 1936–7. Despite their claims, the cloth wasn't always a match for young fingers, or teeth. Their popular logo depicts a Jack Russell playing a tug of war with a British bulldog. This model could be loaned to retailers for a period of one month to promote sales.

Vectis Auctions Ltd, Stockton-on-Tees

Picturing the World

Ever since the first sketches by unknown hands on the walls of caves, pictures have helped humans learn about the world around them. In 1930 an American father-and-daughter collaboration brought photography to the long-established genre of 'object books'.

Picture or object books, as a learning tool for the very young, have long been part of children's publishing. A genre in its infancy with Comenius' *Orbis Sensualium Pictus* of 1658 (see pp. 78–9), which first promoted the idea of learning through imagery, it developed hand in hand with the increasing ease of providing illustrations. By the late Victorian period, with the technological advances allowing good half-tone reproductions from colour artworks, publishing object books had become profitable. In 1930, one American, working with her father, published what would be a turning point in the genre: a wordless concept book with twenty-four starkly modernist photogravures of simple 'Everyday Things': their influential *First Picture Book* introduced photography to children's educational books to striking effect.

The photographer, Edward (Éduard Jean) Steichen (1879–1973), was an emigré American, whose family had relocated to Michigan from Luxembourg in 1880–81, when he himself was at picture-book stage. After a four-year **lithography** apprenticeship with Milwaukee's American Fine Art Company, he found early success, being noticed by the photographer Alfred Stieglitz, with whom he became friendly. From 1911 until 1937 Steichen worked in commercial photography, first with *Art et Décoration* and then for Condé Nast, establishing a considerable reputation as one of America's foremost art and fashion photographers.

At the height of his success as a fashion photographer, Steichen was commissioned

Mary Steichen (Calderone) Martin and Edward Steichen, *The First Picture Book: Everyday Things for Babies*. New York: Harcourt, Brace and Company, 1930. Martin held strong views about a child's education, and this wordless book was designed to be used as a springboard for learning: 'Talk to the child [she wrote] of things which he knows, connected in a pattern of his own experience, in terms with which he is familiar.' Their *Second Picture Book*, again illustrated with Steichen's black-and-white photographs, showed such familiar objects in use.

Private collection

THE GARDEN

The Children's Object Book.
London and New York: Frederick
Warne & Co., 1880. A superb
example of the genre at its
Victorian peak, Warne's book
was lavishly printed in full colour
by G. Loewensohn at Fürth,
Bavaria. It takes the child beyond
the many and varied objects of
the home into the garden and
surrounding countryside, both
reflecting and promoting an
idealised view of life.

Rare Book and Special Collections
Division, Library of Congress,
Washington D.C.

of the object'. Fantasy too was out: Martin proposed a photographic realism (apparently believing the camera doesn't lie), and declared that 'reality is of prime importance in the first three years of life'. Her view of photography as preferential for infants started a vogue for photographically illustrated children's books; but this view is contested by many educationalists today.

In 1927 the Russian Constructivists Alexandr Rodchenko and Varvara Stepanova likewise collaborated, on some delightful 'photo-cartoon illustrations' of paper dolls for the poet-Futurist Sergei Tretyakov's (unpublished) book of poems for children *Samozveri* (*Homemade Animals*). It is unlikely the Steichens saw these (some were printed in the first issue of the avant-garde journal, *Novy LEF* (*New Left Front of the Arts*); but they would have been familiar with the popular tradition of picture books such as Frederick Warne's *The Children's Object Book* (1880) with its lavish look-and-learn type illustrations, or some of the simpler and more modern illustrational styles then gaining ground on the Continent. The later 20th century saw the emergence of **Wimmelbooks** (see p. 13), their hectic complexity a far cry from the Steichens' stylish creations. Ali Migutsch's *Rundherum in meiner Stadt* (*All Around My City*, 1968) is one popular example.

Though photographs have again become popular in recent years, with composite images becoming fashionable, children's fiction remains primarily hand-illustrated, while photography, with its perceived 'truthfulness', is still largely the preserve of factual books.

by his daughter for *The First Picture Book*. Mary Steichen (Calderone) Martin (1909–98) was a realist with wide-ranging interests who held progressive, forthright views about child development and in later life became a key figure in sexual education. She was inspired by a lack of suitable picture books for her two daughters, finding none 'which could be considered either satisfying ... or in line with modern educational theory. Therefore I set about providing a book of such pictures, not only for my own but for other children faced with a similar need.'

Parents creating books for their own children was nothing new (see pp. 86–7), and commercial picture books were widely available. But Mary Martin rejected hand-drawn illustrations as 'inadequate', 'too often ... colored by the artist's viewpoint and personality, thus presenting a falsified image

Tactile, Noisy and Smelly – Books for Babies

One public library offers 'tactile, noisy and smelly' books for babies, but how effective are they in introducing children to reading?

 hen is a book not a book? When it is an object, made of board, rag or other materials (likely), that smells (sometimes), can be chewed (probably), is potentially waterproof (helpful), is sparkly (for magpie eyes and fingers) and feels good to touch. All this and still a book? Certainly, when its purpose is to coax pre- or 'emergent' readers towards one of the greatest of human activities.

Dorothy Kunhardt's *Pat the Bunny*, first published in 1940, was one of the first in this group of interactive books for babies that are now called '**touchy-feely**'. Kunhardt,

biographer of Abraham Lincoln, was an historian, writer and keenly observant mother. Her first children's book, *Junket Is Nice* (1934), was a rather oddball exploration of *why* a man should eat a large bowl of a popular pre-war pudding. Several children's books followed, in conventional format, likewise reflecting the author's lively imagination. But the book about the little cottontail that she wrote for her youngest daughter, patterned after a toy belonging to the elder one, was an inspired departure.

Juvenile publishing has always been inventive. Two hundred years earlier,

Dorothy Kunhardt's original prototype of *Pat the Bunny*, published by Golden Books (Simon & Schuster), 1940. This hugely popular 'interactive' classic, whose all-time sales are second only to *The Tale of Peter Rabbit*, broke new ground in 'developmental' books. Modern touchy-feely offspring include Usborne's *That's Not My ...* (*Penguin*, etc.) series, and many older children's classic books reformatted as tiny board books with few or no words for babies or toddlers.

The Meserve-Kunhardt Foundation

Judy can pat the bunny.

Now YOU pat the bunny.

Jane Johnson (see pp. 86–7), through careful observation of her children and her own ingenuity, created simple literary amusements in order to educate them. Around the same time Thomas Boreman was modifying children's book formats for their greater appeal (see pp. 108–9). A century or so later Deans, McLoughlins and others adopted the use of rag pages to make books 'indestructible' to tiny determined hands. Yet in the nursery books remained primarily something to read (or at least, to look at), regardless of age. Kunhardt's simple bunny tale for babies was an innovation indeed.

Educationalists these days encourage parents to read aloud, so their children may recognise word-sounds long before school age; it gives them a demonstrable advantage in later life. It is now understood too that children learn with *all* their senses. One first instinct of babies (just as with baboons), when confronted with something new, is to grasp at it and try to put it in their mouths. It is 'developmentally appropriate' for children to chew on books – so the place for precious manuscripts is not the nursery! (The scarcity of so many early children's books, and the battered states of those surviving, is testament to a perennial hearty exploration by their readers.) Kunhardt's book contains 135 words, yet draws in the youngest readers by appealing to all other senses too: there is a fluffy cotton-tail to pat, a peekaboo rag to peep under, a squeaking ball, a shiny mirror, and so forth.

The innovations of *Pat the Bunny* encouraged other publishers and authors to follow suit, though sometimes, regrettably, in ugly padded-plastic editions. The flammable or potentially toxic nature (to book-chewing babies) of some cheaper plastic productions currently on the market – quite apart from any aesthetic concerns – are worrying. But sturdy board books are invaluable at this explorative age, either traditionally illustrated, like Helen Oxenbury's baby board books with their acutely observed but simple images, or Eric Carle's *Very Hungry Caterpillar*, or those with all the bells and whistles of the touchy-feely variety. New production processes make such experiments possible, like the scratch-and-sniff technology, developed in the 1960s, which gave rise to books such as Edward Knapp and Manny Campana's *What! No Spinach?* (Little Golden Sniff It Books, 1981), about a sniffable picnic prepared for Popeye by the obliging Olive Oyle. (After three decades, in this well-scratched author's copy, the rye bread still smells faintly of caraway!) Audio features are also popular, like those in Jan Pienkowski's pop-up books, where the reader presses a button to hear the appropriate noise, or the song-and-action books in rhyme to which the right tunes play.

The purist may demur, but sensory books play a vital role in a baby's development of hand–eye coordination, while cultivating a familiarity with books as both a comfort and a source of wonder. The point is not to 'dumb down', but to maintain high standards of illustration and discreetly challenging concepts. Just as it is possible to 'grow into' books first attempted at too young an age, so, with the right encouragement, the words in such sensory books will soon begin, to the very young reader, to take on a much greater life of their own.

Cats in Hats and Other Rhythmic Readers
The Cat in the Hat

'Even though you can't see them or hear them at all, a person's a person, no matter how small!'* – and their needs are often best catered for in verse.

From the earliest lullabies children have enjoyed rhyme. As Iona and Peter Opie have revealed, childhood playgrounds – be they in fields, urban streets, or municipal parkland – have always been home to songs and rhyming games, and time has shown rhyme to be a useful teaching aid for infants and adults alike. Indeed, our ability to remember is aided by setting information in verse (and/or music), as rhythmic responses, influenced by that part of the brain that responds directly to auditory rhythmic cues, require less cognitive processing than non-rhythmic information. (Intriguingly, recent research shows verse and music assist in fighting memory loss in dementia patients too.)

Along with a love of rhyme children delight in the absurd, their attention ensnared by the bizarre – as Comenius knew, who included 'blubber-lipped giants' and other monstrous creatures in his influential *Orbis Sensualium*

Pictus (1658; see pp. 78–9). Combining the whacky with the rhythmic is one route for attracting a child's attention in order for them to learn, and to make the lesson memorable and enjoyable too.

The enduring popularity of Edward Lear and Lewis Carroll (see pp. 154–5 and 162–3) is in part due to their ability to tap into this delight for nonsense in their audience (of all ages). One more recent children's writer, who took it to new levels, was Theodor Seuss Geisel (1904–91), an advertising artist who as Dr. Seuss went on to produce some of the most popular children's books of all time.

An article on child illiteracy by John Hersey in *Life* magazine, 24 May 1954, asked 'Why Do Students Bog Down on First R?', laying the blame largely on 'pallid' Dick and Jane-type **primers**. Responding to this, the educational director of Houghton Mifflin commissioned Geisel to produce a book using words he felt were important for 'first-graders' to recognise, but also one that would foster their 'inner urge' to read. 'Bring back a book children can't put down!' he said, and within nine months, with an explosive energy, *The Cat in the Hat* was born.

Geisel's 1629-word book (of which 223 came from an original 348-word list) was set to a popular metre, easy for infants to grasp. *The Cat in the Hat* was the first in what became a series of Dr. Seuss's Beginner Books, closely followed by others including *Green Eggs and Ham* (1960), which responded to a challenge for a text of just fifty words. Some of Dr. Seuss's books made subtle protest at injustices, such as the McCarthy-era *Horton Hears a Who!* (1954), and the anti-bigotry *The Sneetches* (1964). Though many parents and school buyers disliked their loud (and heavily marketed) style, they proved hugely popular. Dr. Seuss's Beginner Books quickly expanded to include books in the series by other writers, such as P. D. Eastman's appealing *Are You My Mother?* (Random House, 1960).

The bestselling author of *The Cat in the Hat* was also a 'serious' fine artist whose after-hours 'Midnight Paintings' were revealed only after his death. Dr. Seuss's art, with its roots tangled in Surrealism, was nonetheless firmly grounded in consistency. Seuss recognised that the lack of the former was something children would quickly notice, and adhered to what he called a 'logical insanity': 'If I start with a two-headed animal, I must never waver from that concept. There must be two hats in the closet, two toothbrushes in the bathroom, and two sets of spectacles on the night table.' In rhymes, the best things often come in pairs.

---

* From *Horton Hears a Who!*, 1954.

Dr. Seuss reads his bestselling *The Cat in the Hat* to a group of children at a library in La Jolla, California, in 1957, the year of its publication. Though Geisel's book was regarded by some schools and libraries as too 'irreverent' for children's learning, it proved hugely successful: by 1960, sales neared a million copies, and by 2007 ten times that, with translations (rather tricky perhaps) into twelve different languages. The scene is a timely reminder of the important role played by public libraries in children's literary development.
Archive Photos, Getty Images.

Terra Haptica: Touch-and-Feel Books for Blind Children: *Black Book of Colours*

The natural instinct of infants to absorb information using all their senses – not only sight but also sound, texture and even taste – stands children in good stead when visually impaired. Some publishers are making interesting innovations using this knowledge.

The sense of touch plays a crucial role in children's first access to reading. They have long played with books as toys and, as babies, chewed them and, a little later, scribbled on pages. Yet tactile books specifically for blind or partially sighted children are a relatively recent invention. Valentin Haüy's early innovations in raised lettering, embossed to be read by the fingertips, were produced by his blind students in the Paris workshop of his *Institut des jeunes aveugles* in the 1780s. This model for tactile (or **haptic**) reading was soon followed by others in the 19th century, with varying success. Louis Braille and William Moon, who each suffered impaired vision from childhood (Braille through accident, and Moon through scarlet fever) invented forms of raised alphabets for fingertip reading.

American physician Samuel Gridley Howe (1801–76) took the innovations he saw in Europe in the 1820s back home, and helped set up the New England Asylum for the Blind (the Perkins Institution), America's first such school. In the later 19th century Martin Kunz (1847–1923), director of an institute for the blind in Alsace, and Swedish printer Harald Thilander (himself blind since childhood), each took these early ideas further with the development of relief maps and images, made from paper moulds, with Braille used for their labels. These were widely adopted in the schools for the blind.

Such training no doubt improved the lot of many: deaf-blind Helen Keller is perhaps the most famous example of a child whose world was dramatically opened up by access to knowledge through tactile reading – as well

'Red is sour like unripe strawberries ...' from *El Libro Negro de Los Colores* (Ediciones Tecolote, 2007), published in English as *The Black Book of Colors*, and also produced in a Braille edition. The bold approach and arresting graphics invited numerous awards and commendations, including the New Horizons Award, the Bologna Children's Book Fair Award (2007) and the *New York Times* Best Illustrated Children's Book Award (2008).

Ediciones Tecolote

Pero si el sol se asoma a ver el agua cayendo, salen todos los colores a pintar un arco iris.

Le Petit Chaperon rouge (Little Red Riding Hood). Talant: Les Doigts Qui Rêvent, 2009. Grimms' tale, illustrated by Swiss artist Warja Honegger-Lavater, is adapted by Myriam Colin for tactile interpretation. Using symbols, rather than words, a small red circle represents Red Riding Hood; a large black circle, the wolf; and round, embossed circles represent the trees: using only touch, the reader can trace the characters' progression across the accordion-folded pages.

Les Doigts Qui Rêvent

conjuring up mental images of red things as they are experienced rather than seen, also invoking the other senses of taste and smell and touch. A full Braille alphabet is printed at the end of the book.

Embossed illustrations for tactile reading often take the outlined form of the object itself (just as Haüy's early raised characters were in the forms of Roman letter shapes), and the development of thermoplastics in recent years has meant such illustrations can be readily embossed. For a child without the aid of vision, a linear (or outline) representation of objects may bear little relation to their tactile three-dimensional experience of them, and this innovative work is helpful in 'translating' the objects (or concepts) using a more truly tactile language, as Louis Braille attempted with his raised dots.

In France the publisher Les Doigts Qui Rêvent (Dreaming Fingers) was founded in 1993 to mass-produce tactile illustrated books. The pleasingly rhythmic title of its first book, *Au pays d'Amandine dine dine*, appeals to the aural sense as well. As a charity and publisher with both commercial and social aims, it engages in an active programme of workshops worldwide. Many of its books, whether made of collage, or textured or embossed, are produced in South Africa by people with social disabilities. And as with its version of *Red Riding Hood*, in which the sequence of raised circles symbolises the characters and other elements in the tale, such books explore new avenues, not in order to produce embossed imitations of sighted texts, but with the aim, like that of Louis Braille's alphabet of raised dots, of creating a new tactile language of their own.

as Braille, she also 'listened' to speech by placing her fingers against the speaker's lips.

In recent years technological developments, the rise of new media (such as talking or interactive books) and, not least, changes in approach, have brought many positive changes to the reading world of the visually impaired.

El Libro Negro de Los Colores (Mexico City: Ediciónes Tecolote, 2007), by Venezuelan writer Menena Cottin and illustrator Rosana Faría, is an enterprising attempt to bridge the gap between sighted and sightless children. In this 'bilingual' work, each passage of text, embossed in Braille on matt-black paper, has its alphabetic counterpart, but the relief illustrations become visible (on their black background) only through touch. The sparing text evokes the world of colour as experienced by a blind child named Thomas: 'Red is sour like unripe strawberries and as sweet as watermelon. It hurts when he finds it on his scraped knee.' Thus our understanding of red in a sightless world becomes clear through

Scene from a fable: a cat guards
six geese and a nest of eggs.
Limestone fragment (ostracon)
from Egypt, 19th dynasty,
*c.*1120 BCE. Museum of Egyptian
Antiquities, Cairo.

© Werner Foreman Archive/Corbis

CHAPTER 2

Once Upon a Time, in a Land Far Away

Some stories loved by children have been told and retold for thousands of
years. Their structure still tempts new writers to use the same techniques.

Many adults remember the
time, as children, when
being told to sleep, of secretly
reading by torchlight under the bedclothes.
Only for the past two hundred years or so
has artificial light been widely available for
people to see enough to read with comfort,
at any time they choose. Even in the most
sophisticated of cities, there were many
interminably long dark evenings when
individual reading was not possible. If one
person had enough light to read by, he or she
could share the pleasures of the story with
the listeners. If there was no light, no book,
nor anybody literate, stories and songs could
be told. Storytelling in the dark is in our
communal memories.

These ancient stories take many forms.
Some of the most ancient are fables depicting
animals (and sometimes inanimate objects)
as thinking and speaking beings, often
illustrating their perceived characteristics
('the wily fox'). Most of the fables we
encounter in Europe and America contain
a moral, to teach the listener or reader that
undesirable actions produce bad results.
(We all know, for example, the results of
'crying wolf'.) Just as Percy Muir commented
on Enid Blyton that her stories 'exude morals
in every line', most books written for children
in Europe over the centuries carry a moral –
though sometimes the moral is one we
choose to reject, or sometimes we may have

to debate what the moral actually is.

The writer Elspeth Huxley (1907–97),
brought up as an English girl in Kenya on
Aesop and other English children's books,
found the lack of any moral in the local
African stories of the Wakamba people
disturbing. Few of these stories, often about
a crafty hare who outwitted everyone, had a
point she could understand: events happened
without apparent rhyme or reason; they were
not bound to reality (in the way that Jack, on
his beanstalk, still seems a real boy), and
Huxley found these stories frustrating – with
the stories sometimes ending 'in mid-air'.

Fables taken across from Africa to the New
World by slaves can seem as unsettling as
those of the Wakamba; the 'moral' of these
is often markedly different in the Anansi
stories (see pp. 46–7) from the Caribbean
islands, or indeed in the American Uncle
Remus folk tales collected by Joel Chandler
Harris (1848–1908), though these latter tales
may also, unwittingly, incorporate a European
folk memory of Reynard the Fox, so important in storytelling there in the Middle Ages.

The fables of Bidpai, and the other stories
collected together in the Indian Panchatantra,
are seemingly less highly regarded than the
Aesop fables, but they are as full of treasures.
Some of the most attractive editions are by
Indian publishers (see p. 35). Another great,
almost inexhaustible, well of fables came
from the Arab-speaking countries, which we

know as the *Arabian Nights' Entertainment* or *The One Thousand and One Nights*. These were introduced into the West relatively late, but after translation into French by Antoine Gailland, as *Les Mille et une nuits* (12 vols, 1704–12), the stories spread through Western Europe like an epidemic. The authenticity of these translated stories as folklore is questionable: nobody, for instance, has seen the original Arabic manuscript used by Gailland for the stories of the Forty Thieves or Sinbad. Much later translations by J. C. Mardrus (in French) and Powys Mathers (in English) also added many of the sexier parts, some apparently from Mardrus's own imagination.

Even in Georgian England, many of the Arabian Nights stories were recognised as unsuitable for children, but the technique of these stories-within-stories was so attractive! London publishers saw that, suitably edited, the stories would be steady sellers on the juvenile market (see pp. 42–3). Many later writers used the Arabian Nights stories as a model, such as Captain Marryat's *The Pasha of Many Tales* (1835, not only for children, and now nearly forgotten), or Henry Allen Wedgwood's *The Bird Talisman*, which for a century was privately circulated in the Wedgwood and Darwin families (see p. 43). Even J. B. S. Haldane's hilarious *My Friend Mr Leakey* (1937) echoed early exposure to the Arabian Nights themes.

Arab and Indian folklore spread westward fairly early on, but Chinese tales took much longer to percolate into Europe, with the first translations of Wu Cheng'en's *Journey to the West*, better known as *Monkey*, into English in the later 17th century (see pp. 38–9).

In feudal Western Europe, many other tales found their way into literature. Many were those recited by travelling *jongleurs* and other storytellers; after the invention of printing, chapmen (peddlers) distributed such tales widely, in small, cheap, stitched (unbound) little books. These **chapbooks** were primarily

A *vyasa*, or public reader, recites the *Mahabharata* for an audience of adults and children. From Donald Mackenzie, *Indian Myth and Legend*, London: The Gresham Publishing Company Ltd, 1913. The role of the public storyteller or *dastangoi* is still popular in India today, with some women now taking on this traditionally male role.

aimed at working people, but by no means limited to them. Printers and booksellers quickly learned (as the publishers of *Reader's Digest* were later to rediscover) that there was a steady market for short books summarising much longer texts (such as *Robinson Crusoe*) in twelve- or sixteen-page texts. These sold in the tens of thousands, to children as well as adults, middle-class as well as poor people. Chapbooks ranged from 'the tale for wonder, and the joke for whim', as the poet George Crabbe described them (citing Tom Thumb, Hickathrift the Strong and Jack the Giant Killer) in his poem *The Parish Register* (1807), as well as abridgements of such books as *Pamela* and *Gulliver's Travels*.

Until the notion and study of folklore as a discipline developed in the 19th century, chapbook publication was the best preserver of British folk figures. But the translation of tales gathered in Germany by the Grimm brothers, which appeared first in English as *German Popular Stories* (1823, see p. 181), opened the floodgates for other collections from many other countries and cultures (see pp. 40–41 and 44–5). Like the Grimm brothers, many folklorists did not restrict themselves to repeating verbatim the exact tales of their original informants, and later collectors (in Hungary, for example) found they were gathering tales told to them in good faith as local folk tales which had in fact been retold from the Grimms' collections.

Other writers of juvenile literature have taken the whole field of folk stories from which to draw their own versions, sometimes with very good results. Some of these are original, like James Thurber's *Fables for Our Time* (1940). Many newer fables written recently (particularly those intended for publication as e-books) lack the obvious 'morals' of earlier versions of Aesop, reflecting the (supposedly) non-prescriptive morality of our modern age ('each to their own'). But is this the way for the future? We all seek acceptance and many children enjoy the feeling of being 'virtuous' and the sense of approbation that it brings. Just as in Dorothy Edwards' *My Naughty Little Sister* (1952), where the young reader is made complicit in the suggestion that they would behave 'better' than the Little Sister of the stories, one purpose of folk tales is social guidance: we see the thwarted Fox (sourly) deriding the grapes, or the Hare foolishly cocking a snook at the Tortoise and think, we would do better than that! As long as there are social rules, a thirst for stories, and human invention, so there will be folk tales to pass on the cultural message.

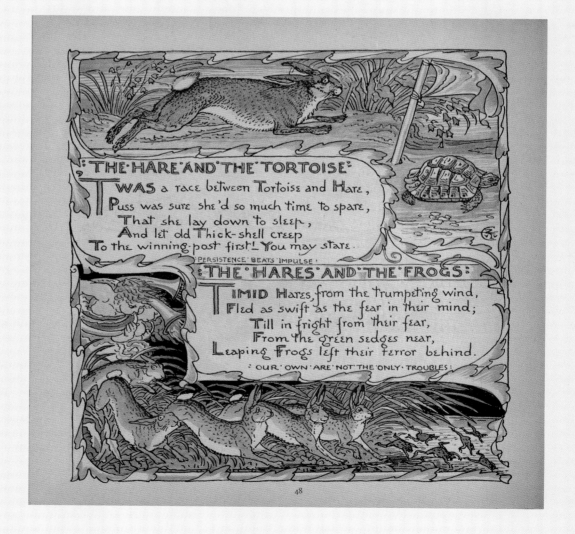

Walter Crane, *Baby's Own Æsop*. London; New York: George Routledge & Sons, 1887. 'The Fox and the Grapes' and 'The Hare and the Tortoise' were well-known fables in the Aesop canon and often illustrated. Some stories in Crane's classically themed picture book, like 'The Fox and the Mask' and 'The Man and the Snake', may be slightly less well known.

A Fabulous Storyteller

Everyone knows Aesop. But when we think about it, we realise we know almost nothing about the most famous fabulist of all time.

The first person to compose a fable, a story about plants or animals which has a hidden inner meaning, was probably a Sumerian or Akkadian, from one of the early civilisations of Mesopotamia that used cuneiform ('wedge-shaped') writing. These fables were often told by nursemaids or professional storytellers, just as they are today by, for example, the griots or storytellers of western Africa. Fables provided a good way for people to comment on aspects of the world as they saw it. The speaker or writer could add a moral, for guidance on the right way to behave, but many of these tales simply illustrate worldly wisdom and the ways to save one's own skin, or make a comment upon clashing cultures.

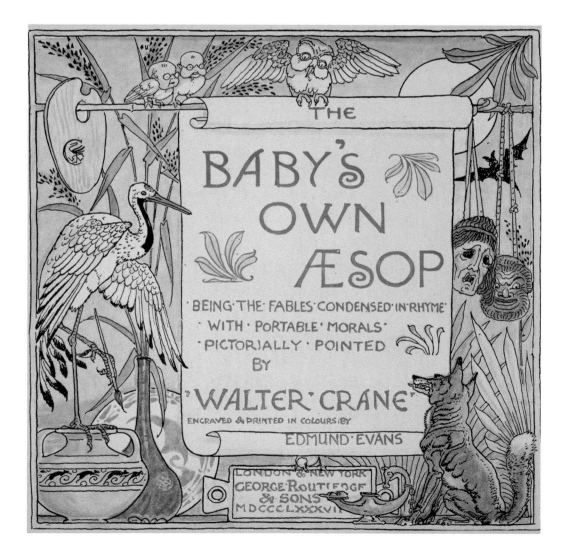

The Baby's Own Æsop: being the Fables condensed in rhyme [by W. J. Linton], *with portable morals pictorially pointed by Walter Crane, etc.* London; New York: George Routledge & Sons, 1887. This version for younger readers with 'portable morals' had the fables translated into verse.

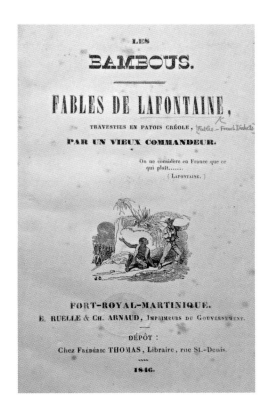

and became a trusted adviser to rulers. It would be pleasant to accept this as fact, but the hundreds of fables attributed to Aesop sometimes come from Indian sources, or are known from Greek and Latin manuscripts. They have been translated into a huge range of languages – with versions in some surprising dialects (such as Martinique Creole, or the patois of Réunion) based on La Fontaine's very popular translation of the fables published between 1668 and 1694. In London, the first known edition in English was published earlier, in 1484.

Translations often varied widely in the selection of fables to be included and particularly in the morals to be drawn from the episodes selected. In effect, a reactionary royalist text could be produced (as many believed the 1692 English version by Sir Roger L'Estrange to be); or others might try for neutrality, like some later politically correct writers, and risk their version becoming dull and lifeless, like that by Samuel Croxall, 1722.

Almost all versions of Aesop's fables intended for children are adapted, rewritten and revised. The present-day buyers of these books pay little attention to the political overtones found by 18th-century readers: it is perhaps more often the design and quality of the illustrations rather than the accuracy of the text which makes the sale. Many publishers of children's books commissioned artwork from their preferred artists. It is possible now to buy an Aesop by Caldecott or Chagall, Griset or Doré, Rackham or Bewick ... The appeal of Aesop's fables is constant; the choice is almost endless.

A wild goat jumps at a tree. Scenes on an earthenware bowl found in an ancient grave in the 5,200-year-old 'Burnt City' of Shahr-e Sukhteh, in Iran. It predates the Assyrian Asurik Tree fable by almost 1,000 years. Yet a 'goat with tree' motif is found in the Indo–Iranian culture of the Haramosh Valley, Pakistan (which had links with the Burnt City), so there may be some credence to this fable having much older origins still.

National Museum of Iran

One of the earliest surviving fables of this kind is about the Asurik Tree; it is a Parthian fable from about 1000 BCE, which recounts the conflict between a palm tree [i.e. agriculture] and a goat [i.e. animal husbandry]. The goat wins. While relatively little known in the West, this story has become central to the body of Persian (Iranian) historical stories and is still told to children.

Aesop's fables were almost as old, dating back to the sixth century BCE. In legend, Aesop was a small, physically repellent man from Samos, and Herodotus said that he had been a slave. In legend again, Aesop earned his freedom through his wit and ingenuity,

Panchatantra: A Forgotten Foundation

Aesop is a name known to all. But another equally important and ancient group of fables from India, still read with pleasure through the Arab world, has never gained the same fame in the Western world.

Ibn al-Muqaffa's *Kalila wa Dimna*, a Persian translation of the Panchatantra/Bidpai tales, from southern Iran (possibly Shiraz), 1307–8. Here, assisted by the Wolf, Leopard and Dimnah, the Lion King treacherously attacks the Camel. Seeking to impress, the Camel has foolishly offered himself up as dinner, anticipating refusal after the Lion King previously declined similar offers by the Jackal and the Crow. The moral: always watch yourself in the company of dodgy characters.

The British Library

About 2,000 years ago, according to tradition, the king of an Indian kingdom was worried about the education of his three 'dullard' young sons. The king instructed an elderly scholar, Vishnu Sharma, to devise a way of teaching the young princes what they would need to know to govern successfully. His method was to produce a series of fables which would painlessly instruct the princes in the skills for successful diplomacy, governance and politics in life: Sharma's *Pancha tantra* or (*Five Principles*) was a very early manual for young rulers-to-be, though very different from the ruthless subtlety of Machiavelli's 16th-century *The Prince*.

There are few accurate details: Sharma's fables were written in Sanskrit, perhaps in Kashmir, and possibly as early as 1200 BCE to 300 CE. We know nothing about him except that his fables were rapidly copied, adapted and translated into other languages. Highly regarded in the Middle East by the 5th century CE, the Persian version was subsequently translated into Arabic by Ibn al-Muqaffa' about 750 CE, and known as *Kalīla wa Dimna*. This Arabic text was in turn translated into old Spanish, Greek, German, English, Hebrew and many other Western languages, and in Asia versions in Javanese, Afghan and Mongolian were also produced. Some of the Persian and Moghul manuscripts are particularly beautiful.

In England, several different translations were published, the earliest being by Sir Thomas North in 1570. The lengthy title of North's *The Morall Philosophie of Doni: drawne out of the ancient writers. A worke first compiled in the Indian tongue (by Sendabar* [Bidpaī]) *and afterwards reduced into divers other languages* gives some indication of the cultural crossovers and mutations of the ancient Panchatantra/Bidpaī/Jatăka tales. Its woodcut illustrations are given a Westernised setting.

The Panchatantra fables appeared under a variety of titles – *The Tales of Bidpai, Les Contes de Pilpay, The Lights of Canopus* – and versions of the fables were used by La Fontaine and the brothers Grimm. But somehow, and unlike Aesop, the Panchatantra seems still to be regarded by publishers only as an adult text calling for scholarly editing. In Britain and America artists and children's writers and publishers have so far failed to recognise the marvellous pictorial possibilities in these very accessible fables. Only in India and the Middle East, it seems, are modern illustrated editions widely produced.

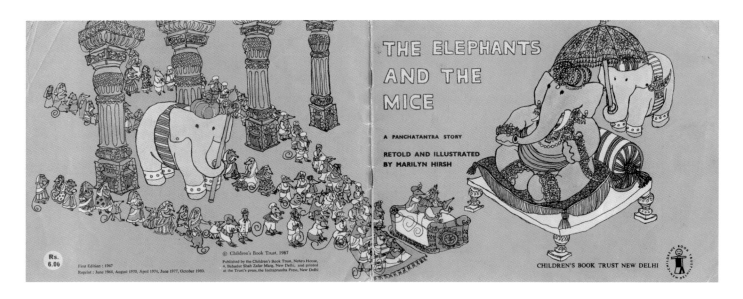

The Romances Which Had It All

Together with the older fables of Aesop, stories of knightly valour were the commonest of all, recounted by minstrels and *jongleurs* – and heard and remembered by children.

The fables of Aesop and others were a frequent form of literary entertainment in the Middle Ages, but they were also used for serious tuition. Almost equally popular, among boys at least, were the (sometimes mythological) exploits, conflicts and battles of famous leaders. Such tales, recounted throughout Europe, told of the triumphs of Christian warriors over their enemies – in the Middle East in the Crusades, such as those of Richard 'the Lionheart'

(1157–99); and of the battles in Spain against the Moors led by Rodrigo Díaz de Vivar (*c*.1043–99), popularly known as *El Campeador* or *El Cid*, after the Arabic word for 'master'. (Schoolchildren in Britain may learn about the Cid in a much less favourable way if they have to study Corneille's 1637 tragicomedy *Le Cid* in French classes; an experience which sadly put this writer off French drama for ever.) In the Arab-speaking countries, and elsewhere in the world,

Sir Bevis of [South] Hampton spearing a lion, with another impaled at his feet; one of three *bas-de-page* scenes which show Bevis, in the *Taymouth Hours* illuminated manuscript, made in south-east England between 1325 and 1340, possibly for Joan, daughter of Edward II. The two lions slain by Bevis are referred to in an earlier verse story, written in what is probably Southampton dialect, *c*.1300.

The British Library, MS Yates Thompson 13

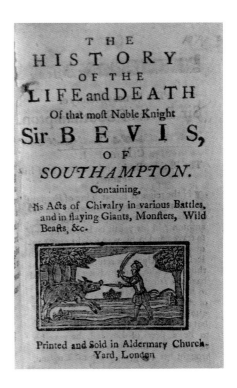

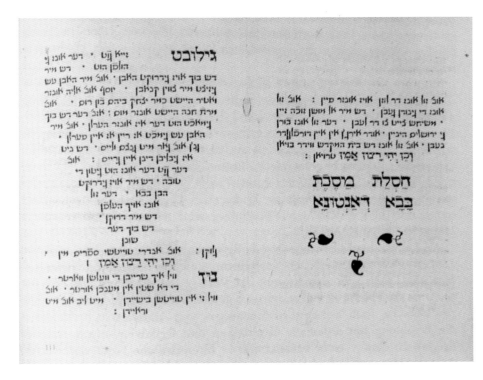

children are exposed to similar tales of valour about their own culture's heroes.

Perhaps even more famous is the French epic, the *Song of Roland,* written about nine hundred years ago. Based very loosely on the Battle of Roncevaux in 778 BCE, the text tells how Roland (Charlemagne's commander) is tricked by a traitor into a battle with a Saracen army. Outnumbered, Roland finally blows his horn to summon help, which ensures eventual victory; in the process he bursts a blood vessel and dies, but for his action he dies a hero. Many manuscript versions of this poem survive, the oldest being in the Bodleian Library at Oxford. Other similar chivalric stories survive in Britain, both those imported from France and home-grown legends: two of the most famous being *Guy of Warwick* and *Bevis of Hampton.*

After the introduction of printing in Britain in the late 15th century, such printers as Richard Pynson and Wynkyn de Worde began publishing such tales in English. The story of the knight Bevis had every exciting feature any boy could hope for: a wicked stepmother, disguises and escapes, countless battles with giants and dragons and (towards the end of the story of Bevis's long life) details of the harrowing death of his valiant horse. Bevis was widely popular, and not only in Britain: a version of the tale was *Bovo-Bukh*, the earliest non-religious book printed in Yiddish (1541). Bevis stories were incorporated into the myths of many countries, with his exploits being recited in French, Dutch, German, Irish and Italian, and especially in Russian.

Though nowadays little known or read by English readers, *Bevis of Hampton* remained amazingly popular in Britain in book form until the 19th century. In **chapbook** form, printed in London or by provincial tradesmen, abridged cheap versions had been peddled around the country in large numbers throughout the 18th century.

An Adventurous *Journey to the West*

Stories of pilgrimage, such as Chaucer's *Canterbury Tales*, have long been popular with children and adults alike. Wu Cheng'en's *Xiyouji* was a rather different sort of journey.

Many Western readers know *The Journey to the West,* the long 16th-century novel by Wu Cheng'en (*c.*1500–82), as *Monkey*. This was the title selected by Arthur Waley (1889–1966) for his 1942 translation of the Chinese classic. Waley's version was bold and adventurous, summarising the story of the pilgrim monk Tripitaka (his English name is 'Three Baskets') on his journey west to India, seeking holy sutras (Buddhist religious texts).

On his journey Monkey encounters the Monkey King and two humanised monsters named Sandy and Pigsy. The story was drawn from tales of the real pilgrim monk Xuánzàng (Hsüan-tsang), who lived from 602 to 664 CE. Armed with a magical staff and shape-shifting powers, Monkey raids Heaven and Hell, perfects his martial skills, and fights demons – such as Sir Bevis of Hampton, a bold and miraculous warrior (see previous page).

Dust jacket by Duncan Grant for Arthur Waley's *Monkey*. London: G. Allen & Unwin, 1942. Grant put the titling on the left of his wraparound cover design at the suggestion of publisher Stanley Unwin, to echo the right-to-left reading of Chinese books. He was commissioned for the jacket alone, but followed this in 1965 with a further twelve illustrations for the Folio Society.

Courtesy of the Charleston Trust

Wu Cheng'en, *Xiyouji* (*Journey to the West*). China, 18th century. *Journey to the West* was one of the 'Four Great Masterpieces' of Chinese literature and much illustrated, in a variety of art forms. This 18th-century version, illustrated with woodblocks, shows one of the characters, Pigsy, giving in to earthly temptations by accepting food, as Xuánzàng and Monkey look on.

The British Library

Journey to the West was a very long book and viewed in the West as unpublishable in the conditions of the Second World War: so Waley's *Monkey* was less than a third of the length of the original, and paraphrased the original 100 chapters in a way which still managed to catch enough of Wu's style to captivate critics of the time (Edith Sitwell praised the 'absence of shadow, like the clearance and directness of Monkey's mind'). Wu Cheng'en's convoluted adventure story was never a children's book, but Waley's retelling made it more accessible for the young; rather like some of the compressed versions of episodes in *Gulliver's Travels* or *Robinson Crusoe*, which may be preferred to the 'authentic' full text. For those caught by Wu's story, the full four-volume text is available now in a good English translation.

Monkey, however, has acquired a new and vigorous life which could never have been imagined by Wu Cheng'en when he wrote it. His episodes have great dramatic value, and were long incorporated into Beijing opera. One could almost argue that in the media, *Monkey* has become a permanent feature of television: a popular series not only in Japan, Taiwan and Hong Kong as well as China, but also dubbed into many languages around the world. It features largely in printed form as **manhua** in China and **manga** in Japan, and has been incorporated into interactive games online. Monkey's shape-shifting journey to the West is by no means over.

A Humorist's Arcadia – Folklore in Ireland

The first collections of Irish folk stories were published before Irish life was changed by the potato famine of the 1840s. Well received elsewhere, their importance was overshadowed by the intricacies of Irish politics.

During the increasing commercialisation of Christmas in Britain in the reign of George IV, publishers discovered that elegant, expensive annuals of stories and poems made excellent Christmas gifts. Most were aimed at a female readership, but in 1828 the historical novelist William Harrison Ainsworth (then a publisher) issued the first volume of *The Christmas Box. An Annual Present for Children*, the first ever produced for a juvenile market. Such publishers usually engaged celebrities as editors, and in this case Ainsworth selected Thomas Crofton Croker FSA, an antiquarian already well known for his books on Irish folklore – though, in fact, much of the editorial work on *The Christmas Box* was actually done by his wife Marianne Croker, herself an accomplished artist and writer.

Croker (1798–1854) was Irish, from Cork, and settled to his successful career as a civil servant working at the Admiralty in London, becoming famous for his *Fairy Legends and Traditions of the South of Ireland* (published by John Murray in 1825), tales gathered in the Munster countryside ten years earlier. It was an immediate success, enabling Croker to include a preface to the second edition (1826) in which he reprinted letters whereby both Sir Walter Scott and the Brothers Grimm praised Croker's work. His position as an authority, it seemed, was guaranteed.

Croker's text is still very readable – but before the end of the 19th century the swell of Irish opinion turned against it: in their belief, Croker was the wrong kind of Irishman. The eminent Irish poet W. B. Yeats (1865–1939) later complained that Croker's

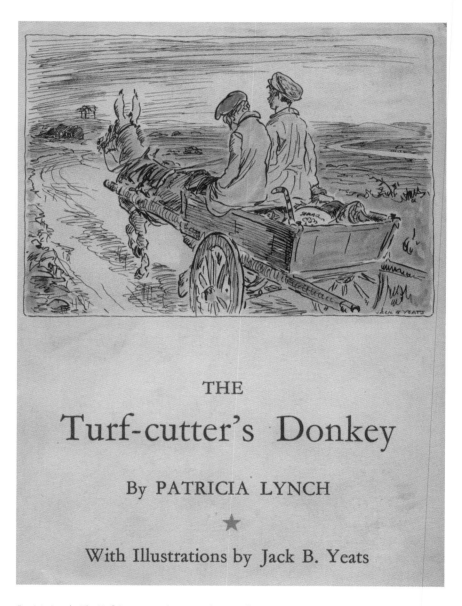

THE
Turf-cutter's Donkey

By PATRICIA LYNCH

★

With Illustrations by Jack B. Yeats

Patricia Lynch, *The Turf-Cutter's Donkey. An Irish Story of Mystery and Adventure.* London: J. M. Dent & Sons, 1934. Illustrations by Jack B. Yeats. Central to Lynch's narrative (originally published as a series of stories in the *Irish Press*) is a wide-ranging Irish traditional mythology, and the tales, charmingly illustrated by Yeats, are now regarded as a landmark in Irish children's literature.
James Adam & Sons Ltd, Dublin

'The Turfcutters' from Thomas Crofton Croker, *Fairy Legends and Traditions of the South of Ireland*. With illustrations by Maclise & Green. London: John Murray, 1826 (second edition). The painter, Daniel Maclise, achieved early success with his intricate book illustrations, reflecting the influence of German illustrators and Romanticism on his work. A Presbyterian, he met Croker in Cork and his own interest in the richness of Celtic mythology coincided with the growing nationalist sentiment in Ireland.
The British Library

work was 'full of the ideas of harum-scarum Irish gentility, [and] saw everything humorised', adding that such writers 'came from a class that did not – mainly for political reasons – take the populace seriously' with 'the dash as well as the shallowness of an ascendant and idle class'. Yeats described Croker as imagining Ireland 'as a humorist's Arcadia; its passion, its gloom, its tragedy, [he] knew nothing of'. In republican Ireland few readers nowadays look at Croker's books.

Later authors, trying to reach the plain people of Ireland, turned back to folk tales in a very different way. Flann O'Brien's brilliant comical adult novel *At Swim-Two-Birds* (1939) has been recognised as a modern classic, with its exuberant mixture of mythology, history and farce, in a way which could never have been imagined by Croker.

The interesting Patricia Lynch (*c.*1894– 1972) was born in Cork, but might be best

described as 'London Irish'. After working as a reporter for suffragette Sylvia Pankhurst's *The Workers' Dreadnought* on the 1916 uprising in Dublin, she played an active role in Irish politics throughout the 1920s. In the 1930s Lynch turned to writing books for children, weaving them from a mixture of folklore and fantasy; among the best known is *The Turf-Cutter's Donkey* (London: J. M. Dent & Sons, 1934) with illustrations by Jack B. Yeats, the younger brother of W. B. Yeats. Lynch later wrote that 'imagination means looking deeper and seeing beyond the veil', a good description of what she essayed. Nonetheless her use of Irish mythology in *The Turf-Cutter's Donkey* received only baffled approval from the American children's reviewer Virginia Kirkus: 'a bit out of the usual line, as Irish history is rarely available for children'.

'To Divert the Sultan': *The 1001 Nights*

The tales in the *Arabian Nights* spread like wildfire over Europe in the early 18th century. But though immensely popular, were its stories suitable reading for children?

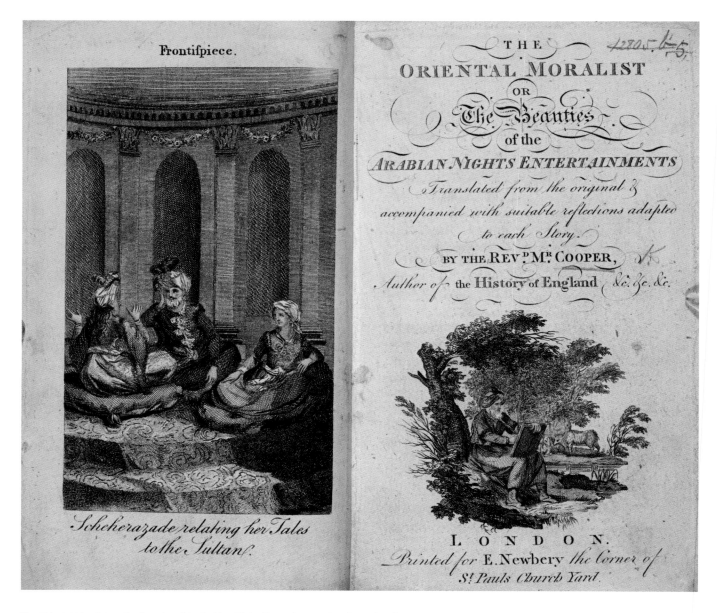

The Oriental Moralist, or the Beauties of the Arabian Nights Entertainments. London: printed for E. Newbery, c.1790. The elaborate title page gives a taste of the sophisticated production and content of this work by 'the Revd Mr Cooper'. The preface claimed that he read the (French) book at an inn in Paris, translating, rewriting and 'reflecting' (and substantially censoring the more lascivious aspects) to 'promote the love of virtue' and 'fortify the youthful heart against the impressions of vice'.
The British Library

After the French orientalist Antoine Galland (1646–1715) published his French translation of the Arabian Nights (*Kitāb ʾalf layla wa-layla*) in 1704, *Les Mille et une nuits*, further versions in other languages were rapidly published throughout Western Europe. Readers were tempted by the title page of the first English translation (1706), and its piquant text continued to attract adult readers. Knowing that it was 'hot', no doubt boys (and even girls) sought it out, but it was not until 1790 that a children's version appeared.

Issued by Elizabeth Newbery (widow of Francis Newbery, who was the nephew of the important juvenile publisher John Newbery), it was dressed up to persuade potential purchasers that it was indeed suitable for children. The title page of *The Oriental Moralist, or the Beauties of the Arabian Nights Entertainments* indicated the text was 'accompanied with suitable reflections adapted to each story. By the Revd Mr Cooper', but this was deceptive advertising – there was no Cooper! The text had in fact been cobbled together by a Grub Street hack writer, one Richard Johnson. (Such deceptions were commonplace enough in juvenile publishing.) Johnson's editorial work on this – and several other books – was competent, but his version was not successful enough to be reprinted (or perhaps the 'suitable reflections' were too off-putting) and the book was soon replaced by other texts intended for children.

The glamour and magic of the *Arabian Nights,* and of both east and west Asia, continued to attract other writers and artists, both indirectly and for further versions of that book. The wood-engraver Gwen Raverat (1885–1957), having illustrated a new edition of *The Cambridge Book of Poetry for Children* (edited by Kenneth Grahame in 1932), then turned to *The Bird Talisman*. It had been written in the 1850s by her ancestor, the lawyer Henry Allen Wedgwood (though neither she nor Wedgwood had ever visited India – its setting). Raverat determined to illustrate it with coloured wood-engravings, a technique very unusual at that time. It was printed by Cambridge University Press for Faber and completed in September 1939. It was disastrous timing: the onset of the Second World War totally overshadowed the book's publication. The charm of Wedgwood's stories and the brilliance of Raverat's engravings in this beautiful book were almost instantly forgotten.

THE
BIRD TALISMAN

An Eastern Tale by
HENRY ALLEN WEDGWOOD
illustrated by
GWEN RAVERAT

Henry Allen Wedgwood, *The Bird Talisman*. Illustrated by Gwen Raverat. London: [printed at Cambridge University Press for] Faber & Faber Limited, 1939. The publisher originally requested the secondary-colour blocks for the wood-cuts from suppliers in Vienna, but the Austrian annexation in 1938 by the Nazis rather messed this up: Raverat objected to doing business with the German-controlled country and found an English block-maker. Production again slowed at the printing stage, with half the staff of CUP called up for military service (a despairing Raverat remarked 'There's always Christmas for children, even in war'), yet the book was eventually completed four months later in September 1939.
Faber & Faber Ltd

Fjords, Trolls and *Nisse*

The folk culture of Norway is rather different from that of the countries to the south, but its legends have had a marked effect on children's literature in English.

The collection of folk stories in Germany by the Grimm brothers had a wide influence throughout Europe. Writers in contact with the Grimms, such as Sir Walter Scott and Crofton Croker, gathered information for British legends, and in 1830s Denmark Hans Christian Andersen was developing his own famous stories, based in part on tales he had heard as a child.

Further north, in Norway, the folk tales often reflected the harsh reality of the climate, and the isolation of small rural communities surrounded by high mountains, places where 'one sat in the darkness by the oven door ... in the endless, lonely winter evenings, where folk still spoke of seeing the *nisse* [a type of wintertime elf], and capturing a sea serpent'. Jacob Grimm, writing to Jørgen Moe in May 1852, commented that 'Norwegian folk tales are the *best* fairy tales there are', adding that 'in our German fairy tales the tradition was often exhausted'.

The cultural and linguistic differences between Norway and Denmark encouraged two local writers to gather their own records of the Norse legends. A glazier's son, Peter Christen Asbjørnsen (1812–85) and his lifelong friend, the clergyman Jørgen Engebretsen Moe (1813–82), published the first edition of their collection, *Norske Folkeeventyr* (*Norwegian Folktales*), in 1845. Immediately popular (Grimm commented that both the representation and substance of their tales were 'admirable'), it was of such significance that it influenced the form of the Norwegian language. 'Asbjørnsen & Moe', as their story collection was commonly known, continued to be expanded and reprinted, but

Norske Folkeeventyr. Christiania [Oslo]: 1874. The compilation by Peter Christen Asbjørnsen and Jørgen Moe includes the well-known 'Three Billy Goats Gruff', originally entitled (rather at length) as 'The three Billy-Goats Gruff who were going to the pasture to fatten themselves up'. This elaborate cover, featuring characters from the tales, is a far cry from the unadorned pamphlet of the first (1841) edition.
National Library of Norway

NORSE WONDER TALES

BY

SIR GEORGE DASENT, D.C.L.

Illustrated by WILLY POGANY

LONDON & GLASGOW
COLLINS' CLEAR-TYPE PRESS

N.W.T.   "A maiden was looking out of a window."   Page 53.

Sir George Dasent, *Norse Wonder Tales*. Tales for the Children, no. 22. Illustrated by Willy Pogany. London; Glasgow: Collins' Clear-Type Press, 1909. The Hungarian-born artist Pogany was a popular choice for this edition of Dasent's translation. His illustration above illustrates 'The Blue Belt'.

The British Library

until 1874 their Norwegian edition remained unillustrated. The Norwegian artists then selected, Erik Werenskiold (1855–1938) and Theodor Kittelsen (1857–1914), though popular in Norway, were (and are) little known in England; a pity because the artists caught the mood and magic of the Norwegian folk tales very well.

For most English readers, these stories are known from *Popular Tales from the Norse* (first published in 1858), translated by the civil servant and Scandinavian scholar Sir George Dasent (1819–96), while he was assistant editor of *The Times*. Dasent had first encountered folk tales as a young boy in St Vincent in the West Indies (see p. 46) and, guided by Jacob Grimm, had specialised in Scandinavian mythology. Dasent's clear, readable version was praised highly by the Norwegians, and earned him a Danish knighthood. In the early 20th century in England editions of his text were illustrated by such artists as Willy Pogany, the Knowles brothers and Kay Nielsen. But for many readers, Dasent's work is often remembered (unwittingly) from the innumerable simplified versions issued of his translation of the story of the 'Three Billy Goats Gruff'.

The Cunning Jumping Spider

When Africans were captured and sent as slaves to the Americas they brought their legends with them. Br'er Fox and Br'er Rabbit are celebrated in the United States, but Anansi the Spider Man, the hero of Caribbean folk tales, is a very different character.

Growing up in the French-speaking islands, children learn about a range of malevolent characters such as 'Papa Bois', or the frightening child-creatures, the 'Duennes'. But in the English-speaking Caribbean islands, the hero is the spider Anansi, celebrated in the stories originating in the forested areas of Ghana and the Ivory Coast in Africa.

Early European travellers were aware of the stories told about Anansi, and it was reported that the Akan people (the Ghanaian and Ivory Coast inhabitants) believed that 'the first Men were made by that Creature'.

As a weak, defenceless animal who, by wit and guile, could dominate much stronger creatures, Anansi was obviously an attractive hero for slaves taken from West Africa to the Caribbean, just as stories about Br'er Fox were celebrated by slaves working on plantations in America. In the islands, stories about Anansi were passed on by word of mouth for generations, and told by nurses and servants to the young white Creole children in their care. The wily spider Anansi became part of their upbringing, in the same way that 'Jack

Anansi and the Alligator Eggs. Kingston: Operation Friendship, 1974. The edition was devised as a fundraiser for the Jamaican charity Operation Friendship. Sir Philip Sherlock's text and Susan Judah's illustrations (and the hard work of the promoters and sponsors) created a memorable book. Forty years later the same method of supporting charities was used to make the text available to a fresh generation of Jamaicans in the Brawta Books 2013 edition.

Author's collection

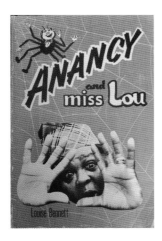

and the Beanstalk' or the 'Sleeping Princess'
became familiar to children born in Europe.

Most Victorian authors telling Anansi
stories had grown up in the West Indies – Sir
George Dasent from St Vincent (1859) and,
from Jamaica, Mary Pamela Milne-Home,
whose *Mamma's Black Nurse Stories* (1890)
reported the difficulty in persuading
Jamaicans to tell Anansi stories to foreigners:
'Dat foolishness; wonder Missus car to har
dat' ('That foolishness; I wonder if Missus
cares to hear that'). The now forgotten but
interesting illustrator and author Patricia
Colman Smith also published her own
version of some of these tales called *Annancy
Stories* in New York in 1899. Such editions
did not circulate widely in the islands, though.

The Jamaican historian Sir Philip Sherlock
wrote down many Anansi stories and thus
made them available to West Indian children

in *Annancy Stories,* issued by Ginn & Co in
their Beacon Supplementary Readers series
in 1936. Another Jamaican, Louise Bennett,
became famous as 'Miss Lou' for her
Jamaican Creole dialect versions of Anansi
stories published in Kingston in 1950. Many
readers dislike the use of dialect as cumbersome to read, as, for example, that in Joel
Chandler Harris's *Uncle Remus* stories, and
'Jamaica talk', or patois, is not easy for
foreigners to understand. Editions of
Sherlock's more accessible versions were
published in both Britain and the United
States in 1954, but as neither the American
nor the English illustrators had personal
knowledge of Jamaica, they could provide
only a pale picture for the stories' setting.

In the 1970s the Kingston learning charity
Operation Friendship had a clever idea: to
produce its own version, printed by a local
firm and illustrated with all the colour and
vibrancy that a local artist (Susan Judah)
could bring to it.

Production costs for special editions were
high, and the local market for such books
was limited. Operation Friendship solved this
problem by having the book sponsored for a
range of children, whose names were then
printed on the endpapers. With over four
hundred direct sponsors or subscribers, as
well as sales to others, copies of this book
reached an unusually large group of Jamaican
book-owners and its publication produced
useful income for the charity. A new edition
by Elethia Rackham's Brawta Press in Jamaica
(2013), also supported by donors to local
charities, demonstrates that modern
technology makes small-scale production
and marketing possible, and allows new
generations of children to read Sherlock's
retellings of Anansi's adventures and the
skills he brings to them.

Chapter 3

Abecedarias and Battledores

Books for very young children were often destroyed or discarded quickly, and easily forgotten as children grew up. Nevertheless, these overlooked publications were among the most commonly issued; though individually insignificant, en masse they could often be very profitable for the publisher, making the difference between commercial success or failure.

Some books intended for use with very young children, long before they are properly conscious of books as such, are discussed in Chapter 1. In this chapter, we move from looking at productions intended to help the young to learn to read, to formats used at different times or in different geographical areas. This chapter also looks at stratagems to interest children in learning; and at some of the novelties introduced in the last three hundred years – sometimes intended for children who were reluctant to read. Some publications, intended to amuse or divert children, were produced by firms on the peripheries of the book trade: productions often not taken seriously enough to be stocked in bookshops or on library shelves, and never added to lists of recommended reading.

While for centuries in all countries the greater proportion of the population remained illiterate, early on many ABCs and similar books to teach reading to the fortunate few were produced. According to antiquary John Aubrey (1626–97), a famous commentator on social life in England, this had changed by the 1630s. He wrote, 'Till a little before the Civill-Warres, the ordinary sort of People were not taught to read.

Now-a-dayes Bookes are common, and most of the poor people understood letters.' But Aubrey saw disadvantages as well: 'the many good Bookes, and [Puritanism] have put all the old Fables out of doors: and the divine art of Printing and Gunpowder have frighted Robin-goodfellow and the Fayries'. Books produced in Aubrey's day would not have caused such a fright (see pp. 54–5); however, much later Puritan texts might have seen off the fairies (see pp. 90–91).

Abecedarias were not just for the boys. Despite a general misconception that women were deliberately left untutored, there is evidence that many girls too were taught their letters (see pp. 52–3). The cult of the Virgin, taught to read her prayer book by St Anne (as often shown in pictures), lent theological authority to the idea of women's literacy.

For teaching, **hornbooks** were often used throughout northern Europe and even in Mexico (see pp. 56–7), and these are often illustrated in pictures. Making these in wood was laborious, though in parts of the Islamic world, similar boards are still used today to help students in madrasas to memorise texts from the Koran. As the book trade in Europe became more sophisticated, makers of hornbooks started using printed pages

Koranic boards. Similar boards, somewhere between a hornbook and a school 'slate', inscribed with Koranic verses and sometimes symbols, are found throughout the Muslim world even today, such as those used by this little girl in a Mogadishu madrasa, March, 2015.

Getty Images

St Anne teaching the Virgin to read. Illumination (detail) from the *Poncher Hours* by the Master of Cardinal Bourbon, Paris, *c.*1500. Tempera, ink and gold on parchment, leaf: 13.3 × 8.7cm.

J. Paul Getty Museum, Los Angeles

mounted underneath the thin horn covering, and bookbinders began making pasteboard to use in their bindings (and, by the late 18th century, using this thin cardboard for board games). In time hornbooks were replaced by printed **battledores**, which by the early 19th century were being sold by the tens of thousands. More attractive than the old wooden hornbooks, cheap to produce, easy to transport and to sell at low prices, these aids to reading nevertheless still wore out. Some enterprising publishers sought to make their battledores 'indestructible', like the **rag books** intended for very young children (see pp. 18–19). But fashions, and educational customs, change: from the middle of the 19th century, battledores dropped out of production, to be replaced by **primers**.

Nowadays, schoolbooks of the past often seem to have been produced with very little awareness (by the compiler or publisher) of the idea that making a book interesting to children is half the battle won. The problem was not with the authors alone, of course; as John Aubrey wrote in about 1670: 'The common way of teaching is so long, tedious, and praeposterous that it breaks the spirit of the fine tender ingeniose youths and causes

'em perfectly to hate learning.' We have all met teachers (and authors) like that. The publishers who conceived these schoolbooks, like the authors commissioned to write them, had ideas about the ways and purposes of education which often seem very strange to us today; indeed, so 'praeposterous' that we wonder what dream-world the publishers lived in. Fiddling around with the letters – replacing alphabets, changing spellings, and other ill-conceived schemes – must often have bewildered children, even causing some to come to hate learning, despite their innate disposition not to do so (see pp. 62–3 and 225).

Publishing for children emerged as a distinct branch of the industry at about the same time that the British first started colonising North America. In the colonial period, and for the first fifty years or so of the United States, British and American publishing for children had a similar and intertwined life, as many of the books illustrated show very clearly (see pp. 62–3 and 78–9, 88–9, 94–7). These schoolbooks naturally echo the preconceptions of their publishers and their purchasers. The Royal Readers series used in Canada, Australia and other settler colonies in the British Empire, for example, echoed the belief, then widely held in the colonies, that the British way was

the best anywhere in the world, and that the British abolition of slavery reflected this. In the US, the McGuffey's Readers series of books were just as patriotic in their tone, but, unlike some Boston-published **readers**, McGuffey's Readers skated over slavery with little comment – 'McGuffey' was read widely in the southern states.

In parts of other European colonial empires, in which a wide range of languages were used, teaching reading to indigenous people was much less straightforward. Books produced in the early 19th century by missionary societies, or bodies like the Calcutta School-Book Society, encouraged the publication of books in local languages, in part as a route to disseminating their own religious message in a language the indigenous people would understand. In time, schoolbooks planned and produced in Britain were seen as 'better' than any created elsewhere and used in India. There was *always* tension between those who believed advance would come through teaching and using English in India (a form of intellectual colonisation), and those others who believed in publishing books in local languages. Printing in local languages increased costs and limited the range of books available; administrators feared it fomented wishes for self-rule. Whether with the British in India, the Dutch in the East Indies, or the French in Indochina, the tension was always there: the methods adopted in each colony changed the whole pattern of book production for children's needs in those areas (see pp. 66–7). The impression received, when visiting ex-colonial countries, is that relatively fewer books are published there (than in Europe and America) which are intended for children's recreational reading. Juvenile publishing is still fragile in much of Asia and Africa.

In societies in which children have ready access to books, sometimes long-preserved

home-created books can be found which were clearly favourite possessions. (This author has warm memories of receiving small booklets about fairies, written and illustrated by an older sister.) Paper dolls and paper cut-outs, for example, gave many hours of pleasure to children wielding scissors or pencils, and they figured largely in home theatricals, often dramatisations of popular stories, ballads or plays. Cut-outs were of great value in opening up children's imaginations, as well as improving their dexterity. Along with panto-mime, they were integral to the emergence of a distinct group of manufacturers and publishers (see pp. 58–9). Such ephemeral items are seldom considered in histories of children's literature: the value of the work done by Jane Johnson in teaching her children in the 1740s has recently been recognised, but surviving examples are very rare (see, for instance, pp. 86–7). The publication in 2015 of *The Adventures of Alice Laselles,* written by Queen Victoria when a child of ten and three-quarters and now illustrated with paper dolls (see above) made by Victoria with her governess, the Baroness Louise Lehzen, throws fresh light on the methods of education chosen for the young

Alexandrine Victoria (later Queen Victoria), *The Adventures of Alice Laselles*, 1829 or 1830. Illustrated by Queen (then Princess) Victoria with doll animations by Felix Petruška. London: Royal Collection Trust, 2015. The princess was a prolific journal and letter writer. Her story, of a motherless girl exiled to boarding school, is dedicated to her own 'dear Mamma', and was written as a composition exercise when Victoria was aged ten. It was first published in 2015, and is illustrated with the hand-coloured paper dolls made by Victoria and her governess, digitally incorporated into newly etched 'sets'.

Royal Collection Trust,
© HM Queen Elizabeth II 2017

princess. Victoria's paper dolls were carefully preserved, and had been among her favourite reminders of childhood – but were they, or the toy theatres marketed by firms like Benjamin Pollock, *really* 'books' at all? Some experts on children's literature dismiss moveable books as pretty poor stuff, because their work is often so crudely conceived and executed. Iona and Peter Opie, for example, write about publishers who sought

> to put life into their books by the crudest of all possible means, by representing life mechanically. Their artists may not be able to depict movement, so the figures in their pictures are made to move in reality; they may not be able to convey the illusion of depth, so they produce pictures that are actually three dimensions; they may be incapable of portraying a cow mooing, so a mooing noise is in fact contrived.

This criticism is by no means limited to the ingenious mechanical books which were available in the 19th century (see pp. 64–5

and 68–9). Children (and adults) at that time *liked* the novelty and the crudeness of the techniques, and some publishers of mechanical or 'pop-up' books made a lot of money.

By comparison, in the 20th century, Disney – and many of the designers and publishers of e-books designed for children – have quite different objectives from those favoured by literary purists. Many traditional publishers of conventional books were (and are) more interested in profit than in producing beautiful or inspiring books. But even espousing the latter ideals can be dangerous. As well as the publishers and booksellers who have attempted to produce good books and made money doing so, there have been others who have completely failed commercially. From the late 18th century onwards, there have been those in the publishing trade who achieved better sales and published poorer books; or those who pandered to undiscriminating purchasers. Children's book publishing is a business, and like all businesses, it has its unsavoury aspects.

Franz Bonn, *Theater-Bilderbuch* (*Theatre Picturebook*). Esslingen: J. F. Schreiber, 1882. This early mechanical book contains four stories pleasing 'for the child's heart': 'Little Red Riding Hood', 'Hansel and Gretel', 'The Wise Men from the East' and 'Christmas Eve'. Below each lithographed pop-up scene is dialogue for different speakers, catching children's interest in both mechanical books and toy theatre.

Collection Ana Maria Ortega

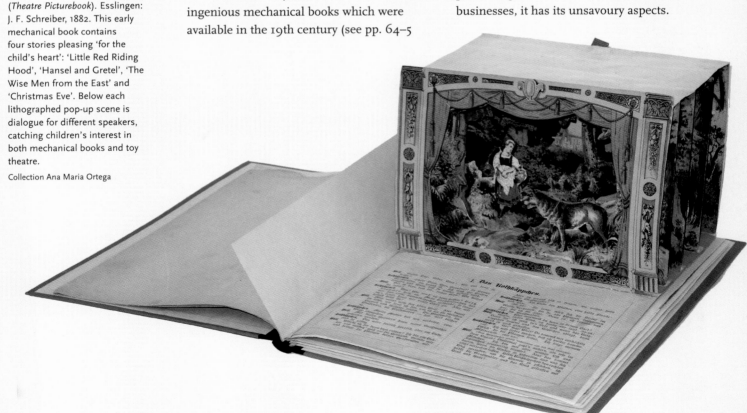

First Steps to Literacy – for Boys *and* Girls

It is a truism that only boys intended for the Church were taught their ABCs, and then how to read. So how and when did girls become literate?

It is often assumed that teaching pupils to understand and speak, and then to read and write, Latin, was only for boy novices in monasteries; and that in a way (after the dissolution of the monasteries during the 16th-century Reformation) this role was passed on to the grammar schools. Perhaps this was generally so, but if that had always been the case, it would be good to know who taught the many outstanding women writers and scholars, such as the German mystic Hildegard of Bingen (1098–1179), or the anchoress Julian of Norwich (1342–*c.* 1416), whose *Revelations of Divine*

Love was the first book by a woman written in English.

Many 15th-century educational books, like Benedict Burgh's *ABC of Aristotle*, were less aids to learning how to read than they were guides to good conduct, like the **courtesy books**, a category of book popular in the period. Yet the structure of Burgh's poem helped even illiterate listeners to recognise and learn the alphabet.

In the Netherlands, as in England, prayer books designed for children started to appear which helped them also with learning to read the vernacular languages. Such books usually

Prayer book with an alphabet and texts in Dutch and Latin for beginner readers (Bruges, *c.*1445). Girls receive a reading lesson from a female teacher, who holds a ferrule, or wooden paddle, for use against disobedient students. A **hornbook** hangs on the wall to her left. On the right, the capital and small letters of the alphabet used in Flemish manuscripts of that time are shown. Note that the different forms of 'r' and 's' are included, and that there is no 'j' or 'w'.

The British Library, Harley MS 3828

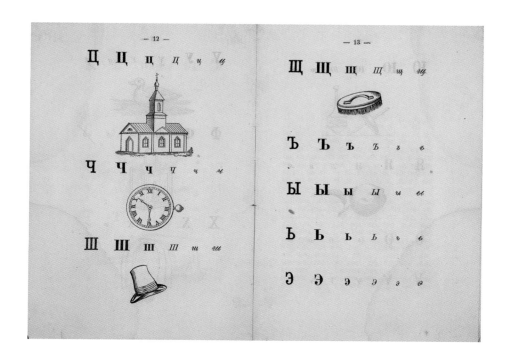

included the alphabet and the sounds of the letters, the three Latin prayers learned by all (the *Pater Noster, Ave, Maria* and the *Credo*), and a range of texts of increasing difficulty. This method placed the child at the centre of image- and text-learning – really the model of most later printed **primers**, like the very attractive and popular *azbukas* produced by Count Leo Tolstoy (1828–1910) for illiterate peasant children in 19th-century Russia.

By the 15th century, in areas of increasing social mobility, ways were being devised to ensure that girls, as well as boys, could read and write. The beautiful vellum manuscript, opposite, now in the British Library, was produced in the 1440s, at the same time as printing was being perfected by Johannes Gutenberg in Mainz. This expensive manuscript was created by a team in Bruges known as the 'Masters of the Gold Scrolls'. One artist produced the miniature, another illuminated the borders and yet another scribe wrote the letters. One is tempted to see the girl shown in the foreground, reading to her teacher, as the child for whom the

manuscript was prepared. It was an asset for girls to learn to read and write: in mercantile classes, it also made it more likely for them to marry well. Literate mothers, too, were able to teach their children the delights of reading; in later centuries the mother's role in teaching reading became ever more important.

Teaching through Pictures: *The Childes First Tutor*

The first illustrated books intended for children started to be published in the 1650s. Despite Puritan influences, some teaching books also intended to amuse their readers appeared.

The dulling effects of Puritanism on publishing in Britain during the period of Oliver Cromwell's rule were marked, but idealistic ideas about teaching spread from the Continent, particularly with the English translation of Comenius' *Orbis Sensualium Pictus* (1658), in 1659 (see pp. 78–9).

The earliest surviving English book of this kind was evidently aimed at parents: *The Childes First Tutor: or, the Master & Mistris*, by 'Festus Corin', published by an enterprising London bookseller, Francis Cressinet, at the Anchor and Mariner in Towerstreet. Cressinet had published an elegy to the memory of Cromwell when the 'Lord Protector' died in 1658, so in *The Childes First Tutor* Cressinet prudently made sure that the text revealed loyalty to the King: for the letter 'K', with an

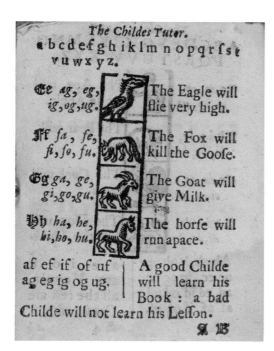

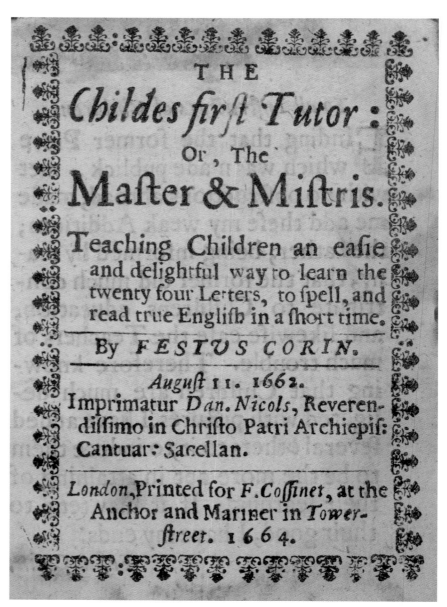

ABOVE AND LEFT
Festus Corin, *The Childes First Tutor*. London: printed for F. Cossinet, 1664. Title page and wood-cut from this rare surviving copy (being the second, enlarged edition), which until the early 1980s was accidentally walled up within an old cottage in Hampshire. The back of the book includes promotion of other books published by Cossinet, setting the tone for publishers to come. The British Library

accompanying image of Charles II, the text read: 'Long may King Charls live, and wear his Crown / To tread all Heresie and Schism down.' Nothing seems to be known of 'Festus Corin' – perhaps the pseudonym conceals a hack writer employed by Cressinet (or perhaps Francis Cressinet himself).

The book's subtitle, 'Teaching children an easie and delightful way to learn the twenty four letters, to spell, and read true English in a short time', promised a lot. Cressinet published several other good educational books, such as Thomas Hunt's *Libellus orthographicus, or, The Diligent school boy's directory* [to spelling] (1661), or *Daniel's Copy Book* (1664), engraved by the famous writing master Edward Cocker. There were other books he published whose titles we know, but no copies are known to exist. Like many of these small books, they were simply read to destruction; only a single battered copy of a second edition of *The Childes First Tutor* survives, and that only because it was immured in a Hampshire cottage shortly after publication, only to be rediscovered in recent years.

Another equally rare teaching book survives, again only in a single copy, in the Bodleian Library in Oxford : *A Play-Book for Children to Allure them to Read assoon* [sic] *as they can Speak Plain,* by 'J. G.', printed for John Harris at the Harrow in the Poultry (London), 1694. Harris did his best to allure purchasers for this book too; the subtitle reads: 'composed of small pages on purpose not to tire children, and printed with a fair and pleasant letter, the matter and method plainer and easier than any yet extant'. Whether this persuaded many purchasers, or if there were other editions of this book, is unknown – true of so many books intended for children – but if John Harris (or later his widow Elizabeth) failed to reprint, other publishers would have been eager to adopt their method for themselves.

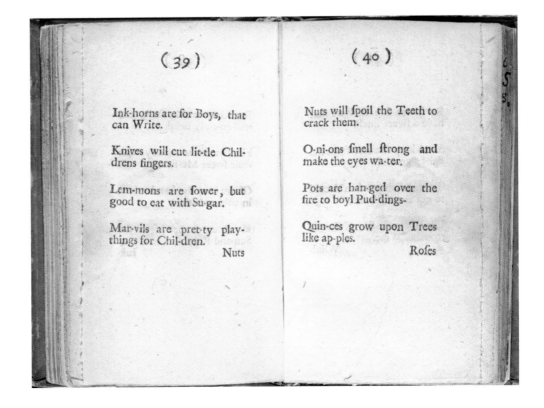

J. G., *A Play-Book for Children.* London: printed for John Harris, 1694. This small book, not enlivened with cuts, progresses from a simple alphabet through vowels, consonants and diphthongs, to lists ('Words of One Syllable', 'Two Syllables' and so on, all the way to 'Six'), and more complicated reading texts such as the one shown here.

Bodleian Library, Oxford, Wing G37

'Gilding the Gingerbread' and the ABC

Paper and books were fragile things in the hands of young children. Hornbooks were devised to make the texts long-lasting – with some tasty exceptions.

Vellum has always been valuable, and paper very fragile. To teach children their ABC, the **hornbook** was invented to carry and preserve texts, using a format which finds its origins in the waxed tablets of ancient civilisations. Later on, more luxurious versions of hornbooks also appeared, and throughout Europe and the Americas too; on some, the lettering was imprinted into metal, or cut in ivory or incised in wood. In time, they became highly collectable, and some cautious experts doubt the genuineness of some added to museum collections in the last hundred years.

In the Netherlands, moulds for letters were cut from wood (and in recent times, copied and sold as antiques), ready for their use by the pastry cooks, to form gingerbread figures, which were then baked and gilded. They were intended as rewards for good children who recognised the letters! The poet Matthew Prior (1664–1721) recorded:

I mentioned different ways of breeding:
Begin we in our children's reading.
To master John the English maid
A horn-book gives of ginger-bread;
And, that the child may learn the better,
As he can name, he eats the letter.
Proceeding thus with vast delight,
He spells, and gnaws, from left to right.

Hornbook, painted wood, Mexico, probably early 17th century. Its former owner, the collector George Plimpton, considered this to be probably the oldest hornbook made in the Americas. It depicts the child Jesus holding a globe surmounted by a cross, with an alphabet below (preceded by another cross, as customary on hornbooks).
Columbia University Libraries, Plimpton Hornbook No. 19

In 1708 the poet William King commented on 'The enticing Gold on Ginger-bread', and a generation later, in *Humphry Clinker,* Smollett remarked 'She don't yet know her letters, but I will bring her the A B C in ginger-bread.' It was a dangerous prize: the cooks used 'orsidue', or Dutch leaf, for the gilding, and this gold-substitute, made from copper and zinc, apparently contained a touch of arsenic as well. The Scottish writer Colin Mackenzie simply commented in his *One Thousand Experiments in Chemistry* (1821) that 'the use of this poisonous material for gilding gingerbread and sweetmeats cannot be too much reprobated'. Yes, indeed.

In their time, hornbooks were to be found in many schoolrooms, as seen in the miniature from the Flemish **abecedary** (see pp. 52–3). In Lyly, Shakespeare and others' work onwards, hornbooks were often mentioned, and the word 'hornbook' both acquired fresh meanings and was used to mean *all* teaching aids of this kind. But by the late 18th century, wooden hornbooks had disappeared.

Advances in papermaking and card production were the reason for the decline. For school use, hornbooks were replaced by **battledores**. Many provincial printers of **chapbooks**, such as William Davison of Alnwick, seized the opportunities battledores offered to them. Schoolchildren must have found that these light cardboard publications made good weapons in schoolroom scrimmages.

Miss Fanny Goes Shopping

The production of paper-cut books or pages is as old as paper itself.
For girls, dolls were favourite toys, and paper dolls had special advantages.

In China, the use of paper has had a long and important role, for example in the making of paper monies, and also household items to be used as surrogates for burning as offerings to the gods in the Hungry Ghosts or other religious ceremonies. In Indonesia, puppet cut-outs were utilised in the *wayang kulit*, or shadow theatres, widely enjoyed by young and old.

Early in Western life, images cut from paper appealed to children, and paper dolls were probably made by many mothers for their daughters. These had advantages apart from play: they enabled women to teach their daughters about fashion – and in the days of Jane Austen (for example), fashion plates of the latest Parisian modes were eagerly purchased by well-to-do ladies.

Paper dolls have other links in history: Jumping Jacks, or *pantins*, in France – figures of paper, card or wood with moveable limbs pulled by strings – had long been popular. (In ancient Egypt, ivory Jumping Jacks have been found at El Lisht.) German publishers reportedly printed paper dolls in the late 18th century, but their manufacture took off in Regency London, at the Fuller brothers' 'Temple of Fancy' in Rathbone Place.

Samuel and Joseph Fuller had previously worked with Edward Orme (one of the most successful print publishers in London) and showed much flair in their business dealing in artists' materials and prints, which started in 1809. Although they were not primarily children's publishers, they published *Little Fanny* in 1810, a moral story about a young

The History of Little Fanny, exemplified in a series of figures. London: Printed for S. & J. Fuller at the Temple of Fancy, Rathbone Place, 1810. This was the first commercially popular paper-doll book produced in England, and a favourite with the young Princess Victoria. It was a series of seven figures, with one separate head designed to be moved from costume to costume as the story progressed. Some of the Fullers' productions included accompanying text, to aid play.
Theriault's Antique Doll Auctions

girl whose love of dress has awful consequences – with the final result that she turns
from idle pastimes to the more productive
one of reading (rather an arch moral for
a **toy book**). The sleeve containing this little
book included hand-coloured cut-outs of
costumes printed separately on card, plus a
single head, which tucked into a slit in each
costume; simple in concept, but enormously
successful. S. & J. Fuller produced expensive
books of this sort for about ten years, before
abandoning the concept to more downmarket
firms to fill the demand.

The closely related toy theatres which were
produced along with play scripts were also
very popular in Regency times, with the plays
enacted by children for themselves or for the
whole family. Ingenious manufacturers found
fold-up cardboard stages (along with their
paper actors) very profitable. The sets were
often immensely elaborate and the dramas
complex; the latter were sometimes topical
ballad enactments, sometimes classics, like
Shakespeare. The firms were often in
business in poorer areas, like Pollock & Co.
who from the 1850s, in a tiny shop in Hoxton,

published the 'penny plain, tuppence
coloured' sheets admired by Robert Louis
Stevenson. Benjamin Pollock's Toyshop,
now in Covent Garden, still sells these toys
which entranced our Victorian ancestors.

Juvenile publishers like Dean & Son,
Raphael Tuck and F. Warne & Co. also
produced toy theatres and paper dolls. In the
United States, *The History and Adventures of
Little Henry* (1812) by J. Belcher was an early
Boston piracy of the Fuller doll-book style,
and from the 1820s onwards huge numbers
of doll books were published in America by
the McCoughlin Brothers.

In the 20th century, manufacturers realised
the commercial value of paper figures, tucked
as freebies into packets of foodstuffs (like
flour) and in newspapers. Paper dolls by
artists such as the cartoonist Grace Drayton
are now regarded as highly collectable.
Although simple in concept, paper dolls
retain their popularity. This early form of
'interactive' play lends itself to the computer
age: indeed, traditionally styled paper dolls,
like those by Tom Tierney, are now even
produced as computer apps as well.

Fighting the Unrighteous – in the Nursery

Moral causes were at the core of Victorian society. In the British Empire
slavery ended in the 1830s, but when would it end elsewhere?

The anti-slavery movement was strong in Britain by the 1780s, long before the British navy enforced abolition of the international slave trade in 1807. Slavery itself finally became illegal throughout British possessions in 1834. In the expanding United States, trade in imported African slaves was prohibited in 1808, yet the use of 'home-grown' slaves continued, particularly in the South. Like the British, many people in America's northern states were appalled by slavery. One abolitionist story, *Uncle Tom's Cabin, or Life Among the Lowly,* was intended to alert people to the reality of slave life: hugely influential, it went on to become the bestselling novel of the century.

EVA PUTTING A WREATH OF FLOWERS
ROUND TOM'S NECK

She will read to Tom for hours on hours,
And sit with him on the grass all day;
You see she is wreathing pretty flowers
About his neck, in her pleasant play.

ABOVE AND LEFT
Pictures and Stories from Uncle Tom's Cabin. Boston: John P.
Jewett & Co., *c.*1853. In the last instalment in *The National
Era* Stowe addressed directly 'the dear little children who
have followed her story'. Her first edition included just six
engravings; later editions were more heavily illustrated and
adapted for very young readers, including revising the ending.

Rare Book and Special Collections Division, Library of Congress,
Washington D.C.

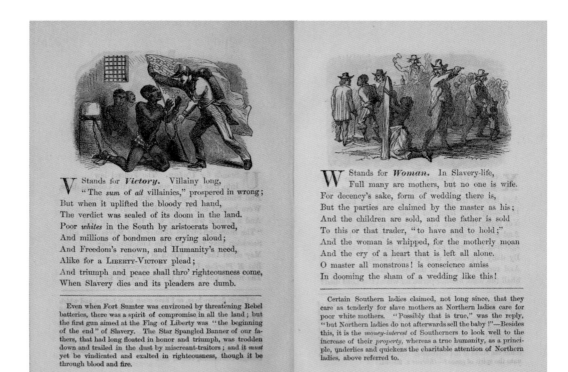

V Stands for **Victory.** Villainy long,
"The *sum of all* villainies," prospered in wrong;
But when it uplifted the bloody red hand,
The verdict was sealed of its doom in the land.
Poor *whites* in the South by aristocrats bowed,
And millions of bondmen are crying aloud;
And Freedom's renown, and Humanity's need,
Alike for a LIBERTY-VICTORY plead;
And triumph and peace shall thro' righteousness come,
When Slavery dies and its pleaders are dumb.

Even when Fort Sumter was environed by threatening Rebel batteries, there was a spirit of compromise in all the land; but the first gun aimed at the Flag of Liberty was "the beginning of the end" of Slavery. The Star Spangled Banner of our fathers, that had long floated in honor and triumph, was trodden down and trailed in the dust by miscreant-traitors; and it *must* yet be vindicated and exalted in righteousness, though it be through blood and fire.

W Stands for **Woman.** In Slavery-life,
Full many are mothers, but no one is wife.
For decency's sake, form of wedding there is,
But the parties are claimed by the master as his;
And the children are sold, and the father is sold
To this or that trader, "to have and to hold;"
And the woman is whipped, for the motherly moan
And the cry of a heart that is left all alone.
O master all monstrous! is conscience amiss
In dooming the sham of a wedding like this!

Certain Southern ladies claimed, not long since, that they care as tenderly for slave mothers as Northern ladies care for poor white mothers. "Possibly that is true," was the reply, "but Northern ladies do not afterwards sell the baby!"—Besides this, it is the *money-interest* of Southerners to look well to the increase of their *property*, whereas a true humanity, as a principle, underlies and quickens the charitable attention of Northern ladies, above referred to.

Just as abolitionists in Britain had used Josiah Wedgwood's medallion 'Am I not a Man and a Brother?' (showing a slave enchained) for their anti-slavery campaigns, so *Uncle Tom's* author, Harriet Beecher Stowe (1811–96), hoped to persuade white Southerners that black people were indeed their 'brothers'. Her story, first written for her own children, about a slave's adventures after he is 'sold down the river', partly based on the autobiography of former slave Josiah Henson, was first published in weekly instalments in the abolitionist journal, *The National Era*, from 1851 to 1852, and in book form in 1852.

Many living in the South believed that Beecher Stowe's melodramatic and highly sentimental tale bore little relation to reality. Several 'anti-Tom' books were produced, one of the most popular being *Aunt Phillis's Cabin or Southern Life as it is* (1852), a defence of slave ownership by Mary Henderson Eastman.

Sales of *Uncle Tom's Cabin* were initially very brisk in America, but then languished for a few years. In Britain, in 1853, in a shrewd move, the young publisher Sam Beeton published the first of several editions, which eventually sold something like a million and a half copies altogether. This was an unprecedented number for such a book: both Mrs Stowe and Beeton made a lot of money, and the success of *Uncle Tom* ensured the success of Beeton's later publishing ventures.

Uncle Tom was one marker for the forthcoming Civil War, and both sides used juvenile publishing to support their beliefs. *The Gospel of Slavery*, the 1864 'primer of freedom', by Unitarian minister Abel C. Thomas, writing as 'Iron Gray', took the form of an illustrated children's **alphabetary** in verse. It pulled no punches. Its publisher, T. W. Strong, was one of the best New York publishers of illustrated books of the time.

Aiming High, with Some Surprising Lows

Writers for children are often idealists. Some, by attempting too much, have failed miserably.

The first English edition by Caxton of Aesop's *Fables* (1484) was an immediate success with readers. It was not until 1585, however, that a schoolteacher, William Bullokar (*c.*1531–1609), produced his carefully planned edition intended for children. Its title page said it all: Æsopz Fablz in tru Ortŏgraphy with Grammar notz. Her-ʋnto ąr also jooinęd the short sentencez of the wýs Cato ... transláteḍ oʋt-of Latin in-too English by William Bʋllokar. Bullokar was, in fact, a very early spelling reformer who thought that reading was made easier if the spelling was adjusted to reflect the sounds. In reality, children using his book had to learn a lot of extra accented letters in the blackletter font used; and, in time, needed to learn to read the ordinary letters as well. Few printers had the range of types to reproduce them.

Bullokar's bold experiment was a total failure, but plenty of later, would-be spelling reformers were to make similar mistakes, such as the 'Initial Teaching Alphabet' (ITA) used by Ladybird Books for some of their books in the 1960s (see p. 227). (ITA was later abandoned, and is today a mystery to all but those of an age to have used ITA in their schooldays.)

Some idealists seek to use special alphabets for cultural or political reasons. In Sweden, the influential Johan Bure (1568–1652), librarian and adviser to King Gustavus Adolphus, deplored the disappearance of the old Runic writing style of pagan times. In 1607 Bure obtained royal support for publishing a **primer** which showed the use of runes, alongside the Roman and Fraktur typefaces normally used then in Swedish texts.

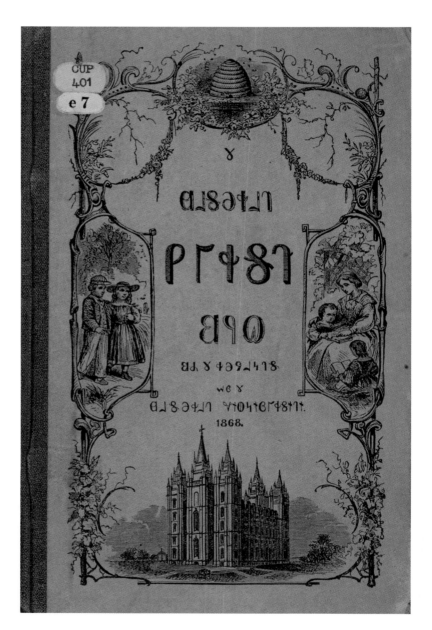

The Deseret First Book. [Salt Lake City]: Regents of the Deseret University, 1868. The Victorian lushness of the illustrations throughout bears little relation to the probable reality of pioneering life in Utah in those days. They were taken from Marcius Willson's Readers, published by Harpers, which in their day were schoolbooks as popular and widely used in Utah as McGuffey's Readers were elsewhere in the United States.
The British Library

Bure's *RVNA ABC Boken* (*Runic ABC Book*) published in Stockholm in 1611 was a creditable piece of work, but it did not persuade many other Swedes to use runes.

To have a range of letters, or language, that can be read only by an exclusive group is always attractive. (Think how many children's games involve the use of secret codes.) Spelling reform was a bee buzzing in many bonnets in the 1840s, and the development of shorthand by Pitman and others encouraged many people to think about changing the alphabet. One was Brigham Young (1801–77), the charismatic President of the Latter Day Saints, who led believers from Illinois to Deseret (round Salt Lake, Utah) to follow their own religion. One of these was the first English convert to Mormonism, George D. Watt (1812–81), who had studied Pitman's shorthand and became Brigham Young's secretary. Watt's influence was crucial in the decision to produce a special alphabet for Mormon use. No doubt it would have been much simpler and cheaper for them to use the ordinary types available from American printers' suppliers, but instead they had a special font cast exclusively for them by the St Louis Typefoundry; in 1854 it was used to print 10,000 copies of a primer for use in the Utah schools.

In the next few years this font was used quite extensively to print editions of the *Book of Mormon* and other Latter Day Saints texts, and a regular section in this typeface was included in the *Deseret News*. A second primer was brought out in 1868, but its production simply reconfirmed that the experiment was very unpopular with young readers. The Deseret font was quietly forgotten and is now remembered only as a quaint memory of early days in Utah.

Animating the Nursery

'Pop-ups' and other moving children's books were invented early on, but German publishers found other ingenious ways to divert the nursery reader.

From the 18th century onwards, book workers, inventors and artists spread from Germany and Austria to London. Even before Alois Senefelder (1771–1834) invented the process of **lithography** in Bavaria in 1796, German printing machines and illustration processes – and the people to work them – were spreading across to the British printing trade. One such emigré in Victorian times was Raphael Tuck (1821–1900), a Prussian Jew who moved with his family to London, opening a shop in 1866, and becoming a British citizen in 1875.

Initially the Tucks sold only picture frames and coloured prints, but soon branched out

Buttercup Pictures, a book of Circling Scenes. Printed in Bavaria, no. 448. London: Ernest Nister; New York: E. P. Dutton & Co., 1899. With verses by Helen Marion Burnside and pen-and-ink illustrations by L. M. Glazier. Nister's 'revolving' or 'dissolving' pictures technique was foreshadowed by Dean & Sons, who produced illustrations divided into several equal 'Venetian blind' sections, with pull-tabs to transform the image. Nister devised a mechanism to reveal pictures in a circular form, creating a kaleidoscope, as here, with ribbons attached to revolve the pictures.

Collection Ana Maria Ortega

into a huge range of stationery items – Christmas cards, Valentines, calendars, picture postcards and gift books, as well as paper dolls, children's books and games and novelties. By 1900 Tuck and his sons had developed a business empire built on the high-quality publications printed for them in Germany, distributing them worldwide through stationers and newsagents (and not through booksellers alone). The Tucks' was a global enterprise, with branches in New York and Montreal, and additional agencies in such other cities as Bombay, Buenos Aires and Cape Town.

Their huge sales of cards bolstered their publication of children's books (at very modest prices), and the firm paid artists and authors generously. But their books were really commercial *products*, not memorable stories: overly sweet, sentimental 'chocolate box' illustrations, in little books which were very popular with casual buyers. Though highly collectable, they seem to have simultaneously been regarded as expendable. Tuck books have hardly ever become classics.

One of the main rivals to the Tucks was Ernest Nister (1842–1909), a Nuremberg printer who had worked with the publisher Theodore Stroefer (who published German translations of English books). In 1888 Nister moved to London and set up to produce English books printed in Germany. In some ways Nister's work was like that of the Tucks (he also published postcards), but Nister perfected and patented a new way of producing 'revolving' or 'dissolving' pictures, as they were known, to illustrate his children's books. Nuremberg printers were adept at this work, and books such as *Peeps into Fairy Land* and *Buttercup Pictures* (both from the 1890s) show Nister's work at its best. He was a difficult employer, modifying artists' illustrations to fit in with his vision – but his books, illustrated by artists such as Beatrix Potter and Louis Wain, were praised for their 'exquisite sentimental beauty'.

Nister's books were distributed in America by E. P. Dutton. After the start of the First World War, anti-German sentiment brought the British publishing of Ernest Nister to a halt in 1915. Nonetheless, the Tuck business continued to flourish until 1940, when a German air raid destroyed the Tucks' premises; stock, blocks, drawings and files were all destroyed. It was a sad end to an impressive attempt to create a publisher for the whole world.

With Father Tuck, In Fairyland. Panorama. London: Raphael Tuck & Sons, *c.*1900. This complex accordion-folded panorama by Tuck comprised eight lithographic scenes (with story text on the reverse) and thirty-six figures to enact within them, including 'The Giant'. The figures were intended for the numbered pockets but the publishers suggested that 'a variety of scenes [...] can be formed, and unending pleasure provided, by placing the figures in innumerable positions'.

Collection Ana Maria Ortega

Colonial Problems, Local Solutions

European colonists settling in the Americas took with them their own ideas about teaching children, and in the 18th century books produced in New England were very similar to those of Britain. But in Asia and Africa things took a different turn.

European colonists moving eastwards had different objectives from the settlers moving to the Americas. The question of whether (or how) to educate indigenous peoples, using unfamiliar languages and scripts, was much debated. At one extreme, assisting indirect rule included sending the sons of Indian maharajahs, Malay sultans or Balinese princes to elite schools in Europe (or prestigious local schools designed with the same public school ethos). Old precepts of 'divide and rule' often applied in governing colonies, with the spread of European-style education restricted to small groups. In both British India and the Dutch East Indies (now Indonesia), it was thought prudent to limit the widespread understanding or use of English or Dutch, and publishing in vernacular languages was closely watched and controlled.

Nevertheless, development demanded an increasing availability of literate staff; and missionary zeal pushed for the spread of teaching. In India, the Calcutta School-Book Society was established, in 1817, to publish textbooks for schools and madrasas in the country, translated into a variety of Indian languages. By the end of the 19th century, through groups such as the School-Book Society, Bengali writing had blossomed, notably in the work of the poet Rabindranath Tagore (1861–1941), the first writer outside Europe to be awarded the Nobel Prize for Literature (1913). In the 1930s Tagore brought out a primer and alphabet book called *Sahaj Path* (*Easy Learning*) that was like no other

Rabindranath Tagore, *Sahaj Path*. [Calcutta]: Visva-Bharati, 1930. The distinctive lino-cuts by Nandalal Bose and Tagore's verse in this classic Bengali primer play on the associative nature of alphabet sounds to stimulate the child readers' imagination and their enjoyment in learning. Here, on a page illustrated with a crawling child, the couplet explores the sounds 'a' and 'aa'.
SOAS, University of London, by permission of Visva-Bharati

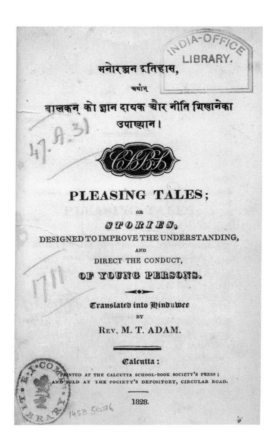

alphabet book. It showed that Tagore was well aware of Lewis Carroll and other English writers, but it also addressed the vernacular culture and its needs. Indian writing for children had reached full maturity.

Starting much later, the Dutch took a different approach to fostering literature in their colonies. In 1917 the colonial government in Batavia (now Jakarta) set up the Balai Pustaka (or Bureau of Literature). A large operation, with hundreds of staff, including a translation section, editorial staff, the provision of library services and a well-equipped printing plant, the Balai Pustaka was largely responsible for developing the national language (Bahasa Indonesia), but also publishing in such other languages as Javanese, Batak and Sundanese.

It published many books by local authors, as well as issuing translations of such books as *Sinbad the Sailor* (1924) and *The Adventures of Tom Sawyer* (1928). When Indonesia became independent, the bureau was incorporated into the Ministry of Education, and the nature of books published by the Balai Pustaka changed over time.

Just as Balai Pustaka hothoused the development of Indonesian literature, something similar was developed later on in Nigeria. Nigeria was governed by Britain from 1903, administered by indirect rule, through local emirs. Education in the north was limited and loyalty to the colonial ethos was questionable. About the time of the Munich crisis in 1938, a troubling local rumour was that the colonial authorities intended handing Nigeria over to Nazi Germany. The government-owned Northern Literacy Agency was set up, to produce a newspaper, *Gaskiya Tafi Kwabo* (*Truth Is Worth More than a Penny*), to counter such rumours. It was written in Hausa, a language understood by many northerners. Its production was passed by the Northern Literary Agency to the Gaskiya Corporation set up in Zaria, an organisation rather like those of the Bureau of Literature in Java. The Gaskiya Corporation proved very effective, and as well as many other Hausa books its publications included some designed for younger readers.

Such attempts by colonial administrators were well-meaning, but propaganda tempts many a politician; unfortunately these ventures enabled later governments to meddle with (or take over) the production of schoolbooks. There are dissatisfactions in many ex-colonial countries today with the quality, accuracy and bias of their (former) educational publications.

Books Designed by Engineers

The latest developments in pop-up and mechanical books were perfected in Bavaria. Much later, paper engineering was reinvented in Soviet-controlled Czechoslovakia.

Moveable books from firms like Dean & Son and Ernest Nister in 19th-century London were an ingenious commercial success. These were sensible business operations whose publication programmes were based on what the partners thought books should be.

One major innovator in the design, development and marketing of books competing in this field was Lothar Meggendorfer (1847–1925), a Bavarian illustrator whose cartoons first appeared, when he was fifteen, in the weekly Munich comic *Fliegende Blätter* (*Loose Sheets*). Meggendorfer was amazingly prolific,

Vojtěch Kubašta, *Sagan om Rödluvan* (*Little Red Riding Hood*). Stockholm: Bok konsum, 1961. Though the paper-engineering seems simple in comparison to Meggendorfer's often more finicky creations, Kubašta's illustrations for these popular fairy tales were very effective, and these tales were translated into many languages with his accompanying illustrations, such as the Swedish version, printed and assembled in Prague by Artia, shown below.

Collection Ana Maria Ortega

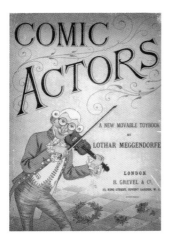

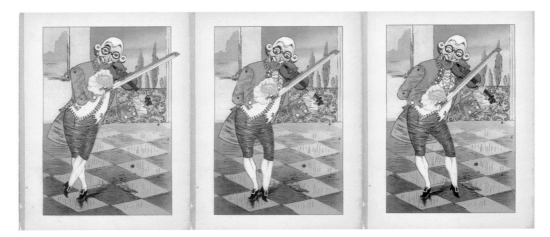

Lothar Meggendorfer, *Comic Actors*. London: H. Grevel & Co., 1891. Meggendorfer's first moving-pictures book was *Lebende Bilder* (*Living Pictures*), in 1878; he later turned his mechanical ingenuity to many more complex pop-up and moveable formats, so influential on contemporary book artists. This production contains eight moveable illustrations to 'The Dancing Master' who 'always keeps a smiling face while teaching steps with vigour'.

Collection Ana Maria Ortega

designing over forty board games and about two hundred pop-up and moveable books; his work was widely published in French and English as well as German editions. While readers may be repelled, sometimes, by the German artistic style of the period, many more marvel at the ingenious complexity of Meggendorfer's constructions – and collectors greatly prize them.

Changes in publishing tastes and the huge social and political upheavals in Europe after the First World War reduced the demand for such complex publications. But by the Second World War there was a marked increase in the range of cut-out books produced.

Before the First World War, Bohemia was part of the Austro-Hungarian Empire, and book design from Prague was widely admired. In the 1950s, when Czechoslovakia was under Soviet control, the architect and artist Vojtêch Kubašta (1914–92) started to produce cut-out and moveable books, marketed by Artia, a state-run publisher which successfully marketed books on Czech art, design and music for distribution by

Western publishers. Kubašta's first pop-up book was *Little Red Riding Hood*, published by Artia in 1956; a London edition appeared in 1960 and other translated editions soon after. He followed this with many other pop-up versions of fairy stories and also 'serious' educational books. His hugely popular books were published in many languages, reportedly selling over 35 million copies worldwide (and collectors pay very high prices when they find them). Almost equally popular was Kubašta's annually published nativity cut-out sheets which allowed children to build a 3-D nativity scene.

Kubašta's work showed that mobile books were not necessarily limited to a past generation's publishing. In 1993, partly because of the interest created by Kubašta's books, the Moveable Book Society was set up. Its work includes deciding upon and giving out the Meggendorfer Award for the best commercially published moveable book. Adults and young children alike continue to delight in the wizardry of these paper-engineered books.

CHAPTER 4

The Childe's First Tutor:
The Education of the Young

Since the earliest days in Sumer and Egypt parents have sought ways to ensure the health, welfare and success of their children. The ways of doing this have always varied widely.

The role of educating the newborn child has always fallen first and foremost to the mother (or wet-nurse or foster-mother), with fathers traditionally taking a secondary role. Yet there have been plenty of male parents scolded for interfering, like the Elizabethan clergyman who fulminated against a father spoiling his young child, who 'dandill hym and didill hym and pamper him and stroke his hedd ... and gyve him the swytest soppe in the dish' ('dandles him and diddles him, and pampers him and strokes his head ... and gives him the sweetest piece in the dish'). Advice on how to bring up children *properly* continues to appear everywhere.

The earliest parental guides were usually **conduct books**; aimed at teaching children to be civilised and not like savage Yahoos (the deformed humanoids of Swift's *Gulliver's Travels*, who only made worse the vices Nature gave them by using their brains). The prime purpose of such books as *The Babees Book* (see pp. 74–5) was to help parents achieve this. As the Elizabethan clergyman Thomas Becon observed, 'learning without manners is as a gold ring in a swine's snout'.

In time such guides became an established publishing genre, particularly in the form of self-help books (as a visit to any contemporary bookshop makes clear). One useful early guide was Edmund Coote's *The Schoole-maister* (1596), a practical aid to teaching reading, aimed at 'men and women of trades (as tailors, weavers, shopkeepers, seamsters and such other) as have undertaken the charge of teaching others'. Coote's manual, by no means the only one, was very successful: by 1737 it was in its 54th edition, at just about the time publishing for children was taking off.

Elias Martin (1739–1818), *Reading Lesson at a Dame School*, 18th century.

Yale Center for British Art, Paul Mellon Collection

Two rather bored young noblemen at their studies: *Serafino and Francesco Falzacappa*, by Pier Leone Ghezzi, *c.*1720. Black chalk, pen and brown ink 16.2 × 26.7cm. Ghezzi came into contact with the family, from Tarquinia, when he was commissioned by them to paint an altarpiece. He made several studies of the family, and in particular of Serafino, shown here practising writing his name.

The J. Paul Getty Museum, Los Angeles

There is ample evidence of the often brutal methods used by teachers in trying to *force* children to learn: Richard Busby, headmaster of Westminster School from 1638 till his death in 1695, was a good scholar, but would not tolerate stupidity in his pupils. The *Oxford Dictionary of National Biography* mildly comments that 'as a disciplinarian [Busby] was feared by his charges (and their mothers).' John Aubrey, in his *Brief Lives*, was less circumspect: 'I have heard several of [Busby's] Scholars affirme, that he hath marred by his severity more than he hath made.' Other masters could be equally harsh, but by the 19th century professional teachers, such as Thomas Arnold at Rugby, or Edward Thring at Uppingham, had adopted the more humane approach to teaching which underpinned the development of public schools in Victorian Britain.

Brutality was, of course, not limited to male teachers, and shocking cases were reported of sadistic behaviour towards children by their nannies or governesses, such as the ill-treatment of Lord Curzon, later Viceroy of India, by his governess Ellen Mary Paraman. ('No children well-born and well-placed ever cried so much and so justly,' Curzon later recorded in some autobiographical notes.)

Schooling for boys was often provided by clergymen, like the 17th-century chaplain at Maidenhead, who supplemented his stipend and 'demanded but 3d. a week for every scholar that learned English only'. Boys could be sent away to schools, and many were. For girls, education was more complicated. There were 'Dame Schools', costing a few pence a week. Some were well run, but the worst were little more than child-minding services run by barely literate women who made little attempt to teach. For Catholics, girls might be sent to schools run by the Poor Clares (an order of nuns), or in Stuart times, the institutions set up on the continent by Mary Ward (1585–1645). For most girls, being taught at home was usual, as Mary Ward herself had been; likewise the Anglican Barbara Johnson, who was taught at home in Lincolnshire by her mother (see pp. 86–7).

For the well-to-do, the provision of a governess was common, and poorer relatives within the household often took on this role. To tutor royalty called for exceptional qualities – including bravery: Katherine Ashley was appointed by Thomas Cromwell to be governess to the three-year-old Princess Elizabeth in 1536, teaching the (exceptionally well-educated) princess her ABC from 'a delicate little horn-book of silver filigree'. The governess's post cost her long spells in prison in the Tower of London during the reigns of Edward VI and Mary; only when Elizabeth came to the throne in 1558 was Kat Ashley's life safe.

British (and especially Scottish) govern-esses were highly esteemed abroad and in Russia, a century after Katherine, tutors to the young Prince Peter (later Peter the Great) ran just as many risks (see pp. 82–3). British governesses continued to be employed in Russia until 1917, and in Latin America until the Second World War. They brought with them their precepts for 'good manners' – and their stories and nursery rhymes. The Argentinian writer Victoria Ocampo, rather a 'wild pony' as a girl, had both French and English governesses; she wrote about her 'Miss Ellis', who grumbled that her pupil would never become a lady and sang 'Pat-a-cake, pat-a-cake, baker's man' to calm her, a nursery rhyme Ocampo remembered all her life.

Beyond rhymes, children had great interest in the world around them, and books about trades and occupations were as interesting for them as for the parents looking to their children's apprenticeships. Many of the best of these were produced in German-speaking countries: Jost Amman's *Der Ständebuch* (or *The Book of Trades*, see p. 76) was a model for many such books produced in Britain. Even more famous was the insidiously successful *Orbis Sensualium Pictus* by the Czech scholar Comenius, first published in Nuremberg in 1658. Once translated into English it became a durable building block for schooling in Britain and America (see pp. 78–9). Comenius's book was *interesting* to children; and his ideas were behind many of the much later informative books for children, such as Arthur Mee's *Children's Encyclopaedia* of 1908–10 (see pp. 92–3).

Throughout much of the 16th and 17th centuries in Britain, religious turmoil was ever present, with martyrdoms on both sides of the Christian faith, during the dissolution of the monasteries under Henry VIII and the counter-Reformation of the 1550s during Queen Mary's reign. Fear of Rome was behind the most famous book of Elizabeth I's early reign: Foxe's *Actes and Monuments* (1563; see p. 91). Usually called Foxe's *Book of Martyrs*, it was a huge undertaking and one never designed in length or physical form for use by children, but it *was* recommended for child readers, and was hugely widely read. Versions of this lavishly illustrated manual, fomenting religious hatred, continued to be published well into the 20th century.

For Puritans, a constant worry about children, for those who did not believe in

The Pilgrim's Progress dissected, or a Complete view of Christian's travels, etc. London: John Wallis, etc.; Leeds: John Binns, 1790. This engraved coloured jigsaw puzzle, with a key, is an allegorical map based on the travels of Bunyan's Pilgrim, and reflects the book's popularity with children and the ready translation of literary subjects, even then, into the toy market.
The British Library

the efficacy of infant baptism, was that only sincere belief in the Christian God would avoid them going to Hell – and yet many parents had children who died too young to reveal their belief. Books like Benjamin Keach's *War with the Devil* (1676) or James Janeway's *A Token for Children* (1671; see p. 91) addressed these concerns. By showing how some 'saved' children had died 'in the arms of Jesus', Janeway hoped to persuade child readers to become sincere believers. His book was very influential, particularly in America, where his beliefs were reflected in other early children's books, such as *The New England Primer* (see pp. 88–9). The beliefs of the early settlers in America permeated their literature for centuries to come.

Only one Puritan book of the 17th century was more popular for children than *A Token for Children*, and that was John Bunyan's *The Pilgrim's Progress* (1678; see pp. 80–81).

This adult book was rapidly taken over for children's reading, and was familiar to almost every British child until well into the 20th century. Unlike many other more provocative Puritan writers, Bunyan's matter-of-fact style was acceptable to young readers, rather in the way *Robinson Crusoe* would be.

The mildness of this Puritan fervour is even more marked in Isaac Watts's *Divine Songs*, first published in 1715. Watts is remembered mostly for the hymns he wrote. In these poems written for children it is clear he recognised that gentleness in tone was far more likely to engage juvenile minds than making them afraid (see pp. 84–5). Many of these simple, innocent verses have stuck in people's memories to the present day, such as 'How doth the little busy bee / Improve each shining hour'; and Victorian child readers would have relished the naughtiness of Lewis Carroll's parody of it in *Alice in Wonderland*. Such readers would hardly have been aware of William Blake's *Songs of Innocence*, as the latter's works were not widely known until the end of Victoria's reign, but Watts's *Divine Songs* were surely in the back of Blake's mind during his composition of them.

By the early 19th century, as printing methods were improving, and governments around the world sought to improve the education of poorer people, the production of schoolbooks emerged as a potentially profitable genre for publishers. Newer firms brought new ideas about how to produce such books economically and well. In America, McGuffey's Readers series typifies (as Henry Ford later did) how mass production worked; by providing texts which helped to bring a growing nation together (see pp. 94–5). In parts of the British Empire, there were other facts to be taken into account. In 1831 the Irish Commission of National Education was set up to produce suitable textbooks (part of an attempt to reduce sectarian differences), and a team selected by a Roman Catholic, a Presbyterian and an Anglican writer devised the Irish National Readers, a series published in Dublin.

It was a success, and in the 1850s it was adopted in Canada (in preference to McGuffey), and in the colony of Victoria, Australia, where the Irish/English/Scottish mixture of immigrants suggested that the Irish National Readers series would be the best choice. It worked well enough, and was adopted in Queensland and New Zealand as well, but the Dublin printers were not well placed to adapt their editions for colonial readers and the Irish and heavily Catholic religious content was soon felt to be unsuitable. By the 1870s Thomas Nelson's Edinburgh-based Royal Readers series had replaced them for colonial use, with modifications (see pp. 96–7). Despite their age, books in this series continued to be used long after one would have expected them to have been superseded by the later schoolbooks produced by the education departments in many former colonial countries.

Decorative opening of Jane Johnson's *George William Johnson his book*. Manuscript 'printed and bound [and illustrated] by his Mama 1745'.
The Lilly Library, Indiana University, Bloomington, Indiana

'Lern, or Be Lewd' – Manners for the Young

Before Victorian times, people knew very little about the way children grew up in medieval England, until antiquaries delved into manuscripts intended for the young.

The early Victorian period was one of great change, and also one of great re-examination of earlier society. Scholars started exploring folk tales and nursery rhymes and, in Britain, the Philological Society was formed in 1842 to study languages (which eventually led to the publication of the *Oxford English Dictionary*). One important Philological Society member was Frederick J. Furnivall (1825–1910), one of the brilliant amateur eccentric and energetic scholars of the age. Furnivall was a volunteer in setting up the first Working Men's College in London (teaching English), and founded many publishing societies. His Early English Text Society (EETS), which put many important unpublished literary manuscripts into print for the first time, underpinned the study of English Literature as an academic field.

Most EETS volumes were purely literary works, but in 1868 Furnivall edited *Early English Meals and Manners*, a collection of short pieces on housekeeping and table manners, and some books like *The Babees Book* written for, or about, the young. These were nothing like the catechisms or **abecedaries** described in Chapter 3; they were really conduct or **courtesy books**.

The Babees Book, or A 'Lytyl Reporte' of How Young People Should Behave was written about 1475, at about the time Caxton was introducing printing to England. The book was aimed not at 'babies', but principally young noblemen, or would-be nobles, and it admonished them to 'Lern, or be Lewd'. It was packed with practical information on the household duties invaluable for a boy (usually one of about eight or nine years of age)

joining the retinue of an important man to master. Ambitious parents hoping for their sons to progress at court and their daughters to make good marriages pored over such instruction books as these.

These 15th-century conduct books gave useful advice on table manners, keeping your hands clean and becoming an acceptable companion. (Learning how to fit in with other

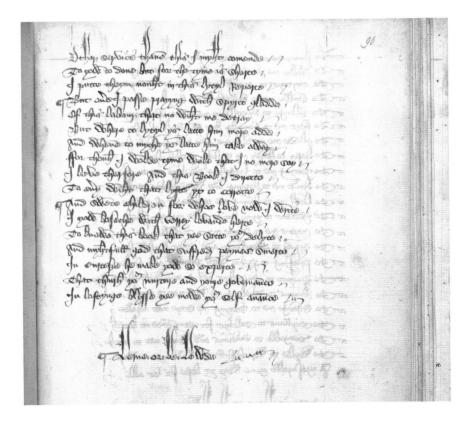

The Babees Book, or A 'Lytyl Reporte' of How Young People Should Behave. This Middle English verse text from the first half of the 15th century formed part of a compilation with a miscellany of treatises relating to 'Hunting, Manners, Human and Veterinary Medicine' (and including the only extant dietary advice for King Henry V).
The British Library

members of the household was as important in future centuries, when middle-class boys, and sometimes girls as well, were sent away to boarding schools.) We look in vain to these medieval authors for any indication of the place of pleasure in children's lives. (This is very different from Furnivall's own attitudes: superficially an irascible pedant spending all his working life poring over medieval manuscripts, Furnivall scandalised his contemporaries by spending time teaching working-class girls how to scull, or row, a boat and by taking them picnicking along the banks of the Thames.)

A similar text included by Furnivall in his collection was another short courtesy book

written about 1480, *The lytille childrenes lytil boke.* Crisp and to the point, the anonymous author repeats instructions ('Pyke not thy teeth with thy knyfe / In no company begynne thow stryfe') very similar to those of *The Babees Book*, and points out the advantages of such behaviour ('Then men wylle say thereafter / That a gentylleman was heere'). We might hear a modern school-teacher droning on in exactly the same way. By the 18th century, writers of books for children were just as anxious to bring up children in the right way, but had found more subtle ways to express it.

The Young Apprentice

With the coming of illustrated books for children in the 16th century,
their world, as viewed from the child's perspective, opens up to us too.

Nuremberg, in Bavaria, was one of the most important cities in Germany, and the *Die Schedelsche Weltchronik* (or *Nuremberg Chronicle*), published in 1493, was famous for its copious and elaborate illustrations. High-quality wood-cuts were a speciality of Nuremberg artists, and the Zurich-born artist Jost Amman (1539–91) did most of his work in the city. One of his most famous books was *Der Ständebuch* (*The Book of Trades*), issued in Frankfurt by Sigmund Feyerabend in 1568, which contained lively and accurate depictions of craftsmen at their work. Children have always been fascinated by how things work or are made, and dreamed of what they would choose to do (or might be apprenticed to do) when they grew up. Feyerabend's formula, together with Amman's skilful pictures and brief poems written by Hans Sachs, proved enormously successful, with children as well as adults. Amman's pictures, like those of Comenius in his *Orbis Sensualium Pictus* published ninety years later (see overleaf), have remained constantly popular, and today are taken as good evidence of what things were like in their time.

Similar illustrated guides to occupations were attempted throughout Western Europe, such as *Het Menselyk Bedryf*, another *Book of Trades*, with attractive copper engravings. This was an **emblem book** produced in Amsterdam in 1694 by Jan Luyken and his son Caspar during the Dutch 'Golden Age' (which reached its height with the elaborate technical illustrations of Diderot and D'Alembert's 1760s *Encyclopédie*).

In Regency England, Tabart published *The Book of Trades, or Library of the useful arts*

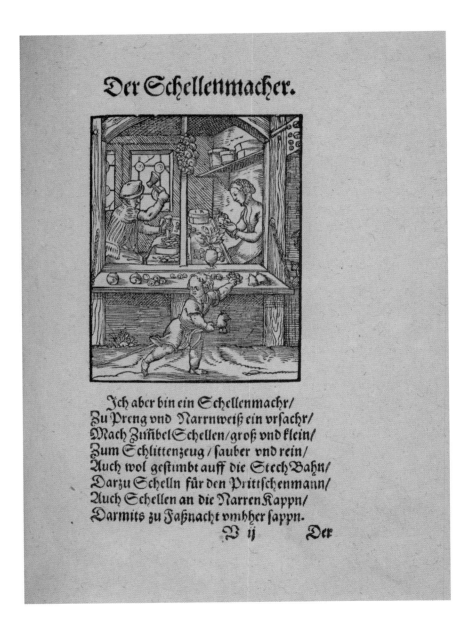

Eygentliche Beschreibung aller Stände auff Erden ... Frankfurt am Main: Sigmund Feyerabend, 1568. While the modern child might recognise many of the occupations in Jost Amman's cuts for the *Ständebuch* – doctor, cook, hunter, shoemaker and so on – the large number of pilgrims, noblemen and knights is typical of an earlier age. Here an infant plays in front of the cowbell-maker's shop, his own hobby-horse apparently adorned by bells.
The British Library

Friedrich Johann Bertuch, *Bilderbuch für Kinder*. Weimar und Gotha: Industrie-Comptoir, 1801. *The Picture Book* described itself as containing 'a pleasant collection of animals, plants, fruits, minerals', and ranged from 'Quadrupeds' (above left) to 'Mixed' items as, here (above right), mythological creatures of antiquity.

Heidelberg University Library

(1804) which went into several editions, and was pirated in the United States. It was rapidly followed by British competitors, as technical innovations made the production of high-quality illustrations economic. *Little Jack of All Trades; or, Mechanical arts described, in prose and verse* (Harvey & Darton, 1823) explained that 'until very lately, children's books were only allowed coarse wooden cuts: but now the copper-plate engraver condescends to work for them also'.

The Germans showed great initiative in the production of their books of trades. Partly because of the success of Rousseau's ideas on education, in 1768 Johann Bernhard Basedow, the German educational reformer and teacher at Dessau, published his *Elementarwerk* (*Elementary Book*), a very influential illustrated textbook for children. Then in Weimar, at the heart of the German

Enlightenment, Friedrich Johann Bertuch started work on his enormous *Bilderbuch für Kinder – A Picture Book for Children*, which appeared in monthly parts during the period 1790–1830. Bertuch was a high official at the Weimar court, able to call on the artistic services of the Zeichenschule (Princely Art School), which he co-founded in 1774. His book was published in French as well as German, and its plates are highly regarded and now collected. Yet in Britain, it seems hardly to have been noted or used (were the Napoleonic Wars partly the reason?), and nothing on the same scale was attempted here until the publication of the *Children's Encyclopaedia* in 1908–10 (see pp. 92–3).

'Instruction Is the Means to Expel Rudeness'

In the early 17th century, a Czech religious refugee wrote a schoolbook which remained important for centuries, and is still interesting today. The author's educational theories underlie many later innovations in teaching.

Jan Amos Komenský, best known as Comenius (1592–1670), was an Elder of the Unity of the Brotherhood Protestant Church (*Unitas Fratrum*) in Moravia during the European religious wars, at a time when the Protestants were being driven out of Bohemia. In 1628 Comenius led members of his church to safety in Poland and, while in exile, wrote *The Labyrinth of the World and Paradise of the Heart* (1631), an allegory which became a Czech classic, not unlike the later English *Pilgrim's Progress* (1678).

For the last forty years of his life Comenius was an exile, working in Germany, Sweden, Hungary, Holland and England. He became widely known for his advanced educational policies, calling for education for all, rich and poor, town-dwellers or country folk, girls as well as boys. But Comenius was not merely a wild visionary. He was able to put his theories to into practicable use, in the production of a celebrated and enduring textbook, *Orbis Sensualium Pictus*, or *The World of Things Obvious to the Senses drawn in Pictures*.

The first edition of *Orbis Sensualium Pictus* was published in Nuremberg in Latin and German (1658), and was soon followed by a Latin and English version (London, 1659), and thereafter, rapidly, editions in other languages. The constant thematic link between the text and the illustrations in the

'The Crow cryeth …': The first instructive illustration from Comenius, *Orbis Sensualium Pictus* (London: John Sprint, 1659) with a table of creatures and the sounds they make. As well as such typically charming illustrations, the author made use of children's curiosity for the bizarre and strange to hold their attention.

The British Library

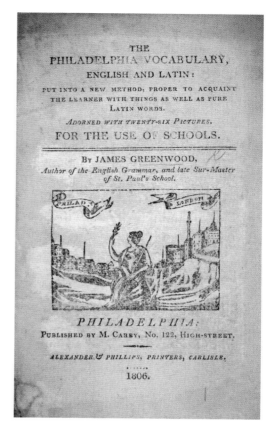

book made study interesting for the child reader; and Comenius' method of leaving readers to work out the connections for themselves was very successful. The book sold well and was influential upon later authors, for example the grammarian James Greenwood, who drew heavily on it for his London and Philadelphia **vocabularies**, or word books. In England, versions of *Orbis Sensualium Pictus* appeared regularly throughout the 18th century, and its fame was not limited to Europe: Comenius' book was reprinted in America, and when Harvard University was set up in Massachusetts, Comenius was recommended as its president.

Orbis Sensualium Pictus is, in essence, a picture-book encyclopaedia of the visible world. The effectiveness of its teaching came from Comenius' arrangement of topics, and the clear, uncluttered text and pictures: 'Children (even from their Infancy almost) are delighted with pictures, and willingly please their eyes with these sights,' was stated in the preface of the first English edition. The author understood that *interested* students would be alert to learning, and pictures focused this interest.

Reprints of *Orbis Sensualium Pictus* are still consulted today, not just 'to expel Rudeness', as the first English edition put it (echoing the sentiments of *The Babees Book*), but because they provide us with a window into 17th-century society, in which young children were invited to teach themselves how to think. We can learn much about many aspects of life in those times, and looking at these pages, if we know Latin, we can improve it at the same time!

'He Who Would Valiant Be': Bunyan Explained to a Child

The Pilgrim's Progress, a Christian allegory, written by a tinker-turned-preacher and published in 1678, turned out to be one of the bestselling religious books of all time. Though intended for adult readers, it was very quickly adopted by children as one of their favourite books.

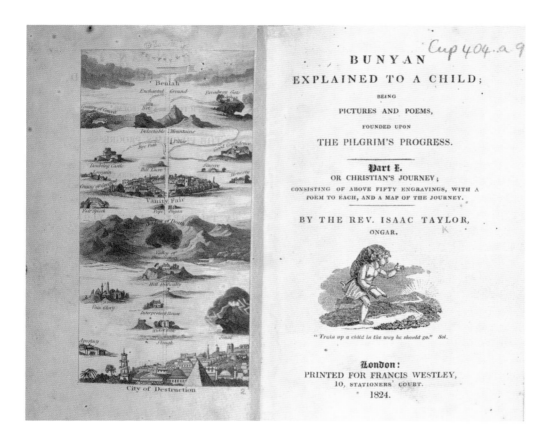

BUNYAN EXPLAINED TO A CHILD;

BEING

PICTURES AND POEMS,

FOUNDED UPON

THE PILGRIM'S PROGRESS.

Part I.
OR CHRISTIAN'S JOURNEY;

CONSISTING OF ABOVE FIFTY ENGRAVINGS, WITH A POEM TO EACH, AND A MAP OF THE JOURNEY.

BY THE REV. ISAAC TAYLOR,
ONGAR.

"Train up a child in the way he should go." Sol.

London:
PRINTED FOR FRANCIS WESTLEY,
10, STATIONERS' COURT.
1824.

Isaac Taylor, *Bunyan Explained to a Child, Being Pictures and Poems, Founded Upon The Pilgrim's Progress.* London: Francis Westley, 1824–5. An 1824 guide, *The Assistance of Education*, recommended Westley's publication as 'a desirable "Picture Book" to give to children, especially as a Sunday book … so exactly fitted for the purpose'.

The British Library

John Bunyan (1628–88) was a fervent Puritan, who served as a soldier on the Parliamentarian side during the long and bitter Civil War of the 1640s. Even during the Commonwealth, when Cromwell was in command, Bunyan ran into trouble for his preaching, and after the restoration of the monarchy under Charles II in 1660, Bunyan spent long periods in gaol. It was during his time in prison that Bunyan worked on the text of

The Pilgrim's Progress, published in London in 1678 by Nathaniel Ponder. The book was an immediate success across the whole Protestant community in Britain, and it was equally popular in North America (German-language translations were published in Germantown and Ephrata in Pennsylvania in the 1750s). After the Bible, it was one of the books most translated into African and Asian languages by missionary groups.

The poet George Crabbe (in his poem

The Parish Register) recorded that *The Pilgrim's Progress* was to be found in every cottage 'on shelf of deal', and he characterised Bunyan as 'a genius rare but rude was honest John'. Bunyan's unsophisticated style did nothing to diminish the book's continuing popularity, and many of the places named by him ('the Slough of Despond', 'the Delectable Mountains', or 'Vanity Fair') have since become part of everyday expressions.

In Britain, where in the 19th century children's behaviour on Sundays was strictly controlled, and the afternoons weighed heavily, the reading of novels was forbidden. However, *The Pilgrim's Progress* was 'safe', permitted reading; it was often selected by children for themselves, usually in adapted or simplified versions. There were innumerable translations into other languages, and the steady sales of Bunyan's book helped to assure the profitability of many colonial and provincial printers and booksellers. Every major British publisher of children's books in Victorian times had its own editions of Bunyan in stock (its popularity was such that even a *Pilgrim's* jigsaw was produced). It's probably safe to say that until the 1940s, or possibly even later, nearly every British child, and many overseas too, read *The Pilgrim's Progress*, or had episodes read to them by parents or in school. Only *Robinson Crusoe* had comparable popularity.

Bunyan's reach to children was not limited to his *Pilgrim's Progress*: eight years later, in 1686, Nathaniel Ponder published *A Book for Boys and Girls, or Country Rhimes for Children* (as by 'J. B.'). The seventy-four short verses, ranging from 'Upon the Ten Commandments' to 'Meditations upon an Egg' and 'Upon a Penny Loaf', call upon the natural and domestic world surrounding the child to serve as 'Divine Emblems' (as the book later became known) for Bunyan's message: 'This Loaf's an Emblem of the Word of God, / A thing of low Esteem, before the Rod / Of Famine smites the Soul with Fear of Death: / But then it is our All, our Life, our Breath.' The extreme rarity of his first edition is perhaps evidence of its early success; later editions were heavily modified, omitting much of Bunyan's original verse (perhaps together with some of his intent): it never achieved the great popularity of his *Pilgrim's Progress* and today it is largely forgotten.

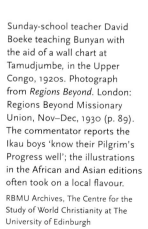

Sunday-school teacher David Boeke teaching Bunyan with the aid of a wall chart at Tamudjumbe, in the Upper Congo, 1920s. Photograph from *Regions Beyond*. London: Regions Beyond Missionary Union, Nov–Dec, 1930 (p. 89). The commentator reports the Ikau boys 'know their Pilgrim's Progress well'; the illustrations in the African and Asian editions often took on a local flavour.

RBMU Archives, The Centre for the Study of World Christianity at The University of Edinburgh

Educating the Romanovs

Most European ruling families have thought carefully about the ways to educate the children who would succeed them. There were many methods tried and tested in the Western countries – but the semi-savage Russian culture was very different. What would be 'right' for Peter the Great?

The role of tutor or governess to royal or noble families has always been a demanding, and even sometimes a dangerous, one. In France, King Louis XIV took special care with his heir Louis *le grand Dauphin* (1661–1711), but the prince's lessons from the theologian Jacques-Bénigne Bossuet bewildered him; while special **bowdlerised** editions of classics subtitled *ad* (or *in*) *usum serenissimi Delphini* ('for the use of the Dauphin'), prepared in the 1670s by Pierre Daniel Huet, simply gave the young prince a lifelong aversion to learning.

At almost exactly the same time, in Russia, Tsar Alexis I appointed a Russian Orthodox priest, Karion Istomin (*c*.1640–after 1718) to prepare textbooks for the young Tsarevich Peter (Aleksey Petrovich), born in 1672. Istomin was one of the great figures in the development of Russian cultural life. In 1683, for Peter's eleventh birthday, he produced *Kniga vrazumeliya* (*The Book of Reasoning*, or *Admonition*), the first Russian conduct book ever published. Istomin also produced *Litsevoy bukvar* (*The Illustrated Primer*, 1684) in which he carefully followed the model of

Karion Istomin, *The Illustrated Primer, or Alphabet Book.* Moscow: Moscow Print Yard, 1694. This primer was lavishly illustrated by Leonti Bunin. Istomin compiled the book, based on the visual method of teaching, for the young Tsarevich Peter. The first edition was of just twenty-five copies, many of which were presented to other members of the Romanov family. It was later published by the Moscow Printing Works, for the use of a less exalted readership.

State Historical Museum, Moscow

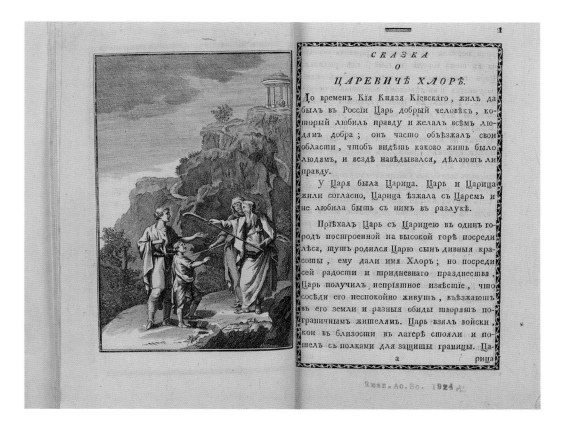

earlier Western **primers**. Istomin may have known Bure's *Svenska ABC boken medh runor* published in Stockholm in 1611 (see pp. 62–3). Evidently Peter was a much more receptive student than *le grand Dauphin* ever was in France: thus, Peter's tutors – including a couple of Scottish soldiers of fortune, Patrick Gordon and Paul Menesius (or Menzies), who ran a vigorous boot-camp for him – Istomin's book and Peter's own lively curiosity all helped to ensure the rapid Europeanisation of his country when he came to rule.

Some later Russian rulers were equally aware of the importance of reading, and of books for children. The Empress Catherine the Great (reigned 1762–96) took many ideas about education and progress from her reading of Locke, Rousseau and Diderot and others, often prompted by Ivan Betskoy (1704–95), who was for many years her advisor. In 1764 Catherine started the first school for girls, the Smolny Institute for Noble Maidens, St Petersburg, and made a start on a programme of national schooling. But Catherine was not just a benevolent despot; she wrote extensively, and composed a Russian primer for children (1781), which was quite widely printed in Russia, and two didactic stories (*The Story of Tsarevich Klore*, 1781, and *The Tale of Tsarevich Fevey*, 1783) which are notable as the first original stories written in Russia for children. The stories owed everything to the Prussian-born Empress Catherine's Western upbringing. There is nothing at all Russian in their content – but they foreshadowed the flowering of Russian children's literature in the 19th century.

'What is Learnt in Verse, Is Longer Retained in Memory'

Rhymes and poetry have always been part of children's upbringing.
Isaac Watts's poems gained popularity everywhere that English was spoken.

Puritan writers of the 17th century often wrote in verse. Isaac Watts (1674–1748) is remembered now mostly for his hymns, well over seven hundred in number, but his attempt to attract children's interest in his writings was unusual – the child's enjoyment of what they read seldom concerned Puritans. The son of a Southampton clothier, Watts was a precocious school student, subsequently educated at a dissenting academy at Stoke Newington, and became a pastor in a dissenting church in London. He spent several years tutoring the son of the nonconformist politician Sir John Hartopp. In 1712 he became the domestic chaplain and tutor to the daughters of Sir Thomas Abney, staying with the Abneys for the rest of his life.

Abney was a very powerful figure in City politics, after the revolution of 1688 (by which King James II was ousted by William of Orange). As Lord Mayor of London and a founding director of the Bank of England, Abney was an influential patron for Watts. Abney's involvement in the New England Company (which sponsored nonconformist missionaries to try to convert Native Americans to Christianity), plus the Abney/Watts links with dissenting ministers in the American colonies, explains the continuing popularity of Watts's books in America.

Divine Songs Attempted in Easy Language for the Use of Children (as it was originally named when published in 1715) was deliberately aimed at a wide audience: 'These Divine songs may be a pleasant and proper matter for their daily or weekly worship,' Watts

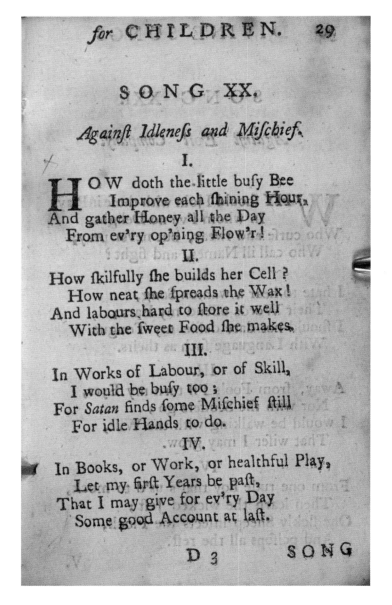

Isaac Watts, *Divine Songs Attempted in Easy Language for the Use of Children.* London: Printed for T. Longman, J. Buckland, and W. Fenner, in Paternoster Row; et al., 1761. The verses within warn against sluggardliness and promote the virtue of obeying one's parents. A copy in the Pierpont Morgan Library, New York, of the first edition (printed at the Angel in the Poultry, 1715), includes an inscription by the author to Mrs Elizabeth Abney.
The British Library

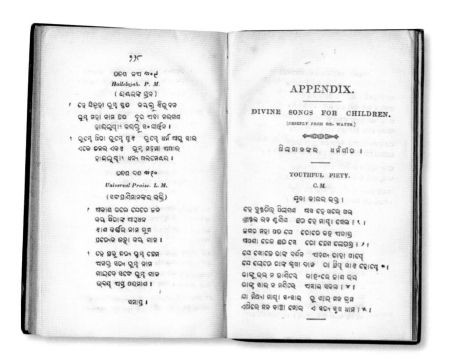

wrote. 'You will find here nothing that savours of a party: The children of high degree or low degree, of the Church of England, or dissenters, baptized in infancy, or not, may all join together in these songs.' Watts was in fact, a Puritan-lite. His work impressed the Tory Samuel Johnson, and even the reactionary Sarah Trimmer reprinted Watts's poems in her tracts. In Britain, and even more in America, the *Divine Songs* were printed and reprinted by many publishers in the provinces and in the colonies; well over 150 editions in the 18th century alone. (A '95th' edition, published in Boston, Massachusetts, in 1800, was advertised at 'Price 12 cents. Great allowance made by the grose or dozen'.)

Watts's *Divine Songs* appealed to children, but equally to teachers. Watts himself suggested that good children who learned a number of the poems by heart should be rewarded by receiving a copy of the book as a prize, and generations of parents sat solemnly listening to their own infants lisping out 'How doth the busy little bee / Improve each shining hour' (or whichever poem it was). The system worked until well into the 20th century, but even by the time *Alice in Wonderland* was published in 1865, tastes were changing. Lewis Carroll's mischievous parodies ('How doth the little crocodile / Improve his shining tail') made gentle fun of Watts's songs. Watts's original poems still bear reading, and no doubt some parents did read a few to their children, but more people today remember Lewis Carroll's versions.

Lewis Carroll was not, of course, the only author influenced by his own childhood reading of *Divine Songs*. One discerning critic has described the book as a piece of grit for the pearl that became William Blake's *Songs of Innocence*, poems which really did not come into general public awareness until late Victorian times. Blake's libertarian and mystical visions were drawn on to his personal images of childhood, and his books were very different from other children's publications of his time.

'Vast Delight in Hearing It Told Over and Over'

Many people believe that modern education was based on Rousseau's theories set out in his *Émile, or Treatise on Education* (1762), but effective publishing in English for children was foreshadowed by an unknown English mother's work some twenty years earlier.

Historians often date John Newbery's publication of *A Little Pretty Pocket-Book* (1744) as the start of book production for children; others point to Thomas Boreman's small books published in London in the 1730s. One contemporary aware of these books, and also that **intaglio** prints were becoming readily and cheaply available for purchase, was Jane Johnson (1706–51). The wife of the Anglican vicar of Witham-on-the-Hill in Lincolnshire, she had four children, one of whom, their daughter Barbara, compiled an album of then

fashionable clothing design and fabrics which is now an important resource for historians in the Victoria & Albert Museum. One can guess that it was her mother, Jane Johnson, who taught Barbara how to make paper dolls.

The Johnsons were a well-to-do couple (both had inherited estates) and Jane was able to devote her time and intellect to teaching and bringing up all four of their children, until her three sons were sent away to school at Rugby, leaving only Barbara at home to be educated by her mother. By great fortune, the books, cards, games and stories written for

LEFT AND OPPOSITE
Opening of *George William Johnson his book*. Manuscript 'printed and bound by his Mama 1745', and, opposite, an alphabet card and some of the many items prepared by Jane Johnson for her children. Mrs Johnson bought patterned papers and intaglio prints which she wrote on and coloured in, cut and pasted into a range of effective teaching toys. Many were personalised; for example, a picture of a couple dancing, captioned 'Lord Mountjoy & Miss Barbara Johnson dancing a menuet together ... in the Hay Market'.

The Lilly Library, Indiana University, Bloomington, Indiana

them by Jane Johnson survived, and were preserved by the members of the family until the late 20th century (and are now in the Lilly Library of Indiana University).

Jane Johnson had obviously read widely, and was well aware of *Les Contes des fées* – the fairy stories by Madame d'Aulnoy published in 1699 (several times translated into English in the next thirty years) – but Jane's writing was of a very different kind. The collection of books and games she used to teach her children to read, and to become moral beings, gives us a rare and attractive insight into the way lucky children were taught in Georgian England. Lucky, not only because they came from a prosperous background, but because of their mother's obvious love for her children (very different from the stern and unforgiving tone of earlier Puritan books): Jane clearly *enjoyed* teaching them.

Her pleasure in her work is evident from a note she made in a copy she kept of 'A Very Pretty Story', in her papers now in the Bodleian Library at Oxford. In it, she records that the story was written in 1744 'on purpose to tell Miss Barbara Johnson and her brother Master George William Johnson, who took vast delight in hearing it told over and over again a vast number of times'. But this enchanting story was never published for others to read until 2001.

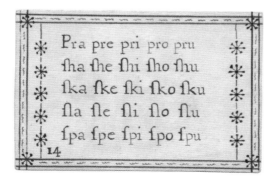

The First American Children's Books

Depending at first on imports of children's books from Britain, the American colonies rapidly started to issue their own, subtly different, children's books.

Quite soon after European settlements formed in North America, bookshops were set up in the main cities, with regular importations from publishers in London, and from Scotland and Ireland as well. Settlers in the West Indian colonies, for example, were well supplied: inventories made of the stocks of Jamaican booksellers in the 1780s included 'Alphabetts and copy books', showing a range of children's books and schoolbooks imported from Britain. Before the American War of Independence, Jamaicans could have ordered primers from Boston as well, because the

production of these schoolbooks had became universal in America.

Well over two hundred different editions or versions of *The New England Primer* were published, and there were scores of others with similar titles. The first was issued about 1690 by Benjamin Harris, a contumacious Puritan who had links with the controversial preacher Benjamin Keach, for whom he had printed some titles. (Keach, who introduced hymn singing into the Baptist Church, was author of *The Child's Instructor*, which in 1664 caused such offence that all copies were impounded and destroyed by the Public

BELOW
The New England Primer enlarged. For the more easy attaining the true reading of English. To which is added, the Assembly's catechism. Philadelphia: Printed and sold by B. Franklin, and D. Hall, in Market-street, 1[7]64. The young Benjamin Franklin, a keen reader of the Bible, Bunyan and **chapbooks**, probably learned his ABC from this primer. Many years later he published the primer himself.

Beinecke Rare Books and Manuscripts Library, Yale University, Franklin 391

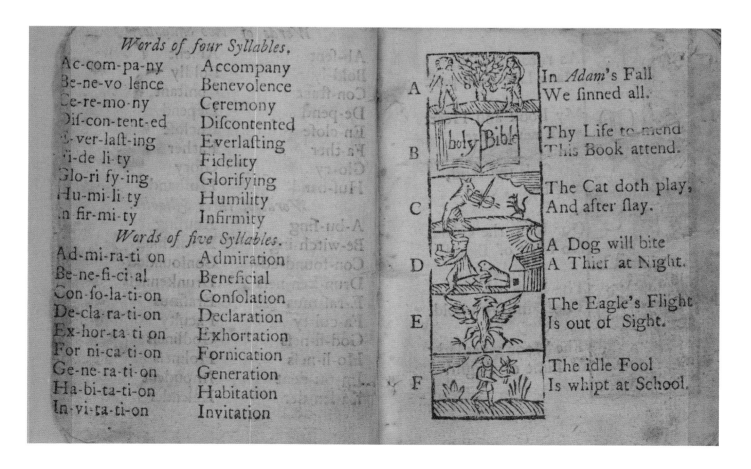

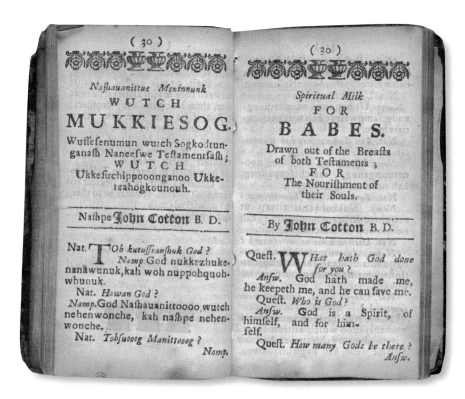

[John Cotton], *Indiane Primer ... The Indian Primer or the First Book. By which children may know truely to read the Indian language. And Milk for Babes.* Boston, Massachusetts: B. Green, 1720. It was translated from English into Massachusetts-Indian by Grindal Rawson.

The British Library

Hangman. Keach himself was imprisoned, and then pilloried. Undaunted, he later republished it under a slightly different title, and had it printed by William Marshall at Newgate.)

Benjamin Harris worked as a printer in London from 1670 until 1686, until, his books too radical to please the majority of the population (for example, they were 'not at all relish'd by the Popish Party'), he found it prudent to emigrate to Massachusetts. (He eventually moved back to London in 1694.) The *Primer* incorporates alphabet poems, probably written by Harris himself, and is illustrated with wood-cut engravings (some were also included in Harris's *The Holy Bible in Verse*, advertised in 1701). Enlarged versions of his *Primer* produced in the 18th century often incorporated some of Isaac Watts's *Divine Songs* as well (see pp. 84–5).

Some editions also include the text of *Spiritual Milk for Boston Babes*, a Puritan catechism (sometimes called *The Catechism of New England*), which took the form of sixty-four questions and answers: 'Q. "What hath God done for you?" A. "God hath made me ...", etc. Its author John Cotton (1585–1652) was a reformist minister who had emigrated in 1633 to Massachusetts to avoid religious persecution in England, and became a pre-eminent minister of the Massachusetts Bay Colony. The first edition was published in London in 1646; the version published in Cambridge, Massachusetts in 1656 was the first book intended for children to be printed in America.

Another was *Indiane Primer ... The Indian Primer or the First Book. By which children may know truely to read the Indian language. And Milk for Babes.* Boston, Massachusetts: B. Green, 1720. Written in Massachusetts-Indian and English, this is often ascribed to John Eliot, who produced the first *Indian Bible*, and was also involved in the publication of the *Bay Psalm Book*. This primer appears to be in the Nope dialect spoken on the island of Martha's Vineyard, and contains a study of the Lord's Prayer, the larger catechism and also Cotton's *Spiritual Milk*.

Dying 'a Good Death'

People often think of Puritans as harsh and unforgiving in their treatment of children. In fact, they cared passionately – about children's lives *after* death.

Parents and guardians usually work hard to protect their children from the ugly realities of life. In the 17th century, there were few families who didn't experience the early loss of children. In Queen Elizabeth I's reign, many clergy and physicians railed against pampering children too much. Only children in a state of grace (many adults believed) could avoid an eternity in Hell.

One of these clergyman was James Janeway (1636–74), one of the most successful Puritan writers of the Restoration period. The subtitle to his *A Token for Children* (1671) advertised the full details of the conversion and exemplary lives – and deaths – of a group of children, which inspired many books on the subject. Janeway knew a great deal about death (he watched several brothers dying of tuberculosis and lived in London during the Great Plague), and his stark accounts must over the years have terrified thousands of children. His book was an immediate success with dissenters throughout Britain, and in America (where many copies of Janeway's book were imported: between 1684–5, some sixty copies by one Boston publisher alone). In Massachusetts, Cotton Mather wrote a sequel, *A Token for Children of New England*, which also continued to be reprinted for many years. John Wesley produced abridged versions; and in all nearly 150 editions of Janeway's book were published until well into the 19th century.

Tastes changed in Victorian times, and by the 20th century Janeway was being described as morbid, gloomy, soul-battering and chilly; certainly not an author whose book would be given to a child today. And yet,

..... et s'il me bat ou me pousse, ne permets pas que je le lui rende : mais que je lui dise : ne fais pas comme cela, mon petit, frère. P. 35.

Les Merveilles de la grâce de Dieu dans un enfant, ou notice sur Marie Lothrop, morte á Boston, le 18 mars 1831, âgrée de 6 ans et 3 mois. Grenoble: Prudhomme, Imprimeur-Libraire, 1834. Victorian children could only aspire to such a 'good death' as little Mary Lothrop, who became extraordinarily pious in the days before she died. First published by the American Tract Society, New York (1832), both American and French versions include the testimony of the Bostonian Baptist pastor who asserts the truth of the account.

Bridwell Library, Perkins School of Theology, Southern Methodist University

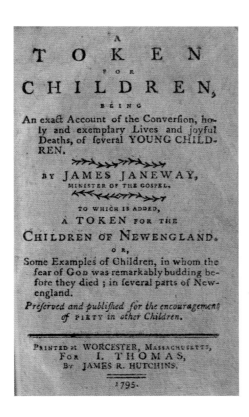

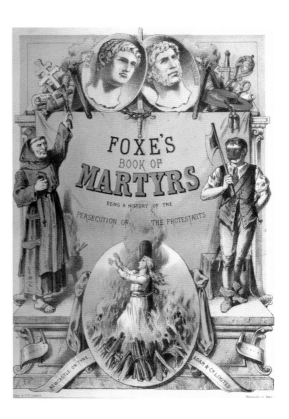

Janeway was not like that at all. The Oxford antiquary Anthony Wood, a contemporary with Janeway as a student at the university, recorded that Janeway was a popular man, especially with the girls ('much resorted to ... and admired as a forward and precious young man, especially by those of the female sex'). Janeway's sincere beliefs and his evident anxiety to save children's souls from Hell made him believe he could help them by writing his frightening book.

Even more frightening to many child readers was the earlier *Actes and Monuments* (1563), usually called the *Book of Martyrs*, compiled by John Foxe (1516/17–87), a Puritan divine who went into exile in Switzerland during the rigours of the Counter-Reformation under Mary I ('Bloody Mary', who reigned 1553–8). Foxe's *huge* book was never designed for children; it was cumbersome to handle. Over twice the length of the Bible, the high quality and number of

its graphic illustrations were notable in Elizabethan publishing. Nonetheless, the *Book of Martyrs* was recommended for children to read, but it was *always* difficult: in his *David Copperfield*, Charles Dickens described kneeling to read the huge folio lying open on a low table: 'I was chiefly edified, I am afraid, by the pictures which were numerous, and represented all sorts of dismal horrors.'

The Book of Martyrs was unashamed anti-Catholic propaganda, which helped to shape enduring perceptions of Queen Mary as a bloodthirsty tyrant, and continued to influence Protestant perception of Catholics. Attitudes change very slowly, and Foxe's book was still thought a suitable choice for a school prize as late as 1900. Protestant publishers continued to republish selections and adaptations from this unsavoury book well into the 20th century.

A 'Store-House of Knowledge'

The period at the start of the 20th century was one of optimism and advance in Britain. Arthur Mee's *Children's Encyclopaedia* distilled the attitudes and beliefs of the people, and continued for generations to influence attitudes and policies.

The form and nature of publishing for a mass market changed in late Victorian times, developing features which became commonplace a century ago. The power of large newspaper publishers, allied with technological innovations, made it possible for them to produce ambitious new forms of publication – if they had the will. Alfred Harmsworth (Viscount Northcliffe, 1865–1922), owner of the *Daily Mail* and *Mirror*, had already made a fortune in publishing cheap magazines such as *Answers*, *Comic Cuts* and *Halfpenny Marvel*, which included the first Sexton Blake stories (see pp. 206–7). Harmsworth intended his Amalgamated Press to have a teaching role and set up a subsidiary company, the Educational Book Company, run by Arthur Mee (1875–1943) and John Hammerton (1871–1949), a very successful creator and publisher of large-scale reference books.

As well as his later series of books on English counties in the King's England series, Mee is remembered largely for the *Children's Encyclopaedia*, originally issued in monthly parts from 1908 to 1910, and thereafter published in eight bound volumes. Harmsworth's publishing business included setting up a paper-mill in Newfoundland to make high-quality papers for use in his publications. The *Encyclopaedia* was designed to include lavish illustrations of an unusually high quality for a children's book. The work was a great success commercially, selling over 800,000 copies by 1920.

The policy of Mee and his collaborators was that children should be respected and

ABOVE AND OPPOSITE BELOW
The Children's Encyclopædia. London: [The Educational Book Co.] Amalgamated Press, *c*.1908. It contained photo essays for the curious such as 'What the Tide Leaves Behind' and 'Happy Homes in the Southern Seas' as well as advertisements for powders, dancing shoes and Mee's *Harmsworth Self-Educator*. These popular magazines, and later books, were aimed at children of empire. Note the warning on the cover against pirated editions. Author's collection

learning should be made interesting. Mee's greatest success was in presenting a picture of middle-class life and values, present as much in British dominions, like Australia or South Africa, as in Britain itself. The underlying theme in the text was that the children growing up in this rich and successful empire, ruling many parts of the globe, had the duty of care for *all* citizens of the British Empire. Indeed, the *Encyclopaedia* was a cornerstone of middle-class upbringing, with the intention of moulding the characters of cadets who might well become district officers, agriculturalists, teachers or railway engineers and spend their careers in colonial service.

Every middle-class child in Britain and its dominions was familiar with it, but its influence went much further: the American publisher Grolier bought the US rights, issuing it as *The Book of Knowledge*, and there were translations into Chinese, French, Italian, Portuguese and Spanish as well. In revised editions, the *Encyclopaedia* continued to be published until long after Mee's death.

The tone of the books is always buoyant: Mee did not foresee that Imperial rule would

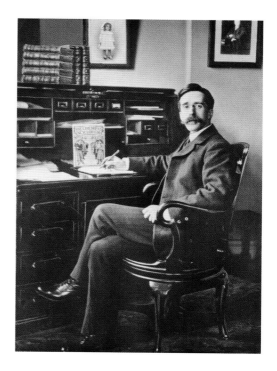

end so quickly, and until the *Titanic* disaster in 1912 he had no doubt that the future would be better than the past: he did not anticipate the horrors of the First World War. Mee was very much a man of his time (he did not, for example, favour the Suffragettes), but nonetheless the influence of this sane, middle-of-the-road man on children's lives was enormous. Yet, surprisingly, the *Children's Encyclopaedia* has been seldom discussed in histories of publishing for children. But apart from some (largely feminist) criticism, Mee's work is remembered with affection by people who grew up with battered copies of the volumes, which introduced to them many topics not discussed in schools' curricula.

The *Reader* Which Went Westward

A bright idea from a Cincinnati publisher enabled an ambitious young school-teacher to create one of the best-known books of the expanding United States.

The idea of publishing anthologies taken from literary works for use in schools seems to have originated with a Prussian landowner and philanthropist, Friedrich Eberhard von Rochow (1734–1805), whose *Der Kinderfreund, Ein Lesebuch zum Gebrauch in Landschulen* (*The Children's Friend, A Reading Book for Use in Rural Schools*, 1776) was widely praised and used throughout Germany. In England, the American-born Quaker Lindley Murray's *English Reader* (1799) was likewise enormously popular, and even more so in America, where it ran into hundreds of editions. There was a market for schoolbooks, and with the rapid spread westward by settlers

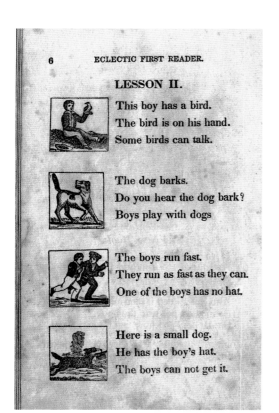

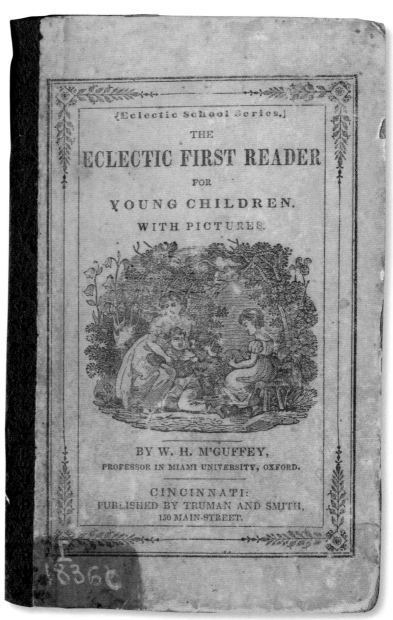

LEFT AND ABOVE
W. H. McGuffey, *The Eclectic First Reader for Young Children, with Pictures*. Cincinnati: Truman and Smith, 1836. This could so easily have been dry. But the promise of the cover engraving, showing a reading group in the open air, was matched by the agreeably illustrated lessons of subjects familiar to the young reader throughout.

Walter Havighurst Special Collections, Miami University Libraries, Oxford, Ohio

in America, many publishers saw the usefulness of producing their own local **readers**.

By the 1830s, Cincinnati was a boom town, rivalling older coastal cities on the eastern seaboard; and dependent on trade with the slave states to the south. After the introduction of steamboats on the Ohio River in 1811, the town was well placed for distributing books down the Mississippi to St Louis and New Orleans, or to the West. In 1833, Winthrop Smith, a partner in the small Cincinnati publisher Truman and Smith, approached a highly respected Presbyterian minister, William Holmes McGuffey (1800–73) to prepare a reader. McGuffey was an unusual man, having started out as a half-educated youth teaching reluctant children in schools on the Ohio frontier. He had proved to be an excellent and energetic teacher and sound scholar, and ended up as a professor of philosophy at the University of Virginia.

By their very nature, books like the readers prepared by Murray or McGuffey were 'cut-and-paste' projects, derived from texts in earlier books. The first of McGuffey's *Eclectic Readers*, which appeared in 1836, was well done, but without much originality. Rival publishers in Boston, who issued schoolbooks by Samuel Worcester, scented danger in the competition and charged Truman and Smith in Cincinnati with 'over-imitation in the McGuffey second and third readers'. The Cincinnati firm was not blameless: Truman and Smith settled out of court, amending several sections in the book, and McGuffey and his publisher ensured texts were not 'lifted' for the revised versions.

Taking care to avoid such mishaps again, Winthrop Smith and his partners marketed the various extensions and revisions of the McGuffey readers very effectively. By taking full advantage of the new printing techniques such as stereotyping, they were able to keep production costs low; they also employed economic marketing devices such as issuing free journals to school-teachers in Ohio (who praised McGuffey's book), and other competitive methods now commonplace in publishing, by which they effectively took control of much of the American schoolbook market. By the time McGuffey's readers eventually ceased in the 20th century, it is estimated that well over 125 million copies had been sold throughout America. Rather like the effect of the *Children's Encyclopaedia* in Britain later, McGuffey's texts helped to educate millions of American children, and his precepts both reflected the moral values of the 19th century and helped to shape them. 'McGuffey' is still used extensively by home-schoolers in America today.

Truman and Smith's partnership was dissolved in 1841; Smith, who took the rights to publish editions of the readers with him, died a very rich man. His firm was absorbed into the American Book Company in 1891. School publishing had become big business.

Friedrich Eberhard von Rochow, *Der Kinderfreund, Ein Lesebuch zum Gebrauch in Landschulen. (The Children's Friend. A Reading Book for Use in Rural Schools.)* New edition, 2 parts in 1 volume. Hanover: Hahn, *c.*1825. By 1880 around one million copies of this successful 'rural schools' reader, frequently revised, had been printed throughout Europe. The original (1776) plain title was improved in this early edition by the addition of an elephant, enhancing its appeal for young readers.

Antiquariat & Auktionshaus Schramm, Kiel

Schoolbooks for the British Dominions

McGuffey's and other readers published in the United States were not thought at all suitable for use in Canada or other British territories. The competition to secure the market was savage, but the rewards for the publishers were considerable.

In his 1963 calypso record 'Dan is the Man (in the Van)', the Trinidadian singer Mighty Sparrow mocked the content of the schoolbooks used in the 1930s West Indian colonies. These books were important to the pupils who used them at school, because for many poor children (particularly those in developing countries) these were the *only* books they ever read.

From the 1830s, and even more following the passing of the Education Acts of 1870 in Britain, the demand for reliable, cheap schoolbooks increased markedly, making their publication profitable to those who contracted to supply them. The competition between one publisher and another was intense, and included dirty tricks (of plagiarism and such) similar to those employed by some American publishers of schoolbooks. The advantage to purchasers was that the publishers worked hard to retain their trade and often modified texts and pictures in their books in order to make them better than those of their rivals. It was not an entirely successful policy: the poet and critic Matthew Arnold, who was a respected inspector of schools from 1851 to 1886, accused these publishers of 'charlatanism and extravagance in the manufacture and supply of our schoolbooks'.

One of the most successful competitors was the Edinburgh firm of Thomas Nelson and Sons, which from about 1800 onwards ran an aggressive and prosperous printing and publishing business, to which Nelson had introduced new equipment and cost-cutting production and distribution methods,

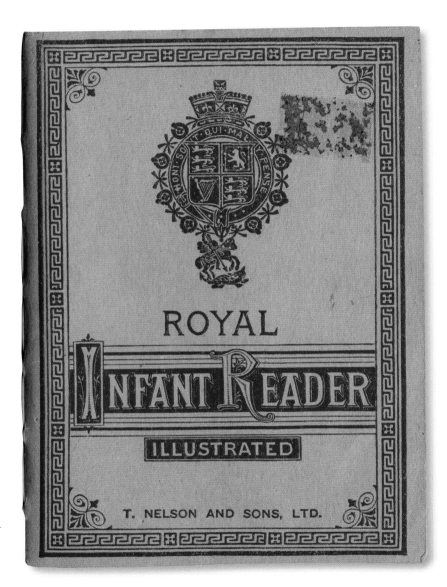

The Infant Reader, Short Stories in Simple Words. Royal School series, London; Edinburgh etc. T. Nelson and Sons, *c*.1890 [?]. This pocket-sized early edition, simply bound in brown card, and probably a reprint, was still being used in Jamaica in the 1960s, and as far afield as Newfoundland. The illustrations within reflect a very different domestic setting than that experienced by the majority of its young West Indian readers. It was the first in a series comprised of eight books, along with *The Royal School Primer* and six titles in the Royal Readers series.
Author's collection

LESSON XIX.

tun	pur	tube	wine	bark
cur	pure	tune	nine	song

I have a long tube. I will put a pea in it, and blow it out. A tun is a large cask. A cur is a kind of dog. This wine is pure. Will Anne give us a song or a tune? Dogs can bark, and cats can pur. Pat will be home at nine.

LESSON XX.

fall	tall	lime
hall	dine	mine

This ball is mine, and not his. I will call for him as I go home. Tom is as tall as you are. We will dine in the long hall. The cat is on the wall; if that slate fall from the roof it will hurt her. The man has got the lime and sand that you sent him for.

LESSON XXI.

born	corn	wants
cord	morn	kind

He was born in a house on the hill. Is rice a kind of corn? He wants a fine kind of cord. Get me a cork for the ink jar. The morn is the first part of the day. This is my son; I hope you will like him. My son, sin not, for if you sin you can not go to God.

First Reading Book for the Use of Schools. Printed and published by direction of the Commissioner of Education Ireland. Melbourne: George Robertson, 1877. These readers, with their heavily Irish content and numerous biblical references, were used in Australian schools until 1878. After an almost unanimous vote by local teachers on their unsuitability, they were replaced by the Collins' Australian Readers series, books which contained (some) local content. From the 1890s these too were replaced by the Nelson's Royal Readers series.

State Library of New South Wales

enabling the firm to compete very effectively. In the years before 1914, with branches in New York, Paris and Leipzig, Thomas Nelson and Sons published very successful schoolbooks in French, German and Spanish, as well as cheap out-of-copyright classics in English, comparable to those in J. M. Dent's Everyman's Library. In the 1870s Thomas Nelson started publishing the Royal Readers series, soon followed by the Royal School series.

The competition and Nelson's prices drove out rival school series, such as the imported Irish National Readers and later Collins' Readers, in the Australian colonies. Millions of copies of Thomas Nelson's School Readers series were sold in Canada, Australia and in many other corners of the British Empire – and beyond: we bought one in Jamaica in 1960, and a copy of a title in the series was seen being used in Roatán, in the Bay of Islands of Honduras, at around the same time. Publishing these readers proved very profitable for Nelson: it was estimated that in the period from 1878 to 1881 the sales of educational books formed 25% of the firm's total output, but brought in 88% of the firm's profit. But there were gains, too, for the purchasers of these often rather drab and uninviting little books: they were good value for money. A poor woman growing up in Labrador in the 1920s praised them highly: 'Anybody who went through those books got an education.'

CHAPTER 5

Small Books for Small People: The Growth of Publishing for the Young

Small books, such as 'Thumb Bibles' and chapbooks, had been around for a while, but it was only in the mid-18th century that canny publishers recognised a need for bright, pint-sized editions for children.

Books read by children came to publication almost by accident. The first of the fabulous histories which came originally through the oral tradition, such as Richard Johnson's *The History of Tom Thumb* (1621), were the antecedents of a huge literary genre, the **chapbooks**, which continued to flourish well into the 19th century. Produced very cheaply and published very widely, they were the most familiar form of publication to many (see pp. 102–5). While many printers and booksellers sought new marketing possibilities for educational books early in the 18th century, most contemplated only textbooks and the books used in teaching.

When in 1730 Thomas Boreman published his version of Conrad Gesner's five-volume zoological study, *Historiae animalium* (1551–58) as *A Description of Three Hundred Animals,* he might have had a child readership in his mind, but by the time of his publication of *Gigantick Histories of Two Famous Giants* in 1740, there is no doubt that this enterprise was well thought out and aimed at children. The very small format and the style of binding attracted children, and the inclusion of children's names in the **subscription lists** surely tickled their vanities. The success of Boreman's enterprise was noticed by contemporary publishers and booksellers, and Boreman's work was soon followed by books produced by the innovative Mary Cooper, whose 1744 *Tommy Thumb's Pretty Song Book* included nursery rhymes and was printed by a different process than that which had been used by Boreman (see pp. 108–9).

By the middle of the 18th century, no doubt inspired by the success of Boreman and Mary Cooper, Francis Newbery and his successors produced a range of books whose names still survive today, in America as much as Britain. Among these, *Goody Two-Shoes* had an enormous and deserved success, and

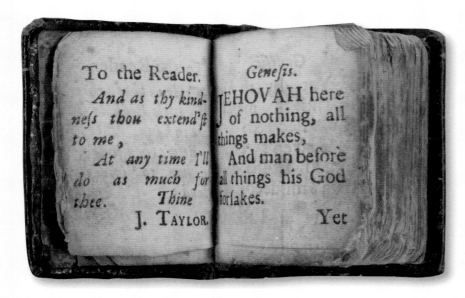

Newbery's *Lilliputian Magazine* was the first of the magazines intended to be read by children (see pp. 112–13).

Schoolboys at boarding schools read Newbery's books, just as they read chapbooks. The growth of chapbook publishing grew, in the same way that the production of adult fiction grew, and rapidly formed part of the core of the book trade. Books like *Gulliver's Travels* and *Robinson Crusoe* (see pp. 102–3 and 106–7), were adopted quickly for the juvenile market, and in themselves adapted for the different types of readers. Many authors were inspired by Swift and Defoe, and the production of 'Robinsonades', derived from tales of savage islands, very soon became a publishing genre. These were not limited to a male readership: women authors too produced Robinsonades as they ventured into writing in other genres. The production of books intended for children did not become limited to female authorship, of course, but it seemed an easier (and perhaps more 'acceptable') field for many. Sarah Fielding, like her brother Henry, wrote adult novels, but she is now better remembered for her rather idyllic *The Governess, or The Little Female Academy* (1749), and her work was later to inspire Mary Martha Sherwood in an audacious, rewritten, 'improved' version (see p. 111).

Sarah Fielding's success was noted by other would-be writers in the later part of the 18th century. The women writers of that time have been extensively studied, and included several good writers (the Kilners and Lady Fenn among them), but as a group they came to irk later readers and historians. Many would concur with Darton, and not altogether unfairly, that these writers 'were far better at telling a story than constructing one. Their very themes made for feebleness of plot'. Percy Muir impatiently commented that 'there is a nauseating fascination about these arch and insipid anecdotes ... whether the

pivot of the story is a child, a mouse, a peg-top, or a pin-cushion, they are all variations on similar themes'. But at the time the books were written, the authors and publishers turned out books which they were convinced would – and indeed did – sell (see pp. 114–15).

At the same time that publishers were producing these rather insipid books, people in the book trade became adept at summarising or abridging the texts of lengthy books. These (much cheaper) versions were read by children, and also by adults, in much the same way as the last century's successful *Reader's Digest*-type versions. In Georgian times, abridging versions was not thought to infringe authors' or publishers' copyrights, so cheap versions were produced in the thousands. The temptation for publishers and editors to 'improve' texts was considerable, and when authors passed their manuscripts to unscrupulous individuals (like Sir Richard Philipps) they could find that the publisher had appropriated the author's pseudonym for use on other books. (This happened to Mary Ann Kilner, and no doubt to other female writers as well.)

Censoring or **bowdlerising** (as it came to be called in the 19th century) was so common as to become part of standard editorial procedure. Filtering out vulgar or overtly sexual expressions from Shakespeare was especially common (and it was by no means only members of the Bowdler family who bowdlerised him). Poetry was also 'purified' by editors ranging from John Wesley (the founder of Methodism) to more recent scholars – and not only in editions intended for classroom use. The redoubtable Sarah Trimmer, producing selections from the Bible for use in her Sunday schools, used these to skate quickly over some of the episodes in the Old Testament (Sodom and Gomorrah, for example), which were thought 'difficult' (see p. 117). Such censorship was by no means undertaken only by reactionaries: would-be

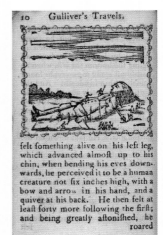

felt something alive on his left leg, which advanced almost up to his chin, when bending his eyes downwards, he perceived it to be a human creature not six inches high, with a bow and arrow in his hand, and a quiver at his back. He then felt at least forty more following the first; and being greatly astonished, he roared

The captain is snared by the Lilliputians, in a woodcut from *The Adventures of Captain Gulliver, in a Voyage to the Islands of Lilliput and Brobdingnag. Abridged from the works of the celebrated Dean Swift. Embellished with cuts.* Gainsbrough: printed at Mozley's Lilliputian Book-Manufactory, 1791.

The British Library

reformers like Mary Wollstonecraft, William Godwin or Charles and Mary Lamb were enthusiastic revisers as well. In the 21st century too, there are plenty of Trimmerites – well-intentioned pressure groups urging publishers to ban or alter books to fit in with their own views.

It is almost impossible to guess at the numbers of chapbook and other abridged versions published, but the projected profits from these persuaded shrewd publishers such as the Newberys (and many others) to produce their own chapbook versions of Fielding's *Tom Jones*, Richardson's *Pamela* and many other books ostensibly intended for adult readers. A single copy survives of *A Catalogue of maps, copy-books, drawing-books, histories, ... printed and sold by Cluer Dicey, and Richard Marshall* (1764), and research by recent scholars on this wholesale catalogue from this Aldermary Churchyard company has revealed the extent of the chapbook trade

to North America as well as in Britain (see pp. 118–19).

Through the activities of Boreman, Newbery and other early developers of children's literature, 'children's books' began to acquire a distinctive format and shape. The physical effort for children involved in tackling the large folios of many adult books was gone: the new volumes from Boreman, Newbery and the rest were all small and often set in larger type more sympathetic to a learning reader's eyes. Traditional chapbooks were always small: *sextodecimos* (or 16s), made from a simple sheet of paper folded to make sixteen leaves, sewn into stiffened paper covers and often accompanied with crude wood-cut illustrations. For the more sophisticated productions of Newbery and his rivals, from the 1760s onwards, a much more attractive dress was devised.

Some books (again small-sized 16s) were bound with a green vellum spine and the boards pasted with green paper; others had '**Dutch gilt**' paper over the boards, a style introduced by Boreman for his *Gigantick Histories*. The binding of schoolbooks was traditionally in sheepskin, but the Newberys also bound these in durable canvas. Such styles were, effectively, publishers' bindings, rather than special bindings bespoke at purchase (as had been one tradition). Later publishers of small children's books, marketed for the miniature libraries, used bindings selected by themselves together with the binders, who were now getting into edition binding, which was to become so important in Victorian times.

Bookcase of Instruction and Delight. London: John Marshall, *c.*1802. Six of a series of twelve books, each with lively covers, which were issued in a cloth box as part of John Marshall's infant library series.

PBA Galleries, San Francisco

Small Heroes for Small Readers: Tom Thumb and Gulliver

Children have always been fascinated by tiny people, but two of the most popular stories about them were originally written for adults.

Dwarves and giants figure largely in stories worldwide, but we don't know who told the first stories about very small people, before the invention of printing. In 1621, more than a century before printers and publishers identified 'juvenile literature' as profitable to cultivate, *The History of Tom Thumbe, the Little* was published in London. At the end of the text was a note stating that 'the second part shall be followed with tales of more maruell, by the author hereof. R. I.'. R. I. has been identified as an obscure writer, Richard Johnson (active 1592–1622), but no further

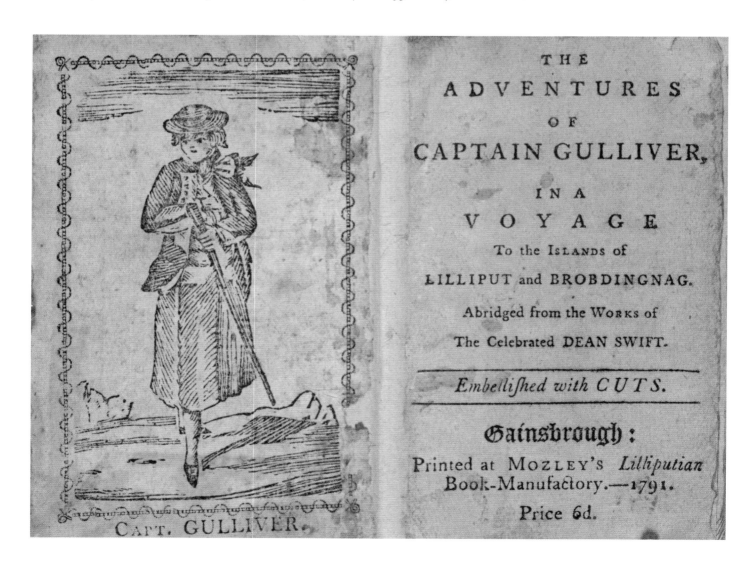

CAPT. GULLIVER.

THE ADVENTURES OF CAPTAIN GULLIVER, IN A VOYAGE To the ISLANDS of LILLIPUT and BROBDINGNAG. Abridged from the WORKS of The Celebrated DEAN SWIFT.

Embellished with CUTS.

Gainsbrough: Printed at MOZLEY'S *Lilliputian* Book-Manufactory.—1791.

Price 6d.

OPPOSITE
Jonathan Swift, *The Adventures of Captain Gulliver, in a Voyage to the Islands of Lilliput and Brobdingnag. Abridged from the works of the celebrated Dean Swift. Embellished with cuts.* Gainsbrough: printed at Mozley's Lilliputian book-manufactory, 1791. The 'cuts' are a simpler affair than the more lavish and well-known engravings of the adult editions. Note the title of the provincial publishing firm. J. & H. Mozely, booksellers, also reprinted titles such as *The History of Whittington and his Cat,* and *The History of Little Goody Two-Shoes* (see p. 112).

The British Library

RIGHT
[Richard Johnson?], *The History of Tom Thumbe, the Little, for his small stature surnamed, King Arthur's Dwarfe* ... London. Imprinted at London: [by Augustine Mathewes?] for Tho. Langley, 1621. The brave Tom, in gossamer dress and mouse-skin boots, is carried off by a crow, on the title page of this **chapbook**, the sole surviving copy of the first English folk tale to appear in a complete printed version. In recognition of its importance, its provenance has been scrupulously recorded by no fewer than ten previous owners, including the pioneering collector Narcissus Luttrell (1657–1732).

Pierpont Morgan Library, New York

tales 'of more marvel' have been identified. Johnson's story, almost certainly drawn from existing folklore, of a boy no bigger than a man's thumb, became so widely popular that retellings followed in cheap editions in Britain and America well into the 20th century. It was so popular that nobody thought it strange that in 1830 Americans should name their first steam locomotive 'Tom Thumb' (like the British 'Puffing Billy'), or P. T. Barnum his dwarf boy 'General Tom Thumb' for his touring live show, or Messrs Longman & Co., in 1849, their miniature abridged 'Thumb Bible' (see p. 99): the name was by then part of everyday consciousness.

The fame of the story came partly from the writer Henry Fielding, who wrote a tragedy on the subject of Tom Thumb; in time Fielding's work provided Beatrix Potter with the characters' names for her *Tale of Two Bad Mice* (1908). Fielding's play was said to make Jonathan Swift laugh when it was performed in 1730 at the Haymarket Theatre; something very rare for the author of *Gulliver's Travels.* Swift (1667–1745) was an author of bitter political satires, who intended his *Travels into Several Remote Nations of the World ... By Lemuel Gulliver* (1726) for a cultivated, sophisticated readership. Political satire was dangerous stuff, and both Swift and his publisher, Benjamin Motte, anticipated it would sell very well, but it was clearly provocative: Motte redacted Swift's text to lessen the risk to himself and arranged for the book to be printed at five separate workshops, to speed it through the process of publication. Nonetheless, the stories were, for children, enthralling tales told with great ease and simplicity – far too compelling to be left to adults alone. Very quickly publishers of juvenile books started issuing abridged editions, often including only the stories of the very small people in Lilliput and of the giants in Brobdingnag. Children seldom read the later stories of Laputa, or about the

intelligent horses called Houyhnhnms, so they seldom saw the best of Swift's satire.

Nonetheless, the splendid tales about Lilliput were possibly the most readable of all the 18th-century classics, and Swift's name was quickly taken into everyday English use. John Newbery, the most famous of all publishers for children in the 18th century, made frequent use of the term 'Lilliput' in his books (see pp. 112–13); and the publisher John Harris described his own miniature books of 1802 for sale as 'The Cabinet of Lilliput'. Swift's book was equally popular on the Continent, and over time translations and adaptations of *Gulliver's Travels* have appeared worldwide, in a variety of Asian languages as well. The continuing publication of versions of Swift's work in less-common languages (such as Basque, Georgian and Tajik) illustrates the continuing power of the story of the Lilliputians.

'Abominable Absurdities'

In the early 18th century, chapbook publishers introduced many children to familiar tales. But was *Jack the Giant Killer* really very old? And why did it cause a spat in children's publishing in Victorian times?

As printing spread out from London to the provinces at the end of the 17th century, local printers often took to printing small, cheap books which had a ready sale in markets and small towns. They were cheap to produce and easy to transport, and **chapbooks** were often distributed very widely by pedlars. Country printers issued extraordinary numbers of different titles, and it is estimated that over 15,000 were published in Scotland, though fewer than half still survive.

One canny provincial printer who understood what would sell well in the north-east was John White, a printer who moved from York to Newcastle upon Tyne, establishing a printing /publishing business which lasted for generations. As well as his hundreds of **broadside** songs which were hawked around the quays, White is notable for his range of chapbooks. In 1711, he issued a cheap version of *Jack and the Giants*, the second-known printing of the Jack the Giant Killer tale; an earlier printing is recorded as having been in 1708 (although any copies of these two editions are now lost). The tale's early provenance is supported by the fact that Shakespeare had known of the phrase 'Fee fi fo fum' as being what giants say (*King Lear*, III.iv), but it was in use before that.

The story is a gruesome tale set in the reign of King Arthur, about a young Cornish lad who kills not only one giant, but (aided by his cap of invisibility and his swift shoes) manages to dispatch *six* of these tiresome critters. As the poet Robert Bloomfield complained, the tale had 'abominable absurdities', and historians of children's

The Chronicle of … Jack the Giant Killer, etc., in the Home Treasury series, p. 32. London: Felix Summerly [Henry Cole], 1845. Jack gets to grips with the giant in this coloured wood-cut. The fairy tales were designed and printed by Charles Whittingham the Younger at the Chiswick Press. Cole also published books for adults, often on a 'day excursion' sort of theme.

The British Library

by 'Peter Parley' (the pseudonym of Samuel Griswold Goodrich, 1793–1860, though at least six other writers pirated the Parley name). Goodrich was very much in the Puritan New England tradition, and as a ten-year-old he had been lent *Jack the Giant Killer*, *Red Riding Hood* and 'other of the tales of horror, commonly put in the hands of youth, as if for the express purpose of reconciling them to vice and crime'. Goodrich complained in the 1840s at the English revival of traditional nursery rhymes; he also found fault with the new, well-designed and illustrated editions put out by 'Felix Summerly's Home Treasury of Books'. This was a venture by the entrepreneurial Henry Cole (1808–1882), soon to be a key lobbyist and manager for the Great Exhibition of 1851.

Cole had no patience with Goodrich and his plea for a new, purified type of children's literature ('Such a thing is unheard of'). Cole explained what the books in his Home Treasury would be – 'the character of which may be briefly described as anti-Peter Parleyism'. It was a declaration of war. In the end, Cole prevailed: his work was important for the development of children's publishing in Britain, and today it is still a pleasure to handle his Home Treasury edition of *Jack the Giant Killer*. One can buy many versions of *Jack* in contemporary publishing today. However, Goodrich's ideas are not dead: some modern writers on children's literature, and librarians, still share Goodrich's moral disquiet, and see censorship as a solution to the problems faced by parents presented with what they may still see as 'tales of horror'.

literature still debate the sources used for the writing of the story. (There were innumerable giant stories in European folklore. In Britain there were many chapbook editions of the story of Tom Hickathrift, a giant-slayer from the Isle of Ely, as well as versions of the later *Jack and the Beanstalk*.) Jack the Giant Killer's popularity was such that he also appeared as 'author of two letters, to "Jack" and "Polly"' in John Newbery's *Little Pretty Pocket-Book* of 1770.

Bloomfield's views were shared across the Atlantic as well. Few people nowadays read the once-popular American children's stories

Crusoe Adrift: The Father of the Modern Adventure

Daniel Defoe was a failed London tradesman turned government spy.
He also wrote the most famous novel of his time, *and* a Parisian village
was named for his hero.

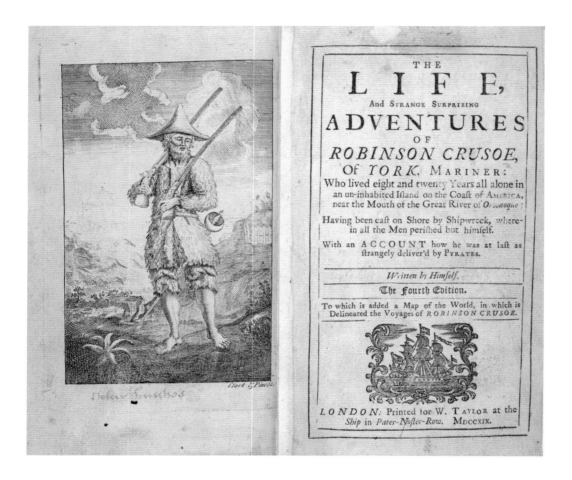

Almost all English-speaking children grew up reading a version of *The Life and Strange Surprizing Adventures of Robinson Crusoe, Of York, Mariner ... Written by himself*, by Daniel Defoe (1660–1731), first published in 1719, though many read it only in an abbreviated form, which left out much of the author's (sometimes tedious) moralising. Puritanism had had its effect on Defoe.

There were earlier stories of shipwrecks and tropical adventures – the tale of Inkle and Yarico (from the *True and Exact History of the Island of Barbados*, 1657, was one). But it was *Robinson Crusoe* which caught the imagination of Europe, for Crusoe's adventures, but also for Defoe's 'Language plain, artless, and honest, suitable to the Story, and in a Stile easie and free' (as he put it). As in his later novels, *Colonel Jack*, *The Journal of the Plague Year*, or his proto-feminist *Moll Flanders* (all published in 1722), Defoe persuades the reader that he is telling the truth, a valuable talent for any writer.

THE
HERMIT:
Or, the Unparalled
SUFFERINGS
And Surprifing
ADVENTURES
OF
Mr. *PHILIP QUARLL*,
An *Englifhman*.

Who was lately difcovered by Mr. *Dorrington*
a *Briftol* Merchant, upon an uninhabited
Ifland in the *South-Sea*; where he has
lived above Fifty Years, without any
human Affiftance, ftill continues to
refide, and will not come away.

CONTAINING

I. His Conferences with Thofe who found him out, to whom he recites the moft material Circumftances of his Life; as, that he was born in the Parifh of St. *Giles*, educated by the charitable Contribution of a Lady, and put 'Prentice to a Lock-fmith. II. How he left his Mafter, and was taken up with a notorious Houfe-breaker, who was hanged; how, after this E- fcape, he went to Sea a Cab-

bin-Boy, married a famous Whore, lifted himfelf a com- mon Soldier, turned Singing- mafter, and married Three Wives, for which he was tried and condemned at the *Old- Bailey*. III. How he was pardoned by King CHARLES II. turned Merchant, and was fhip- wracked on this defolate Ifland on the Coaft of *Mexico*. With a curious Map of the Ifland, and other Cuts.

WESTMINSTER:

Printed by J. CLUER and A. CAMPBELL, for T.
WARNER in *Pater-nofter-row*, and B. CREAKE
at the *Bible* in *Jermyn-ftreet*, St. *James's*. 1727.

Philip Quarll and Beaufidell

The timing was lucky: the story of Crusoe, the castaway who learns to live alone in the wild, meets Man Friday and converts him to Christianity, struck a chord with many readers, including children. Within a couple of years of the first edition's publication, translations of the book had been published in France, Germany, Italy, Holland and Portugal. Others rapidly followed (for example, a Serbian translation made from an early German version). New London editions followed and **chapbook** publishers recognised that there was a readership for a much briefer text; simplified editions also appeared, aimed at a younger audience (for example, *Robinson Crusoe in One Syllable*). By 1900, it is estimated that well over 700 versions had been published; some French and German versions became classics in their own right.

Defoe's book gave rise to a special word, 'Robinsonade', for the many stories which followed after it about being marooned on an island – and the term is not always limited to adventure stories. The almost-forgotten English writer Penelope Aubin seized on *Crusoe* as a way to instruct and delight readers; her 1723 *Life of Charlotta Du Pont* was one of the earliest castaway novels with a female protagonist. In turn Prévost's *Manon Lescaut* drew from Mrs Aubin. Robinsonades by two German women followed in the 1720s, and *Die Insel Felsenberg* (*Felsenberg Island*, also published as *Rock Castle Island*; 1731) by Johann Gottfried Schnabel acquired a life of its own, translated even into Icelandic. In England, *The Hermit or the Adventures of Philip Quarll* (1727), probably by Peter Longueville, and often preferred by children, continued to be reprinted in cheap editions until the 20th century. It is still worth reading.

Robinson Crusoe's influence was far-reaching, interpreted by readers according to their own cultural concerns, famously so by Jean-Jacques Rousseau, whose own enthusiasm for *Crusoe* is seen in *Emile, or Education* (1762).

While Defoe's novel was inspired by the true story of the hot-tempered Scottish mariner Alexander Selkirk, many Robinsonades were utopian fictions. The best known, perhaps best loved, in Britain was *Der Schweizerische Robinson* (*The Swiss Family Robinson*, 1812–13) by Johann David Wyss. Its appeal is no doubt in part due to the fact that the (often implausible) adventures are experienced by an everyday, middle-class family (rather than the experienced and capable mariner Crusoe) and it lacks the gripping realism of Defoe's story.

Frederick Marryat's *Masterman Ready* (1848) attempted to correct Wyss's romantic depiction of shipwreck. Much later writers have often used *Robinson Crusoe* to craft their own fiction, from Robert Louis Stevenson (*Treasure Island*) to William Golding (*Lord of the Flies*) and Patrick O'Brian for his Aubrey/ Maturin novels: not a bad record for Defoe's novel, now three hundred years old.

Small Books, Gigantick Ideas

How to tempt a new readership is always problematic. Thomas Boreman's ways of attracting his young readers were novel and successful, and inspired generations of future publishers.

[Thomas Boreman?], *The Gigantick History of the two famous Giants and other Curiosities in Guildhall*. London: Printed for Thomas Boreman, 1741. (Second edition.) The first of the *Gigantick* series; Boreman owned a shop in the Guildhall and may have written the text, perhaps to draw visitors to it. The giants are Gog and Magog, the Old Testament figures who in folklore became the guardians of London. The original papier-mâché figures (destroyed in the Great Fire of 1666) were superseded by the sturdier oak 'curiosities' of the title. These, gnawed by mice and later destroyed in the Blitz, were replaced by David Elms's 9ft-tall, lime-wood giants, 1953, which still guard the Guildhall today.

The British Library

It is always interesting to look at the travel trophies sold in tourist centres; whether in Venice, Paris or London, one is struck both by the ways hucksters attempt to attract prospective buyers, and the range of pretty things and rubbish displayed for sale. With only a small book stall in Georgian London, Thomas Boreman devised several ways of making his books attract attention in order to persuade people to buy copies as gifts for children. Publishing books specifically for children was in itself novel. Boreman began in 1730 with a profusely illustrated natural history, *A Description of Three Hundred Animals*. It was a publishing success and was supplemented by several later volumes. By the end of the 19th century, there had been thirty-eight editions.

Boreman was more innovative with his next publications. He must have realised that small books would attract children, and (in combination with printers, illustrators and bookbinders) he developed a very small format, with the books' pages measuring around 6 × 5cm. These very small books dealt with very large subjects – giants and monuments – and the books' miniature charms were increased by their attractive bindings. Finally, Boreman included in the volumes the names of subscribers (or their children). Such **subscription lists** were becoming common in Georgian publishing.

Many of Boreman's customers were Londoners, but there were some from the English provinces and further afield: 'Miss Henny Hitchcock of Oporto', 'Master Jack Stewart Campbell of Jamaica' and 'Miss Nabby Davenport of Boston, New England' were among the lucky recipients of these miniature volumes. Adult subscribers (and their children) must often have felt a sense of reflected glory as members of the nobility were among the customers: imagine the pleasure for Master Tommy or Miss Polly to see their own names printed alongside those of other, highly born subscribers to the *Gigantick Histories*! Priced at 4d., these miniature books must have seemed very good value.

'During the Infant-Age, ever busy and always inquiring, there is no fixing the attention of the mind, but by amusing it', Boreman observed in the preface to *Gigantick Histories*. Already a master of puffery and self-advertisement, there is some evidence that Boreman got his publications noticed in North American newspapers as well as in London. Then, suddenly, in the early 1740s, Boreman's name disappears from publishing history. Other booksellers and publishers further developed Boreman's ideas about new ways to amuse child readers – but Boreman was the first real founder of publishing for children.

One publisher influenced by Boreman was Mary Cooper, who took over running the family business in 1743 when her husband Thomas Cooper died. Mary Cooper's *Tommy Thumb's Pretty Song Book* (1744, see pp. 16–17), like the *Gigantick Histories*, was small in size (just 7.5cm tall), but printed by a quite different **intaglio** method: its text, along with the pictures, was punched on to copper plates with individual letter punches – a technique more common for making music scores and satirical prints.

This little book has been studied closely, both because of its rarity and because it was for many years the earliest-known book of nursery rhymes. With Mary Cooper's name on the volume, some writers have guessed that she was the author, but there is no evidence that she was involved in the choice of rhymes. It may possibly have been produced by the satirist George Bickham, who illustrated the 'companion' volume, *Nancy Cock's Song-Book* (also 1744), with which there are many correlations. Another close business associate at the time who also used the name of 'Tommy Thumb' when it suited him was John Newbery. He, rather than Mary Cooper, was the person most responsible for developing publishing for children.

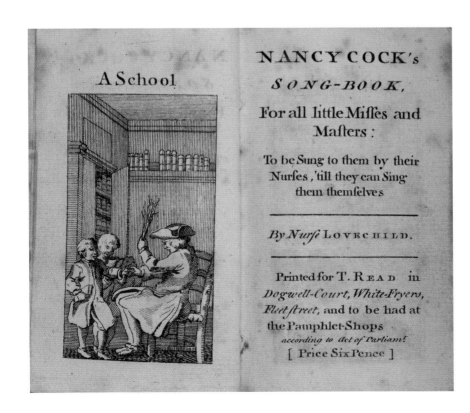

A School

NANCY COCK's
SONG-BOOK,

For all little Misses and Masters:

To be Sung to them by their Nurses, 'till they can Sing them themselves

By Nurse LOVECHILD.

Printed for T. READ in *Dogwell-Court, White-Fryers, Fleet street,* and to be had at the Pamphlet-Shops according to Act of Parliament
[Price Six Pence]

'Not ... Too Wise to Be Taught': Taking Girls' Education Seriously

As the first school story written for girls, Sarah Fielding's novel broke new ground – but a new generation of children's writers decided to rewrite it altogether.

As a second novelist in the Fielding family, Sarah Fielding (1710–68) became well known for her novel *The Adventures of David Simple* (1744), but she had already appeared in print for a letter inserted in Henry Fielding's *Joseph Andrews* of 1742. Her brother Henry had links to the literary and dramatic world, and a role in the administration of justice (together with their younger half-brother, the blind Sir John Fielding, Henry was famous for forming the Bow Street Runners, the first effective police force in London). Through these Sarah was more widely experienced than many women of her time who learned, as she put it, to 'work and read and write and to talk French and Dance and be brought up as Gentlewomen'.

Sarah followed *David Simple* with *The Governess; or, The Little Female Academy. Being the history of Mrs Teachum, and her nine girls, with their nine days amusement* (1749), based partly on her own school experiences at Salisbury. It was openly didactic in tone, as her preface made clear: 'consider with me, what is the true Use of Reading; and if you can once fix this Truth in your Minds, namely, that the true Use of Books, is to make you wiser and better, you will then have both Pleasure and Profit from what you read'. Sarah sweetened her teaching by inserting a few fairy stories: in the 17th century Puritan sentiment had driven out fairies altogether (as John Aubrey noted), and in Georgian England the use of fairies was becoming more acceptable, if the method helped a girl 'not to be apt to fansy yourself too wise to be taught'.

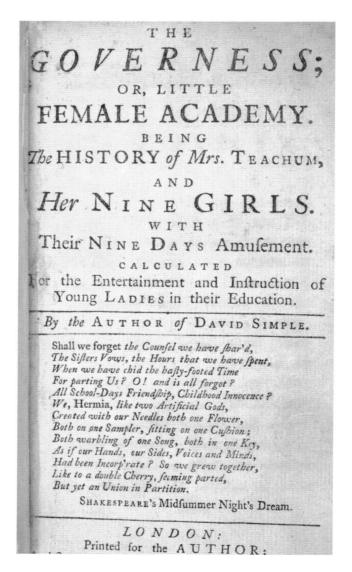

THE
GOVERNESS;
OR, LITTLE
FEMALE ACADEMY.
BEING
The HISTORY *of* Mrs. TEACHUM,
AND
Her NINE GIRLS.
WITH
Their NINE DAYS Amusement.
CALCULATED
For the Entertainment and Instruction of
Young LADIES in their Education.

By the AUTHOR of DAVID SIMPLE.

Shall we forget *the Counsel we have shar'd,*
The Sisters Vows, the Hours that we have spent,
When we have chid the hasty-footed Time
For parting Us? O! and is all forgot?
All School-Days Friendship, Childhood Innocence?
We, Hermia, *like two Artificial Gods,*
Created with our Needles both one Flower,
Both on one Sampler, sitting on one Cushion;
Both warbling of one Song, both in one Key,
As if our Hands, our Sides, Voices and Minds,
Had been Incorp'rate? So we grew together,
Like to a double Cherry, seeming parted,
But yet an Union in Partition.
SHAKESPEARE's Midsummer Night's Dream.

LONDON:
Printed for the AUTHOR:

Sarah Fielding, *The Governess; or, Little Female Academy. Being the history of Mrs Teachum, and her nine girls.* London: A. Millar, 1749. Regarded by many as the first novel in English for children, it is perhaps also the first girls' school story, in the form of a ten-day narrative at the school. A keen student herself, Fielding had been tutored in Latin and Greek (by the Anglican priest Arthur Collier) and later published a translation of Xenophon's *Memoirs of Socrates*, as 'one of the only women in England with sufficient Greek' to complete such a translation.
The British Library

Mary Martha Butt (afterwards Mrs Sherwood). *The Governess; or, the Little Female Academy. By Mrs. Sherwood*. Wellington, Salop: F. Houlston & Son, 1820. Recast by Mrs Sherwood from the work of the same name by Sarah Fielding, its title page draws attention to *Little Henry*, Mary Sherwood's earlier success.

The British Library

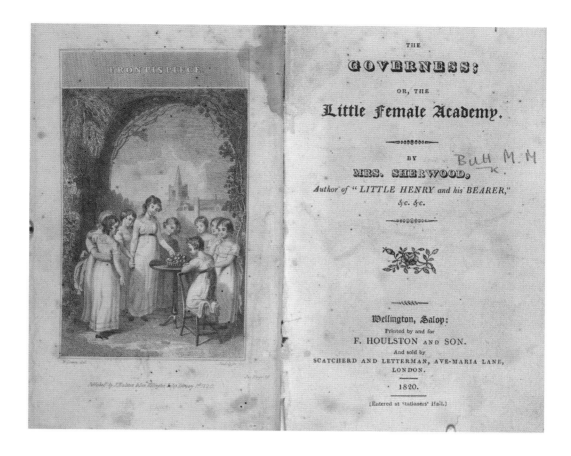

Sarah was a really good writer, and when, after each day's tale, the girls (Jenny Peace, Sukey Jennett, Dolly Friendly, Lucy Sly, Patty Lockit, Nancy Spruce, Betty Ford, Henny Frett and Polly Suckling) recount their own personal histories, one's attention is caught.

For the 18th century, Fielding's book worked well, and there were several other editions in Britain, Ireland and America – but changes in religious fervour in England had an enormous effect. One very successful children's writer in Regency England, Mary Martha Sherwood (1775–1851) became a fervent evangelical Christian. Her *History of Little Henry and his Bearer* (1814), about the conversion by a young British boy of his Indian bearer, written while Mrs Sherwood was resident in India, was hugely popular. Subsequently she rewrote and 'improved' *The Pilgrim's Progress* (see pp. 80–81) shortly after

her return from India, adapting it for an Indian context (*The Indian Pilgrim*, 1818), and again for the very young (*The Infant's Progress*, 1821). A firm based in Wellington (Shropshire) issued several editions of *The Governess* under her name as author, a rewritten version of Sarah Fielding's story, stating that all but one of the fairy stories were being omitted 'since such fanciful productions of this sort can never be rendered generally useful'.

Instead, Mrs Sherwood set about 'substituting in their place such appropriate relations as seemed more likely to conduce to juvenile edification'. These were the days when **bowdlerising** books was thought to be the right thing to do. Publishers of books for children still today rewrite and adapt books for fiscal or moral reasons, but seldom so destructively as with Sarah Fielding's tale.

'Jack Whirler' Publishes Some Books

An apprenticeship as a bookseller and printer in Reading led John Newbery to found a dynasty, which dominated juvenile publishing in the 18th century and beyond.

The London publisher Allen Lane is often described as the inventor of the paperback, through the Penguins he started in the 1930s. It is often forgotten that part of Lane's success was in taking other people's ideas and running with them (the idea for Penguins came from John Holroyd-Reece's slightly earlier Albatross Editions, and Noël Carrington's Puffin Picture Books were inspired by Soviet books of the 1920s.) Lane's greatest success was in engaging brilliant assistants to work with him, and in persuading bookshops to distribute his publications.

One should not push the parallels too far, but in his day John Newbery (1713–67) was a similar visionary, one highly respected and liked by his peers. Dr Johnson's description of him as 'Jack Whirler' was an affectionate reference to Newbery's constant activity in the manifold aspects of his business. By 1730 Newbery was employed by William Carnan (printer of the *Reading Mercury*), and after Carnan's death Newbery married his employer's widow and ran the Reading business for a couple of years. After time spent touring England looking for new business opportunities (including the sale

The History of Little Goody Two-Shoes. London: John Newbery, 1765. F. J. Harvey Darton described the book, priced at sixpence, as not far off being a great one and 'an extraordinary picture of rural England painted by, so to speak, a sentimental democratic conservative'. Margaret Thatcher would have approved.

The British Library

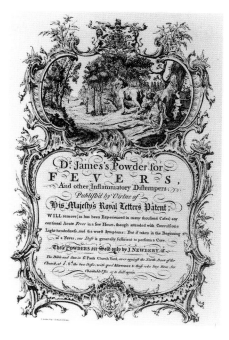

of patent medicines) he set up a bookselling and publishing business in London, where his first publication was *A Little Pretty Pocket-Book* (1744) 'intended for the instruction and amusement of Little Master Tommy and Pretty Miss Polly'. The first of Newbery's books designed specifically for children, it was one of several reprinted in Massachusetts by Isaiah Thomas, becoming as well known and popular there as in Britain.

Newbery was an assiduous promoter of his books, of which he issued hundreds, by no means all intended for children (he also published schoolbooks and adult **readers**). While obviously influenced by the juvenile books of Thomas Boreman and Mary Cooper, Newbery never adopted their very small formats, but he recognised the importance of illustrations, commissioning many for his own children's titles.

Establishing the authorship of Newbery titles is often difficult: some were written by the poet Christopher Smart (who became Newbery's stepson-in-law), some by Oliver Goldsmith, more by other competent but less well-known writers of the time. Stealing the name from Swift's *Gulliver's Travels* of 1726, Newbery adopted the word 'Lilliput' for many of his books. One pioneering effort was *The Lilliputian Magazine* (1751–2), the first periodical aimed specifically at a child readership, issued in parts priced at 3d. each. The editorial control of the magazine was probably by Smart. Historians of children's literature have described it as a failure because only three numbers appeared – but as records show 4,000 copies were printed, it was far from a failure.

Newbery's marketing was almost always aggressive, undercutting other publishers' prices. *Nurse Truelove's Christmas-Box* (1750) was advertised as 'free' – 'only paying 1d. for the binding'. His *Renowned History of Giles Gingerbread* (1765), priced at 1d., would appeal to many children. Another undoubted success was *The History of Little Goody Two-Shoes* (1765), possibly written by Oliver Goldsmith, or perhaps by Giles Jones or Newbery himself. It was a rags-to-riches story, which was enormously popular in the 18th century. Often thought to be written for girls, records of sales show it was also consumed eagerly by schoolboys at Rugby School. Though almost forgotten today, it has been highly praised by readers who enjoyed it in their childhood. The Newbery imprint lasted into the 19th century, continued by Elizabeth Newbery (John's niece-in-law) until 1801–2 when the business was taken over by her manager, John Harris. Newbery's son Francis moved from the book business in 1779 to concentrate on patent medicines (making a fortune from Dr James's Fever Powder). Other members of the Carnan and Newbery families continued in publishing: 'Jack Whirler' had shown how publishing books for children could be highly profitable.

Pins and Perambulations: Mary Ann and Dorothy Kilner

In the last quarter of the 18th century, increasing numbers of children's books were written by women. Two sisters-in-law took storytelling in fresh directions.

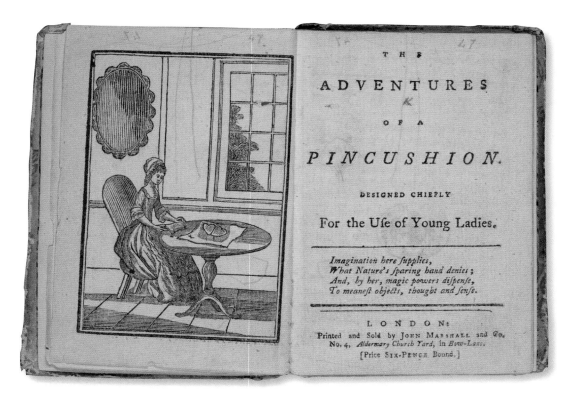

Mary Ann Kilner, *The Adventures of a Pincushion*. London: Printed and sold by John Marshall and Co. No. 4, Aldermary Church Yard, in Bow-Lane, [between 1779 and 1789]. As a Huguenot (with their trade in silks and lacework), it is perhaps no surprise that a pincushion should be uppermost in the writer's mind when choosing her subject. The copious wood engravings give a clear picture of the routines of life for a young girl in the Georgian period.

The British Library

When juvenile book publishing developed as a speciality, many of the authors were from East Anglia and suburbs developing to the east of London. At the same time, many booksellers in earlier times concentrated round St Paul's Cathedral, long a centre for small booksellers and publishers, relocated to the new fashionable parts of the West End. Some of the best children's books were written by two long-term friends and correspondents. One was Dorothy Kilner (1755–1836), who wrote as 'M. P.' or 'Mary Pelham', a pseudonym based on her village home of Maryland Point in Essex (now in Newham). The other was Mary Ann Maze (1753–1831), or 'S. S.', a bilingual Huguenot whose father was a prosperous silk throwster, or silk yarn worker, who had moved into the developing prosperous district of Spittal (now Spital) Square. In 1774 she married Dorothy Kilner's brother Tom Kilner (also a silk merchant at Spital Square).

Working at Spital Square, and later in Margate, the two sisters-in-law produced an impressive range of books, apparently written in collaboration. While Mary Ann was bringing up her children, Dorothy (who never married, preferring 'darling liberty') had sought advice from the redoubtable Sarah Trimmer (see overleaf), and Mrs Trimmer recommended she approach the publisher

John Marshall. It was a valuable introduction, and Marshall became a close friend to the Kilners, publishing many of their little books (see pp. 118–19).

Marshall's business in Aldermary Churchyard, in Aldgate, was an old one, with close and prosperous links to the chapbook trade and the sale of books to the provinces. Its success was largely built on quantity of sales, but the Kilners' books were well written and intended for attentive children who were being well educated. Dorothy Kilner's earliest publications were pious and didactic, intended for use with children, but these were followed by livelier works: *Poems on various subjects, for the amusement of youth* (1783) was aimed at the very young, and her best-known story, *The Life and Perambulation of a Mouse* (1784) was aimed at much older readers with a good vocabulary – as the title makes clear. It was the first book to give characters and names to the mice described – but Dorothy Kilner evidently did not expect readers to believe her characters actually spoke: 'I must beg and assure young readers that *in earnest*

I never heard a mouse speak in my whole life, and only wrote the following narrative as being far more entertaining and more instructive than my own life would have been.' Dorothy's device was the first sprouting of a genre for much later writing such as Kenneth Grahame's *Wind in the Willows* (1908) or E. B. White's *Stuart Little* (1945).

Mary Ann Kilner's *Adventures of a Pincushion* (1780) used an inanimate object (a pincushion) as the vehicle for various adventures in places not normally familiar to young middle-class girls. It was equally as inventive as her sister-in-law's book, and hundreds of later Victorian children's writers would adopt a similar device. Other books by Dorothy and Mary Ann Kilner were popular in their time, and continued to be republished for fifty years or so. But fashions change. Unlike some of the emerging feminists such as Mary Wollstonecraft, the Kilners tend to be overlooked by modern scholars interested in children's literature: they were good, pious women who sought Christian contentment and to make the world better by teaching children the rewards for goodness and honesty, and the punishments for selfishness and misconduct. The Kilner stories were the sort used by the governesses portrayed in Jane Austen's novels (such as Miss Taylor in *Emma*): the development of middle-class values in Regency times owed much to these writers, who tried 'to promote the cause of virtue ... with incidents of an amusing nature'.

[Dorothy Kilner], *The Life and Perambulation of a Mouse*. London: Printed and sold by John Marshall and Co., No. 4, Aldermary Church-Yard, in Bow-Lane, 1784. In two volumes, with a book list at the back advertising further titles by 'M. P.' and 'S. S.'. Mary Wollstonecraft, rejecting too-early reading of the Bible for children, instead favoured animal stories (singling out the *Perambulation*), noting their 'best effect in forming the temper and cultivating the good dispositions of the heart'.

The British Library

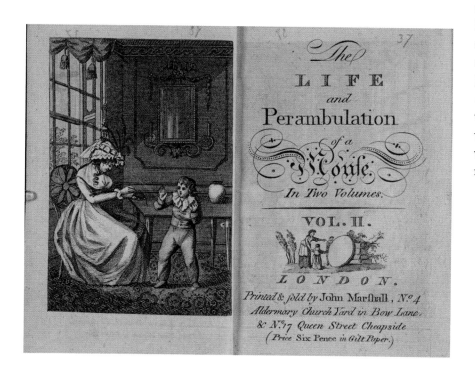

Fighting the Revolution: Hannah More and Sarah Trimmer

In the late 18th century, a split developed between those supporting Locke's and Rousseau's ideas on children's education and literacy, and those who disagreed with them strongly. At the same time, the French Revolution affected writing for children, and not only in France.

The 18th century saw many women of remarkable ability. One, Hannah More (1745–1833), was active in several fields: running a successful boarding school; as a poet, playwright and novelist; as an anti-slavery activist; and as the founder of a group of Sunday schools. Despite lacking beauty, wealth or high social standing, More was popular with fashionable London Society, counting Samuel Johnson, David Garrick, Edmund Burke, Joshua Reynolds and Horace Walpole among her friends.

One of the original 'Bluestockings', Hannah More wrote extensively, including several plays based on Old Testament themes for the girls at the More sisters' boarding school (where she later taught). She then turned to writing for women, on their rights and education, often in conflict with Mary Wollstonecraft, whose views were the antithesis of her own. More, a sincere Anglican, and horrified as events unravelled in the French Revolution after 1793, believed sincerely that the British social structure was best, with a monarch at its head, and strove to convince the working classes to share these views.

Following her mockery of Thomas Paine's *Rights of Man* (published in 1792 in her *Village Politics* under the pseudonym of 'Will Chip, a country carpenter'), from 1795 to 1797 Hannah More concentrated her counter-revolutionary fervour into a long series of 'Cheap Repository Tracts', distributed freely and very widely. *The Shepherd of Salisbury Plain* (1795) was the most famous of these,

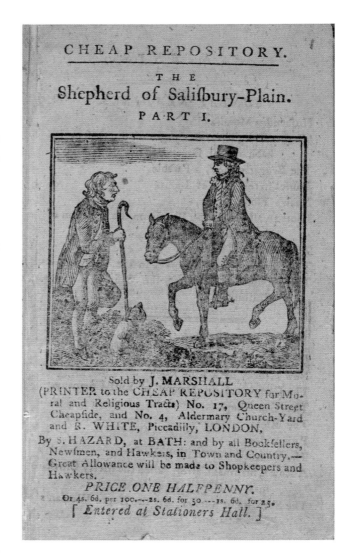

Hannah More, *The Shepherd of Salisbury-Plain*. London: J. Marshall and Bath: S. Hazard, 'and by all booksellers, newsmen, and hawkers, in town and country', 1797. More's evangelising tracts, enlivened with wood-cuts, aimed to undermine the salacious halfpenny **broadsides** so popular at the time. Supposedly a true tale of David Sanders, a modest shepherd who tended his flock in Wiltshire (inspired to his peaceful life by his Bible), this was later satirised as 'The Washerwoman of Finchley Common' by W. M. Thackeray in his novel *Vanity Fair*.
The British Library

CHAPTER VIII.

MASTER FREDERICK VIEWING THE YOUNG ROBINS IN THE CURRANT-BUSH.

WHILST all the business related in the last chapter was going on in the Redbreast family,

Mrs Sarah Trimmer, *Fabulous Histories, By Mrs. Trimmer; or, the History of the Robins. Designed for the Instruction of Children, respecting their treatment of animals With Wood Cuts by Bewick.* London: Thomas Ward, 1839. The charming engravings here were cut but not designed by Bewick (whose name had yet to become an advantageous selling point). This natural history was intended to lead one 'to contemplate the perfections of the Supreme Being, and [to furnish] ... useful hints for the conduct of human affairs'. Continuously in print from 1786 until after the First World War, later under the title *The History of the Robins*.

Author's collection

intended as 'an antidote to the poison continually flowing thro' the channel of vulgar and licentious [chapbook] publications'. Their efficacy has often been questioned, however, and the importance of this early instance of moral panic in children's publishing has also been doubted. In 1799 the Religious Tract Society (RTS) was established to produce further 'antidotes'; its later wholesome children's books and magazines, such as the *Boy's Own Paper* and the *Girl's Own Paper*, were important and effective. The decline of **chapbook** publishing in the early 19th century may have been in part a result of competition from the RTS.

The often rather clumsily propagandist RTS tracts were sometimes written by other members of the More family or other writers (two by Mary Ann Kilner). The organisational skills required to produce and distribute these were considerable, as many millions of copies were published throughout Britain, the West Indies and Sierra Leone. Their effect was curiously muted, however: much sincere effort with few discernible results.

In the 1790s, Hannah More's patriotic, conservative stance was well supported by most of her contemporaries, but in her later years her diatribes on moral decline earned William Cobbett's reference to More as 'the old bishop in petticoats'. Her later strongly paternalist views on education, on women's role in society and the poor, make her unattractive to modern academics, but in her time her views were shared by many, and a reassessment of her significance is surely overdue.

The now equally unfashionable Sarah Trimmer (née Kirby, 1741–1810), whose father taught perspective drawing to the young Prince of Wales (later George III), had considerable influence at the Royal court. Holding strong ideas on suitable books for children (she raised twelve of her own), Trimmer disapproved thoroughly of Rousseau's ideas. The historian Percy Muir commented that Mrs Trimmer 'was terrifyingly familiar with what had been written for [children] in the past, and she disapproved of most of it'. This 'preposterous woman', as Muir described her, had a marked effect on children's publishing: her reviews could make or destroy a publisher. She was not just a theoretician, however. Her strong disapproval of fairy stories led her to writing fables as a substitute, and her *Fabulous Histories* (1786), was a near-classic: a charming anthropomorphic tale which survived in regular publication for well over a century.

Aldermary Churchyard: From Chapbook to *The Infant's Library*

Aldermary Churchyard in Bow Lane in London was an early centre for producing cheap books and chapbooks for sale throughout England. By the late 18th century, the trade was being transformed and gentrified.

The little, cheap Aldermary Churchyard books, though produced by the tens of thousands, were seen as so insignificant that hardly anybody mentions them. One exception was Samuel Johnson's biographer, James Boswell. In the entry for 10 July 1763, in his London journal, Boswell recorded that he had been to:

the old printing-office in Bow Church-yard kept by Dicey, whose family have kept it

fourscore years. There are ushered into the world of literature *Jack and the Giants*, *The Seven Wise Men of Gotham*, and other story-books which in my dawning years amused me as much as *Rasselas* does now.

The press was run by the Dicey and Cluer families, both of them based in the Aldermary Churchyard and, from 1720 onwards, with another branch in Northampton, which acted as a supply depot for a colossal range of maps

The Infant's Library. London: John Marshall, 1800. The second of several successful miniature bookcases published by the self-styled 'Children's Printer' in the same year. By now, the boundary between books and toys was becoming blurred, and other publishers adopted the profitable trend established by Marshall, with close copies of his titles made by John Harris and others.

The Lilly Library, Indiana University, Bloomington, Indiana

and prints. (The prints bought by Jane Johnson for her teaching work – see pp. 86–7 – could well have come from either of these sources, or she might have had recourse to the extensive catalogue of their available publications produced soon after Boswell's visit, in 1764.) The Cluers and Diceys had become wholesale dealers.

Under Richard Marshall, already in partnership with Cluer Dicey, the Aldermary business followed the earlier foray by John Newbery into publishing, and like the earlier Aldermary-based venture, it began producing large numbers of children's books. Richard Marshall's son, John Marshall, worked with Hannah More on her Cheap Repository Tracts, with Sarah Trimmer as well on several of her books, and on a host of other children's

books with the Kilners and Ellenor Fenn (1743–1813). The latter was a prolific author whose many titles by 'Mrs Teachwell' and 'Mrs Lovechild' included *Cobwebs to Catch Flies,* a **primer** published first in 1783. It was to prove John Marshall's bestselling work and he kept it in print until 1815. However effective he was as a publisher, Marshall was also disliked and distrusted by some of the writers he worked with, and (unlike Newbery), he seems to have preferred rapid profits over producing good books. Yet he had one simple but brilliant idea: as he was publishing these very small volumes intended for children, why not package them in a miniature bookcase, which would make an elegant addition to a nursery?

By the last years of the 18th century, with increased prosperity and changing attitudes towards education, the aspirational middle-class were willing to spend money on equipping their nurseries. Marshall produced several of these miniature libraries: *The Juvenile or Child's Library, The Infant's Library* (also translated into Latin, German and French) and several others which he issued in around 1800, were an immediate success – with the consequence that they were rapidly copied by other contemporary publishers! John Harris, describing himself as 'successor to E. Newbery', was one, with his *Cabinet of Lilliput,* a miniature library of twelve volumes of stories, published in 1802. This effective gimmick still works today; Frederick Warne's boxed set of the 'Original Peter Rabbit Miniature Collection' (for instance), still attracts children – and the adults, too, who are usually the purchasers of the boxed sets, whether for themselves or others.

CHAPTER 6

Tales of Tails: Animal Stories for Children

Animal stories are probably the oldest tales of all, as cave paintings show plenty of evidence of early human interest in the animal world.

In the pre-industrial West, every child became familiar with a range of domesticated or farm animals. No doubt mothers dandling young children made up stories about the family's cats or dogs; even in town children knew about cattle, horses and donkeys. Sometimes their introduction to animals was pretty horrifying, with bear-baiting, badger-baiting and cock fights common and popular spectator sports from Tudor times until the end of the 18th century (the first British laws protecting animals were passed early in the next century). Only in the 18th century did authors start to write sympathetically about the lives of animals: Sarah Trimmer's *Fabulous Histories* of 1786 was influential in many ways (see p. 117).

Many other early books dealt with aspects of animal life. Francis Coventry's *The History of Pompey the Little, or, The Life and Adventures of a Lap-Dog*, caused a stir when this lively novel of fashionable life was published anonymously in 1751, but it was not really intended for a juvenile audience. Nor were the fantastical verses about insect life by William Roscoe (first published in *The Gentleman's Magazine* in 1806), but the publisher John Harris seized upon them, and *The Butterfly's Ball and the Grasshopper's Feast* (1807) proved enormously popular with

children. This led to many early imitations: some were good, like Catherine Ann Dorset's *The Peacock 'At Home'* (1807), but many others, such as *The Fishes Grand Gala* [sic], by a Mrs Cockle (1808), were rather inept things, even when they were produced merely to amuse rather than educate.

For the continuing health of their businesses, all children's publishers tried to ensure that their lists included a tempting selection of animal books. Competition was intense, so many of these were published in series, with one volume on dogs, another on cats, bears, ponies and so on. Alfred Elwes, a translator and compiler of language dictionaries, branched out into writing children's stories, and had some success with his *Adventures of a Dog and a Good Dog Too* (1854), and various other books which went into several editions, but he is now totally forgotten. The same could be said of other rather good books consumed by Victorian children, such as Charles Bennett's *Nine Lives of a Cat: A Tale of Wonder* (1860), which deserves to be revived, or Mrs E. Burrows's *Tuppy, or the Autobiography of a Donkey* (1860). Both were published by Griffith & Farran (successors to the old Newbery firm) and continuously reprinted until the firm eventually disappeared at the end of the 19th century.

The Tribulations of Tommy Tiptop. London: Myra & Son, 1887 (see p. 129). The ready ability of children to empathise with the characters makes this story of the naughty young Tommy an uncomfortable introduction to animals.

The British Library

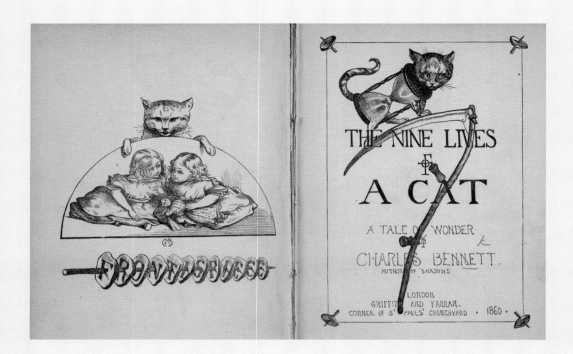

In the first animal stories to reach a cultivated adult audience, two centuries earlier, the protagonists were not described as real animals, but rather people in the guise of animals – and a very select, upper-class group of animals they were, like Puss in Boots and the other figures in Perrault's stories, or the later fairy tales by the Baroness d'Aulnoy, all rather grand beings (see pp. 126–7).

However fanciful in their notions, the success of the 'papillonades', or butterfly stories, by Roscoe and Mrs Dorset at the beginning of the 19th century surprised everybody, including their publisher John Harris, who claimed to have sold 40,000 copies immediately after publication. In this febrile boom period in juvenile publishing, *Old Mother Hubbard* (1805) by Sarah Catherine Martin (1768–1826) was almost equally successful; its nonsensical content obviously appealed (see pp. 128–9). But Harris did not always get it right. His choice of the industrious Elizabeth Sandham as a regular writer was on the whole successful, with her *Adventures of a Bullfinch* and

Adventures of Poor Puss (both 1809) typical of her output. Why then did her translation of Florian's *Selected Fables* (1806) fail to attract English readers? Coming from a successful and enterprising publisher, and by a competent, readable author, this translation ought to have succeeded (see pp. 130–31). Some other excellent foreign-language books in translation also failed to break into the English market, and vice versa.

With the exception of a few books discussed in this chapter, few of the 19th-century animal books have survived and been read with pleasure by contemporary children. Anna Sewell's *Black Beauty* (1877), on the other hand, is a notable exception (see pp. 166–7). Gifts of Charles Kingsley's children's book *The Water Babies* (1865) were inflicted on many English-speaking children. Though its chimney-sweep hero turns into a fish-like 'water baby' it is less an animal story than an overtly moralising Christian fable: Kingsley had dreams of helping to make the world a better place, but many readers found his book poor, maudlin stuff, full of prejudices against religious and ethnic groups the author disliked: Kingsley simply could not resist over-egging his arguments, nor stop himself preaching when trying to tell a story. Kingsley had many gifts as a writer, however, and *The Water Babies* is still available today – usually in an abbreviated form, wisely omitting many of the author's tiresome digressions.

We don't think of *The Water Babies'* near-contemporary *Alice in Wonderland* (1865) as an animal book – Alice herself, as depicted by Tenniel, is so very convincing as a real child – but Lewis Carroll's influence is marked upon the development of other zany writers of children's books. T. S. Eliot's *Old Possum's Book of Practical Cats* (1939), or Edward Gorey's rather unsettling picture books, and even Maurice Sendak, owe a great deal to *Alice*.

Many Victorian children's books introduce animals which people had come to know via colonisation, even if they had only seen them in real life in zoos (the world's first scientific zoo was set up in the capital in 1828 by the Zoological Society of London). Such animal displays stimulated European writers' interest in the '*Pourquoi*' or '*tingi-tingi*' ('Why' or 'How Did ...') type of stories so typical in Africa and in the Anansi stories of the West Indies (see pp. 46–7). By far the most famous, though, were those drawn from India by Rudyard Kipling in his *Just So Stories* and *The Jungle Book* (pp. 134–5). Kipling set very high standards for other writers of animal books: even in the dumbed-down Disney versions, his animal kingdom seems 'real' and the stories as appealing today as when they were written. In the context of Kipling it is worth mentioning the Detmold brothers, prolific and meticulous illustrators of exquisite nature scenes, who illustrated Kipling's *Jungle Book*, among other works.

The real Christopher Robin and his grandfather with Pooh. Uneasy with his role as the inspiration behind his father's books, in later life Christopher Milne came to dislike the commercialisation and Disneyfication of the characters.

Peter Harrington Rare Books, London

Whether *The Wind in the Willows* is doing as well nowadays is a matter of debate (see pp. 136–7). Some aspects of Kenneth Grahame's fantasy are very modish, of course, such as the nostalgia for an older, simpler country life (not altogether unlike that of *Goody Two-Shoes*); and his close and loving observation of animal life pointed the way for later writers such as Henry Williamson with his *Tarka the Otter* (1927). Grahame also influenced Richard Adams's *Watership Down* (1972). Surprisingly, for a first book from a new writer by an unknown publisher, this was a great success, in Germany and Scandinavia as well as in Britain (though much less so in France). American reaction was far more equivocal: Adams's treatment of relationships between the male and female rabbits was regarded by some as evidence of societal flaws deliberately introduced by the author; if the story is to be regarded as an allegory for human behaviour, as is often the case, they did have a point. It brings to mind how the Nazi authorities disliked *Bambi* enough to ban it (p. 137).

To include Michael Morpurgo's sombre *War Horse* (1982) as an animal story is perhaps to stretch a point, but his tale of a farm horse on the Western Front during the First World War brought a new dimension to the hitherto often cosy world of animal stories. Any realistic treatment of war in children's books has by and large been avoided or condemned. Even in the most jingoist days, when Britain was involved in the Boer War in South Africa (1899–1902), a reviewer in the *Spectator* sternly rebuked the publisher and the (Canadian) author of *Ten Little Boer Boys* (1900):

We must own to not caring for the fun of pictures which show them blown to pieces by lyddite [a form of explosive] and the like. Mrs. Ames should find worthier ways of employing a patriotic pencil.

Authors who served in the forces in the First World War included Hugh Lofting (1886–1947), an English engineer trying to make a career as a writer in America, who returned to Britain in 1916 to enlist with the Irish Guards, but was invalided out in 1917. Lofting's way of dealing with the horrors of the Western Front was to blot out the war totally from the letters he wrote to his young children while convalescing. Instead, his *Story of Doctor Dolittle* (published in New York in 1920) was set in an imaginary village in the England of a century earlier. A series of Doctor Doolittle stories appeared over the years until Lofting's death and were very popular in America (never quite so much in Britain), but the stories of the man who could talk to the animals, and the image of the pushmi-pullyu, live vividly in many people's minds – aided, perhaps, by the very popular musical film of the story starring Rex Harrison as the doctor (1967). Like *The Water Babies*, this novel has suffered from the passage of time. Lofting used imagery drawn from his time working in West Africa, and some scenes are now found to be offensive. Even the revised (more politically correct) editions prepared by Christopher Lofting have not revived the popularity that the book once enjoyed.

Considering the great success of the *Winnie-the-Pooh* stories, it is perhaps rather surprising that the combination of A. A. Milne and E. H. Shepard in the production of these stories of an innocent small boy and his teddy bear have been given little critical attention. Despite the crass distortions of the later Disney film versions of these books, Milne's stories survive in print, though other teddy books, despite being published in book form even earlier, may have a shorter shelf life ahead of them (see pp. 140–41 and 145). However, both the Winnie-the-Pooh and the Teddy Robinson books have been readily adapted to manifest all the features of modern 'manufactured' books (that is, published in many formats, as buggy books, as lift-the-flap titles and as books which make interesting noises – aimed at younger readers) and their characters successfully used to create other related merchandise, which is often as important in cash terms as the books themselves. Newbery and Harris had some good marketing notions as long ago as the 19th century; Beatrix Potter's *Peter Rabbit* series, consisting of delightful books in themselves (see pp. 132–3), has given itself over to modern merchandise marketing with the greatest of ease. But other

Mrs Rabbit and Peter – Beatrix Potter merchandise modelled by Warren Platt for Royal Doulton, after 1997.
AlamyBest/Alamy Stock Photo

series produced between the wars also illustrate clearly that the production of children's books today calls for a complex manufacturing and marketing approach, not a chief consideration at that time, and one itself which often shows little connection with the simple attempt of parents to tell new stories to their children (see pp. 142–3).

Books first devised in one country may succeed equally well in another, and many animal (and other children's) stories have been successfully exported. However, the range of books originating in developing countries which go on to succeed in Europe or America remains disappointingly small (see pp. 146–7). Eighty years ago, several British and French publishers sought new markets in the emerging ex-colonial countries, and worked hard to attract authors from those countries, many of which enjoyed longstanding and immensely rich oral traditions, particularly of animal stories and folklore. Yet despite their efforts, and no doubt for complex cultural and economic reasons, by and large the successful profitable publication of such stories for children, either by small local publishers or larger 'umbrella' companies, remains a hope rather than reality. Awards made by the Swedish government for children's literature (the Astrid Lindgren Award) have been valuable in encouraging book production overseas, for example the 'Little Hands' books in South Africa. New media formats may make inroads, but at present how to foster and develop the reading habit in African and other children in the developing world remains an unsolved need.

A Cabinet of Fairies – from *Mother Goose* Onwards

Were animal and fairy stories invented in France? Or just gentrified there?
And were they even intended for children?

e now tend to think of fairy and folk tales as something for children, but curiously, many of our most popular children's tales, like those of Perrault and the brothers Grimm, were originally nothing of the sort.

The antiquary John Aubrey alleged that in England, fairy folk were 'driven out' before the English Civil War of the 1630s, meaning that they had dropped out of the oral tradition of working people. At the same time, it is often said (correctly) that the fairy stories we use today were first published in Paris in 1697, in the *Histoires ou contes du temps passé* (*Stories or Fairy Tales from Times Past*) of Charles Perrault (1628–1703). Yet in the sixty years between Aubrey and Perrault, the nature of fairy tales changed completely.

Modern scholars, looking for earlier origins of fairy tales, claim to have found them in the 15th-century stories by the Venetian Gianfrancesco Straparola (1480–1557), and the Neapolitan Giambattista Basile (1566–1632), but Perrault's stories were of a very different kind. Readers of Denis Diderot's 18th-century comic novel *Jacques the Fatalist* note how the author utilised the wide gap between the (at times uncouth) life of the peasantry and the idealised aristocratic view of the *ancien régime* to give the stories an earthy humour, but Perrault's *Contes* were gentrified stories, written in a dignified style, with royal or at least noble characters; and his tales showed the exquisite modes of behaviour and feminine elegance typical of the writings of the Parisian '*précieuses*' ('wits'), such as Madeleine de Scudéry (1607–1701). The idea of groups of educated, literary

Charles Perrault, *Contes de ma Mère l'Oye*. Paris, 1695. Frontispiece of Perrault's manuscript, containing stories such as 'Red Riding Hood' and 'Bluebeard'. It was presented by Perrault to Elisabeth Charlotte, daughter of Philippe, Duc d'Orléans, when she was about nineteen. Perrault's dedication suggests that these simple, 'irrational' tales, so pleasing to children of the lower orders, also offer an instructive picture for those designed to rule them. Here the young audience (and cat) listen to the storyteller; the first known reference to the name 'Mother Goose' is in the sign above her head.
Purchased as a gift of the Fellows, 1953. Pierpont Morgan Library, MA 1505

Jane Johnson (see pp. 86–7). But the pedigrees of some of the best-known tales are very complicated: 'Beauty and the Beast', first written as a very long story in 1740 by Gabrielle-Suzanne Barbot de Villeneuve (one of Aulnoy's followers) was drastically abridged and altered by Jeanne-Marie Leprince de Beaumont in 1756, when this prolific and influential children's writer was working as a governess in London. Her version became the basis for most later editions of the story, whether it appeared in cheap **chapbooks** or in rather more luxurious publications.

In the three hundred years since Perrault and Aulnoy's tales were first printed, many publishers, book designers and illustrators have adapted their work for their own editions of the stories. Many authors have also written their own new tales. Oscar Wilde's fairy tales, for example, were written not only for children, but also for a cultivated adult audience who could relish the author's wit, like Perrault's: fairy stories still attract artistic interpretations of all kinds, in versions for readers of all ages.

women meeting to listen to such rose-coloured tales now seems ridiculous, but in the days before modern media and artificial lighting, the telling or recounting of tales (and it is from '*contes*' we derive our verb 'to recount') was very popular – and remained so well into the 19th century. Charles Joseph Mayer's forty-one-volume *Le Cabinet des fées: ou, Collection choisie des contes de fées* (*The Cabinet of Fairies, or, A Chosen Collection of Fairy Stories*), published in Geneva in 1787–9, in the last years before the French Revolution, was testimony to the continuing popularity of fairy stories for adult readers.

Many fairy tales were first written down by the Baroness d'Aulnoy (Marie-Catherine Le Jumel de Barneville; 1650–1705) in her books, *Les Contes des Fées* and *Contes nouveaux ou les Fées à la mode*, published in 1697–8, at almost at the same time as Perrault. Perrault's stories were first published in English, translated by Robert Samber, in London in 1727, twenty years after the first English version of Aulnoy's collections; and these became well known in Georgian times by readers such as

Devonshire Diversions

Old Mother Hubbard is one of the best-known Regency books for children, and an improbable fruit of the Napoleonic Wars.

As a Member of Parliament and Comptroller of Portsmouth Docks in the 1780s, Sir Henry Martin (1733–94) was a busy, harassed man. With his port full of naval midshipmen and officers, having a pretty, precocious, outgoing seventeen-year-old daughter to attract their attention could lead to trouble. And it did, when his daughter Sarah Catherine Martin (1768–1826) told her father that she had received protestations of eternal love from one of them. Bad enough, but the situation was far worse than Sir Henry could have imagined, for the lieutenant in question was Prince William Henry, one of the sons of King George III, who was serving in the Royal Navy at Portsmouth. Marriage was impossible, so Sir Henry rapidly sent his

ABOVE AND LEFT
Sarah Catherine Martin, *The Comic Adventures of Old Mother Hubbard and her dog ...* London: Printed for J. Harris, Successor to E. Newbery, Corner of St Paul's Church-Yard, 1806 [1805]. Sarah Martin published sequels, but these never achieved the same success as her first book, which had objections from some over-serious readers: 'I wish I had not chosen that silly book,' wrote *Lucy, or the Enquirer*, 1815, 'it says a great deal that I am sure is not true. Dogs cannot dance; can they, George? It says in the book that a dog danced.' Didacticism casts a long shadow.
The British Library

M. B. [Myra Browne], *The Tribulations of Tommy Tiptop*. London: Myra & Son, 1887. The production of this book was excellent. The sixteen fine – though often alarming – **chromolithographic** plates show the animals taking their revenge on the cruelly mischievous Tommy. By an unnamed, perhaps French or Swiss, illustrator, they are printed by the Leighton Brothers of Drury Lane.

The British Library

daughter away to the safety of Devon to live with relatives.

In Devon, the high-spirited, talkative Sarah Catherine seemingly drove her host to distraction. Her brother-in-law, John Pollexfen Bastard, also an MP (for Devon), was a serious man: he is reported to have told the girl to 'run away and write one of your stupid little rhymes'. Martin obeyed, and the result was her written text for *Old Mother Hubbard* (but it was not immediately published). Whether the author based the published poem (1805) on her own early work is much debated. There were similarities to *Old Dame Trot and her Comical Cat*, first published in 1803, but the Dame in Sarah Martin's jingle was said to have been modelled on the housekeeper at Bastard's Devon house.

Many years later, Sarah Martin passed the text to John Harris, successor to the Newberys' business, and in 1805 he published a sparkling little edition, illustrated by hand-coloured washes from drawings by the author. Nonsense verse of this kind has always been popular with children, and Sarah Martin rather audaciously dedicated the book to Bastard, 'at whose house these Notable Sketches were design'd'. The dedication intrigued book-buyers, and Harris's edition was a great success – the publisher claimed that 'upwards of ten thousand copies' were distributed. Later chapbook versions, and reprints of *The Comic Adventures of Old Mother Hubbard and her Dog*, continued to appear throughout the 17th century. What Mr Bastard (or his housekeeper) thought about it has not been recorded, and whether Prince William Henry remembered the young Martin girl at all is doubtful; but Sarah Catherine herself never married.

Animal rhymes and tales remained very popular with children throughout the 19th century: indeed, ever since Sarah Trimmer's *Fabulous Histories* (see p. 117) of 1786.

A century later, the rather effective (and sometimes quite terrifying) *Tribulations of Tommy Tiptop* was published by Myra and Son in 1887, about a little boy who mistreats animals and, in a series of dreams, is in turn mistreated by them. *Tommy Tiptop* came from a firm based in Covent Garden which specialised in fashion magazines and dressmaking and knitting patterns, and was scarcely known for children's books at all. The story was almost certainly written by Matilda Browne (1836–1936), known as Myra, a close friend of Isabella and Samuel Beeton (see p. 61), and one of the now-forgotten gifted women journalists of the period. Calling herself 'The Silkworm', she took over editing the *Englishwoman's Domestic Magazine* when Isabella Beeton died, and was herself to publish a cookery book. It is a pity that 'Myra' apparently never published any other books for children; her popular fashion journal continued to appear well into the 20th century.

Forgotten Authors – and Artists

'Puss in Boots' and other stories taken from the French became totally naturalised as English children's stories. But Florian, famous in France, is almost unknown in England today.

Almost every British child knows some of the fables written by Perrault and La Fontaine in the 17th century, but it is a safe bet that none of them have ever heard of Jean-Pierre Claris de Florian (1755–94), one of the victims of the French Revolution. Florian's name does not appear in any of the standard books on English children's literature – yet some of the phrases in his *Fables* (published posthumously in 1802) have become catch-phrases in French usage, rather in the way the English quote from the *Pilgrim's Progress* or *Alice in Wonderland*.

Though the Napoleonic Wars interrupted cross-Channel publishing, books by Florian were published (in French) by the emigré French community in London; and in 1806 John Harris published Florian's *Select Fables*, translated by Elizabeth Sandham. Sandham was a popular and successful writer, described by Harris in 1812 as 'the author of many approved works for young persons'. Possibly these young persons were repelled by her subtitle to the *Select Fables*: 'written for the purpose of instilling into the minds of early youth a true sense of religion and virtue', for there were no further editions of this rather scarce translation. For the English market, Florian's *Fables* settled into a sort of library purgatory: used as a teaching text for those studying French, but never read for pleasure.

Florian is to be remembered as much for the illustrations in a Paris edition of his *Fables* (1842), by the brilliant caricaturist Jean-Ignace-Isidore Gérard (1803–47), known as Jean-Jacques Grandville. Grandville flourished under King Louis Philippe at a

'An evening's conversation': *Fables de Florian, illustrées par J.-J. Grandville* (*Fables of Florian, illustrated by J.-J. Grandville*). Paris: J.-J. Dubochet, 1842. The artist suffered great personal loss in the last years of his life, and perhaps sought refuge in his surrealistic visions. His friend Alexandre Dumas recounted in his *Memoirs*: 'Others find fault with the world as good God has made it, but, powerless to refashion it, they rest satisfied with railing at it; Grandville not only did not scoff at it, but even re-created one of his own.'

The British Library

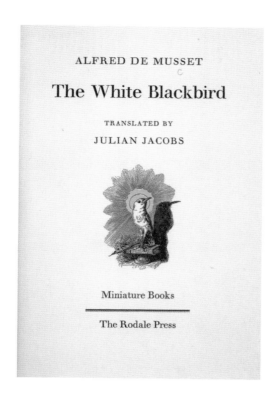

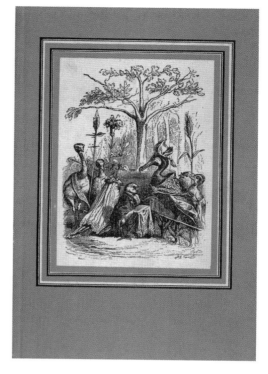

time when French printing and book illustration was at its best. He achieved early success with his *Les Métamorphoses du Jour* (*The Metamorphoses of the Day*; 1828) and his most striking illustrations often showed anthropomorphised animals in human dress. His extraordinary engravings are often regarded as the first Surrealist illustrations (the Surrealist Max Ernst adored him, and his influence is evident in particular in Ernst's collage-novel *Un Semaine du Bonté* (1934) illustrated in our previous *100 Books*). In his own time, Grandville's style was influential upon the work of such British book illustrators as John Tenniel and Richard Doyle.

In the early 1950s, a century after Grandville's tragically early death at the age of forty-four, one enterprising London publisher, the Rodale Press, gave fresh exposure to some of his work with a couple of volumes in its Miniature Books series. An offshoot of a firm based in Emmaus, Pennsylvania, the Rodale Press was different from most of the other new publishing companies starting up in the years after the end of the Second World War. Its prices were relatively high, and so was the quality of its books; much effort was taken with the selection of unfamiliar titles and interesting illustrators. The (beneficial) Dutch influence on their use of illustration and typography was marked. The Rodale edition of *The White Blackbird* (1955) by Alfred de Musset (1810–57), with Grandville's striking illustrations, was typical of the series.

Florian, Grandville, Musset – all died young.

Peter – the Bunny That Ran and Ran

Books illustrated by Randolph Caldecott, Walter Crane and Kate Greenaway marked a change in children's publishing, but Beatrix Potter's *Peter Rabbit* in particular offered exciting new marketing opportunities.

By the 1870s, new styles of illustrating and printing children's books were appearing. The printing firm of Edmund Evans (1826–1905), which had made its name owing to the covers of the 'yellow-back' novels sold at railway stalls, was famous for its fine wood-engravings and colour printing. Warne and Routledge used Evans to print their sixpenny **toy books**. When public demand for these toy books expanded, Evans began commissioning and publishing such books himself.

Beatrix Potter (1866–1943), probably the most famous of all children's authors of the 20th century, was a remarkable woman: a mycologist and botanical artist, and a founder of the National Trust, as well as the author and illustrator of many children's books.

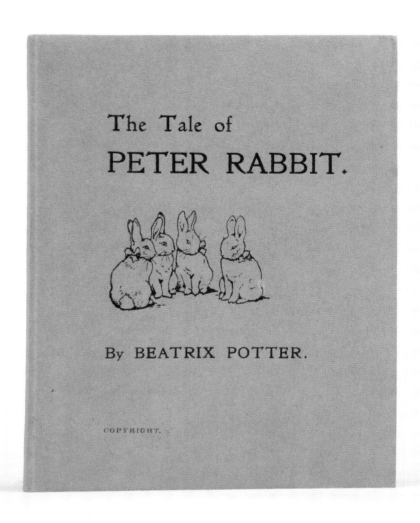

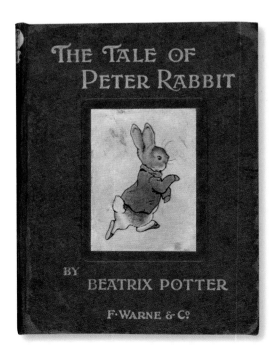

She sold sketches of her own pet animals (rabbits, mice, frogs) to two publishers: Hildesheimer & Faulkner for Frederic Weatherly's *A Happy Pair* (1890), and Ernest Nister for *Changing Pictures* (see p. 65). This success, and the stories she wrote in 1892 for Noel Moore, the son of her former governess Annie Moore, stimulated her wish to produce her own children's books. Her tale for Noel about 'four little rabbits whose names were Flopsy, Mopsy, Cottontail and Peter' in time became *The Tale of Peter Rabbit*.

Beatrix Potter had strong views about the format of her book. She was attracted by the size of Grant Richards's Dumpy Books (from 1897; see pp. 172–3), so she created a dummy book, and in 1901 printed a private edition of *The Tale of Peter Rabbit* for family and friends. Although Frederick Warne & Co. had originally rejected the book, on the recommendation of Leonard Leslie Brooke (a highly regarded illustrator), a contract was signed, and the first trade edition, of 6,000 copies, was published in October 1902. Potter's delicate watercolours were printed

by Edmund Evans, using the (then new) three-colour half-tone process developed by Carl Hentschel.

Potter found an instant rapport with Norman Warne, her editor (and later fiancé), and until his untimely death in 1905 Warne took an active part in planning the design and illustration of her 'bunny books'.

Beatrix Potter's bunnies were not just images on the pages of her books, of course. *The Tale of Peter Rabbit* was an immediate success, and has remained so, with more than 45 million copies sold. Beatrix Potter's later tales were widely translated, but owing to a disastrous oversight, costing Potter and Warne many millions, Frederick Warne's New York branch forgot to register the copyright in the United States. American publishers quickly produced pirated editions (the first being by Henry Altemus in 1904). Potter learned the lesson, and soon produced and patented a Peter Rabbit soft toy and related merchandise: nursery wallpaper, painting books, pottery and other spin-offs, which sold very widely. Despite the copyright oversight, the publication of *Peter Rabbit* made both Warne and Potter wealthy.

Importantly, in 1938, Potter prevented Walt Disney from producing an animated version similar to *Snow White*. But copyright is a dwindling asset, and the rights in Beatrix Potter's published works expired in 2014. Warne, who inherited her copyrights, cannot now prevent their use. Fortunately for Penguin Books (which acquired Warne in 1983) one unpublished story by Beatrix Potter was recently unearthed in the Victoria & Albert Museum collections: *The Tale of Kitty-in-Boots*. Written in 1914, put on one side at the start of the First World War and then forgotten, it was finally published in 2016 to mark the 150th anniversary of Beatrix Potter's birth. In 2016 a new 50-pence coin, showing Peter Rabbit, was minted, the first UK coin to celebrate a children's book.

An autographed letter from Beatrix Potter to Noel Moore, London, 8 March, 1895, pp. 1 and 4. The books based on the tales inspired by Benjamin Bouncer and Potter's other pets retain the playful immediacy of her private letters to the son of her former governess.

The Pierpont Morgan Library, New York, MA 2009.3

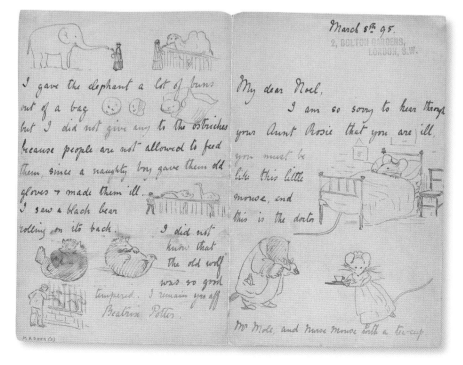

Bringing the Jungle Home

Readers often assume that Kipling's *Jungle Books* and the *Just So Stories* were written in India. In fact, they were first created in Vermont.

In 1865 the artist John Lockwood Kipling (1837–1911), newly married to Alice Macdonald, moved to India to take up his new appointment as Professor of Architectural Sculpture at the Sir Jamsetjee Jeejebhoy School of Art in Mumbai (then called Bombay), the first art school to be established in India. Their first son, Joseph Rudyard Kipling (1865–1936), was born in December of that year.

Rudyard Kipling's early childhood in India was in many ways idyllic, but like many children of the British Raj he was sent back to England to school at five years old, and he hated it: 'I had never heard of Hell, so I was introduced to it in all its terrors.' Subsequent schooling at the United Services College at Westward Ho! was happier; its headmaster, Cormell Price (a friend of Edward Burne-Jones, who was married to Rudyard's mother Alice's sister) fostered his reading, reviving the school paper so that Kipling could edit it.

It was a prescient move: Rudyard had a great facility for verse, and his attempts in the style of Keats, Swinburne and other poets impressed his parents enough to have his *Schoolboy Lyrics* privately printed in Lahore in 1881. The Kiplings had moved up in Indian society: in 1875 Lockwood Kipling was appointed Principal of the new Mayo School of Art in Lahore, and Curator of the Lahore Museum, and he and Alice were heavily involved in arrangements for the great display of Imperial pomp that was the Delhi Durbar of 1877. It was relatively simple for them to persuade the Lahore *Civil and Military Gazette* to engage Rudyard as a sub-editor in 1882.

Rudyard worked a journalist in India for the next seven years, and this time and his

Rudyard Kipling, *Just So Stories*. London: Macmillan & Co., 1902. Cover illustration by the author. Many subjects for these *Pourquoi* stories, such as 'How the Leopard got his Spots', were apparently suggested to the author by Nelson Doubleday, the eight-year-old son of Kipling's American publisher. On publication Nelson received a 'two-cent-a-copy' share from his father on the Doubleday edition, which, given their popularity, must have served him well.

The British Library

Rudyard Kipling, *The Jungle Book*; *The Second Jungle Book*. London: Macmillan & Co., 1894; 1895. Lockwood Kipling was very proud of his son's books, and his illustration for *The Jungle Book* shows his skill in portraying animals. Later artists, like the talented Detmold brothers (in 1903), brought different interpretations of jungle life to Kipling's text, as did Disney Productions in 1967 with their film.

The British Library

childhood memories of Bombay informed many of his later books. He soon became known for the fresh tone in his work, which drew heavily on his Indian experiences. One romance, *The Naulahka* (1892), was written jointly with an American friend, Walcott Balestier, who helped to secure American copyrights of Kipling's works (at a time when American publishers were not bound by international copyright agreements). Kipling married Walcott's sister Carrie (who had taught Kipling to use a typewriter), and their first child, Josephine, was born in 1893 while they were visiting Carrie's family at Brattleboro, Vermont. They stayed on in Vermont until 1896. There Rudyard wrote and published *The Jungle Book* (1894), and *The Second Jungle Book* (1895), with illustrations by Kipling's father Lockwood, which show just what a good illustrator he was.

The *Just So Stories* (1902) were drawn from the bedtime stories Kipling had devised for his 'Best Beloved' Josephine. In 1899 he and his daughter were both struck down with pneumonia (for Josephine it proved fatal), and the stories were written by a grieving Kipling after his recovery, from 1900 on, and published with his own decorations.

Time and attitudes change; Kipling, the once enormously popular and Nobel-prizewinning author, was for generations condemned by many as 'a jingo imperialist', as George Orwell (who likewise was born and spent time in British India) described him, concluding that his writings were 'morally insensitive and aesthetically disgusting'. Others share Michael Morpurgo's view that these **Pourquoi** stories were among the best ever written, and that Kipling's amazing ingenuity and inventiveness have made the *Just So Stories* the ideal bedtime book.

An 'Admirable Hieroglyphic': Moles, Toads ... and Fawns

When Kenneth Grahame's *Wind in the Willows* was first published, some critics thought it a miserable failure. It took time for it to be recognised as a (flawed) masterpiece.

Kenneth Grahame (1859–1932) seemed always something of a misfit. A friend described him in London as looking like a large dog who should have been playing in the countryside: 'he was too big for London, and it hardly seemed kind of Fate to keep him there'. He always wanted to live in the Thames Valley, where he grew up.

Coming from a prosperous middle-class Scottish family, and brought up by a fond grandmother, Grahame was found a well-paid post in the Bank of England, where he ended up as Secretary. As well as banking success, he wanted to be a 'man of letters', and the essays and articles reprinted in his books (*Pagan Papers*, 1893, *The Golden Age*, 1895, and *Dream Days*, 1898, all published by John Lane at the Bodley Head) were well received, so Grahame made the decision to become a full-time author.

His early books, though written for adults, included many articles about children and childhood, largely derived from his childhood memories of growing up in the countryside on the Thames, near Cookham. Following marriage and the birth of his son, he started writing bedtime stories for him, and these became the book known as *The Wind in the Willows*. The publishers of his adult books did not like it at all, and turned it down, but Grahame's literary agent persuaded Methuen & Co. to take on the book. When it was published (unillustrated) in 1908, critics were bewildered: was it an adult satire, or was it written for children? Reviewers in such

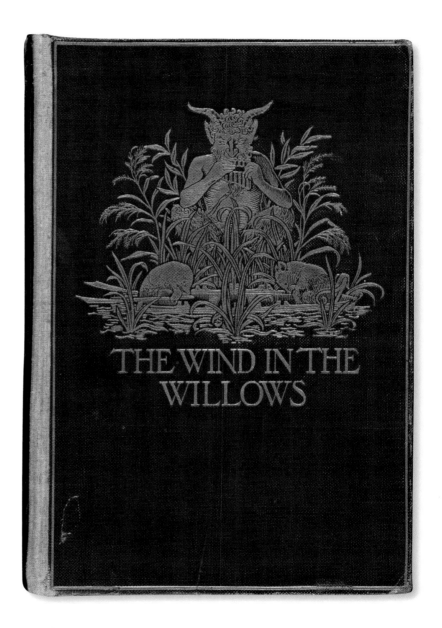

Kenneth Grahame, *The Wind in the Willows*. London: Methuen, 1908.
This edition was not illustrated, save for a headpiece by W. Graham Robertson. It has since been widely illustrated by many artists with varied success. The illustrations by E. H. Shepard perhaps come closest to catching the author's mood.
The British Library

journals as *Punch* and *The Times Literary Supplement* condemned it. It took luck and warm praise of the book's charm from (of all people) Theodore Roosevelt before readers discovered its pleasures for themselves.

As a children's book, *The Wind in the Willows* was a mixed success: it was long, and contained literary allusions which young readers could hardly hope to grasp, and it mixed together several quite different themes. The riverside domestic saga of the water rat, mole and badger was totally different from the tale of the vulgar and extravagant Mr Toad, and surely many child readers have been baffled by the Wild Wood episodes. Yet Grahame's book had much to attract children. C. S. Lewis later praised it as:

an admirable hieroglyphic ... The child who has met Mr Badger has ever afterwards, in its bones, a knowledge of humanity and of English social history which it could not get in any other way.

The book has since been mined by many publishers, with one of the strands of the

story within the novel produced as a children's play (*Toad of Toad Hall*, written by A. A. Milne, 1929), and another popular version 'retold for easy reading' published by Ladybird Books.

Animal stories often bemuse authorities as well as critics. *Bambi. Eine Lebensgeschichte aus dem Walde* by the writer Felix Salten (Siegmund Salzmann, 1869–1945) was first published in Vienna in 1923. Salten's ostensibly innocent little story, which introduces children to the brutal realities of nature, was published in America as *Bambi, A Life in the Woods* by Simon & Schuster in 1928. It became very popular, and was selected there as a 'book of the month'. Yet Salten was an Austrian Jew, and the book was banned by the Nazis in 1936 as a 'political allegory on the treatment of Jews in Europe'.

But *Bambi* became most widely celebrated not for Salten's text, nor for its illustrations, but for the animated film Disney made of it in 1942. Disney found the Salten story too sombre and realistic for children, so he extensively altered and prettified the storyline. Children may still weep about the death of the eponymous fawn's mother, but (like many Victorian writers, in fact), Disney shied away from realism. Salten's book gave its name to the 'Bambi effect' (our struggle with seeing 'cute' animals suffer), which is still of interest to psychologists and sociologists today.

A Warren of Women Writers

The success of Beatrix Potter's *Peter Rabbit* of 1901 inspired several writers to build other stories about rabbits, both real and toy.

Possibly Sarah Trimmer's *Fabulous Histories* of 1786 'designed for the instruction of children respecting their treatment of animals' was the earliest book to anthropomorphise animals. But many later writers used talking, thinking animals as characters in their stories (such as the White Rabbit in *Alice in Wonderland*), and Beatrix Potter's genius as author and illustrator encouraged other writers to attempt similar tales.

One of the most enterprising was an aspiring young writer and mother, Margery Williams Bianco (1881–1944). Though she was born in London, her family had moved, after her father's death, to rural Pennsylvania, and there, after her schooling, the strong-willed Margery had determined to become a writer. At the age of nineteen she took herself back to London, where she got her first book published by Heinemann (*The Late Returning*, 1902). She had many further adventures – marrying the Italian Francesco Bianco in 1904, moving to Italy in 1907 (where, some years later, her husband was caught up in the First World War) and having two children, before the family finally returned to settle in the United States.

Margery Williams wrote *The Velveteen Rabbit; or, How Toys Become Real*, for her children, and it was published by Heinemann in 1922. In London, the Biancos formed a friendship with William Nicholson (1872–1949) and his family, and the painter made a portrait of Margery's daughter Pamela, then celebrated as a child prodigy, whose art was displayed in London in 1919. Nicholson agreed to illustrate Margery's rabbit book. His early graphic work, as one of the

Margery Williams, *The Velveteen Rabbit*. With illustrations by William Nicholson. London: Heinemann, 1922. Margery Williams's early books were published in London, but after the success of *The Velveteen Rabbit* she followed it with thirty more intended for the American market. Many were illustrated by her daughter, Pamela Bianco.
The British Library

Alison Uttley, *The Squirrel, the Hare and the Little Grey Rabbit.* Pictures by Margaret Tempest. London: Heinemann, 1929. Uttley rejected comparison with Beatrix Potter, whom she felt was primarily an illustrator who wrote words 'around' her pictures, whereas Uttley believed that storytelling was of much greater importance. For many readers, however, the charm of both series of books comes equally from author and artist.

The British Library

pseudonymous Beggarstaff Brothers (with James Pryde), and on his own titles (such as *The Square Book of Animals*, 1900), was bold in its approach. By contrast, for Margery's rather sad story of a battered toy rabbit, Nicholson used a more tentative style. The book was an immediate success in America, and though she never produced any other successes on this scale, Margery Williams's later books continued to sell well. But it has not been universally liked, dismissed by one critic (children's literary historian Brian Alderson) as a 'sentimental play with a dud concept of Reality as applied to nursery toys'.

From 1929 onwards, a charming series of children's books from Alison Uttley (1884–1976) provided some strong competition for leporine tales. Alison grew up in rural Derbyshire, and in her adult books (such as *A Country Child*, 1931, and *A Traveller in Time*, 1939), Uttley drew heavily on her countryside memories. For her *Little Grey Rabbit* children's series, reworking tales she had devised for her son, Uttley recreated a rural society largely peopled by animals, writing 'I always try to give some specially English touch of country life, which might be forgotten.'

Alison Uttley's books were illustrated by Margaret Tempest (1882–1982), an artist based in Chelsea. Though not as fine work as Beatrix Potter's, her drawings are delightful – but (apparently feeling that the books' fame was attributed to the artist, not herself), Uttley's journals reveal her jealousy of the illustrator, and she came to dislike Tempest and her paintings intensely. For the last few *Little Grey Rabbit* books, the pictures were drawn by Katherine Wigglesworth, with perhaps rather less lightness of touch.

From Harrods to Pooh Corner – a Bear's Tale

A. A. Milne's Winnie-the-Pooh rapidly became a favourite with readers in the 1920s. When copyrights in the book were later passed to the Disney Company, the Californian (film) version was to be totally different.

There are some easy ways to recognise whether an English children's book has really been established as a classic: has it been translated into Latin (*Winnie ille pu*)? Has its language led to the invention of new words recorded in the *Oxford English Dictionary*? A. A. Milne's stories of the teddy bear Winnie-the-Pooh and his friends were such: many children have played at Poohsticks; and if one of your colleagues is described as being 'a bit of an Eeyore', or being 'Tiggerish' – or even the *Spectator* writing about 'a heffalump-trap' – most English-speaking people will understand perfectly what was meant.

On the face of it, Alan Alexander Milne (1882–1956) was an unlikely man to become best known for his children's books. A mathematician who was expected to become a school-teacher, while studying at Cambridge Milne started writing for the magazine *Granta*, and in 1904 had his first article published in the weekly satirical magazine *Punch*. His success at writing humour was such that in 1906 he was made *Punch*'s assistant editor. Another frequent contributor to *Punch* was the artist E. H. (Ernest Howard) Shepard (1879–1976). Both men had served in the army in the First World War (Shepard being awarded a Military Cross), and at a crucial point the critic E. V. Lucas suggested Shepard should illustrate a book of verse for children which Milne had written, *When We Were Very Young* (1924), in which the teddy-bear character first appeared.

Milne had married Dorothy (Daphne) de Sélincourt in 1913, and in 1920 their son Christopher Robin was born. Milne bought

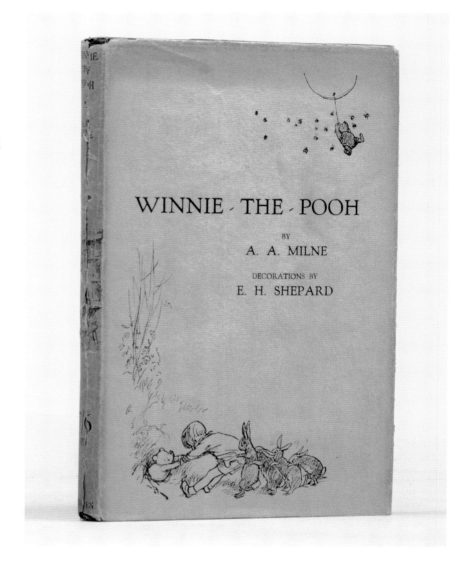

A. A. Milne, *Winnie-the-Pooh*. Decorations by Ernest H. Shepard. London: Methuen & Co., 1926. This and its companion volume *The House at Pooh Corner* (1928) are some of the most successful stories for children ever written. Shepard's illustrations, pleasingly shown on the jacket, were modelled upon the actual toys owned by Milne's son, and now seem inseparable from the text.

Peter Harrington Rare Books, London

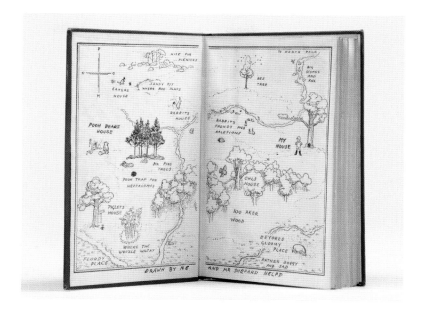

Endpaper map of the '100 Aker Wood', drawn by E. H. Shepard, for A. A. Milne's *Winnie-the-Pooh*. Methuen & Co.: London, 1926. Perhaps the most rewarding entry into the imaginary world of Pooh is through the original text and drawings.

Peter Harrington Rare Books, London

a toy teddy bear in Harrods for his little boy for his first birthday, and like many other fathers (including Kipling and Kenneth Grahame) he made up simple bedtime stories for him, which he later wrote out as the *Pooh* stories. The first story was published in the Christmas Eve 1925 issue of the *London Evening News*, and in book format by Methuen in 1926, as *Winnie-the-Pooh*. *The House at Pooh Corner* followed in 1928.

The books were an instant success, in the United States as much as in Britain. (In time, the New York Public Library was to acquire the collection of the 'original' Christopher Robin's stuffed toys of Eeyore, Piglet and the others to enrich its resources.) Milne recognised how much Shepard's sensitive drawings caught the mood of the book, and arranged that a proportion of the royalties should be paid to Shepard – a rare case of an author and the publisher acknowledging the importance of the illustrator's role.

Methuen, Shepard and Milne all benefited from the sale of the *Pooh* books. Other firms noted the stories' commercial value, and after Milne's death, Walt Disney bought the copyright. In the 1960s, when Disney's

companies were working on the film of Kipling's *Jungle Book*, the first short *Pooh* films were prepared. Disney himself had strong views about work for children, even though this was of an unsubtle and sanitised kind, and it has been suggested that the later Disney Company abandoned Walt Disney's values, and had no interest in fidelity to Milne's stories. Many experts on children's literature regard Disney's books and films as appalling travesties: vulgarising and dumbing down the action, and changing the appearance of the characters.

Nonetheless, the Disney versions had tremendous commercial success (*Forbes* magazine has described Winnie-the-Pooh as the most valuable fictional character of all) and the company's merchandising skills have ensured that for many children, Pooh Bear *is* the Disney character. Commercial success of this kind has had an enormous effect on other producers, authors and illustrators of books for children throughout the world. It remains to be seen whether future generations of children will come to prefer the Milne/Shepard version in place of that created by Hollywood.

Urbane Animals

Some authors write about animals as wild, red in tooth and claw. In others'
books, they are really people in animal guise. Some of the most effective
stories have urbane, sophisticated characters as their protagonists.

There is no doubt that Babar the
elephant, probably the most
famous animal of the early
twentieth century, was an urbane, highly
civilised animal, just as his creators were
cultured Parisians. The inventor of the story
was Cécile de Brunhoff (1903–2003), a piano
teacher married to the artist Jean de Brunhoff
(1899–1937); together they devised the story
of an orphaned elephant to tell to their young
sons. They were a well-connected, prosperous
family living in Neuilly, and through Jean's
father (a respected Paris publisher) and his
brother Michel (already famous as the editor
of *Vogue*), the Brunhoffs were in touch with
many aspects of the musical, artistic and
cultural life of the Belle Époque and of
interwar Paris.

Babar was a family affair: Cécile composed
the story, Jean wrote it out and provided the
pictures, and Michel arranged for it to be
printed for a private edition and urged the
production of a public edition. Though
produced as an over-large (and expensive)
book, *L'Histoire de Babar, le petit éléphant* was
warmly welcomed on its publication in Paris
in 1931, and in 1933 in London, with the
English edition introduced by A. A. Milne.
It was followed by six more *Babar* books, but
in 1937 Jean de Brunhoff died suddenly of
tuberculosis, aged only thirty-seven.

The artist had been commissioned by the
London *Daily Sketch* for two further sets of
pictures, in black and white. Under Michel de
Brunhoff's direction, Jean's eleven-year-old
son, Laurent, produced colour interpretations
which were used in *Babar and his Children*
(1938) and *Babar and Father Christmas* (1940),

Jean de Brunhoff, *L'Histoire de Babar, le petit éléphant* (*The Story of Babar, the Little Elephant*). Paris:
Éditions du Jardin des modes, *c*.1934. [1931] The story's originator, Cécile de Brunhoff, insisted
her name be taken off the title page for the first edition, believing her contribution to the book too
slight. The pictures and text for later *Babar* books were all by Jean de Brunhoff or his son Laurent,
but they remained essentially whole-family affairs.

The British Library

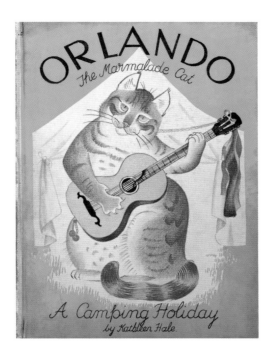

Kathleen Hale, *Orlando the Marmalade Cat: A Camping Holiday*. London: Country Life, 1938. Country Life was an unusual publishing company, and in the 1930s it was one of the vehicles Noel Carrington used to push into publication his own ideas about children's book design. Kathleen Hale's book charmed generations of children and adults in Britain. Strangely, *Orlando* has never gained the same fame in the United States.

Private collection

produced by Random House in New York. After the end of the war, Laurent resumed the unusual inter-generational partnership by teaching himself to paint in his father's style, and from 1946 continued to produce these delightful volumes.

Whether by father or son, it hardly matters to the *Babar* stories – which all look back to the Belle Époque. Critics grumble that the stories were imperialist propaganda; they were certainly self-conscious comedies about the difficulties of a bourgeois life and the French consciousness of Africa and its culture.

It would be hard to find an artist and author more different from the Brunhoffs

than Kathleen Hale (1898–2000), whose *Orlando* stories were inspired by their books. The daughter of an impoverished piano salesman, Kathleen had a rebellious childhood and left school at eighteen to join the Land Army, then from the early 1920s worked in commercial art.

Hale later said she had 'a talent for being in the right place at the right time'. Loathing the poor quality of Enid Blyton's books ('the Pied Blighter'), Hale was determined to attempt to create better books for her own children, which, encouraged by Noel Carrington, she began to do, with *Orlando the Marmalade Cat: A Camping Holiday* (published by Country Life in 1938). Carrington was crucial for Hale's development, but equally for improvements in children's book illustration in general (see pp. 230–35). Hale's early *Orlando* books were the first models for his Puffin Picture Books.

The Brunhoffs had enough printing expertise for the illustration of their *Babar* books to work beautifully. However, driven by Carrington, Kathleen Hale painstakingly had to learn the techniques for preparing colour separations for the **lithographs**, at W. S. Cowell, the printers in Ipswich (a firm with a high reputation for colour printing). Hale spent 'four to five months of working seven hours a day, seven days a week' on the plates for each *Orlando* book, but her efforts paved the way for the very first Puffins, and for a new school of illustrator–storytellers of the next generation.

Teddies Everywhere

Winnie-the-Pooh was not the first book to be based on a stuffed bear; other writers and artists also tried to make use of this toy's popularity.

Teddy bears form so large a group within the range of children's stuffed toys that it is hard to remember that they did not exist in Victorian times. Named for Theodore 'Teddy' Roosevelt, the American president, stuffed toy bears originated in the United States and Germany at around the same time (around 1902–3). Those sold in English toy shops originally came from the Steiff factory in Germany, but by the start of the First World War British firms had begun making them as well. It was one of the 'British' teddy bears that A. A. Milne had bought and used for the Winnie-the-Pooh stories, but a teddy-bear story had been published much earlier, by the now little-known but prolific illustrator Grace Marsh (1888–1981), who during the war had illustrated several books for Deans, and after her marriage signed herself as H. G. C. Marsh Lambert.

Her *Story of Teddy Bear* was printed in about 1921, as a twelve-page, **shaped book** issued by an obscure publisher (Alldays, based in Birmingham) and almost certainly sold by stationers and newsagents rather than booksellers. It always meant facing stiff competition for artists to get their work commissioned by publishers, and it seems that Grace Marsh Lambert had followed in the footsteps of the slightly older Mabel Lucie Attwell (1879–1964), producing postcards of children's nursery rhymes, or of girls dressed in the national dress of the Allied countries – Belgium, France, Italy, Russia and so on – during the war years. In the 1920s Marsh Lambert showed much initiative in her illustration work (she produced a children's

A. C. G. Marsh Lambert, *The Story of Teddy Bear*. Shakespeare Series, no. 1903. Birmingham: Alldays, 1919–21. This might be seen as a 'bad' cheap book; its illustrator's style, emulating the very popular Mabel Lucie Attwell, is now rather dated, but such **die-cut** shaped toy books were popular with young children themselves. The publishers, primarily of law books and pictorial local guides, were obviously trying their hand at the juvenile market, with others in this series illustrated by W. Arthur Fry.
Author's collection

pictures of chubby, dimpled babies and infants', noting that Attwell's name 'became synonymous in Britain with the sentimentalization of childhood'. Marsh Lambert's stickily sentimental tale of *The Story of Teddy Bear* no doubt attracted many a child in the 1920s, but the printer's choice of typeface and bulky paper shows some of the faults in book design which typographers were then trying to persuade publishers to improve upon.

Some later teddy-bear books became far more popular, like the *Teddy Robinson* stories by Joan G. Robinson (1910–1988), an author now best known for her older children's novel, *When Marnie Was There*. She had trained with Margaret Tempest at the Chelsea Illustrators Studio (see p. 139), and her *Teddy Robinson* stories, the adventures of her daughter's toy bear, were adored by English children sixty years ago, when first published by Harrap (and later by Puffin); they still have a considerable following among book collectors.

The stories of *A Bear Called Paddington* written by Michael Bond (born 1926) were, like those by Robinson and Milne, based on a real toy bear, and appeared from 1958 under the Collins imprint. For Bond's rather endearing stories, the publisher selected Peggy Fortnum as the illustrator, which proved an ideal marriage of author and illustrator. Fortnum's pictures caught the mood of the stories, in the same way that E. H. Shepard was 'right' for *Winnie-the-Pooh*. More than twenty Paddington Bear stories have appeared, in over forty languages, and selling over 35 million books; they also inspired a television series and more recently (2015) a film. Bond was not an exclusive teddy-bear man (many children also enjoyed his rather preposterous stories of a guinea pig, Olga da Polga), but Paddington Bear will live long in children's memories.

book for Ovaltine, and was one of the early designers of dot-to-dot books for Ward, Lock & Co. – a group of juvenilia usually left out altogether in studies of children's publishing).

Unluckily, Marsh Lambert was not a first-class artist: she modelled her work on that of Attwell, very popular for what the *Oxford Companion* describes as 'endless

The Leopard with No Claws

As African countries developed higher education and acquired independence, people looked forward to a rosy future which would include books written by Africans for Africans. But what happened?

For almost all British or American children, although Africa was often used as the setting for savage or exotic adventure stories, the significant characters in them were almost all Europeans. While animals often figure largely in the plots, in these stories they were seen only as trophies, to be shot or taken to a zoo. Even in books written by Europeans who had devoted much of their lives to working in Africa, their views of African culture and folklore were often those of the West, and their books intended for children seem incompatible with traditional African values. One exception was in the books printed in Northern Nigeria by the Gaskiya Corporation (see pp. 66–7).

In their schools, books provided by missionaries were (at best) peripheral to the needs of African societies. Even the very popular stories written in French by René Guillot (1900–69), such as *Kpo the Leopard* (first published in Paris by Magnard as *Kpo la Panthère*, 1955), gave their readers only a European perspective. This was despite the fact that Guillot spent twenty years teaching in Senegal and in 1964 received the prestigious Hans Christian Andersen Award for his children's books. Although other authors, such as Peggy Appiah, Barbara Kimenye and Mwenye Hadithi, identified themselves with the local peoples, and wrote respectively for Ghanaian, Ugandan and Kenyan children, they and their illustrators were all expatriates. Their approach was inevitably more European than African.

In the period immediately after the Second World War, colonially educated students at

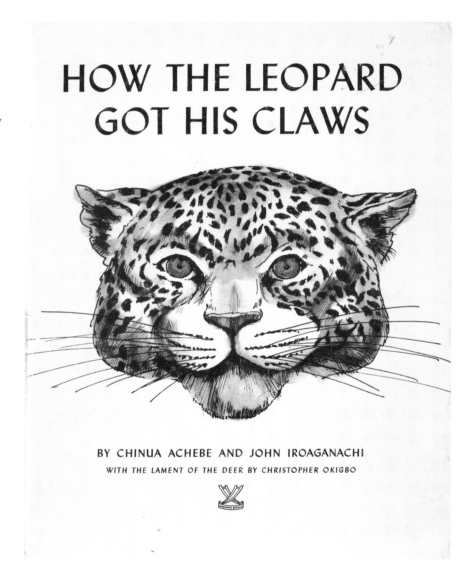

Chinua Achebe, *How the Leopard Got his Claws*. Enugu, Nigeria: Nwamife Publishers, 1972. Though Nigerian writers such as Cyprian Ekwensi and Chinua Achebe wrote books intended for use in Nigerian schools, Achebe's hopes to produce children's books in Nigeria were dashed by the Biafran war.
The British Library

René Guillot, *Kpo the Leopard* (*Kpo la Panthère*). Oxford: OUP, 1955. With illustrations by Joan Kiddell-Monroe. *Kpo* was a very successful book, translated into many languages, but its artists were European, without first-hand experience of Africa. With Guillot's many years in Senegal, his story drew closer to the African landscape but could hardly enable local readers to experience the scent of the bush.

Courtesy Q's Books, Hamilton, NSW, Australia

the new universities set up with the (British) Colonial Development and Welfare funds in Nigeria, Ghana and elsewhere, anticipated the benefits of independence, and, as African writers, attempted to develop an African-oriented literature, often for series of **readers** intended for use in schools. Two such children's stories (written in English) were published by Cambridge University Press, written by Cyprian Ekwensi (1921–2007) and Chinua Achebe (1930–2013). Ekwensi's *The Drummer Boy*, about slum life in contemporary Lagos, became very popular with Nigerian schoolboys; Achebe's *Chike and the River* (1966) looked at traditional Igbo life (as did his earlier adult novel, *Things Fall Apart*, 1958, which has sold more than 8 million copies and is held to be the most widely read book to have come out of Africa).

Achebe was alert to the faults of colonisation, but he was essentially nostalgic, looking forward to a new Africa, but one which retained old Igbo values. He resented the ways in which Africa was represented by European writers, particularly Joseph Conrad and Joyce Cary. He wanted books for African children to be written from an African

perspective and feared the continuing (colonial) influence of books issued there by British publishers. In a position of some power and influence, Achebe in 1962 became the first editor of Heinemann's African Writers Series, and so fostered many indigenous authors. For children, Achebe planned a series of such books, to be written by himself and his brother-in-law, the poet Christopher Okigbo, and produced by an African publisher, the Citadel Press, which would publish works 'relevant' to African readers. The popular street literature already being produced in Onitsha pointed the way for the spirited children's books Achebe wanted to see.

The dream was splendid: many African and West Indian leaders looked forward to a democratic and better future for their countries. In Nigeria, political murder, corruption and civil war – all soon to be the realities of life in independent Nigeria – killed Achebe's hopes stone dead. The street literature of Onitsha ceased to be produced; Achebe's brother-in-law, the poet Okigbo, was killed fighting in the Biafran war; and Achebe himself was lucky to survive relatively unscathed.

How the Leopard Got his Claws was finally published in Enugu in 1972. (It redeveloped an earlier manuscript, *How the Dog Was Domesticated*, by John Iroaganachi, one of the first submitted to Citadel Press.) Though its title, perhaps deliberately, calls to mind Kipling (perhaps the best known of colonial writers), it bears little resemblance to his *Just So* stories. Instead, it can be read as a political allegory in the guise of a children's tale. It was a brave attempt, but Achebe's story attracted little attention. Like other Nigerian writers, Achebe later concentrated on adult fiction. Even in that area, the hopes of the 1960s have been disappointed: poor sales made Heinemann discontinue production of these novels in the 1990s. Successful African publishing has not developed.

CHAPTER 7

Innocence, Experience and Old-Fashioned Nonsense

By the 1830s, juvenile publishing was a well-established and often profitable genre. The Victorians introduced some welcome innovations, and a world market emerged for children's books.

Apart from a few enthusiasts such as Sarah Trimmer (see p. 117), before the 19th century few people paid much attention to children's books, but by the 1840s they were being reviewed, and educated adults were increasingly aware of them. The trade had a vital commercial interest in them – American publishers pirated many British publications, paying no fees to authors: in the 1840s, between 40% and 50% of books published in the United States were British, and in the hidden and unscrupulous commercial war between Britain and the United States, British publishers reprinted American titles with equal gusto.

The American Samuel Griswold Goodrich (1793–1860), who wrote as 'Peter Parley', made a considerable fortune from sales of his books: several millions were sold in the United States (so Goodrich affirmed), and untold numbers in Britain. Goodrich was incensed, though, that the name of 'Peter Parley' was taken over by hacks who used it on books issued in Britain – at least six different Peter Parleys seem to have been published in London. The name had really become a brand, rather than a person.

The name 'Peter Parley' came to represent a style of writing which was cordially disliked by one very influential Englishman, who proclaimed that his objective in publishing *his* children's books was 'anti-Peter Parleyism'. As Goodrich claimed in his *Recollections of a Lifetime* (1856), 'a quaint, quiet, scholarly gentleman, called Mr Felix Summerly – a dear lover of children – was invented to preside over the enterprise, to rap the knuckles of Peter Parley, and to woo back the

'He is gone, Patience!' – frontispiece for Mrs [Mary] Sewell, *Patience Hart's First Experience in Service*. London: Jarrold and Sons, 1862. At a time of high infant mortality, young girl readers 'in service' would strongly empathise with the prospect of the death of their young charge.

The British Library

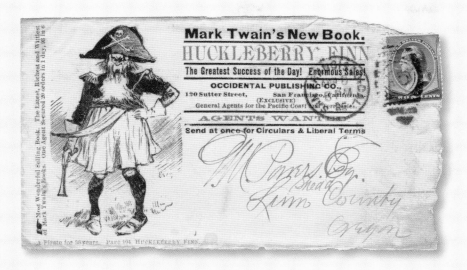

Agent-recruiting advertisement by Occidental Publishing Co., San Francisco, c.1885, for Mark Twain, *Adventures of Huckleberry Finn*. The lucky book agent would be sent the outlines of the permitted territory to canvas (which could be in very rural areas), and a kit containing the prospectus materials to hawk from door to door.

Courtesy of Kevin MacDonnell, Austin, Texas

erring generation of children in the good old orthodox rhymes and jingles of England'. Goodrich could hardly have been more wrong: 'Felix Summerly' (Sir Henry Cole, 1808–82) was then a young, energetic civil servant who was worried about the poor quality of books available for his own children. Under the pseudonym of Felix Summerly, Cole set out to issue his *Home Treasury*, a series of exceptionally well-produced children's illustrated story books, published by Joseph Cundall, and which proved the high-water mark for children's illustrations for many years. But Cole was an exceptionally busy man – at the same time he was developing the Penny Post, improving the railway services and inventing the Christmas card. Cole's later career – as the king-pin in the organisation of the Great Exhibitions of 1851 and 1862, *and* as a founder of the Royal College of Art and the Victoria & Albert Museum – took him away from children's books; but his part in juvenile publishing should not be forgotten.

Others of the period shared Cole's views about the importance of tradition and imagination in juvenile publishing. William Makepeace Thackeray's writing, as in his novel *The Newcomes* (1855), or his book reviews for *Fraser's Magazine* as 'Michael Angelo Titchmarsh', showed a keen eye for what was good or bad in new children's books. Thackeray wrote for adults, and only his *Rose and the Ring* suggests what he could have done as a children's writer (see pp. 156–7). Other contemporary writers also mocked aspects of foreign children's books: Charles Kingsley's parody of two very popular American books by Susan Warner, writing as 'Elizabeth Wetherell' (*The Wide, Wide World*, 1850, and *Queechy*, 1852) did not prevent British girls reading and weeping copiously over these sentimental tear-jerkers.

Of course, there were many British books with sad aspects. Mary Sewell's *Patience Hart's First Experience in Service* (1862) was a sensible tale well aimed at young girls (and their mothers) who felt apprehensive about leaving home for the first time. This forgotten little tale shows the innocence of early Victorian society (which had never heard of the 'grooming' so feared in our present age): on her train journey to London, Patience entrusts herself to a kindly middle-aged man who befriends her and, taking her bag, whisks her off from the railway terminus on an omnibus to Islington. (All ends happily, but there is no suggestion by Mrs Sewell that young girls should be cautious of new, especially male, friends.)

There was Innocence and Experience in plenty in Victorian juvenile books. And also Nonsense: the pleasure of being hilarious or inconsequent, or simply silly, seemed a rare joy to children exposed to the preaching of Mrs Sherwood and other writers of the Regency age. Edward Lear's verses for the Stanley family (see pp. 154–5) must have felt liberating to read; as also the books by Lewis Carroll (see pp. 162–3), which changed the future of writing for children.

Though not averse to Fun, writers of books intended for boys were (on the whole) serious in style and intention. Such books were about heroes, however flawed. The schoolbooks such as Thomas Hughes's *Tom Brown's School Days* (1857; see p. 158), or those by the scarcely less talented Talbot Baines Reed, started a long sequence of such books, often first serialised in magazines like *The Boy's Own Paper* (see pp. 168–9).

The whole string of adventure stories written for boys (and young men) were very similar in their perceived readership. The naval and military yarns written by men of action like Captain Marryat (a naval officer) or G. A. Henty (a war correspondent) often appeared in magazines and annuals, while such authors as R. A. Ballantyne (see pp. 160–61) made their living from their books. Later authors such as Rider Haggard, Anthony Hope and John Buchan also enjoyed much popularity with their tales of derring-do.

Some American stories are now largely forgotten, such as the Rollo series of boys' stories by Jacob Abbott (1803–79). They had a long publishing life in America, but were at a lower literary level than those by 'Mark Twain' (Samuel Langhorne Clemens, 1835–1910). In America, the development of **subscription publishing** enabled door-to-door salesmen to distribute books (which alarmed some librarians and bookstores): Twain's *Huckleberry Finn* (1885) and the earlier *Adventures of Tom Sawyer* (1875; see pp. 170–71) were such. They aroused intense criticism. In Concord (Massachusetts), *Huckleberry Finn* was banned by the Public Library as being 'rough, coarse, and inelegant, dealing with a series of experiences not elevating, the whole book being more suited to the slums than to intelligent, respectable people'.

Public libraries have not been mentioned before, but their emergence in America in the 1840s, and in Britain from 1850 onwards, led to the free availability of reading matter and also had an effect on the publishing trade. In England, the first public library which paid special attention to children's reading was in Nottingham, where in 1882 the pioneering city librarian John Potter Briscoe set up the Nottingham Library for Boys and Girls, which had a stock of 3,000 volumes and was staffed by a dedicated children's librarian. Frances Catherine Hill (who started there as a library assistant, with a weekly salary of 12s. 6d, which eventually increased to £1) was the first of the many children's librarians who were to foster and guide children's reading in the 20th century.

Frances Hill was capable and hard-working, and her work in Nottingham was recognised as valuable, but by no means did all librarians promote reading as necessarily good. In 1879 Miss M. A. Bean, the Librarian of Brookline (Massachusetts) wrote eloquently on 'The evil of unlimited freedom in the use of juvenile fiction'. Her proposal, to lessen the quantity and improve the quality of the books they bought, had marked effects (both positive and negative) on libraries' book selection policies – librarians naturally identified themselves with the 'intelligent, respectable people' mentioned in the Concord Public Library ban on Mark Twain's books. Commercial circulating libraries, like those operated within their shops by Boots the Chemist in

Boots Booklovers Library, Pelham Street Branch, Nottingham, *c.*1906. Commercial libraries like Boots's and Mudie's developed in conjunction with the private collections built up by tradesmen's societies, which for many poorer families might be their only access to books (beyond the family-owned copies of *The Pilgrim's Progress* and a hymnal). Boots catered for the better-off, but like most libraries they were hugely important in providing access to reading for children.

The Boots Archive

the first half of the 20th century, respected the conventions of the time.

Censorship was always present, of course. 'Intelligent, respectable people' had always found ways to limit access to 'unsuitable' books, and many publishers and booksellers acted as self-censors. But there has always been a market for pornography, and some newsagents stocked some fairly unsavoury publications, of the sort displayed in shops in Holywell Street, off Fleet Street. The Obscene Publication Act of 1857 ('Lord Campbell's Act') controlled, but did not wipe out altogether, their distribution – and the production of 'Hank Janson' books in the 1950s illustrates the continuing secret world of boys' books kept hidden from the authorities (see p. 207), and often left out of discussions of children's books.

In the 18th century, the stories intended for girls and set in girls' schools had a very different history, as did their writers' literary intentions (see pp. 110–11). Many were to figure largely in girls' magazines, such as *The Girl's Own Paper*, or *Aunt Judy's Magazine* (see p. 169). No doubt because girls' boarding schools developed later in Britain, it took a generation after the publication of *Tom Brown's School Days* before L. T. Meade wrote her *A World of Girls* (1886; see p. 159). Meade's book was the first of scores written and enjoyed in the early 20th century, 'both enthralling to the young and easy to grow out of' (as Angela Brazil's school stories were later described).

Equally enthralling but slower to be outgrown were some 'coming of age' books from North America, like Louisa May Alcott's *Little Women* (see pp. 164–5), which became very popular with readers on both sides of the Atlantic. As Simone de Beauvoir wrote,

I identified myself passionately with Jo, the intellectual [who] clambered up into trees when she wanted to read ... I shared her

horror of sewing and housekeeping and her love of books.

She read the book in French translation, and one wonders how the translator (or de Beauvoir herself) comprehended the extent to which in *Little Women* Alcott employed motifs from *The Pilgrim's Progress*, a book not familiar to French readers. (One wonders, too, how faithful Japanese **manga** versions have been to Alcott's text.)

After family tales, stories about animals were particularly attractive to women writers and their audiences, though Jack London's *The Call of the Wild* (1903) showed that male writers could also shine in that department. Anna Sewell's *Black Beauty* (1877; see pp. 166–7) pointed the way for many other writers of pony books, which (like Angela Brazil's school stories) were enthralling to the young, but soon to be discarded.

Many histories of juvenile literature take 1865, the year *Alice in Wonderland* was published, as marking a revolution in the production of children's books. But this development was not a destructive real-world revolution of the 1789 or 1917 kind. The earlier children's books, the fairy stories, *The Pilgrim's Progress, Robinson Crusoe* (see pp. 80–81 and 106–7) and many others continued to be republished in new editions and enjoyed by generations of fresh readers. Many of these old favourites were the bread-and-butter which helped keep publishers of children's books in business.

Technical developments in printing and bookbinding sustained such trade. The general adoption of stereotyping (or **electrotyping**) simplified and made much cheaper the production of new reprints, and some enterprising publishers augmented their stock of stereo plates by buying them from defunct publishers. The introduction in the 1840s of type-casting machines and other ways of producing typefaces made it easier for printers to use a range of typefaces in children's books. The steady cheapening of paper and the introduction of larger powered printing presses likewise helped to drive down production costs for juvenile publishing.

In illustration, the extensive use of wood-engraving, and the skill of the engravers, meant that the publishers and printers could produce superb black-and-white illustrations for *Alice in Wonderland*, which would satisfy its author, and Edmund Evans perfected the printing of coloured wood-engravings. The colours of the **chromolithographs** in such a book as *Alice* were often rather garish compared with the hand-coloured engravings of the 1820s, but Victorian chromolithograph books could be produced and sold much more cheaply. Child readers became used to seeing colour in their books, and many might have repeated the eponymous Alice's question: 'What is the use of a book without pictures or conversation?'

In the second half of Victoria's reign, the number of women illustrators steadily increased, and the best of them – Kate Greenaway and Beatrix Potter – surpassed their male contemporaries. Less-talented female illustrators were often very cheap to employ, a fact noticed by many publishers of books for juveniles. As soon as photo-mechanical illustration processes were developed, at the end of the century, they were adopted for children's book illustrations, which were often very fresh and attractive (see pp. 132–3 and 172–3).

Books changed on the outside, too, in the bindings and endpapers used. Bookbinding changed from being a skilled hand-craft to an industrial process, allowing publishers to provide attractively and enticingly decorated cloth bindings for their wares at relatively low costs. Just as some publishers added printing to their businesses, several of the most successful publishers of juvenile literature

The Children of the New Forest, by Captain Marryat. London: Blackie and Son, [n.d.]. One of the Blackie's Library of Famous Books series, with a binding designed by Talwin Morris. Signed with three-dot device on spine.

Author's collection

started out as stationers or bookbinders and expanded into publishing. In the United States, the Henry Altemus Company of Philadelphia produced a very wide range of children's books in pictorial bindings, closing eventually in 1936. In Scotland John Alexander Blackie, in charge of book production at William Blackie & Son, devised an ingenious and efficient bookbinding system which gave Blackie the edge over rival publishers. (When Blackie appointed Talwin Morris to take charge of design in 1893 the firm's books became internationally famous for the Art Nouveau 'Glasgow style' often associated with the architect Charles Rennie Mackintosh, and Blackie books are now regarded as very collectable.)

Other publishers imitated Blackie's innovations as best they could, with their own **stereotyped** reprints of standard classics – such firms as William Collins & Sons in Glasgow, and Thomas Nelson & Sons in

Edinburgh, or J. M. Dent in London. All of them produced good, cheap series which were easy to reprint, and as publisher of the Royal Readers, Nelson had a firm hold of educational publishing (see pp. 96–7). Unusually, Thomas Nelson & Sons had a branch in Paris, and in the early 20th century they published a range of children's books translated into French (and also Spanish), which were all printed in Edinburgh for export to the Continent.

Commercial experience showed that the numbers of 'classics' which could be sold to families were limited – books already owned by families were passed on to younger children to read when they reached the right age. Publishers, naturally, disliked this, and sought ways to make their own new publications attract potential purchasers. Using better, more striking bindings helped, and fresh illustrations to a classic by an eminent artist often seemed the best lure a publisher could provide. By the last decades of the Victorian era, lavishly illustrated children's books intended to tap into the gift

market started to appear: when *Alice in Wonderland* came out of copyright in 1907, no fewer than eight different illustrated editions were published at the same time to compete with the Tenniel pictures always used in the book's earlier editions (see p. 163).

The production of these books was always a bit of a gamble. The fees paid to artists such as Arthur Rackham or Edmund Dulac could be very high: in 1909 J. M. Dent paid Rackham £500 for his pictures for *Gulliver's Travels* and *Lamb's Tales from Shakespeare* (that is, about £17 per picture), so publishers needed to sell a lot of highly priced copies of the books they produced to ensure that their books brought them a profit. In the years before 1914, such publications sold very well; but with the exception of those titles illustrated by a few very popular artists, from the 1920s onwards the market for such illustrated gift books became less certain.

Looking back at children's books produced at the end of Victoria's reign, they seem to have a golden glow about them. The Dumpy Books put out by Grant Richards, or the Beatrix Potter books published by Warne (see below and pp. 172–3) looked to the future, not the past; while many books intended for older child readers also reflected the changing mood of the times. As well as the books written by people like Mrs Hodgson Burnett and E. Nesbit (see pp. 174–5), titles by newer authors such as Walter de la Mare (*The Three Mulla-Mulgars*, 1910) and John Masefield (*Martin Hyde: The Duke's Messenger*, 1910, and *Jim Davis*, 1913) held a hint of their authors' future greatness.

'This is a motor air-ship. Some day we shall all have them', from T. W. H. Crosland, *The Motor Car Dumpy Book. Illustrated in colour by J. R. Monsell.* London: Grant Richards, 1904.

The British Library

How Pleasant to Know Mr Lear

Many people grow up learning Edward Lear's limericks, but some of his other nonsense verses were even more popular in their day.

Edward Lear (1812–88) was an unusual man: a melancholic, with persistent and serious health problems, and an extensive traveller; he was largely self-taught as an artist. Lear first came to attention for his work for the Zoological Society of London, producing *Illustrations of the Family of Psittacidae, or Parrots*, in 1830, when he was only nineteen years old. His large **lithographs** (which he hand-coloured from his watercolour drawings) were masterly, and his ornithological illustrations comparable to those of the slightly earlier

American artist Audubon, and his work was praised by Darwin. His topographical paintings, too, are now highly prized.

Lear's work attracted Lord Stanley (later 13th Earl of Derby), president of both the Linnean Society and the Zoological Society, who, as an eminent natural historian, had formed a very extensive private zoo at his home, Knowsley Hall, near Liverpool. Lord Stanley invited Lear to come and stay whenever he wished. While living at at Knowsley, Lear painted birds, and wrote. Guests staying at great houses were often

Edward Lear, *A Book of Nonsense*. London: Routledge, Warne and Routledge, 1846. The third edition, with additional nonsensical illustrations, of the verses first published as being by 'Derry Down Derry', depicted here on the cover.

The British Library

expected in some way or other to sing for their suppers, and as a frequent visitor to Knowsley Lear soon discovered he could charm the younger members of the large Stanley family by writing and illustrating nonsense verses. His first book of nonsense verse (1846), published under the pseudonym 'Derry Down Derry', was dedicated to them.

Lear did not invent the limerick form (the first limericks probably dated to those in the picture book, *The History of Sixteen Wonderful Old Women,* published by John Harris in 1820), and Lear claimed that he had first seen limericks in *Anecdotes and Adventures of Fifteen Gentleman,* a book from John Marshall, with illustrations by Cruikshank (1821). But many readers prefer Lear's other nonsense verse to his limericks, partly because of Lear's imaginative new words with which he enriched the English language: 'They dined on mince and slices of quince, / Which they ate with a runcible spoon', one of the many examples from 'The Owl and the Pussycat' (and the origin of his nonsense words has invited much speculation). Lear's nonsense has been (and still is) highly regarded by the Germans and the French too, and Francis Steegmuller's free translation of *Le hibou et la poussiquette* (1961) has been relished by many.

It was not only the people in the English-speaking world who enjoyed writing and reading nonsense. One of the most effective and successful nonsense writers was a young man from Bengal, Sukumār Rāy (1887–1923). His father, Upendrakishore Ray Chowdhury, was a multi-faceted man, a successful children's writer and musician who also owned a printing and publishing business in Calcutta (and later on Sukumār's own son was to become one of India's most famous film directors). Sukumār, a very precocious boy, who translated 'Hickory Dickory Dock' into Bengali at the age of nine, was sent to London in 1911 by his father to study

process-engraving and lithography. Once there, in swift succession he joined the Royal Photographic Society, and contributed several articles to the graphics arts journal the *Penrose Annual*. On his return to Calcutta he joined his father in the printing trade.

With an interest in nonsense verse already apparent when he was still in school, Sukumār formed a 'Nonsense Club' in 1907 soon after graduation, and went on to write several works which play with language and nonsense verse. Nine days before his death from leishmaniasis (a parasitic disease) in 1923, his *Abol Tabol* (*Nonsense*) was published. This Bengali collection rapidly became very popular in India and, in English translation, has its devotees in Britain too. It is likely Sukumār had come across Lear's poems in India, but it may have been in London that he got hold of a copy of his verse; there were very cheap editions available there, in W. T. Stead's Books for the Bairns series and others by British publishers. Surely Sukumār's own delightful addition to the nonsense verse tradition would have pleased Edward Lear too.

Fireside Fables for All the Family

In the early reign of Queen Victoria, there were many changes in publishing for children. Significant writers of adult fiction such as Dickens and Thackeray were now tempted into producing stories intended as entertainment for the whole family.

The idea of the characteristic British Christmas crystallised at about the same time as the marriage of Queen Victoria and her consort Prince Albert. Technical developments, such as powered printing machines, mechanised bookbinding, and the development of **stereotyping**, **electrotyping** and **lithography**, all enabled the development of illustrated magazines – and the production of special 'Christmas' books, which coincided with the first commercial production of Christmas cards, introduced by 'Felix Summerly' (Sir Henry Cole) in 1843.

This was a time when British fiction writing for children was coming into full flower. Charles Dickens's *A Christmas Carol*

was written in 1843; another story by Dickens's literary rival William Makepeace Thackeray (1811–63), *The Rose and the Ring*, was also published as a Christmas gift book; it is dated as having been published in 1855, but in fact was issued in time for the 1854 Christmas season. Now best known for his novel *Vanity Fair* (1848), Thackeray had a long journalistic background, and his biting social comment for *Fraser's Magazine* and for the satirical weekly *Punch* was appreciated by many readers (if not always by the targets of his satire). His Christmas story, issued under his pseudonym 'Michael Angelo Titchmarsh', described itself as 'A fire-side pantomime for great and small children', and, with its over-the-top burlesque character, it was an

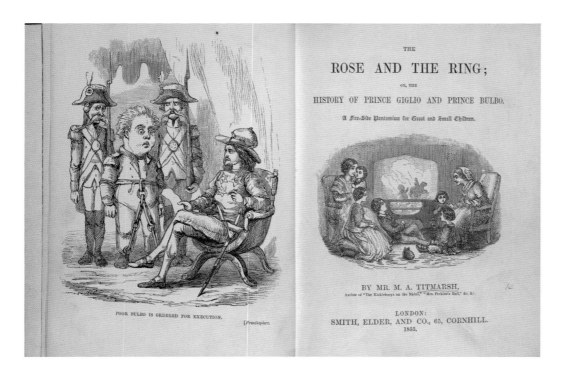

POOR BULBO IS ORDERED FOR EXECUTION.

[Frontispiece.

THE
ROSE AND THE RING;
OR, THE
HISTORY OF PRINCE GIGLIO AND PRINCE BULBO.

A Fire-Side Pantomime for Great and Small Children.

BY MR. M. A. TITMARSH,
Author of "The Kickleburys on the Rhine," "Mrs. Perkins's Ball," &c. &c.

LONDON:
SMITH, ELDER, AND CO., 65, CORNHILL.
1855.

W. M. Thackeray, *The Rose and the Ring*, London: Smith, Elder & Co., 1855. Thackeray signed his pictures with a pair of spectacles. As with his illustrations for *Vanity Fair*, the influence of 'Dicky' Doyle's artistic style is very marked. Thackeray had all his work engraved by Joseph Swain, one of the best trade wood-engravers of the time. Electrotyped copies of Swain's vulnerable boxwood blocks enabled the pictures to be easily reusable for both reprints and new editions.

The British Library

John Ruskin, *The King of the Golden River*. London: Smith, Elder & Co., 1851. Ruskin's fairy story set in the Austrian province of Styria has attracted many book illustrators. The earliest were by 'Dicky' Doyle in the first edition (published in time for Christmas 1850, but dated 1851), which has some of his finest work in it.

The British Library

journalism). Clearly attentive to what was new in the genre of children's books, Thackeray also wrote some trenchant critiques of children's books of the 1840s as a journalist writing for *Fraser's Magazine*. *The Rose and the Ring* became immediately popular, and remained in print in both Britain and America until well into the 20th century. It is little read in Britain today, but in other political climates, things have been different. In Russia and the Soviet bloc, Thackeray was read, studied and translated, partly because Marxists regarded him as a 'safe' author who had often been strongly critical of aspects of British society, as in *Vanity Fair*. With *nine* different Polish translations of *The Rose and the Ring* published between 1945–65, plus several in Czech and Russian – and with Moscow editions in English of Thackeray's work also being widely available – this 'fire-side pantomime' has had a much longer and wider life than most people would realise.

Even more popular, and still read today, was John Ruskin's story *The King of the Golden River*, which he wrote in 1841 for the twelve-year-old Effie Gray, whom Ruskin married just seven years later. (Their marriage was famously annulled for non-consummation in 1854.) Written at Effie's request, this fairy tale illustrated the triumph of kindness, love and goodness over evil; perfect for the prevailing Victorian mood. When published in 1851 *The King of the Golden River* rapidly became a classic. It was soon adapted for younger readers and translated into numerous languages (including Hindi, Kikuyu and Esperanto), while its text cried out to be illustrated, making it a natural choice for artists such as Willy Pogany and Arthur Rackham. But perhaps the original illustrations by 'Dicky' Doyle are best suited to Ruskin's tale. It was Ruskin's only book for children.

enormous success at the time. This fantasy, about four royal cousins in the kingdoms of Paflagonia and Crim Tartary, had all the usual elements of pantomime, including a Good Fairy, the witchy Blackstick as the baddie, and characters such as the Princess's governess, 'Countess Gruffanuff' and the Head of the Guard, 'Kutasoff Hedzoff'. Victorians of all ages, not only children, seem to have found these ponderous jokes amusing, and the contemporary references to events and places around the Black Sea were reminders that the book's production coincided with the outbreak of the Crimean War.

For many readers (including other authors) the illustrations, by Thackeray himself, added much to the interest of the book. His style of drawing was strongly influenced by that of his friend, the famous illustrator Richard ('Dicky') Doyle, who designed the original cover of *Punch*. Thackeray's illustrations demand and repay close attention. It should be remembered that in his twenties Thackeray had studied art both in Paris, at the Ecole des Beaux Arts and other *ateliers*, and in London too, intending to become a full-time artist, but he gave up the idea, then turning to book illustration (as a side-line to his

Such, Such Were the Joys?

School stories could be very influential: was *Tom Brown's School Days* the reason Baron de Coubertin started the modern Olympic Games in 1894?

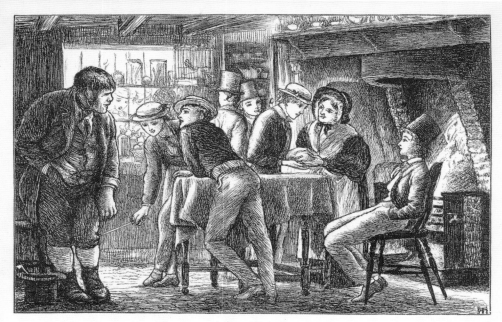

WAITING FOR ROAST POTATOES IN SALLY HARROWELL'S KITCHEN.   P. 116.

Although some of the 'great' boys' schools such as Charterhouse, Harrow, St Paul's or Winchester had existed for centuries, early Victorian England saw a steady increase in public *boarding* schools catering for the expanding middle classes, such as the United Services College at Westward Ho! to which Rudyard Kipling was sent (see p. 134). With more and more boys being sent to these schools, there was a natural gap in the market for 'improving' books about schoolboys' lives, which fitted very well with the evangelical, 'muscular Christianity' of Charles Kingsley and others. The most famous of these was a story published in 1857 by the social reformer Thomas Hughes (1822–96), *Tom Brown's School Days*.

This was an heroic tale which used Rugby School as a metaphor for Britain itself – with the unwritten understanding that Rugby boys were learning self-reliance there and that such self-reliance would ensure that authority could safely be delegated to them – it was almost a manual for those who would, when mature, go abroad to govern the Empire. For a former pupil (and especially at the time when Thomas Arnold, as headmaster, was reforming Rugby School), Hughes's uncritical admiration for Arnold was unusual. He noted that it was 'a very rough, not to say brutal place when I went there', but Arnold's methods (for example in giving older boys responsibility for disciplining the younger, in an atmosphere of moral earnestness and self-questioning) were certainly effective.

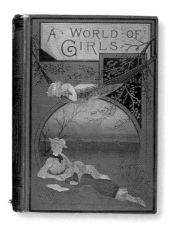

Elizabeth Thomasina Meade, *A World of Girls*. London: Cassell & Co., 1886. For the first half of the 20th century, school stories were a popular theme with girls as well, and readers had the choice of books (targeted for girls) by Angela Brazil, Elinor Brent-Dyer, Dorita Fairlie Bruce, Elsie J. Oxenham and many other women writers.

The British Library

Hughes's book created the popular idea of Arnold's work, emphasising that competitive games were essential to public-school spirit – an idea subtly different from Arnold's own views. It was also different from another didactic school story published soon after, Frederic Farrar's *Eric, or Little by Little* (1858). Though originally a very popular book, the author's earnestness (wishing to display the effects of boys' moral turpitude) eventually proved counter-productive, his piety mocked by later writers such as Kipling. For many years, both *Eric* and *Tom Brown's School Days* were very widely read, and exerted a considerable influence beyond Britain. In Japan, Hughes's book and its precepts had a marked effect on that country's educational methods, while in France, Pierre Frédy, Baron de Coubertin saw Arnold's methods as an enabler of Britain's Imperial success. Especially interested in physical education, Coubertin wrote that 'organised sport can create moral and social strength'. His beliefs led to the development of the modern Olympic movement, with the first games of the modern era held in Greece in 1894.

Tom Brown's School Days has since dropped out of fashion. But it has survived in a strange way, through the series of books about Flashman written by George Macdonald Fraser (published from 1969 onwards). Flashman was a bully and a minor character in Hughes's story; but Fraser seized on him as an anti-hero, as a braggart, a lecher, a thief and a coward – more like a nastier version of Farrar's Eric than Tom Brown. Fraser's stories (not intended for an adolescent audience, but nonetheless relished by them) caught the mood of post-colonial Britain perfectly.

School stories for girls included games in their content, but never to the extent of those for boys. Sarah Fielding's *The Governess* (1749) pointed the way (see p. 110), but it was only in the late Victorian period that girls' boarding school stories really developed. An early book in the genre might be taken as representative: *A World of Girls* (1886) by Elizabeth Thomasina Meade (1844–1914), who always signed herself as L. T. Meade.

Now as an author she is largely forgotten, but in Meade's day she was one of the best-known women writers, and she is credited with nearly three hundred books. These were issued by more than thirty publishers, beginning in the 1870s with her 'Street Arab' stories about the waifs and strays of East London. Meade ranged widely in her books, writing both good detective stories (which bear comparison with the *Sherlock Holmes* tales of Arthur Conan Doyle), and **problem novels** for an adult audience. From 1887 to 1893 Meade edited *Atalanta*, one of the best girls' monthly magazines of the period.

Inevitably, much of Meade's writing was stereotyped (and the later books reflect that she had started dictating her text to a secretary). Had she written less, her books might have survived longer. Nonetheless, *A World of Girls* is still readable more than a century later, because Meade represented the 'new woman' of the 1880s and could write convincing dialogue. Turning to it now is like turning to one of the well-crafted detective stories of Agatha Christie or Dorothy L. Sayers: few surprises, but comforting memories of a life now long past.

Successful Scottish Adventurers

From about 1820 onwards, Scottish authors and publishers played a major role in children's publishing, particularly in the area of adventure stories.

London booksellers and publishers dominated the market for recreational books in general, but from about the end of the Napoleonic Wars, Scottish authors and publishers based in Edinburgh and Glasgow often set the tone for books intended for adolescent boys. The poetry and novels of Walter Scott were already popular by the time of George IV's public relations visit to Edinburgh in 1822, and *Blackwood's Magazine* (established in 1817) had already become one of the most important and influential of British literary magazines.

One early success of *Blackwood's* was *Tom Cringle's Log*, with its first anonymous instalment published in 1829. Its author, Michael Scott (1789–1835), had been a land agent and merchant in Jamaica; and the authenticity of his account of adventures in a slave colony, and capture and imprisonment by the French navy, rang true.

Michael Scott's work set the tone for other Scottish writers who had worked in exotic places, such as R. M. Ballantyne (1825–1894), who at the age of sixteen went to Rupert's Land (in British North America) to work for the Hudson's Bay Company. His long descriptive letters to his Edinburgh family telling them about his travels by canoe and sleigh, and of fur-trading with the First People, formed the basis of his first adventure book, *Snowflakes and Sunbeams, or, The Young Fur Traders*. He sold the copyright to this for £50 in 1856 to Thomas Nelson & Sons, already well reputed for adventure stories, and Ballantyne became known for the authentic quality of his writing. However, the payments he received from Nelson & Sons for his copyrights remained modest: in 1858

THE STORM.

Page 215.

Robert Michael Ballantyne, *The Coral Island: A Tale of the Pacific Ocean.* With illustrations by the author. T. Nelson & Sons: London, 1858 [1857]. Ballantyne's own lovely illustrations for his frontispiece and title page hinted at the colourful stories contained within. His book was a great success, and Ballantyne became something of a celebrity, yet much of his income came from giving talks and lectures rather than his royalties.
The British Library

they paid £60 for his *Coral Island*, probably the most successful of all his books, often selected for school prizes, and which remained in print well into the 20th century. Nelson & Sons made handsome profits from their well-produced and modestly priced editions of *The Coral Island*, but refused to pay anything to Ballantyne (or to allow him to buy back the copyrights), so the author turned to other, London-based publishers for his later works.

Though Ballantyne's earliest books were based on his own experiences, he enlarged his scope by immersing himself in research to give his stories authenticity. He had never visited a coral island, but his readers believed his account, as they did in his African stories. One of Ballantyne's most enthusiastic readers as a child was Robert Louis Stevenson (1850–94), who was to transform the nature (and intellectual quality) of adventure stories. Ballantyne was a sincere Elder of the Free Church of Scotland, and this was seen clearly in the texts of his tales. No doubt his piety appealed to Victorians selecting his books as gifts; but 20th-century readers were put off by it, and by the sentimentality in Ballantyne's tales, and their readership ebbed away.

By contrast, in Stevenson's *Treasure Island* the author's touch was much lighter, and much less censorious. The story was first published serially in *Young Folks* magazine in 1881–2 and actually received some complaints about the story's violence, in its treatment of treasure-hunting and pirates (or the vividly realised characters of Long John Silver, Ben Gunn, and the sinister and frightening Blind

Pew). Yet he showed his villains as not beyond redemption – an idea rare in Victorian adventure stories. 'I'll make this boys' book business pay,' he wrote. It caught readers' imaginations, and from the time Cassell first published *Treasure Island* in 1883 the book has never been out of print. Innumerable translations and adaptations have appeared. Whether upon the *Pirates of the Caribbean* film series, or the adventure stories by John Buchan or others, the influence of Stevenson was extensive. He was overpraised in his lifetime, but the quality of Stevenson's writing has since been undervalued – though not by readers of *Treasure Island*. It remains a magical book.

Curiouser and Curiouser

The year 1865 marked a watershed for the production of children's books: since *Alice*, juvenile writing has changed completely.

Charles Lutwidge Dodgson (1832–98), better known as Lewis Carroll, went to Rugby School soon after Thomas Hughes, the author of *Tom Brown's School Days*, who flourished there under its headmaster Thomas Arnold. Unlike Hughes, however, Dodgson hated his every minute there. His books for children were a direct refutation of the Arnoldian ideals of duty (which were to be carried out with true missionary zeal as the route to a 'successful' life).

Dodgson became a mathematical lecturer at Christ Church, Oxford, and might now be all but forgotten, but while at Oxford he became keen on photography, and photographed the daughters of the Dean of Christ Church. His friendship with the Liddell girls developed, and in 1862, while taking the children on a boating trip on the Thames, Dodgson told them a story about a young girl who fell down a rabbit hole and embarked on a fantastical adventure. The ten-year-old Alice Liddell loved the story, and asked Dodgson to write it for her.

Dodgson showed the manuscript to a friend, George MacDonald, who was to become the author of *At the Back of the North Wind* (1871), and he urged him to get it published: 'Lewis Carroll' was born. After some false starts, Dodgson/Carroll obtained an unusual contract with Macmillan to publish his books at his own expense, which allowed him control over their design and production. Carroll first turned to Oxford University Press to print the book (again at his own expense), but insisted on several printings being withdrawn because he was dissatisfied by their presswork.

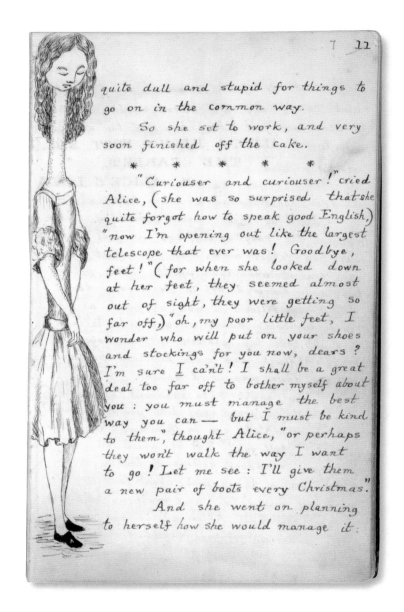

Lewis Carroll, *Alice's Adventures Under Ground*, 1862–64. Manuscript, in sepia ink with thirty-seven pen-and-ink illustrations and a coloured title page. This manuscript was given by the author to Alice Liddell in November 1864 as an early Christmas present. The following year it was published as *Alice in Wonderland* (after all the Liddell family references were removed). Alice Liddell kept the manuscript until 1928; just after the Second World War it was resold and presented by a group of benefactors through the Library of Congress to the British people in gratitude for their war efforts.

The British Library

And that reminds me. There's a little lesson I want to teach *you*, while we're looking at this picture of Alice and the Cat. Now don't be in a bad temper about it, my dear Child! It's a very *little* lesson indeed!

Do you see that Fox-Glove growing close to the tree? And do you know why it's called a *Fox*-Glove? Perhaps you

Lewis Carroll was an exacting author, exerting close supervision over both John Tenniel, the illustrator, who was selected on the advice of the wood-engraver Orlando Jewitt, and the Dalziels, who engraved Tenniel's designs (see p. 262).

When *Alice in Wonderland* was published in 1865, the 'funny pretty book', as Christina Rossetti called it, acquired instant popularity. It had a young, spontaneous mood, its plot suggesting that Carroll had improvised rapidly on the first version of the story told on that golden afternoon in Oxfordshire. Its successor, *Through the Looking Glass, or, What Alice Found There* (1871) has a less free-spirited plot; the author ranges through aspects of growing up and its mood becomes more autumnal; but it proved equally popular, on the Continent and in America as well as in Britain.

Carroll continued to adapt his *Alice* stories, also rewriting them for a younger audience (*The Nursery 'Alice'*, 'to be read by Children aged from Nought to Five', 1889). One of the great virtues of his illustrator Tenniel was that he read the texts assiduously before he started his sketches, and the quality and force of his illustrations make it almost impossible for readers now to imagine any other characters than those Tenniel drew, despite numerous attempts to re-illustrate the books.

Many later illustrators attempted *Alice* as soon as (and even before) it went out of copyright, and the *Alice* theme has remained attractive to a range of artists, illustrators and filmmakers, ranging from Mervyn Peake (1946), to Tove Jansson (1966), to filmmaker Jan Švankmajer (1988), as well as many more mediocre interpretations. One of the most interesting is that of the American wood-engraver Barry Moser (b. 1940) who produced both the *Alice* books for his own Pennyroyal Press (1982), and later for the University of California Press. Moser's interpretations of Carroll are sombre, and his books are really intended for adult readers; but the 'Pennyroyal Alices' provide magnificent illustrations, and are models of intelligent, scholarly and thoughtful presentation – all too rare in the production of children's books.

An American Girlhood

Little Women, first published in 1868, was the first major success in American coming-of-age novels, and is still enormously influential.

Louisa May Alcott (1832–88) had an unusual childhood; episodes remind one of the extraordinary characters in Thomas Love Peacock's novels. As the offspring of a New England transcendentalist, Bronson Alcott, Louisa and her sisters experienced great poverty, as Bronson, who believed in 'the sweetness of self-denial', tried to live out a good life in a remote rural farmhouse, combining plain, unheated living with high thinking – an experiment which failed before the end of one Massachusetts winter. At the same time, the Alcott girls grew up with exposure to such writers as the early feminist Margaret Fuller, Ralph Waldo Emerson, Henry David Thoreau and Nathaniel Hawthorne.

Given their poverty, it was essential for the young Louisa to earn a living and after time spent working as a hospital nurse (during the American Civil War), and as a seamstress and governess, she turned to writing. Her first book, *Flower Fables* (1854), was a collection of stories written for Ralph Waldo Emerson's daughter, Ellen. For several years Alcott edited the illustrated children's magazine *Merry's Museum* (established by Samuel Griswold Goodrich, 'Peter Parley', in 1841) (see p. 105), to which she contributed a few stories, but her real success came with *Little Women*, written in 1868 at the suggestion of Thomas Niles, her editor at the Boston publisher Roberts Brothers.

Loosely based on the lives and characters of herself and her sisters, but also closely linked to *The Pilgrim's Progress* (important in the Alcotts' thinking), *Little Women* had an immediate success in America, and soon after in Britain. Despite the echoes of

They all drew to the fire, mother in the big chair, with Beth at her feet; Meg and Amy perched on either arm of the chair, and Jo leaning on the back. — PAGE 12.

Frontispiece to Louisa May Alcott, *Little Women or, Meg, Jo, Beth and Amy*. Boston: Roberts Brothers, 1870 [1868]. A family affair, the novel was furnished with line drawings (like the frontispiece here) by the author's youngest sister, May Alcott Nieriker, who figures largely (as Amy) in the text. The 'loose' perspective here has a rather homespun charm.

The British Library

Louisa May Alcott, *Nisā sạ ghīrāt* (*Little Women*). Translated by Amīnah al-Saʿīd. Cairo: Dar al-Māarif; New York: Franklin Press, 1954–8. Four volumes. This Arabic translation reflects the enduring popularity around the world of Alcott's vision of a 19th-century Bostonian girlhood. The translator, a feminist activist, also founded the first women's magazine in Egypt. The books were distributed throughout the Arabic-speaking world in the 1950s as part of the Franklin Book Program.

African and Middle Eastern Division, The Library of Congress, Washington D.C.

Bunyan, the author avoided the evangelical tone so common in children's books of the period, and vividly captured the squabbles and mishaps of real family life. Alcott's easy colloquial style was ideal for the readership of the time – *Little Women* was discussed in the streets and in the parlour, just as Dickens's novels had been, and British readers found the characters intriguing. Though scholars have expressed horror at the alterations and mistranslations in some German and French versions, Alcott's work was also very popular on the Continent.

Little Women rapidly became a world classic; a version for the blind was published very soon after its publication in Boston, and simplified versions were produced for school use. It joined such books as *Robinson Crusoe*, with many competing editions available, and as a favourite book for school prizes. It is still so well loved that paper dolls of the characters were published as recently as the 1990s, while in Japan, **manga** versions have been published.

Little Women, and its sequels, were hugely influential. Like E. Nesbit later (see pp. 174–5), Alcott's skill lay in writing about children who were convincingly real. Her work influenced the young Henry James, who described her in 1875 as 'the novelist of children – the Thackeray, the Trollope, of the nursery and school-room'. Her books lit the way for many other authors' coming-of-age stories, from Susan Coolidge's early *What Katy Did* (1872) to Laura Ingalls Wilder's 1930s *Little House on the Prairie* series and *Anne of Green Gables* (1908) by the Canadian writer Lucy Maud Montgomery, which enjoyed similar success with its account of childhood on Prince Edward Island.

'Be Kind to Animals'

Children's writers were already trying to teach children to care for animals, but Anna Sewell's *Black Beauty* started a fashion which still survives and flourishes.

What could educated women do when suddenly their family's prosperity disappeared? This happened to Mary Sewell (1797–1884): when her father became insolvent, she became a governess ('a great descent in the social scale'). In turn, when her husband failed as a draper, and needing to buy books to teach her young children, Sewell wrote *Walks with Mamma, or Stories in Words of One Syllable* (1824), as a series of nature walks (largely around then semi-rural Dalston) for her young daughter. She sold the copyright for £3 to the publisher John Harris (see p. 119).

Many years later Mary Sewell resumed writing children's books, in verse, which were popular and successful in their day. She is now remembered more for her role in completing *Black Beauty*, written by her daughter Anna Sewell (1820–78). Anna had been crippled in her teens and thereafter had a life of debilitating invalidism (rather like the heroine in Susan Coolidge's *What Katy Did*). What Anna did do was to edit her mother's books for publication ('a very severe critic'). Over a period of six years she also composed her only book, *Black Beauty: His Grooms and Companions. The Autobiography of a Horse. Translated from the Original Equine*, which she dictated to her mother, or wrote partly on slips of paper for Mrs Sewell to transcribe. Mrs Sewell sold the copyright in *Black Beauty* for £40 to her own publisher, Jarrold & Sons, based in Norwich.

Anna Sewell died a few months after its publication in 1877, but lived long enough to see it was successful. *How* successful was a

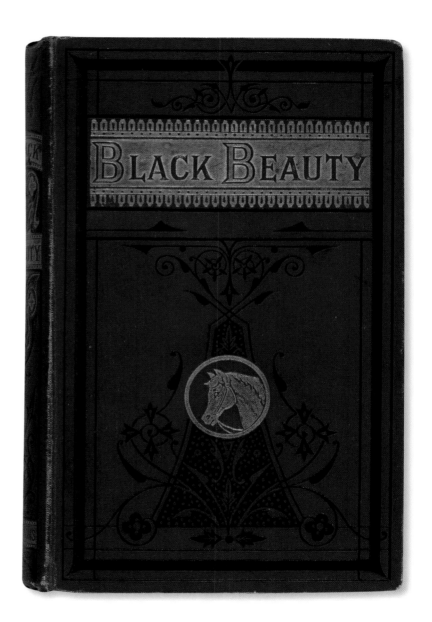

Anna Sewell, *Black Beauty: His Grooms and Companions. The Autobiography of a Horse. Translated from the Original Equine*. London: Jarrold and Sons, [1877]. The first edition appeared in two elaborate blocked and gilt bindings. Anna recorded, shortly before her death, 'I have for six years been confined to the house and to my sofa, and have from time to time, as I was able, been writing what I think will turn out a little book, its special aim being to induce kindness, sympathy, and an understanding treatment of horses.'
The British Library

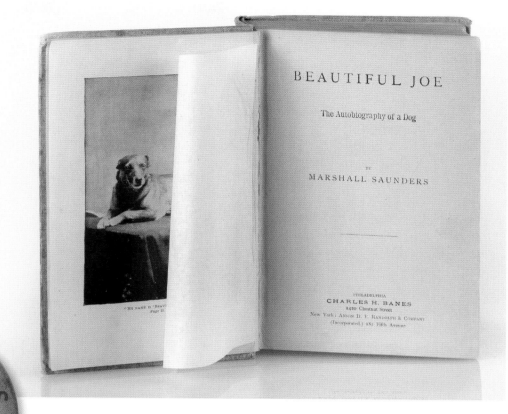

BEAUTIFUL JOE

The Autobiography of a Dog

BY

MARSHALL SAUNDERS

PHILADELPHIA
CHARLES H. BANES
1420 Chestnut Street
New York: ANSON D. F. RANDOLPH & COMPANY
(Incorporated.) 182 Fifth Avenue

surprise even to Jarrold & Sons, who sold many millions of copies before their copyright ran out; it was an extraordinary phenomenon. Anna Sewell's story was translated and adapted in many different languages and became well-enough fixed in people's minds for later gentle mockery, as in H. G. Wells's description of it as 'the sympathetic story of a soundly Anglican horse'.

The success of *Black Beauty* had two marked effects on juvenile publishing. The first was the production of other books whose main concern was animal welfare. Perhaps the most important was *Beautiful Joe* (1894) by the Canadian Marshall Saunders (1861–1947). Another 'autobiography', based on a true story about a mistreated dog, it won an award from the American Humane Education Society and was the first Canadian book ever to sell a million copies. Like *Black Beauty*, it was hugely successful. Through the English editions published by Jarrold & Sons, *Beautiful Joe* became very well known in Britain too.

The second result of the success of *Black Beauty* was perhaps less meritorious: a plethora of (often rather poorly written) horse books, produced for sale to pony-mad girls. After the Second World War, for half a century, the Pullein-Thompson sisters (Josephine, Diana and Christine) each made their careers from writing scores of 'pony stories' which sold by the tens of thousands. They still have their enthusiastic readers today.

Journalism for the Young

Attempts were made in the 18th century to produce children's magazines, but they only became important as a publishing proposition for the juvenile market in Victorian times.

With the success of such journals as *The Gentleman's Magazine,* published in London from 1731 onwards, the idea of a periodical press aimed at younger readers became attractive to the book trade. By the 1830s there were already effective methods (newsagents) to distribute magazines and journals. Publishers in both Britain and the United States sought profitable ways to tap into the growing juvenile market.

One of the earliest profitable journals was *Merry's Museum,* started by Samuel Griswold Goodrich ('Peter Parley') in Boston, Massachusetts, in 1841 (see p. 164). The success of this was noted in Britain and inspired similar ventures. One of the better English attempts was *The Boy's Own Magazine,* started in 1855 by William Clarke and Samuel Beeton (1831–77), the latter of whom is more often remembered as the husband of Isabella Beeton (who wrote bestsellers on household management). As the first magazine for children targeted at one gender, *The Boy's Own Magazine* was a success, at its height selling 40,000 copies, but Isabella Beeton's death and a bank failure forced Samuel to sell the copyrights to Ward, Lock & Tyler, who continued to publish the magazine for a few more years.

Many in Victorian society worried about the content and level of magazines aimed at adolescents (boys, in particular) – the '**penny dreadfuls**' in England, the **dime novels** in the United States. In London the Religious Tract Society (founded in 1799) decided to produce its own magazine, *The Boy's Own Paper,*

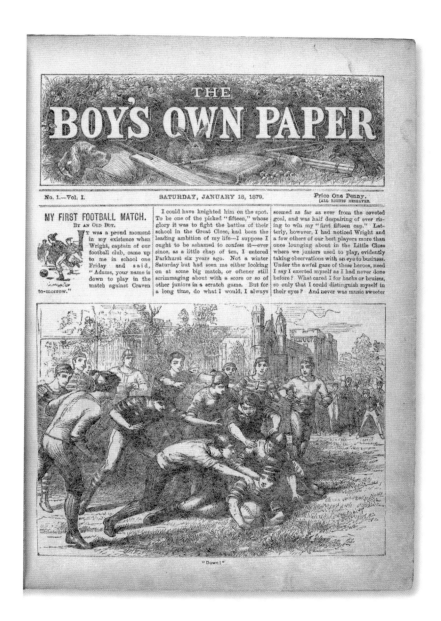

The Boy's Own Paper. London: Religious Tract Society, 18 January, 1879, no. 1, vol. 1. The cover story 'by an Old Boy' in this first issue recounts a match between fictitious rival schools of the newly popularised game of rugby (started in 1823).

The British Library

MATCHMAKING AT A GARDEN-PARTY

started in 1879 and continuing until 1967, followed by *The Girl's Own Paper* in 1880. At its height, the *BoP* (as it became known) sold 250,000 copies of each issue. Initially aimed at boys of all classes, it appeared weekly, with the parts being gathered up yearly in a bound volume and sold as *The Boy's Own Annual*. Its first assistant editor, Talbot Baines Reed (1852–93), was a brilliant writer who shared the same views as Thomas Hughes, as expressed in *Tom Brown's School Days* (1857, see p. 158), and Reed was even more important in the development of school stories. His *Fifth Form at St Dominic's* (1881) and his other novels remained in print for well over half a century. Later boys' stories owed much to Reed, and the Religious Tract Society also gained greatly from them, as Reed gave them his copyrights.

The *BoP* had many commercial rivals, and their output is still treasured by collectors today. *Chatterbox*, started in 1866 and surviving until 1955, was one of the best, and popular in North America. A strong rival was *Chums*, published originally by Cassell (and modelled closely on the *BoP*), which appeared as a magazine from 1892, along with a yearly annual, until it was discontinued during the Second World War. The instantly recognisable

scarlet bindings of its annuals can still cause a gleam in the eye of elderly readers who remember *Chums* fondly.

The Girl's Own Paper was intended 'to foster and develop that which was highest and noblest in the girlhood and womanhood of England'. From 1880 until the 1950s it published stories and articles, which are still of interest. Many English children (like Rudyard Kipling, as a homesick and unhappy schoolboy) preferred *Aunt Judy's Magazine*, started in 1866 by the interesting writer and naturalist Margaret Gatty (1809–73). She was a good writer, and *Aunt Judy* had contributions from Lewis Carroll and other eminent writers. It was worth reading, partly for the articles and stories by her daughter Juliana Horatia Ewing (1841–85), also famous in her time for *her* children's stories. But tastes change: as a *Spectator* review commented on the 1883 annual, 'the editors should be careful to remember [the annual] is intended for the hours of recreation, and not of instruction'. Publication ceased a few years later.

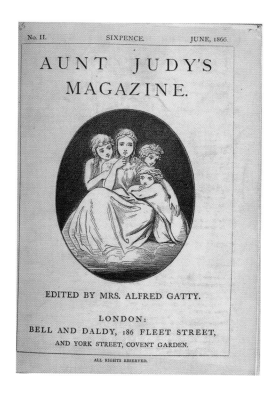

Bad Boys on Subscription

Mark Twain wrote *Tom Sawyer* (1876) as one of the new genre of
'bad boy' stories which were starting to be published in the United States.
But his sequel was to be much more controversial.

The establishment of public libraries in America called for people with courage and a strong missionary zeal. Their faith in the rightness of their cause included the old, widely held belief that the bookless masses had to be guided to share the same values as the better-educated classes – the views of earlier writers such as Sarah Trimmer and Hannah More had not been superseded. The 'rags to riches' theme of many American books by Horatio Alger and others fitted well with these feelings, but the writers of 'bad boy' stories were regarded with suspicion. The recent growth in the United States of **subscription publishing** increased the fears that the formerly bookless masses would now be exposed to books which retail bookshops chose not to stock.

'Mark Twain' (Samuel Langhorne Clemens, 1835–1910) was not the only author of 'bad boy' stories: *The Story of a Bad Boy* (1870) by Thomas Bailey Aldrich was the first American book to concentrate on a young miscreant as the chief character. It had a marked effect on Twain, whose early experience was of growing up in a small town on the Mississippi, working as a printer and journalist, and then becoming a pilot on a river steamboat, until the river traffic was curtailed by the onset of the American Civil War.

Twain admired Aldrich, and his reading of *The Story of a Bad Boy* was the genesis of Twain's *Adventures of Tom Sawyer*, published in 1876 by Elisha Bliss at the American Publishing Company in Hartford (Connecticut). The edition was sold only by door-to-door salesmen: Twain believed that subscription

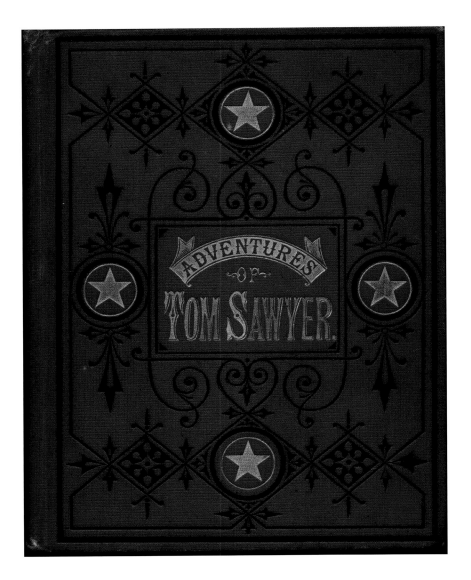

ABOVE AND OPPOSITE
Mark Twain, *The Adventures of Tom Sawyer*. Hartford, Conn.: American Publishing Company, 1876. The prospectus for *Tom Sawyer*, put together in the autumn of 1876, allowed potential customers to preview 84 of the novel's 274 pages, including the lovely frontispiece of Tom fishing on the title page opposite. For the binding, depending on the style, prices for *Tom Sawyer* ranged from $2.75 to $4.75. One filled in one's order on the last page of the prospectus.
Special Collections, University of Virginia, Charlottesville, VA

THE ADVENTURES

OF

TOM SAWYER

BY

MARK TWAIN.

THE AMERICAN PUBLISHING COMPANY,
HARTFORD, CONN.; CHICAGO, ILL.; CINCINNATI, OHIO.
A. ROMAN & CO., SAN FRANCISCO, CAL.
1876.

publishing was more profitable for authors, though later he alleged that Bliss defrauded him of thousands of dollars.

The book sold very well indeed. Despite his misplaced faith in Bliss, 'Mark Twain' was a canny businessman as well as a good writer. He secured British copyright by having his book issued by Chatto & Windus – and published on the Continent by Bernhard Tauchnitz. Translations, adaptations and illustrated editions have followed ever since: *Tom Sawyer* remains popular worldwide.

Mark Twain was by no means entirely satisfied by *Tom Sawyer*. The author's restless imagination suggested exploring the adolescence of a more interesting, questioning boy, using the same tense background of growing up in a slave state. The result was his *Adventures of Huckleberry Finn*, first published in London in 1884, and in the United States in 1885. Told in the first person by 'Huck' Finn, a friend of Tom Sawyer, and deliberately written in coarse, vernacular American English, it is full of

satire about the nature of a slave society, and proved to be a great subversive masterpiece. *Huckleberry Finn* was strongly disliked by many public librarians, and condemned by Louisa May Alcott, who missed the point, writing that if Twain could not 'think of something better to tell our pure-minded lads and lasses he had best stop writing for them'.

Some critics found the last chapters of the novel to be very weak, almost as though Twain knew he was on dangerous ground. Ernest Hemingway has observed that the end of *Huckleberry Finn* became 'little more than minstrel-show satire and broad comedy'. Sadly, many African Americans also disliked the book, because of Twain's use of the offensive word 'nigger'. Because censors in the United States still call for it to be banned from libraries or school curricula, the American Public Broadcasting Service (PBS) and the Ford Foundation have prepared *Huck Finn in Context: A Teaching Guide* to help rebut attacks on what is arguably the greatest American novel.

What's in a Name?

In the 1890s, a Scottish woman in India wrote a story to amuse her children. It still has its enthusiasts for its earliest version, but is also much disliked and often banned.

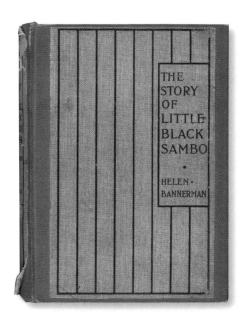

In the 1890s, Helen Bannerman (1862–1946) was escorting her young daughters by bullock-cart from their hill station (where her husband was in the Indian Medical Service) to the coast at Madras (Chennai), a tedious, two-day journey. Mrs Bannerman made it more interesting by composing a story about a little Indian boy who outwits some tigers. She subsequently wrote the story out for the girls, illustrated it with her own drawings, and eventually the manuscript was entrusted to a friend to take it to show to a new London publisher, Grant Richards. This was an enterprising and ambitious company (Richards started the World's Classics series, later taken over by

The Story of
Little Black Sambo.

ONCE upon a time there was a little black boy, and his name was Little Black Sambo.

2   3

ABOVE AND LEFT
Helen Bannerman, *The Story of Little Black Sambo*. London: Grant Richards, 1899. A young Indian boy outwits some tigers, who take his clothes and are themselves eventually reduced to a golden puddle of ghee. Despite later allegations of racism, in Bannerman's original, charmingly simple tale, the treatment of Sambo is no more derogatory or reductive than many other characters (of all racial origins) in children's books: the sensitivities lay *outside* the book, fed by the later mis-adaptations.

The British Library

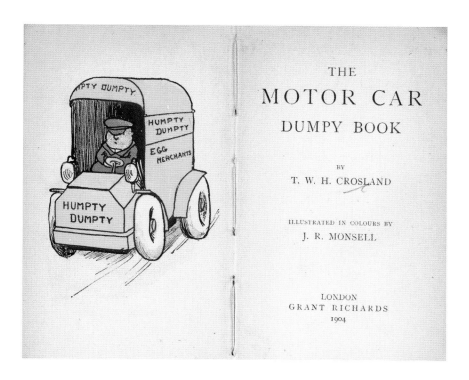

THE

MOTOR CAR
DUMPY BOOK

BY
T. W. H. CROSLAND

ILLUSTRATED IN COLOURS BY
J. R. MONSELL

LONDON
GRANT RICHARDS
1904

'This is a motor car that won't stop': from Thomas William Hodgson Crosland, *The Motor Car Dumpy Book ...* Illustrated in colours by J. R. Monsell. London: Grant Richards, 1904. Grant Richards's Dumpy Books were forward-looking in many ways. But, as *Sambo* was, Monsell's characters have been reduced to simplified visual stereotypes, a form of literary shorthand which thoroughly exercises modern cultural commentators.

The British Library

Oxford University Press), and on the spot Richards paid £5 for Helen Bannerman's manuscript.

The book was published in 1899 as *The Story of Little Black Sambo* in Richards's Dumpy Books series (then in its second year). The small book immediately became popular: Beatrix Potter was so taken by it that it inspired her to start to write her own small books in the style that she later adopted for the *Peter Rabbit* books published by Warne. Mrs Bannerman was disconcerted to find her friend had inadvertently parted with the copyright in the book (against her wishes): the £5 was all she was ever paid for what would become a wildly successful book. It was also widely pirated by American publishers, who used Mrs Bannerman's text but added other, very different, illustrations to their editions.

The text and Mrs Bannerman's illustrations clearly set her story in the Indian countryside, but some of the illustrations in the American pirated editions place it in plantations in the deep South (no doubt misled by the word 'Sambo', then pejoratively used to mean a docile slave). Some of these later editions, particularly by Stoll & Edwards, displayed a racial contempt which has been found deeply offensive: thus *Little Black Sambo* has often been censored or banned.

Attempts to produce a rewritten, politically correct, version were made in the United States, resulting in *The Story of Little Babaji* by Fred Marcellino (1996). Other publishers (including Penguin) have produced their own sanitised versions, nothing like the original charming, innocent book written by Helen Bannerman. Those who want to read her version must search for it very carefully.

Other volumes in Grant Richards's Dumpy Books series seldom created such antagonism. Like other publishers of juvenile books before him, Richards wanted to create a series which would be instantly recognisable, and at the same time would include a range of forward-looking and different titles to attract potential customers. He appointed the young journalist E. V. Lucas (1868–1938) as its series editor, and (as well as writing Dumpy Books himself) engaged other authors and illustrators whose names are still remembered a century later – among them Honor Appleton, Nellie Benson, T. W. H. Crosland, J. R. Monsell, Jessie Pope and Mary Tourtel, who invented the *Rupert Bear* books. In 1904 Richards published *The Motor Car Dumpy Book* by Crosland and Monsell, a very early automobile book for children. Dumpy Books were a success, but Grant Richards himself ran into financial problems, and eventually had to sell the series to Chatto & Windus.

Advanced Women, Looking Backwards

Changing codes of behaviour for women at the end of the 19th century and the growth of magazine publishing had a profound effect on writing for older children.

Throughout Queen Victoria's reign such women as the novelist Caroline Norton and the publisher Emily Faithfull were working for improved rights for women. By the 1870s educated women could acceptably make their living (however precariously) by writing. The growth of magazine publishing afforded new opportunities to such authors.

Edith Nesbit (1858–1924) represents the 'advanced' woman of the times. Coming from an impoverished middle-class family, Edith spent a lot of her childhood at boarding schools: 'When I was a little child,' she wrote later, 'I used to pray ... that when I should be grown up I might never forget what I thought and felt and suffered then.' This sentiment underlay her later writing for children. In 1880 she married Hubert Bland, a charming

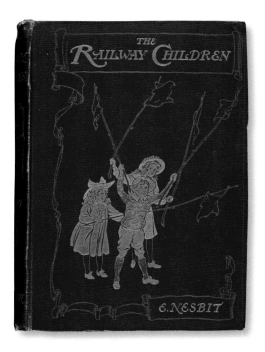

LEFT AND ABOVE
E. Nesbit, *The Railway Children*. With drawings by C. E. Brock. London: Wells Gardner, Darton and Co., 1906. Her fellow Fabian, Oswald Barron, is credited with providing Nesbit with the plot, though close parallels have been identified with *The House by the Railway* (1896) by Ada J. Graves, serialised in *The Child's Own Magazine* in 1904. Whether borrowed or invented, the children's adventures and their wistful yearning for an absentee parent have struck a chord with readers ever since.

The British Library

Frances Hodgson Burnett, *The Secret Garden*. New York: Frederick A. Stokes, 1911; London: Walker Books, 2007. Likewise, first serialised, and also nostalgic, Burnett's story is one that lends itself to illustration, from this first American edition with cover and inside illustrations by M. L. Kirk, to the full-blown, lavish garden scenes by Inga Moore for the Walker Books edition.

Houghton Library, Harvard University

journalist who introduced her to the 'Fellowship of the New Life', a group aiming at 'higher' personal and ethical ideals, which later formed the Fabian Society. She became friends with people such as Eleanor Marx, Olive Schreiner and George Bernard Shaw.

Bland's earnings were often unreliable: Nesbit's writing for children was a necessity. She wrote about her own childhood for *The Girl's Own Paper* (see p. 169), in 1896–7, which stimulated her to attempt to write longer stories. For her first, *The Story of the Treasure Seekers* (1899), she created a highly original way of writing about and for children, treating them as equals, and its tone was neither pious nor judgemental.

From the early 1900s several of Nesbit's stories were serialised in the *Strand Magazine* (famous for publishing Arthur Conan Doyle's *Sherlock Holmes* stories), including the *Five Children and It* trilogy, still widely read today. The best-loved, in Britain at any rate, is *The Railway Children* (1906; first serialised in the *London Magazine*, 1905) – partly because it was made, sensitively, into a film. The plot revolves around a family of children (with an

absent, much-missed father) moving to live in genteel poverty in unfamiliar countryside – near an ever-present country railway, which plays a crucial role in the story. There was not the same nostalgia for steam trains in 1906 as for readers today, but Nesbit cleverly caught the differing hopes and fears which affected the children – elements often part of the best books for the young.

Something of the same sense of being left out of Eden also pervades *The Secret Garden* (1911), by Frances Hodgson Burnett (1849–1924). Born in Manchester, Burnett had similar childhood misfortunes (loss of father, fear of destitution) in a more exaggerated form, including a period of real poverty in Tennessee after her widowed mother emigrated. Burnett, like Nesbit, turned to writing as a way to earn money, starting in 1868 with stories for *Godey's Ladies Book*, a popular Philadelphia fashion journal.

Burnett became 'a pen-driving machine' (as she put it), producing a huge range of novels, short stories and plays for both adults and children. Though often superficial and at times melodramatic, Burnett's writing caught the mood of the times and was very profitable, with highly successful books such as the rags-to-riches tale *Little Lord Fauntleroy* (1886) supporting her in the opulent, extrovert lifestyle that was then becoming fashionable.

In 1911 she published a book which drew upon her own unhappy memories of her Manchester childhood: *The Secret Garden* showed, with a touching intensity, how two unloved and unhappy children were changed by the discovery of a hidden garden, which they appropriated, and in which they watched the plants grow as the year progressed. Based partly on an abandoned garden near her own childhood Manchester home, Burnett's picture of this lost Eden is still very readable today.

CHAPTER 8

Fairies and Frighteners: Tempters, Tearaways and Cautionary Tales

Féeries and frightening tales have always existed in folklore and oral histories. In the 19th century they became central to children's literature.

The poet George Crabbe mentioned 'those little stories and ballads about ghosts, witches and fairies, which were then almost exclusively the literature of youth'. Crabbe was writing of the 18th century, but visionaries looked for a much better future world. 'Think what you would have been now,' wrote Charles Lamb to Samuel Taylor Coleridge in 1802, 'if instead of being fed with tales and old wives' tales in childhood, you had been crammed with geography and natural history!'

At the same time, the London bookseller Benjamin Tabart was puffing up the virtues of his *Popular Fairy Tales* (1804) as being much better than those published in the 18th century, 'so obsolete in their style, so gross in their morals, and so vulgar in their details, as to be altogether unfit for the purposes to which they seem to have been adapted'. Tabart claimed that his version was intended 'to elevate the language and sentiments to a level with the refined manners of the present age'. This was very different from the much earlier experience of the antiquary John Aubrey, who reported in *Brief Lives* that 'the fashion was for old women and mayds to tell fabulous stories nighttimes, of Sprights and walking of Ghosts, &c... Now children fear no such things, having heard not of them; and are not checked with such feares'.

For most of the 19th century, publishers of fairy tales played safe, and followed the policy suggested by Tabart. The prolific London playwright and theatrical impresario James R. Planché (1796–1880) published translations of both German and French *féeries* and between 1825 and 1871 produced many 'grand, comic, romantic, operatic, melodramatic, fairy extravaganzas in two acts' (such as Hoffmann's *King Nut Cracker*), no doubt delighting many children lucky enough to be taken to them. These retained their place in panto and other forms of theatre for children – Barrie's *Peter Pan, or, The Boy Who*

The cast of *Peter Pan* performing for the patients at the hospital in Helena Ward, Great Ormond Street Hospital, in 1929, the year Barrie gifted them the copyright. Jean Forbes Robertson took the starring role as Peter, with Gerald du Maurier as Captain Hook. Barrie was in the audience, seen in the shadows at back left.

Great Ormond Street Children's Hospital

Wouldn't Grow Up (1904; see pp. 192–3), is a later example. The Swedish-born Anthony Rubens Montalba (1813–1884) edited *The Famous Fairy Tales of all Nations*, with illustrations by Richard Doyle (1849; see pp. 190–91). These fairy books achieved a solid, continuing readership, precisely what juvenile publishers always sought; they would be steady sellers for many years, provided the publishers avoided design or pricing mistakes. So Alexander MacMillan commissioned his friend the writer Dinah Maria Craik (1826–1887) to edit what he hoped would become the ultimate anthology for his own list, sending her copies of Planché and Grimm, and suggesting that she should consult the vast pre-Revolution *Cabinet des Fées* in the British Museum.

Though her books are now largely forgotten, Mrs Craik was an able writer. Her collection, entitled *The Fairy Book: The Best Popular Fairy Stories Selected and Rendered Anew* (1863), was very successful, and continued to be reprinted until the 1920s. Mrs Craik left out 'Blue Beard', the story so often alleged to cause bad dreams and night terrors, but she included 'Snow White' and 'Puss in Boots', which were both pretty gruesome in many ways. She was not a **bowdleriser**, nor fearful of frightening her readers. Her publisher, MacMillan, did very well from the contract.

Another publisher who noted Mrs Craik's success was Longman, who commissioned the well-known folklorist and scholar Andrew Lang to produce a similar collection. In fact, much of the writing was by Mrs Lang, but *The Blue Fairy Book* of 1889 was enormously popular – and Lang's other, later coloured fairy books were equally successful (see p. 191). Like Mrs Craik, Lang refused to include modern fairy stories – believing them markedly inferior to the old favourites – but stayed with the old, classical, out-of-copyright stories. This simply opened the field to

authors who wanted to try their hands at writing new fairy tales, and to publishers wanting to break into this very profitable niche market.

The now largely forgotten *Diamond Fairy Book* (1897), *Emerald Fairy Book* (1901) and others published by Raphael Tuck enabled such writers as Margery Williams to get their work into print (see pp. 138–9). Other writers and illustrators created their own markets, notably in Australasia (see pp. 194–5), and enterprising Japanese publishers, too, ensured that Western booksellers would have access to Japanese stories (see pp. 182–3).

By the mid-Victorian period there was an abundance of juvenile literature, as Mrs Molesworth made clear in her *Carrots* (1876):

I should think *everybody's* grandfathers and grandmothers had an 'Evenings at home' among their few, dearly-prized children's books. Do you know how very few these books were? ...

Now-a-days, when you have galloped through all the brilliant blue and green and scarlet little volumes that have been given to you on birthdays and Christmas Days, you come with a melancholy face to your mother and tell her you have 'nothing to read.' And then, most likely, when your mother goes to the library, she chooses a book for you out of the 'juvenile department,' and when it is done, you get another, till you can hardly remember what you have read and what you haven't ...

Not so was it long ago. Not only had no children many books, but everywhere, children had the same!

By Edwardian times, when books for children were cheaper and more widely available than ever before, children might have felt they were better off; but they did not always, as

Edith Stokes (echoing Mrs Molesworth) commented, on her own mother reading to the children:

We took turns in sitting beside her so that the one sitting beside her could see the book and she read to us. Reading was quite a feature, all the traditional things of course: George Macdonald and Mrs Gaskell ... *Lob-by-the-Fire* and *Jackanapes* and Mrs Ewing and Mrs Molesworth and the fairy tales. The Andrew Lang fairy tales were a great feature, the blue one and the red one and Grimm's and Andersen. But not books again like the children have today, I mean; you didn't really have any *new* books for children. It was just all those books.

'Just all those books': Victorian children, of course, found their own ways to interpret books available to them. M. V. Hughes, writing about her childhood holidays in Cornwall in the 1880s, recalled how the group of children would take a book into a secret treehouse:

... a great point being read aloud in turn. We took much pleasure in prophesying the events. We could rely on Providence to punish the naughty and bring to notice the heroism of the good, and generally grant an early death to both. Why was there a bull in the field? *To gore the disobedient.* Why did cholera break out? *To kill the child who went down a forbidden street.* The names told us much: Tom, Sam and Jack were predestined to evil, while a Frank could do nothing but good ...We had bettings of gooseberries on such points.

Those games in Cornwall were fun, but also provided a way for the children to inure themselves to the frights they encountered in their other reading. Being frightened is a part of almost every child's early life. It might be

quite unconscious: the fear in the timorous, young Maurice Sendak of his boisterous uncles who, when coming to dinner, told him he 'looked so good we could eat you up' was the episode which eventually led to him writing *Where the Wild Things Are* (see pp. 196–7).

Many authors, of course, deliberately use fear or apprehension to attract readers and make their work successful. Even though it can be argued that such masters as Sheridan Le Fanu, M. R. James, Edgar Allan Poe or Ambrose Bierce wrote for adult audiences, there's no doubt that children took possession of their stories, as they did *Gulliver's Travels*. Testing yourself to overcome fear is commonplace, but it doesn't always work: writing in the 1930s, Harvey Darton confessed that after fifty years he couldn't rid his mind of the 'fearful creation ... endowed with terror' in one of Lucy Clifford's *Anyhow Stories* of 1882; not the reaction intended by the publisher, but reported by other children scared by Mrs Clifford's writing.

Mrs W. K. [Lucy] Clifford, *Anyhow Stories: Moral and Otherwise.* London: MacMillan and Co., 1882. The stories were perhaps unintentionally frightening, yet there is certainly something unsettling in the contortions of the gauged-eyed children on the rail in Dorothy Tennant's frontispiece.
The British Library

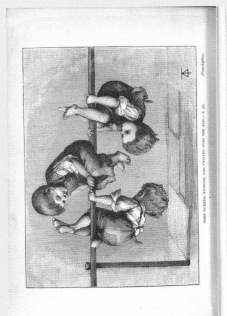

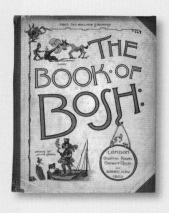

The Book of Bosh. London; Sydney: Griffith Farran Okeden & Welsh, 1889. The cautionary tales demonstrate the consequences of 'bad' behaviour by naughty children, who invariably get their comeuppance. The transgressions are often fairly minor – and the punishments not as harsh as those meted out by *Struwwelpeter*'s Great Long Red-Legged Scissor Man to Suck-a-Thumb (he chopped those digits off) nor Belloc's Matilda (who told lies and was burned).

The British Library

One well-known frightener, *Struwwelpeter*, has its admirers and detractors, but was also taken deliberately as a model for later books, such as *The Book of Bosh* issued in 1889 and Hilaire Belloc's hilarious *Cautionary Tales for Children*, 1907. Though dedicated to Edward Lear, *Bosh* has much closer similarity to Hoffmann's book. Its success came from its inclusion of laughably severe punishments for minor peccadilloes (such as 'The Piteous Story of Willie Cootes', 'who never, never wiped his boots'.

Later authors and illustrators of frightening tales included the American Edward Gorey, whose version (posthumously published in 2002) of Belloc's *Cautionary Tales* delighted his adult admirers too; many young Gorey readers continue to gain pleasure from his beautifully drawn pseudo-frighteners.

Victorian sentimentality was exploited by many children's authors: Kingsley's *Water Babies* and several of Mrs Ewing's stories did just this (see p. 187). As Francis Jacox commented in *Temple Bar* (1868), 'if anybody can get a pretty little girl to die prattling to her brothers and sisters, and quoting texts of Scripture with appropriate gasps, dashes, and broken sentences, he may send half the women in London, with tears in their eyes, to Mr. Mudie's or Mr. Booth's'. These fashionable circulating libraries were of great commercial significance, and authors, often quite unconsciously, adapted their work to perceived demand.

Kate Greenaway, in her illustrations as much as in her writing, took a different approach, and the extreme and unrealistic innocence she conveyed set a new model for life, brilliantly exploited commercially by Liberty & Co. (and others) for a range of clothing (see p. 188). Though the inspiration was often tacit, Liberty & Co. directly acknowledged it in some instances, such as the wording of an advertisement for a 'Kate Greenaway ... frock in muslin with a silk sash'

(borrowed from her *Marigold Garden*) in Liberty's 'Fancy Dress for Children', 1899, Sheet 35. Such modest, pretty clothes were popular with parents. Greenaway herself was not unaware of the comic side of such costumes, writing in her poem, 'Three Bonnets', of rude little boys who mocked the girls in their outfits, '"My Eye! Three Grannies out to-day!"' Walter Crane put it more delicately: 'May I confess that (for me at least) I think she overdid the big bonnet rather.' Greenaway's prim, over-sweet and immaculately clean little girls charmed many women, but male readers generally preferred the more robust work of Caldecott and Crane. They, along with Greenaway, can be regarded as the founders of the modern picture book.

Producing such books drew on the skills of publisher, author, illustrator, printer and binder; the increasing size of editions, and the number of children's books being printed, introduced fresh pressures. The developing mechanisation of book production could lead to substantial financial losses: a mistake in the process could destroy a publisher.

In large integrated businesses, such as Blackie or Collins, or Nelson in Scotland, or Marcus Ward in Belfast, employing a good design manager (such as Talwin Morris for Blackie, or Thomas Crane for Marcus Ward) was of great significance. Sometimes a staff artist would undertake some of these duties. Most publishing firms were family-owned or partnerships, and one of the partners would look after production matters. Disagreements between partners could result in firms ceasing to trade (as with Marcus Ward in 1899). Effective management of sales was vitally important, too. The development of **subscription publishing** had a very considerable effect on book distribution in the United States: we know quite a lot about Mark Twain's foray into this area (see p. 150), but its effect on book production overall seems to have been little studied.

The Fairy-Tale Revival

When the Grimm brothers started to collect stories in Germany, they founded the study of folklore. Their collection has been quarried by authors, translators and artists ever since.

It is impossible to know how Jacob Grimm (1785–1863) and his brother Wilhelm Grimm (1786–1859) first became interested in traditional tales while they were students at Marburg University. Much of their research was done as librarians at Kassel and their *Kinder und Hausmärchen* (*Children's and Household Tales*) was first published in 1812. The Grimms' technique was not well developed in scholarly terms, nor at first was their text composed to be read by children. However, the Grimms adapted their stories for a juvenile readership, and in 1825 published their *Kleine Ausgabe* ('small edition') with fifty tales selected for children. *Kinder und Hausmärchen* attracted people throughout Europe, just as the folk tales collected by Sir Walter Scott and Crofton Croker appealed widely to readers (see pp. 240–41).

In England, the first translations were made (anonymously) by a lawyer, Edgar Taylor (1793–1839), whose sister Emily was well known for her children's books. Taylor's capable translation, published in 1823, was illustrated by the caricaturist and illustrator

BELOW
Jacob and Wilhelm Grimm, *Kinder und Hausmärchen*, 1819. The frontispiece and lovely title-page decoration is by the Grimms' brother Ludwig Emil (engravings by L. Haas). The 1840 edition featured Ludwig's portrait of Dorothea Viehmännin, one of the main sources of the tales. In the original German, the tales – not intended for children – were grimmer by far than many readers are aware (or Disney's anodyne versions would ever allow): Cinderella's stepsisters, for instance, cut off parts of their feet to fit them into the glass slipper, and it was Snow White's natural mother, not her stepmother, who wanted her dead.

Dr Ralph Schippan, Düsseldorf

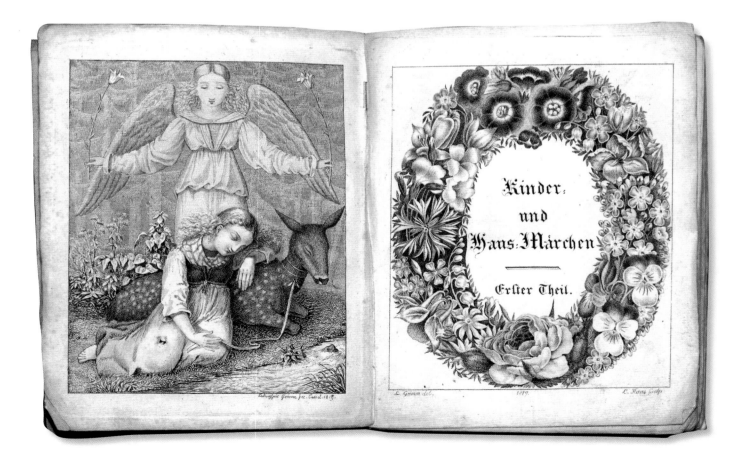

George Cruikshank (1792–1878), already
famous for his engravings (in June 1820
King George IV had Cruikshank paid £100
'not to caricature His Majesty in any immoral
situation'). Cruikshank's delicate etchings
for the *German Popular Stories* (1823), as it
was titled in English, were particularly fine.
John Ruskin, in his *Elements of Drawing*
(1857) recalled the vignettes, remembered
from his nursery days, as 'the finest things,
next to Rembrandt's, that ... have been done
since etching was invented', and advised
readers chancing across the books to 'pounce
on them instantly' – high praise indeed.
The Taylor/Cruickshank version of the
Grimm stories has since been reprinted in
innumerable editions.

The stories collected by the brothers
Grimm have always attracted young readers:
every child must have memories of Rapunzel
letting down her hair, and of Rumpelstiltskin,
or Snow White, or Cinderella trying on her
glass slipper – even if only from the debased
versions marketed by Disney.

The graphic possibilities of the Grimm

stories have attracted many artists, as well as
the publishers of juvenile books, throughout
the world. English readers, tired of, or
frightened by, Cruikshank's etchings could
find a huge range of editions illustrated by
artists of mixed abilities and sensibility, such
as Walter Crane (Macmillan & Co., 1882),
Arthur Rackham (Freemantle & Co., 1900)
Helen Stratton (Blackie, 1903) or Charles
Folkard (A. & C. Black, 1911). These
illustrated editions were often aiming at the
gift-book market. Although the production
of such editions diminished after 1914, they
were still produced, a notable one being a
version of *Hansel and Gretel* by the Dane Kay
Nielsen (Hodder & Stoughton, 1925).

Later artists, writers and publishers have
also been attracted by the challenge presented
by the Grimm brothers. Some of the most
memorable (and frightening) illustrations
were by the brilliant writer and artist
Mervyn Peake (1911–68), made for Eyre &
Spottiswoode in 1946, when Peake's work
was at its best. Reportedly, Peake was paid
very poorly (his drawings for Lewis Carroll's
Hunting of the Snark earned him only £5 in
1941), and the publisher seems to have
thought that any version of the Grimms' tales
would be good enough to form their edition.
A tart review of a 2012 edition produced to
celebrate the centenary of the Grimms' work
welcomed the reprinting of Peake's lively and
characteristic line illustrations, but pointed
out that the publisher had used a mixture of
stories by different translators, some in an
arch, high-Victorian style, others in more
colloquial English. This is not the way to
produce a good book for children, but was all
too common in the past, and, as this example
shows, is not unheard of in the present day.

Japonisme for the Nursery

The fashion for Japanese arts and crafts swept into Europe from the 1860s onwards, and the little books published by Hasegawa Takejirō introduced Japan to Western children.

The opening up of Japan in early Victorian times enabled Europeans to see the exquisite art of the country. Japanese arts were first introduced to the West through Dutch traders, and displayed in London, and later Paris, at the International Exhibitions of Art and Industry in 1862 and 1867. Very soon people were collecting the wood-cut *ukiyo-e* prints by Hiroshige or Hokusai being sold in La Porte Chinoise (a smart Parisian shop selling Japanese articles and prints), and in London Arthur Liberty built his shop from the sale of Japanese fabrics. Puccini's opera *Madame Butterfly* and Gilbert and Sullivan's *The Mikado* reflected the fascination with

LEFT AND ABOVE
The Boy Who Drew Cats. Japanese Fairy Tale Series, no. 23. Rendered into English by Lafcadio Hearn. Tokyo, T. Hasegawa, 1898. A *chirimen-bon* (crêpe-paper) edition beautifully illustrated by Suzuki Kason, it was the first of five books translated for Hasegawa by Hearn, who enlarged on a traditional tale – his eerie warning 'Avoid large places at night, keep to small' thrilled this author as a child.
The British Library; Tokyo Printing Museum

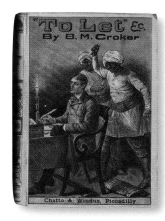

Japan, while artists inspired by the *ukiyo-e*
prints ranged from Degas, Manet, Monet and
Pissarro to Tissot, Klimt and Van Gogh.

In the 1880s, an enterprising Tokyo
importer of Western goods and publications,
Hasegawa Takejirō (1853–1938), began
publishing a series of what would become
nearly thirty small books of Japanese fairy
tales, with the texts translated into English,
and illustrated with traditional wood-cuts
made for him by Kobayashi Eitaku (1843–90)
and Suzuki Kason (1860–1919). Hasegawa's
translators (mostly American) included
Lafcadio Hearn. One of the best known was
the very scary *The Boy Who Drew Cats*, first
published in 1898. Its plot concerns a
farmer's boy who compulsively draws cats,
and only cats, rather than attend to his
studies: the habit gets him into hot water, but
is ultimately his saving grace. (It seems
Hearn made this gruesome story more

frightening with the additions he made:
'translation' is an imprecise word for writers
dealing with children's books.)

Hasegawa marketed his books through
a variety of overseas publishers he knew
through his book importation business.
In London, they were distributed by the
long-established firm of Griffith, Farran &
Company; Kelly & Walsh (in Shanghai)
distributed them in eastern Asia. Elsewhere,
versions in French, German, Portuguese
and Swedish also appeared – Hasegawa's
marketing skills were strong, and the stories
in his Japanese Fairy Tales series were very
beguiling, particularly when printed on crêpe
paper (**chirimen-bon**). The use of this
traditional format and of bright, water-based
inks for printing created books for the
nursery quite unlike anything else published
for children. They must have been issued in
the thousands, but they were (like so many
small children's books) fragile, and few
people valued them. Their attrition rate must
have been very high, but today they are
treasured.

Western children's books dealing with
Asia were totally different. They ranged from
the early moralising of Mrs Sherwood's
amazingly successful *Little Henry and his
Bearer* (1814) to ghost stories, not necessarily
written specifically for children, but spine-
tinglingly enjoyed by them, like the works of
Kipling. His *The Phantom Rickshaw & Other
Eerie Tales* was first published in India in the
Indian Railway Library Series in 1888.
Another writer of ghost stories who used
an Indian setting to enrich their plots and
atmosphere was the Irish Bithia Croker
(c.1848–1920), who whiled away her many
years following her husband from one
military cantonment to another by writing
romantic novels and stories which (though
now forgotten) had quite a loyal readership a
century ago.

Grim Tales before Bedtime

Many children's books have frightened their child readers, but one Victorian book, by a Frankfurt physician, became a world classic.

When Prince Albert of Saxe-Coburg-Gotha married Queen Victoria in 1840 there were already significant links in Britain with printing and publishing in Germany – such as Edgar Taylor's translation of the Grimms' *Kinder und Hausmärchen* (1812–15), omitting some of the scarier passages, as *German Popular Stories* (1823). It was so successful that 'Grimm' became known to all English children.

Then in 1844 Heinrich Hoffmann (1809–94), a physician working in Frankfurt, wrote some rhymes to entertain and instruct his three-year-old son. A friend persuaded Hoffmann to publish them, which he did, as *Lustige Geschichten und drollige Bilder* (*Funny Stories and Droll Pictures*, 1845), with his own crude, amateurish pictures as illustrations.

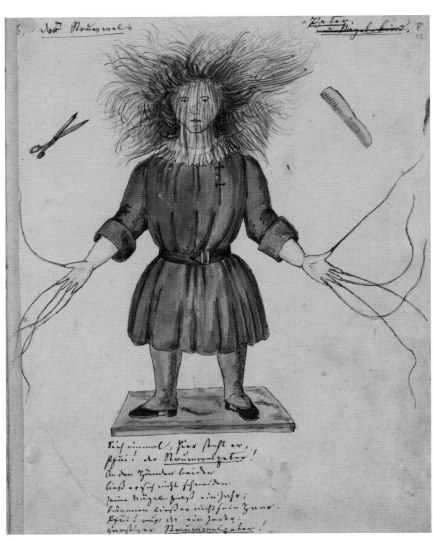

ABOVE
Heinrich Hoffman, manuscript drawing for *Funny Stories and Droll Pictures*. 1844. Pencil, watercolour and ink on paper. This drawing of an unkempt 'Shock-headed Peter' was made by Hoffmann on Christmas Eve that year as a gift for his three-year-old son. It is instantly recognisable as the cover image of what, from the third published edition (in 1876) became known as *Der Struwwelpeter*: a worldwide success, with numerous editions and endless pastiches.
Germanisches Nationalmuseum, Nuremberg. HS 100921

LEFT
Heinrich Hoffman, *The English Struwwelpeter, or Pretty Stories and Funny Pictures for Little Children.* After the ... German ... of H. H. Leipzig: 1848. With tight control over the copyright, this early (fourth) edition was printed under license.
The British Library

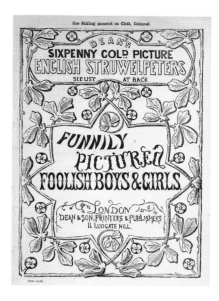

Hoffmann had discovered early on that using laughter and nonsense helped to deter children from undesirable habits, such as cruelty to animals, playing with matches, or sucking their thumbs. The cautionary message was reinforced by his arresting and often frightening pictures.

As an author, Hoffmann was almost as demanding as Lewis Carroll was to be about *Alice in Wonderland*. He had strong beliefs about the bookbinding (not too strong), and insisted the price should be set low, so purchasers would think 'Why! It costs less than one guilder'. He supervised the illustrations very closely, saying that 'the artist was compelled to copy stroke by stroke exactly, and I checked every one of the stones'. Despite (or perhaps because of) Hoffmann's fussiness, his intentionally 'amateurish' book was a great success, selling over 20,000 copies in Germany before an English edition appeared in February 1848. Prussia, Saxony and Brunswick had signed a copyright convention with Britain in 1846, so Hoffman had legal protection for the English edition. Hoffmann and his German publisher could therefore control the distribution of *The English Struwwelpeter* in Britain, and so, for

the rest of the century, all copies of the English-language version (nominally published by a variety of London publishers) were printed in Germany. Later London-based publishers such as Raphael Tuck and Ernest Nister used German printers for their work until the First World War.

The English Struwwelpeter was more than a straight translation: its translator (possibly the Anglo-German Alexander Platt, 1819–83) skilfully integrated the outlandish comedy of Hoffmann's drawings with the text, making the English book funnier than its original. Hoffmann's book was assimilated into the British comic-verse tradition, and the word 'Struwwelpeter' into the British vocabulary. Nonetheless Hoffmann's book always remained troublesome to some adults, listed on one website (in 2016) under the heading of 'recommended inappropriate books for kids'. While the internet is full of dire warnings about its effects on the child's imagination, *Struwwelpeter* continues to delight generations of children, and provides ongoing food for debate for scores of psychological and literary interpreters. Much can also be said about the American artist Edward Gorey (1925–2000). His *Gashlycrumb Tinies* (1962) is likewise a recommended 'inappropriate' book for children's enjoyment. The listing could include any one of Gorey's unsettling picture books written between the 1950s and his death in 2000. Beautifully crafted, sophisticated and witty, many of his picture books, like *The Unstrung Harp* (1953) or the hilarious *The Curious Sofa: A Pornographic Tale* (1961), were clearly intended for an adult readership. His large range of alphabet books, and small books such as *The Pious Infant* or *The Chinese Obelisks*, reveal his familiarity with Victorian children's books, but Gorey's work is much more than a pastiche of these: for grown-ups or children, his books continue to please in later life.

Chimney Sweeps and Boy Soldiers

The Water Babies was one of the most discussed, admired and read children's books of the Victorian era, but its fame has not helped it to survive; and *Jackanapes* is nearly forgotten.

The clergyman Charles Kingsley (1819–75), with Thomas Hughes, the author of *Tom Brown's School Days* (see pp. 158–9), was one of the best-known 'Christian Socialists' who emerged in response to the failure of the Chartist movement in 1848. Kingsley's propagandist novels, such as *Yeast* (1848) and *Alton Locke* (1850) attracted much attention; and his enthusiastic and well-prepared introduction to natural history, *Glaucus, or, The Wonders of the Shore* (1855) showed another facet of this extraordinary man. *Glaucus* persuaded Darwin to send Kingsley an advance copy of *On the Origin of Species* in 1859, and this was the trigger for him to start work on *The Water Babies*.

Kingsley was widely read and fervently interested in many fields; but he was also easily distracted. His *Water Babies*, serialised in *Macmillan's Magazine* (1862–3), started as a story for his own children, attacking the use of small boys to sweep chimneys. By the end of this very long, discursive book, Kingsley had sent the little chimney sweeper on an evolutionary moral journey, with lengthy passages on the nature of scientific evidence, American politics, fashion, sanitation, school examinations and many other irrelevancies. The book had many virtues, yet was a failure. Kingsley, writing the instalments as MacMillan was publishing them, needed (but never received) a much more severe editor to eliminate its faults. With his well-intentioned garrulity, the book was meandering and overlong. He also made no attempt to avoid giving offence – freely attacking Africans, the Irish, Catholics and others.

'Oh don't hurt me!' cried Tom, 'I only want to look at you; you are so handsome!', from Charles Kingsley, *The Water Babies: A Fairy Tale for a Land Baby*. New York: Dodd, Mead & Co., 1916, p. 140. The first edition (1863) contained just two line drawings, but it was later often richly illustrated, by Mabel Lucie Attwell and Heath Robinson among others. This edition was one of the most successful, with its delicate watercolours by Jessie Willcox Smith (1863–1935), a popular illustrator who had studied under Howard Pyle.

Library of Congress, Washington D.C., Prints & Photographs Division, CAI – Smith (J. W.), no. 4

Juliana Horatia Ewing, *Jackanapes*. With illustrations by R. Caldecott. London: Society for Promoting Christian Knowledge, 1884 [1883]. It first appeared in *Aunt Judy's Magazine* in October 1879, and was published separately by the SPCK four years later, priced at one shilling. It was superbly illustrated by Caldecott, whom Ewing met in June 1879, immediately commissioning from him an initial illustration for her tale of the boy soldier Jackanapes while it was still, as her sister recorded, 'simmering in [her] brain'.

The British Library

Despite this, in abridged forms *The Water Babies* continued to be recommended until the mid-20th century. Attempts to revive his book as reading for children have failed, but in the academic world, Kingsley's chaotic text (and particularly his irrelevancies) provides a rich field for those who want to understand better the nature of Victorian culture.

Almost equally popular in its day was the short *Jackanapes* by Juliana Horatia Ewing, daughter of Margaret Gatty (who, like Kingsley, wrote on natural history for children, notably her popular *Parables from Nature*, produced between 1855 and 1871). Mrs Gatty started *Aunt Judy's Magazine* in 1866 (see p. 169), intending that every article should have a moral for its young reader. Many were written by Juliana (for whom the magazine was named), a children's author whose very readable work strongly influenced Kipling and E. Nesbit. Ewing was the author of the short story 'The Brownies', whose name was adopted by Baden-Powell for the younger Girl Guides. Mrs Ewing had a life linked with the military, spending years with her husband in New Brunswick (Canada) and later in Aldershot (England). Disliking the increasingly material and commercial attitudes she found in contemporary Victorian civilian life, she saw the military ethos as a source of strength.

Jackanapes, the tale of a boy soldier, was written while British society was buzzing with gossip about the death of Napoléon, the French Prince Imperial, killed in a skirmish in the Zulu War of June 1879. It was set during the Battle of Waterloo, rather than later during the colonial campaigns. Less cloyingly sentimental than many Victorian heroic books, it continued to be read by British children for many years. National moods have changed about war, duty and sacrifice, and it is unlikely that future generations will find the same rewards as Kipling did in Mrs Ewing's work.

Innocence, Untouched by Poverty, Illness or Sin

Under the Window formed the model for a popular (but very unreal)
view of children's life.

Kate Greenaway (1846–1901) is one of the best known of the Victorian children's illustrators, and famous also for the way Liberty and other fashion shops seized on her images to create a new range of children's clothing.

At first, there was very little to point forward to her success: the daughter of a poor wood-engraver working in Islington, Kate studied art at Finsbury School of Art (following the curriculum devised by Henry Cole for designer-craftsmen), and in 1869 her first pictures were published. By the 1870s she was producing illustrations for Frederick Warne & Co.; and also for greetings cards for the Belfast-based firm of Marcus Ward, first notable for the copybooks it printed for Vere Foster for use in the Irish school system (see pp. 96–7). Kate was encouraged by Hugh Loftie, editor of *People's Magazine* (1867–73) by the Society for Promoting Christian

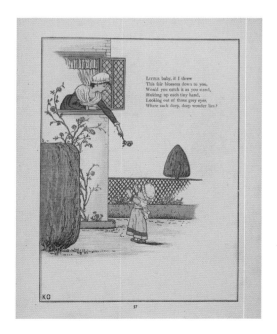

LEFT AND ABOVE

Kate Greenaway, *Under the Window*. Pictures and Rhymes by K. G. Engraved and printed by E. Evans.
London: Frederick Warne & Co., [1879], title page and p. 38. The infants, including small boys too
young for trousers, wear Greenaway's neo-Regency dress (quickly adopted by Liberty & Co. for its
progressive 'Aesthetic'-leaning customers). Evans reproduced the paintings by chromoxylography,
from hand-engraved wood-blocks, with charming results. Greenaway's nostalgic style is not without
its critics; Maurice Sendak, referring to the later *Mother Goose* (1881), described her work as 'a lovely
but antiseptic affair ... [with] a chilly Victorianism at the heart of her prim interpretation'.

The British Library

Knowledge, who published her work in it.

Kate was ambitious. She quarrelled with Marcus Ward & Co., who turned down some of her verses, and turned instead to the engraver/printer Edmund Evans, a friend of the Greenaway family, to publish her *Under the Window*. Her text was less than perfect, but was polished up by the poet Frederick Locker. Edmund Evans's book was very well executed, and displayed the artist's illustrations at their best. Her mixture of pictures and text was unusual, and the book attracted buyers right from its first publication in 1879. It sold very well, with initial sales of 70,000 copies (the publisher's initial printing of 20,000 (viewed as optimistic for a 6s. book) had to be rapidly increased) – earning Greenaway £7,000, and creating the 'enchanting and enchanted private nursery world', as Harvey Darton described it. 'The Greenaway vogue' was under way.

Success of this kind created immediate imitators; notably in the United States, where the McLoughlin Brothers issued their own distortions 'after Kate Greenaway', as they proclaimed on the covers of their books. American piracies were nothing new, but Edmund Evans, Greenaway and others

complained bitterly about the English pastiche created by the artist J. G. Sowerby. Sowerby (1850–1914) was a good painter, and his *Afternoon Tea*, published by Frederick Warne in 1880, seized on the Greenaway style. Though inferior in the quality of its colour printing, the book bore comparison with Greenaway's work.

Modern feminist critics, deeply interested in Kate Greenaway and her style, suggest that Sowerby didn't really understand or like what Greenaway was doing; instead *Afternoon Tea* showed male figures taking charge on the page, guiding girls in their play, or leading fearful females, or getting into mischief. Possibly Sowerby, like many male readers, found the idealism in Greenaway's prim, over-sweet pictures too false for his own view of child life; but his attempt at a more 'masculine' interpretation of Greenaway's style has received little support.

Although *Afternoon Tea* was never reprinted by Warne, Sowerby produced some other Greenaway-influenced books. These were published by Marcus Ward & Co., then under the artistic direction of Thomas Crane (the older brother of the artist Walter Crane). Thomas Crane was a very capable book designer, and such books as *At Home* (1881) and *At Home Again* (1886) have been described as among the loveliest books of the period. Whether they made money for the publisher is unknown, but the competition with Greenaway disappeared: the partnership of Marcus Ward & Co. ceased publishing in 1899 and Sowerby's books went out of print.

BELOW AND BELOW RIGHT
Afternoon Tea. Rhymes for Children, with ... illustrations by J. G. Sowerby & H. H. Emmerson. London: Warne & Co., [1880] and *At Home* [in verse]. Illustrated by J. G. Sowerby; decorated by T. Crane. London: Marcus Ward & Co., [1881]. Sowerby's images had less innocence, and a somewhat more knowing tone, than Greenaway's illustrations. Here, children sit before empty tea-plates, and one errant little girl is in the corner, presumably sent there to 'mend her ways'.
Author's collection (below)
The British Library (below right)

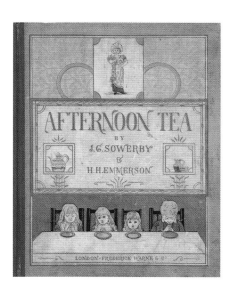

When Fairies Became Fashionable

Until Victorian times, publishing fairy tales was not a commercial success, but a growing demand persuaded publishers, artists and writers to give them serious attention.

Of the many men and women involved in the Victorian production of fairy books, two stand out for their roles in the continuing growth of the genre: one as an artist, the other as editor or re-teller of classic fairy stories.

Richard 'Dickie' Doyle (1824–83), famous for his cover design and other graphic work for the magazine *Punch*, became well known for his illustrations for children's books, including a selection from Grimm, Anthony Montalba's *Fairy Tales from All Nations* (1849) and Ruskin's *King of the Golden River* (1851; see p. 157). These were widely admired, and when Doyle discussed the possibility of a large expensive fairy book for the Christmas market with the publishers Longmans, they were enthusiastic.

In Fairyland: A Series of Pictures from the Elf-World (dated 1870, but published in December 1869) was one of the most elaborate and technically complex children's

Richard Doyle, *In Fairy Land: A Series of Pictures from the Elf-World. With a Poem by William Allingham*. London: Longmans, Green and Co., 1870. Frontispiece for this lavish production. Allingham's verse, as an afterthought of the publisher, in part failed to contain Doyle's magnificent and capricious vision, but nonetheless the result has been described as 'the most impressive children's book of the 19th century' – if not the most commercially successful.

The British Library

Andrew Lang (ed.), *The Blue Fairy Book.* With Numerous Illustrations by H. J. Ford and G. P. Jacomb Hood. London: Longmans, Green and Co., 1889. The 12-book series drew widely on the wealth of fairy lore worldwide; it was the first time many of these tales appeared in English. This volume contains some of the best-known tales. Modern reprints are available and, as seen from the Folio Society's new editions using fresh illustrations, the market for well-printed fairy books is still strong.

Private collection

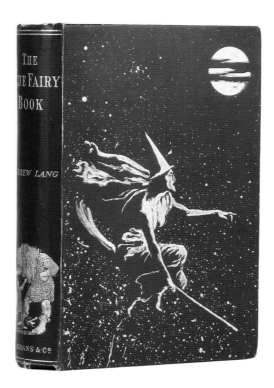

three-quarters were still unsold when Longmans attempted to relaunch the book in 1875. Longman and Doyle never worked together again.

One man well aware of Doyle's *In Fairyland* was the Scot Andrew Lang (1844–1912). Anthropologist, poet, historian, brilliant essay-writer and journalist, Lang was active in the Folk-Lore Society. Whether the idea for the stories came from Lang or his publishers is uncertain, but Longmans made sure to avoid the problems they had earlier faced with Doyle. They commissioned Henry Justice Ford (1860–1941), a successful English illustrator (like Lang, with a background in the classics), whose work was very much in the pre-Raphaelite style.

Lang's *Blue Fairy Book* was published in 1889, at a price of 6s., in a relatively small edition of 5,000 copies. It was followed in 1890 by the *Red Fairy Book* in an edition of twice that number. The Longman/Lang/Ford formula was very successful, and though Lang wrote in the *Green Fairy Book* (1892) that it would probably be the last, ten Fairy Books had been issued by 1910, with all of the volumes remaining in print.

But were Lang's Fairy Books really by Lang at all? His name was well known in the publishing world; his wife Leonora Blanche Alleyne Lang (1851–1933) was a willing helper, and Andrew Lang acknowledged that they had been 'almost wholly the work of Mrs. Lang, who has translated and adapted them ...' As an Oxford don, he adopted a calculatedly effete manner, and his throwaway description of his own role was, 'My part has been that of Adam, according to Mark Twain, in the Garden of Eden. Eve worked, Adam superintended. I also superintend. I find out where the stories are, and advise, and, in short, superintend.' Few feminists are likely to find this remotely amusing – but nonetheless the volumes are still called Andrew Lang's Fairy Books.

books of the century. But when the publishers first saw Doyle's beautiful drawings they were perplexed by their episodic nature, and (perhaps) whether the pictures were really intended for children, or just *about* children. Alarmed as well as enchanted by Doyle's work, Longmans recruited the Irish poet William Allingham (1824–89) to write a poem to provide a backbone for the pictures. Allingham was a good choice, but, unfortunately, Longmans failed to bring the artist and the poet into personal contact, so the poem was hardly integral to Doyle's envisaged work.

Despite this setback, with its plates superbly produced by Edmund Evans this folio volume (unusual in books for children) was very attractive. It received warm reviews, but priced at a guinea and a half (£1-11s. 6d.), it was too expensive, when most children's books then cost around 6s. It proved a commercial failure, and of the small edition printed (just some 2,000 copies), nearly

'An Awfully Big Adventure': Peter Pan, the Boy Who Wouldn't Grow Up

J. M. Barrie's tale became a perennial classic, yet few readers are aware of the tragic provenance of the quixotic boy-adventurer.

For readers unfamiliar with J. M. Barrie's 1902 novel *The Little White Bird*, Peter Pan's provenance is obscure. It is Peter's first appearance, as a week-old baby. He, 'like all infants' once part-bird, is still able to recall his powers of flying and flits through his nursery window into Kensington Gardens. There, befriended by fairies, he is stranded, unable to return to his grieving parents, and so becomes 'lost' and motherless. The theme of lost boys pervades the tales; indeed, Peter in origin is 'only half human' – a psychopomp figure who serves to carry other 'lost' children to Neverland. The death of Barrie's elder brother David when Barrie was just six was a tragedy which deeply affected his own mother. Barrie later recalled that she took comfort in knowing her son would now never grow up and leave her, and Barrie's tale begins with loss and ends with the mention of childhood death.

Barrie enlarged on the character with his play, *Peter Pan, or, The Boy Who Wouldn't Grow Up*, first performed at the Duke of York Theatre in London on 27 December 1904,

'Away he flew, right over the houses to the gardens'; from J. M. Barrie, *Peter Pan in Kensington Gardens*. London: Hodder & Stoughton, 1906. The wayward Peter eventually attempts a return, to discover his mother has given birth to another child. Barring the windows to prevent a second escape, she has unwittingly shut Peter out, and is unable to hear, at the window, the cries of her heartbroken son. For this author, at least, as a child his mother's rejection was a tragedy of unthinkable proportions. The book contains fifty colour plates and three line drawings by Arthur Rackham, who picks up the impish, anarchic nature of Barrie's goat-riding Peter.

The British Library

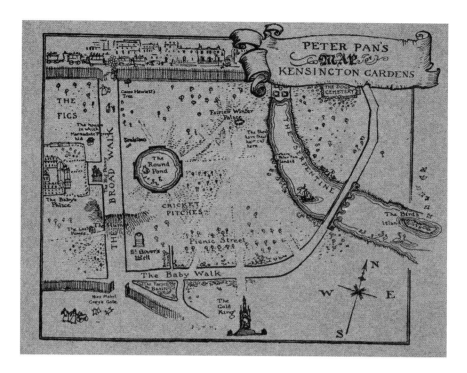

'Peter Pan's Kensington Gardens'; from J. M. Barrie, *Peter Pan in Kensington Gardens*. London: Hodder & Stoughton, 1906. The map from *The Little White Bird* is revised for the 1906 book, turning the whole of the Gardens into a fantasy land for its young readers. By the Round Pond are old parish boundary stones, turned by Barrie into grave markers ('I think that quite the most touching sight in the Gardens is the two tombstones ... Here Peter found the two babes, who had fallen unnoticed from their perambulators ...').

The British Library

and then in his book *Peter Pan in Kensington Gardens* (1906) which repeats the text of chapters 13 to 18 of *The Little White Bird*.

But it was through *Peter and Wendy* (1911) that Peter perhaps became best known. In it, the considerably older, fly-by-night and motherless Peter attaches himself to the Darling family children, and in particular to Wendy, whom he leads to Neverland to mother other abandoned children known as the Lost Boys. The children's dog Nana, based on Barrie's Newfoundland Luath (often portrayed as a St Bernard), is a reassuringly ever-present companion, to some extent filling the maternal gap as the children play.

Peter is complex, a mysterious and hardly likeable protagonist: a somewhat sly outsider whom the children take into their world, as he, more dangerously, takes them into his. Walt Disney's anodyne and two-dimensional, though hugely popular, film (RKO Pictures, 1953), shies away from the complexities of Peter's character and instead takes the viewer

on a thrilling animated ride. Life, for Peter, *is* always and expressly, 'an adventure'.

Peter's underlying anarchy appeals to children's need to test boundaries, and the frisson of pleasure and fear with which they meet the dreadful Captain Hook only adds to the appeal of the story. Fictional dangers may serve us as a rehearsal for later real-life difficulties or frights, to which we may respond as we learned to in childhood – or, frightened, by yearning for childish comforts. It is no accident, perhaps, that during the First World War (that most awful adventure of them all), trenches and blockhouses were named after characters from the book: Peter Pan House, Hook Copse and Wendy Cottage among them.

One of the many killed in action at Flanders was Gerald du Maurier's nephew George Llewelyn Davies (1893–1915) of the Kings Royal Rifles. Barrie first met George (then aged four), his younger brother Jack, baby Peter and their nurse Mary Hodgson, in 1897, whilst walking his dog in Kensington Gardens. George became the inspiration for Peter (a fact he later came to resent) in the stories Barrie told to the boys and later developed in his play. George is supposed to have once exclaimed 'To die will be an awfully big adventure!', which became one of the book's most famous lines (though cut from the play during the 1914–18 war). When the boys' parents died (both from cancer in their forties), 'Uncle Jim' Barrie, by then close to the family, took on their guardianship. George, himself barely grown at twenty-one, was later shot through the head at St-Eloi outside Ypres, on 15 March 1915. It was less than eight miles from Peter Pan House.

In 1929, eight years before his own death, Barrie bequeathed the rights for *Peter Pan* to Great Ormond Street Hospital, made in perpetuity, a hugely valuable gift.

Fairies Flourishing Down Under

In America, the Puritan traditions discouraged the production of fairy tales for children. In Britain's Australasian colonies, the early settlers brought with them stories from 'home' and authors acclimatised them to their new surroundings.

Until the late 19th century, settlers relied largely on books imported from Britain and Ireland, and the links with 'home' remained very strong (see Chapter 4). The earliest successful children's books from 'down under' were for older children: Ethel Turner's *Seven Little Australians* (1884) set in New South Wales, which inspired the New Zealand novelist Esther Glen in 1917 to set her own story, *Six Little New Zealanders*, on a sheep farm in Canterbury. Both Turner and Glen's books were published in London before the First World War; having an English imprint was

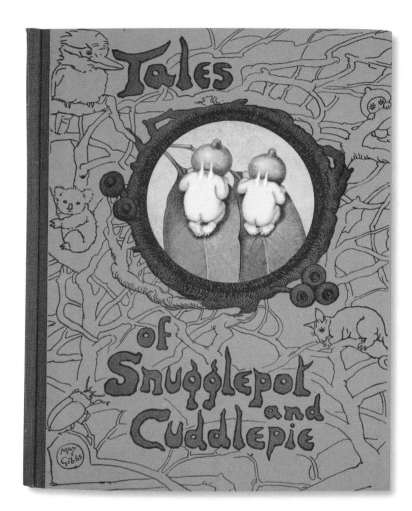

OFF TO THE WAR
Goodby my little Gum Blossom
And don't you fret for me
We'll soon be back together
In the Old Gum Tree

Copyright   May Gibbs

The beauty of the garden took her breath away.

thought essential for success in both countries.

For both authors and artists in the southern hemisphere, the call of London was very strong. The first important (Anglo-) Australian book illustrator, Cecilia May Gibbs (1877–1969), was born in Kent to two artist parents, and trained in London as an illustrator. Her first book, *About Us* (1912, originally entitled *Mimie and Wog, their Adventures in Australia*), was published in Britain by Ernest Nister, who had it printed in Bavaria, like so many children's books at that time.

May Gibbs had seen the huge range of fairy books being produced in London at the time, and when she returned to Australia in 1913 at the age of thirty-six she started drawing Australian fairies, the eucalyptus gumnut creatures first shown as a headpiece to Ethel Turner's story, *The Missing Button*. Gibbs's cute homunculi, or miniature 'bush-babies', which first appeared on the cover of the Australian literary magazine *Lone Hand* in January 1914, were enormously popular in Australia, where, reflecting some flavour (however far-fetched!) of the local landscape, they found a home in the local imagination. During the First World War she designed

many gumnut postcards; these were often used to boost the morale of Anzac troops overseas. Of the many books for children that she wrote and illustrated, her most successful, *Tales of Snugglepot and Cuddlepie*, published in Sydney by Angus and Robertson (1918), has remained in print in Australia ever since.

Equally popular in her time was Rhona Olive Harris (1903–91), always known as Pixie O'Harris. A Welsh-born commercial artist who moved to Australia in 1920, Pixie was the daughter of a very successful portrait painter. Pixie had her work exhibited in Wales by the age of fourteen, but her style was quite different from her father's. When settled in Sydney, Pixie worked in commercial art, and her later fairy paintings reflect both her early exposure to Art Nouveau, and her experience in fashion illustration.

O'Harris's first book was *The O.K. Fairy Book: New Rhymes and Pictures for Kiddies* (1923); her ambitious *Pearl Pinkie and Sea Greenie* (1935) was the most lavish children's book published by Angus and Robertson during the Depression. Pixie's drawings of fairies and sea sprites clothed in seaweed were all very pretty (in a rather knowing, Lolita-ish way), and appealed to young readers in Australia. But O'Harris was working at the end of the period when fairy books were in fashion, so she needed to find another field for her books. Her *Marmaduke the Possum* (1942) and other animal books also sold well. These were published in black and white originally, but several decades later they were republished in full colour, as part of Angus and Robertson's 1970s Young Australia Series of home-grown classics. Her books are still remembered fondly, and today the Australian Publishers Association gives the Pixie O'Harris Award to new authors and illustrators 'for Distinguished and Dedicated Service to the Development and Reputation of Australian Children's Books'.

Where the Wild Things Are

Children often enjoy being (gently) frightened – especially from the comfort of their bedtime stories. It is part of the learning process. One masterly example of such imaginative storytelling can be found in Maurice Sendak's most famous work.

Children have for generations been frightened or alarmed by uncertainties and threats in plots, or scary pictures. Most readers have memories of illustrations that as children they wished they hadn't seen, or of stories they don't want to remember in bed in the middle of the night. One might recall, for example, the terrifying ogre in Doré's illustrations of Perrault's tales, or even, at the lower end in the scale of frighteners, 'Dr Fell', with his cat-o'-nine-tails menacing from behind his back, in the otherwise (mostly) harmless *Ladybird Book of Nursery Rhymes*. 'Incipient darkness' is a spice which attracts many authors and illustrators. Perching somewhere at the more comfortable end of this wide scale of apprehension is

Maurice Sendak's *Where the Wild Things Are*.

For a book famous for its rumpus on the wild side, it had surprisingly anodyne beginnings: it was after seeing Disney's *Fantasia* that the twelve-year-old Maurice Sendak (1928–2012) decided to become an illustrator. This prolific Jewish-American artist and writer rapidly developed a very successful career, with his first book of illustrations (*Atomics for the Millions*) published when he was nineteen. His own writing for children started with *Kenny's Window*, published by Harper & Brothers in 1956. By the time of his death, Sendak had illustrated and written more than a hundred children's books. A thoughtful, intellectual artist, his enthusiasm for many writers and artists inspired his own large collection of

The former President and First Lady act 'wild' for a rapt young audience during Barack Obama's reading of *Where the Wild Things Are* at the annual Easter Egg Roll, at the White House, 2016. This tradition of Easter entertainments dates back to 1878, more recently including the First Families reading books to the children. Maurice Sendak's rambunctious *Wild Things* proved immensely popular, not least with the former President himself, who has selected the book on successive occasions.

Getty Images News

" She could not help noticing how strangely her grandmother seemed to be altered."

books by William Blake, Beatrix Potter, Meggendorfer, Caldecott and many others.

In some ways, with its darkly humorous undercurrents, Sendak's work reflected the earlier Yiddish work by the Nobel prizewinner Isaac Bashevis Singer. In 1966 he illustrated Singer's *Zlateh the Goat and Other Stories*, and later his own father's memoirs (*In Grandpa's House*, 1985), drawing on his Eastern European *shtetl* roots for both; but Sendak's undoubted masterpiece was his *Where the Wild Things Are*, published in 1963. Having sold 20-million-odd copies worldwide, this thrillingly vivid and sometimes dark tale, described as 'simply the epitome of a picture book', has received many awards and seals of approval: the Caldecott Medal, Hans Christian Andersen, and Astrid Lindgren Memorial awards in 1964, 1970 and 2003 respectively. The story was read aloud by President Obama to children attending the White House Easter Egg Roll in March 2016.

Sendak's status as one of the most important 20th-century children's illustrators is unquestioned.

In Britain, *Where the Wild Things Are* was equally lauded, though Sendak's later books, while widely admired, have proved less popular. One English obituarist, who perspicaciously described Sendak as 'at his finest a *shtetl* Blake', noted that his plots were full of worries (children being kidnapped, a dog going missing, or parents disappearing) and his pictures often unsettling. Another took a much more critical tone: while noting 'the immense artistry of the elaborate picture books' he condemned the later volumes in the trilogy *In the Night Kitchen* (1970) and *Outside Over There* (1981) for their ease of multiple interpretations, and for their incipient darkness. He argued that they had a self-indulgent quality absent from *Wild Things*. Only time will tell how well these books will continue to be read and enjoyed.

CHAPTER 9

Heroes in Action: Time-Travel, Detection and Derring-Do

In this chapter, we concentrate on the stories written for older children and adolescents in the mid-20th century. Authors and readers were familiar with the disastrous effects of the conflicts of the First World War, but though its themes of trench warfare, social collapse and revolution had their place in writing for adults, it was largely seen as an unsuitable subject for children's books.

Where war was the setting, glorifying it was not part of most writers' intentions: escapism was often the objective – although individual acts of courage at sea or in the air remained a strong element in many stories. Indeed, there was a widespread appetite for heroism in the culture at large: newspaper reporters wrote extensively about the skills and gallantry of individual pilots on both sides, from Baron von Richthofen to Captain Ball, giving rise to a whole new genre, that of adventure stories.

Captain Frederick S. Brereton (1852–1957), who had served in the RAMC in the Boer War and in the First World War, was well known for his rather tight-lipped, Henty-like adventure stories about conflicts, including *The Great Aeroplane* (1910), but his books seem now to have dropped out of memory. The rather appallingly fecund 'Herbert Strang' or 'Mrs Herbert Strang' (pen-names of both C. J. L'Estrange and G. Herbert Ely, staff members of the relatively new children's books section of Oxford University Press) wrote books ranging from *Boys of the Light Brigade* (1904) to *The Rose Fairy Book* (1912)

and also aircraft stories, such as *Burton of the Flying Corps* (1916); but these (deservedly) have also largely been forgotten.

One writer for children who is still well remembered is Percy F. Westerman (1876–1959; see pp. 204–5). Westerman, from a naval and Royal Flying Corps background, effectively exploited the emerging technology

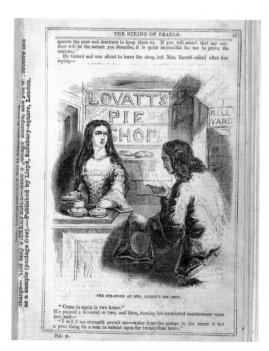

'Lovatt's Pie Shop', from [James Malcolm Rymer (attrib.)], *The String of Pearls; or, The Barber of Fleet Street. A Domestic Romance*. London: E. Lloyd, Salisbury Square, Fleet Street, c.1850. A penny dreadful's often dodgy contents had a wide and unseen trade. This one, the earliest version of the tale of the murderous Todd and his pie-selling accomplice, offers a free sample by post in exchange for three stamps and an envelope. Production of such penny serials – produced for adults but read by children too – would have been cheap and rapid: note the misspelling of the pie-shop name.

The British Library

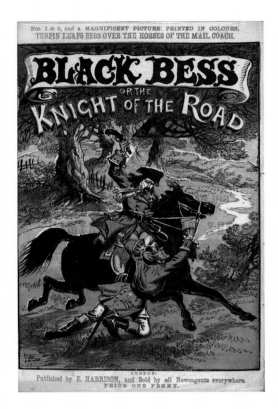

[Edward Viles], *Black Bess, or, The Knight of the Road: A Tale of the Good Old Times*. London: E. Harrison, [1866–8]. Tales of the exploits of Essex-born highwayman Dick Turpin, who was executed at Knavesmire in York in 1739, were a favourite with children and adults alike and much reprinted in penny-dreadful form. In this version, he did not meet his fate until page 2,207.

The British Library

NOS. 1 & 2, and a MAGNIFICENT PICTURE, PRINTED IN COLOURS.
TURPIN LEAPS BESS OVER THE HORSES OF THE MAIL COACH.

BLACK BESS
OR THE
KNIGHT OF THE ROAD

LONDON:
Published by E. HARRISON, and Sold by all Newsagents everywhere.
PRICE ONE PENNY.

of submarines, airships and the wireless in his many adventure stories published by Blackie. In many ways, Westerman was a simple, traditional, uncomplicated man (he wrote all his stories out in longhand in notebooks before having them typewritten to be sent to the publisher); but like many writers of boys' stories, his books were tolerated rather than admired by critics.

The same was even more true of the slightly later, and very prolific, W. E. Johns (1893–1968), whose knowledge of flying came from his service in the RFC and later in the RAF. Johns was a great advocate of flying, and his 'Biggles' stories were so successful that it was reported that the Spitfire pilots in the Battle of Britain in 1940 used his stories to learn his technique in aerial combat. Certainly, Johns wrote his 'Worrals' stories about a fictional female aviator (see p. 205) to help persuade girls to enrol in the WAAF. Despite this, like Westerman (or indeed

Blyton), Johns was not regarded highly for the quality of his writing, and children's librarians discouraged the reading of his work – a vain hope, for there are still active readers of both Johns and Westerman.

Wary of books by such authors, children's librarians had no place at all on their shelves for those other adventurous stories: the descendants of the Victorian '**penny dreadfuls**'. Combining escapism with profitability had been typical of the Victorian downmarket, but immensely popular, penny dreadfuls (the rough equivalent of the American '**dime novels**'). With their whiff of lawlessness and rebellion, and often a touch of cruelty or even sadism, such stories were a worry to many. Charles Knight (1791–1873), the benevolent provider of *The Penny Magazine* (1832–45), *The Penny Cyclopaedia* (1828–43) and many other books published under the auspices of the Society for the Diffusion of Useful Knowledge, despondently wrote in the 1860s that he had been too hopeful about the benefits of the increasing general ability to read. Knight blamed writers of 'the most vulgar and brutal' popular fiction for 'diffusing a moral Miasma through the land'.

It is now very hard to recognise how much of this undergrowth of literature figured in the publishing business for, by and large, it was produced outside the regular trade. Books issued by printers and publishers such as James Catnach or Edward Lloyd, or stories of 'Sweeney Todd, the Demon Barber of Fleet Street', or 'Dick Turpin and Black Bess' were known to everyone (and widely read, not only by children), though you would not find them in a bookshop, reviewed in magazines or on library shelves. Such books were invisible to most people; the fact that a few precious copies survive in the British Library is due to one persistent book collector, Barry Ono, who preserved them and bequeathed his collection in 1941.

Two descendants of these nasties we show here, also absent from school libraries (and seldom discussed in the histories of children's literature), were strongly influenced by their Victorian antecedents. The first, *Sexton Blake* (see pp. 206–7), was an attempt by the Harmsworth Press to provide something more wholesome than the penny dreadfuls, but it too was pretty poor stuff. *Hank Janson*, on the other hand, simply illustrates the fact that, despite all best Victorian efforts to control pornography through the Obscene Publications Act of 1857, people could and did still find ways of providing 'dirty' books for the youth, before another moral panic in the 1950s attempted to remove them from sale.

The British penny dreadfuls and the American dime novels (which also had a considerable circulation in Britain) featured such fictional characters as Ally Sloper or Charley Wagg, and were of real importance in feeding adolescent boys' imaginations. So too were the stories about cowboys, Indians and the 'Wild West' (see pp. 208–9), a significant element of dime novels. The Westerns written for adults by such authors as Will James or Zane Gray, and more recently by Larry McMurtrie, were often adopted by adolescent boy readers. Both Gray (famous for his *Riders of the Purple Sage*, 1912) and James (*Smoky the Cowhorse*, 1926) also wrote for a juvenile audience. Hollywood seized on these Westerns with great enthusiasm.

For girls, pony stories and their like were immensely popular, from *Black Beauty* (1877) or *Beautiful Joe* (1894) onwards, but girls' perceived interests in theatre and dance also supported a range of well-crafted English stories which were very popular in the middle of the 20th century; no doubt because of the authenticity of their authors' texts, based on personal experience. This success was increased by BBC radio serialisation. The work of Noel Streatfeild (1895–1986), with her *Ballet Shoes* (1936) and later books about

child actors, members of a circus troop, ice skaters and tennis stars, was widely praised. Pamela Brown (1924–89) started writing *The Swish of the Curtain* (1941) while still a student at RADA, giving an enthralling account of working in a young theatre company, which must have prompted many readers to think of acting as a possible career.

Both Streatfeild and Brown were significant for the high quality of these 'career' stories. Others, such as Helen Dore Boylston's *Sue Barton, Student Nurse* (1936) or Helen Wells's *Vicki Barr, Flight Stewardess* series (from 1947) were very popular in their day, but were

The Children's Hour Annual, edited by 'Uncle Mac' of the BBC – Derek McCulloch, etc. London, BBC [1936]. In the programming since the BBC's inception, *The Children's Hour* was designed for 'the citizens and the licence holders of the future'. It serialised popular books like those by Masefield, C. S. Forester's *The Commodore* (about Captain Hornblower) and Barbara Todd's *Worzel Gummidge*, gave nature talks, and made outside broadcasts. Sunday programmes took a more devout turn, adapting *The Pilgrim's Progress* and L. du Garde Peach's *Paul of Tarsus*.

Author's collection

seemingly manufactured to a publisher's notion of what the public would buy; not a recipe for good, memorable writing.

This was perhaps inevitable, for by the mid-20th century it was clear that there was a large group of children's publishers (and booksellers and would-be writers) who found that good profits could be made from quite run-of-the mill books. The literary standard was often not very high, but it seems parents and booksellers were not always discriminating, and librarians' attempts to raise standards were only slowly felt. From the 1930s onwards in Britain the influence of the BBC and its selection of work for its radio programme *The Children's Hour* was hugely beneficial. In the United States, the American Library Association's Newbery Award (first given in 1922, for Hendrik Van Loon's *Story of Mankind*, 1921) went some way to counteract the poor quality of writing for children.

This improvement was badly needed. In America, the effect of the work of the book-packager Edward L. Stratemeyer (1862–1930) – almost a Henry Ford of the literary world – was profound, and depressing. Having edited some of the American writer Horatio Alger's last books for publication, Stratemeyer devised a ghostwriting technique for mass-producing books for children. For a fee of $75 to $250 (around £60 to £250) ghostwriters were employed to produce, within a couple of months, mystery stories, written to strict guidelines and to plots outlined by Stratemeyer himself. Having had all the rights signed over to him, Stratemeyer would then invent a pseudonym for the author, and edit and prepare the text for publication. He was a busy man: his syndicate, founded in 1905, created more than 1,300 novels for adolescents, which are said to have sold more than 200 million copies – for the Stratemeyer Syndicate's books included those titles about the Bobbsey Twins, the Hardy Boys, the Dana

Girls, Nancy Drew and a host of equally well-known books read avidly by young Americans (and British) over the generations. After Stratemeyer's death the syndicate was continued by his daughters until the 1980s when the business was bought by the publishers Simon & Schuster; production of the Nancy Drew and Hardy Boys stories has since been continued by another book packager, Mega-Books.

In providing a consistent quality and at modest prices, mass production had its advantages. Some in the British library world believed, mistakenly, that Blyton or W. E. Johns had engaged ghostwriters to augment their supply of titles, as Newnes had done for the downmarket *Sexton Blake* stories. The authorities at the BBC certainly shared the values of professional children's librarians who wanted to raise the standard of children's literature, and indeed instituted their own award – the Carnegie Medal (first awarded for Arthur Ransome's *Pigeon Post* in 1936). *Children's Hour* adhered to solidly middle-class, traditional values; as its producer Derek McCulloch ('Uncle Mac') wrote in the *B.B.C. Quarterly*:

> Our established policy is that nothing but the best is good enough for children ... our wish is to stimulate their imagination, direct their reading, encourage their various interests, widen their outlook, and inculcate the Christian principles of love of God and their neighbours.

Importantly, the parents who encouraged their children to listen to the daily *Children's Hour* broadcast from 5 p.m. to 6 p.m. were buyers (or at least borrowers) of books. Sales improved as books were serialised, including those written by such writers as 'Romany' (George Bramwell Evens), Pamela Brown and John Masefield, and adoption by the BBC both increased authors' incomes and the shelf-life of their books. Masefield's *The Box of Delights*, published in 1935 (see pp. 212–13), and broadcast from 1943, led readers on to his earlier children's novel, *The Midnight Folk* (1927) and his other stories and poetry.

These books also encouraged readers and writers to explore other fantasy and time-travel stories. One of the earliest was J. R. R. Tolkien's *The Hobbit* (1937) and the later *Lord of the Rings* (1954–5), phenomenally successful with both adults and children. Having sold well over 150 million copies, and with both radio and film adaptations, Tolkien's commercial success was staggering, and his work has continued to influence other writers such as Stephen King and J. K. Rowling. His near-contemporary and friend at Oxford C. S. Lewis had almost equal success with his *Chronicles of Narnia* (published 1950–56), and, more recently, its own film versions. Lewis's influence on later writers such as Philip Pullman and Rowling has again been very notable. In a happy moment, Collins (the publisher) commissioned Pauline Baynes to illustrate both Tolkien and Lewis's very successful fantasy series (see p. 213). It is hard to overstate the importance of these books: without them, it is difficult to imagine that later books by Madeleine L'Engle or indeed Pullman or Rowling would have appeared in the forms they did (see pp. 218–19).

Hendrik Van Loon's *Story of Mankind* (1921), mentioned above as a prizewinner, received the Newbery Award because it broke new ground in its attempt to provide children with *interesting* non-fiction. Between the two world wars, other attempts were made to provide school textbooks to (it was hoped) enthral pupils. These had some success, like Mason Gray's *Latin for Today* – and many educators strove to produce books that would be attractive to young readers. To represent the books on prehistory and dinosaurs which attract so many children, we chose

Whirlaway, by H. C. F. Morant (see pp. 210–11). This little-known book by an obscure Australian writer, which never got beyond its original small edition, has to be regarded as a publishing 'failure'. Indeed, it seems many copies were destroyed during the Luftwaffe air-raids on London, when millions of books went up in flames – but *Whirlaway* has a touch of magic which in the 1940s worked brilliantly for at least one British reader, and subsequently inspired several younger generations.

Recreational reading for British children in the 1930s was frequently much more pedestrian. The quality was dependent on the policies of the publishers or editors of children's annuals and gift books, so often the main source of children's reading. At the low (but nonetheless hugely popular) end came annuals derived from comic strips in newspapers, such as Mary Tourtel's 'Rupert Bear' for the *Daily Express* in 1920, the slightly earlier 'Teddy Tail' for the *Daily Mail*, and 'Pip, Squeak and Wilfred' in the *Daily Mirror*. All these led to the creation of annuals (often published after the Second World War) which are still eagerly collected today. There were also more 'upmarket' anthologies or annuals, containing poetry and stories by notable authors, and these often gave children their first introduction to writers they had not previously encountered.

One of the best series of anthologies published each year came under the title of *Joy Street: A Medley of Prose & Verse for Boys and Girls*, published by Basil Blackwell and edited by Michael Lynn. *Number One Joy Street* was published in 1923, and each volume was individual in content and authorship. This unusually well-designed series eventually ended with *Number Fourteen* in 1936 when the book trade declined.

Competing for children's attention were the books by Arthur Ransome (1884–1967), whose *Pigeon Post* (the sixth in his series of twelve innocent, middle-class stories about a group of children having sailing adventures in the Lake District), won the first ever Carnegie Medal in 1936. Its successor, the winner in 1937, clearly selected by judges who were aware that children's books were being criticised for their traditionalist, middle-class assumptions, was *The Family from One End Street* by Eve Garnett (1900–91). Garnett wrote in 1938:

> It is true that the average child of well-to-do parents to-day – particularly the country child – is extraordinarily ignorant of the conditions under which the less fortunate children live.

Garnett's text and her own lively illustrations made an attractive book. There were other left-wing writers such as Geoffrey Trease (whose 1934 *Bows Against the Barons* was a powerful attempt to produce a revisionist history of Robin Hood) and John Rowe Townsend (author of *Grumble's Yard*, 1961), who claimed Garnett showed an outsider's condescending view of the working class. It

was reported that in Germany, Dr Goebbels prescribed Garnett's book as a reading book for German schools as providing valuable 'anti-British propaganda'; but in Britain *The Family from One End Street* remains a classic. More typical recreational reading was provided by writers with no political intentions: authors such as Richmal Crompton (with her 'William' books) or Enid Blyton (see pp. 214–15).

From 1931 Flammarion's innovative *Albums du Père Castor* began to appear, under the direction of editor Paul Faucher, as a series of stories told by the 'Father Beaver' of the title, revealing the wider world to his three children. *Babar*, also from 1931, was issued in translation from 1933 (see pp. 142–3), but few other European books attracted British publishers. Some, like Rose Fyleman's 1942 translation of the Czech classic *Broucci* (*Fireflies*) by Jan Karafiát, seemed to sink without trace. Progressive and attractive publishing for children became typical of Swedish publishers, but it took a very long time before Selma Lagerlöf's *Wonderful Adventures of Nils* was sold in Britain; while Astrid Lindgren's *Pippi Longstocking* (see pp. 216–17), published in Stockholm in 1945 to instant success, did not make her own feisty way on to British bookshelves for another nine years. Shortages of paper and post-war conditions were partly the reason for the delays, no doubt, although British children were very attracted to Pippi when they finally met her. There were similar delays in publishing English editions of the *Moomin* books by Tove Jansson, first published in 1945 and hugely popular throughout the world.

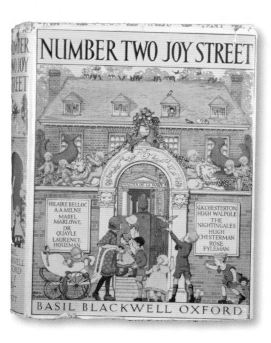

G. K. Chesterton et al., *Number Two Joy Street: A Medley of Prose & Verse for Boys and Girls.* Oxford: Basil Blackwell, 1924. The fourteen volumes in this series, published from 1923–36, featured lively, full-colour wrapper designs and colour illustrations within, with stories and verse by Laurence Housman, G. K. Chesterton and A. A. Milne, among others.

Rooke Books, Bath

New Ways of Being Heroes

Boys' stories had a strong military content in Victorian times, but the coming of aerial warfare opened up fresh subjects for plots with which to enthral young readers.

The stories of such popular Victorian writers as W. S. Kingston and G. A. Henty were avidly read by schoolboys (and sometimes their sisters too), and the events of the Boer Wars (1880–81 and 1899–1902) and the Russo-Japanese War (1904–5) provided much recent material to exercise authors' imaginations; but the real catalyst came from the Wright brothers' first flight in 1903, which sent the plots soaring off in new directions.

Percy F. Westerman (1876–1959) was among those who sought to write adventure stories like those made so popular by Henty. From a naval background at Portsmouth (where his father was a Master-at-Arms), Westerman was prevented by poor eyesight from joining the navy. Instead, he became a clerk in the naval dockyard, and started writing sea stories for sailing magazines. Living a rather Spartan life on a Thames barge at Wareham with an Admiralty salary of £90 a year – and a wife and son to support – the money he earned from his spare-time journalism was very welcome.

Westerman's novels started to appear in 1908, and by 1911 he felt secure enough to give up his clerical job and (apart from wartime duties in both world wars) to devote his time to writing. Over his lifetime, he wrote more than 170 books; the majority sea stories, often traversing the same topics as Joseph Conrad. Increasingly, Westerman wrote aircraft stories as well – for in 1918, Westerman became an instructor in navigation for the RFC. In a poll run by the *Daily Sketch* through various children's libraries, Westerman was voted the most

Percy F. Westerman, *Unconquered Wings*. London; Glasgow: Blackie & Son, [1924]. This early edition, *c.*1930, contains six illustrations by Edward Smith Hodgson, who illustrated many of Westerman's books for Blackie, and other ripping yarns by Conan Doyle and others.
Author's collection

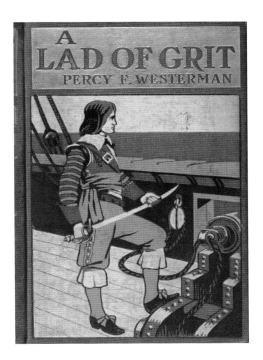

popular boys' author: despite his pedestrian style, his emphasis on patriotism, discipline and tenacity provides a revealing picture of British character and culture between the wars.

One of Westerman's innovations was to write about 'Colin Standish of the Air Police', which he did first of all in *The Amir's Ruby* (1932). It was a good idea, also used by Westerman's son, John F. C. Westerman, who between 1929 and the 1950s published many aircraft stories, lots of them involving an air detective, John Wentley. Nowadays, Standish and Wentley are almost forgotten.

Many readers today will remember the slightly later 'Biggles', the hero of the majority of stories written a little later by W. E. Johns (1893–1968) and published in *Popular Flying*, the magazine which he founded. The basic idea for using an air-pilot detective was lifted from Westerman's stories, and the character of Biggles first appeared in Johns's *The Camels are Coming* in 1932. Johns, who had served in the RFC during the First World War and was captured as a prisoner of war in Germany in 1918, seems

clearly to have been damaged emotionally by his wartime experiences. In his recounting of his war exploits he showed a tendency to romanticise, and some of his claims about his experiences are dubious, but he remained in the RAF until 1927 before turning his hand to illustration and journalism.

A phenomenally prolific writer, Johns wrote well over a hundred Biggles books, with many of them serialised in *The Boy's Own Paper* and *The Girl's Own Paper*. In the late 1930s he was involved in the setting up of the Air Training Corps. His popularity was so great that during the Second World War he was asked to write stories to help recruitment for the WAAF and produced eleven books about Flight Officer Joan Worralson (a.k.a. 'Worrals'), based on women aviators Pauline Gower and Amy Johnson. He went on to create a further ten 'Gimlet' stories around his character, Captain Lorrington, King of the Commandos, who was known as the 'Gimlet' King for his keen eyesight (and perhaps based on Johns's own commanding officer Major 'Gimlet' Champion). Johns's attempts at science fiction were much less successful.

Johns was a very careful and thorough writer who worked efficiently to see that his stories were widely published. Despite murmurings from public librarians and booksellers about Johns's stereotyped characters, his old-fashioned imperialism and his xenophobic attitudes, in the 1960s Biggles books were the most popular children's reading of the time. There is a thriving group of Biggles book collectors even today, and there is little sign that Biggles will join Standish and Wentley among the forgotten aircraft heroes any time soon.

Under Covers: Books Hidden from Parents and Teachers

Down the years, children have often wanted to read books which their parents thought unsuitable. In the 19th century, street literature and penny dreadfuls were shunned by guardians, but later there were other, fresh dangers.

Access to books intended for middle-class children was, in the 18th and 19th centuries, strictly controlled by publishers, librarians and booksellers, and throughout the Victorian period there were both individuals and organisations whose greatest aim was to promote 'good' reading for the young. Yet the history of street literature (and of pornography) shows that at the same time there were many other firms and individuals much more interested in making profits than in providing wholesome reading.

In his magazine, *The Halfpenny Marvel*, started in the 1880s, the publisher Alfred Harmsworth tried to drive out the nasty Victorian **penny dreadfuls** with something better, sold at half their price as an incentive. Conan Doyle's *Sherlock Holmes* stories were then popular and, as Doyle had by then apparently killed off his hero, Harmsworth asked Harry Blyth, a journalist, to write a suitable similar detective story for *The Halfpenny Marvel* as a replacement. 'Sexton Blake', who first appeared in Issue 6 in December 1893, soon became one of the best-known fictional detectives, but only a few of these stories were actually written by Blyth. Instead, Sexton Blake stories were commissioned from a wide range of writers, in the same way that later a New York book packager, the Stratemayer Syndicate, created the Nancy Drew and Hardy Boys books.

Sexton Blake stories appeared in *The Halfpenny Marvel, Union Jack* and other magazines, and in book format too. They

Hal Meredeth [pseud. Harold Blyth], 'The Missing Millionaire', in *The 'Halfpenny Marvel'*. London: Amalgamated Press, 13 December 1893, issue 6. This is the first appearance of Sexton Blake, published by Alfred Harmsworth in the same month that Sherlock Holmes died (toppling over the Reichenbach Falls with his arch-enemy Moriarty, which this cover, by an unknown illustrator, echoes). But as a debut it is hardly a literary triumph: as one critical commentator puts it, 'Sexton Blake ... does virtually nothing and the plot resolves itself without his help. Who could possibly have predicted his fabulous future from this?'
The British Library

Hank Janson [Stephen Daniel Frances], *This Woman is Death*. London: Ward & Hitchon, [1948]. This first full-length Hank Janson novel was strictly *not* for children, but was certainly read by adventurous older boys. Frances was sole author from 1946 until about 1953, when other writers took on the Hank Janson pseudonym. Titles like *Skirts Bring me Sorrow*, and *Slay-Ride for Cutie*, set the tone (superbly parodied by Dennis Potter in *The Singing Detective*), and contained much to exercise modern-day critics.

Courtesy of Telos Publishing

were certainly profitable, but the literary quality of these stories was, at best, mediocre. Complex plots, wooden characters and stilted diction made parents and public librarians regard them as trash. But office boys and schoolboys loved them, and continued to buy them by many thousands until production eventually ceased in the 1960s. Today, old copies and modern reprints are avidly collected; often by elderly men, who remember them fondly from their youth.

This was pulp fiction, but of a relatively innocuous kind; however, in Victorian times, there was enough concern about pornography to lead to the passing of the Obscene Publications Act of 1857 (see p. 151). In the 1940s, there was a similar outbreak of moral panic about horror comics in the US, and Fredric Wertham's *Seduction of the Innocent* (1954), an American book about the impact of popular comic fiction on children, led to changes to the law in Britain and Ireland as well in the United States. Despite these

controls, in the 1940s stories started to be published in London about the tough pseudo-American Hank Janson. They offered a marked, and raunchy, response to post-war austerity. Very close to pornography in their text, their girly-magazine-type covers by Reginald Heade indicated both to the initiated and perhaps to the not-so that they were pretty hot stuff.

Schoolboys buying Hank Janson books – and they did so – prudently removed their covers and concealed the books from their parents, just as later generations would do with copies of *Penthouse* or *Playboy*. But copies of Hank Janson books were destroyed by the police or military authorities as well as by concerned parents. The author's name was hidden by a pseudonym (in fact he often wrote the books under the name of his character 'Hank Janson'); the publisher's name was frequently a false one and there was no printer's imprint given on the page where such details would usually be found (or, in other cases, the books were stated as having been 'printed in Paris'). Their instigator was one Stephen Daniel Frances (1917–89), a Londoner with a vivid imagination and a style which titillated adolescent boys. In the early 1950s, Frances found it prudent to leave Britain and move to Spain, where he continued to produce these tales at the amazing rate of one volume every month, and with great success (by 1953, the print runs of each new novel were reaching 100,000). In the terms of our contemporary attitudes, and the ready availability of pornography on the internet, the Hank Janson books now seem pretty mild stuff, but not so in the 1950s. As with the Sexton Blake novels, there is now a strong collectors' market for this pulp fiction.

Opening up the West

The expansion of the United States westwards created many topics which had to be included in children's books.

When the thirteen colonies became independent of Britain after 1776, new writing for children was needed to convey the story of how the expanding United States developed. Some of the American books for children described parts of America or ways of life which seemed enough like Britain to be incorporated into British children's reading without the children finding them exotic: *The Wide, Wide World*, *What Katy Did* or *Little Women* had plenty of English readers (see pp. 164–5). But these 'girls' books' described settled communities in New England. Reading for boys was more meaty and much more exotic in content. When visiting the United States in the 1830s Frederick Marryat commented unfavourably on seeing boys reading magazines 'mostly confined to the lower orders', which he thought most unsuitable. Among these would have been copies of the popular and widely published Davy Crockett almanacs, named for the Tennessee 'king of the wild frontier' who was killed in the Mexican attack on the Alamo in 1836.

The wild tales about Crockett, Daniel Boone, Jim Bowie, Kit Carson and other frontiersmen helped to give them iconic status, and their lives became the subject of dozens of later American **dime novels**, which were condemned (or ignored) by polite society in America. By contrast, the 'Leatherstocking Tales' by James Fenimore Cooper (1789–1851) created a new American form of historical fiction, which looked at American history, rather as Walter Scott's popular Waverley novels had done for British history.

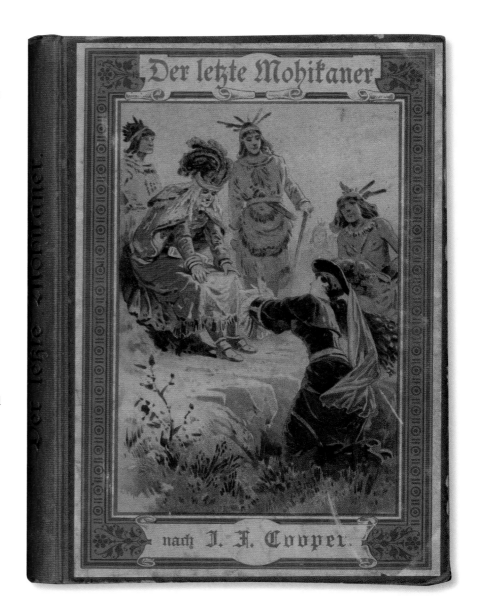

James Fenimore Cooper, *Der letzte Mohikaner. Eine Erzählung für die Jugend. (The Last of the Mohicans. A Story for the Youth.)* After J. Fenimore Cooper, 'freely edited by Paul Moritz'. With plates after watercolours by G. Franz. Stuttgart: K. Thienemanns Verlag, 1889. The book, defining a dying culture, quickly captured the public imagination, becoming one of the most widely read novels. It inspired numerous illustrators and artists, such as Emanuel Leutze (who depicted the brooding chieftain Uncas on a rocky outcrop in a famous painting of the same name) and was translated into many languages, such as the German edition 'for youth' here.

Reproduced by kind permission of the Syndics of Cambridge University Library, Waddleton.d.1.74

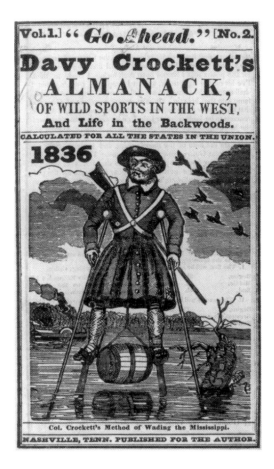

Cooper was later mocked by Mark Twain (see pp. 170–71) for his verbose style and stereotyped characterisation, but Cooper's books – and particularly his *Last of the Mohicans* (1826) – were immediately admired in Britain and on the Continent. Writers such as Balzac and Victor Hugo were enthusiastic in their praise. Successful in many countries (and particularly in Eastern Europe), his *Last of the Mohicans* continues to be produced in abridged versions, large formats, and cartoon and **manga** forms. Re-interpreted in film, television and radio versions, Cooper's work is very much alive.

Well over a hundred years after Cooper wrote the 'Leatherstocking Tales', the Wilder family lived through the perils and privations of pioneer life, initially in Wisconsin, and later in Kansas, Minnesota and eventually the eastern Dakota Territory. Laura Ingalls Wilder (1867–1957) grew up as a member of a poor farming family, and after a few years teaching in rural schools married the farmer Almanzo Wilder. As an established farmer's wife she started writing about farm topics for the *St. Louis Star Farmer,* and the *Missouri Ruralist,* and with this improbable background – as an expert on rearing chickens – she perfected her writing skills.

In the anxious and money-strapped years of the early 1930s, Wilder produced her first book based on her reminiscences of pioneer life: *Little House in the Big Woods* (1932). It was well received, and was soon followed in 1935 by *Little House on the Prairie* (1935), the title used for a series of semi-autobiographical stories that grew eventually to a multi-million-dollar franchise for many television and radio versions. In writing these books, now regarded as some of the best American books written for children, Laura was certainly helped by her daughter Rose Wilder Lane (1886–1968). But Rose was no ghostwriter; Laura Ingalls Wilder was that very rare thing, an untutored genius. The *Little House* stories remain consistently popular.

Making Sense of Dinosaurs

Fossils seem to have always fascinated children, and 19th-century discoveries of dinosaur bones to have increased their interest still more. But was it possible to make palaeontology attractive?

D inosaurs are undoubtedly popular. Almost every bookshop these days has a range of 'dinosaur books' from which to choose, from those for the youngest readers to serious scientific (and expensive) volumes for the committed adolescent enthusiast. One, a favourite since the 1940s with this author's family, but hardly known today, is *Whirlaway: A Story of the Ages,* by H. C. F. Morant (1885– 1952), published by Hutchinson in 1937.

Though published in Britain, *Whirlaway* was an Australian book, which explains why the eleven-year-old heroine, Helen, had a pet koala bear which accompanied her on her adventures. Possibly inspired by Kipling's *Puck of Pook's Hill* in its narrative construction (and similarly using a sprite as a narrative guide) the adventure begins with Helen's meeting with Whirlaway, a sprite-like lump of coal, and her discovery of a hidden lift in the cellar of a house named for Sir Charles Lyell (the geologist who was so influential upon Darwin's development of the theory of evolution). The lift carries them downwards, back in time, through successive geological strata to the dawn of life. Their return journey takes place through a series of doors, each opening into a new geological epoch, which the party explores, discovering the extinct plants, fishes and animals of each period.

British-born Morant, of St Kilda, Australia, was a man of diverse interests: a commercial photographer and author of several photographic works, but no other writings. *Whirlaway* seems to have been a one-off. An ingenious writer, Morant packed a great deal of factual information into this light-hearted

'Jurassic – 60 Million Years to Cretaceous', illustrative chapter opener, from H. C. F. Morant, *Whirlaway: A Story of the Ages.* Illustrated by Jean Elder. London: Hutchinson, 1937. How envious we were of their adventures! Unusually, the cheery colour plates, with their 'fairy-book' feel, were less interesting to the author himself and other family members as children than the peculiar creatures depicted in the black-and-white drawings. Morant was careful with accuracy and the book's palaeontology was checked by authorities in this subject. A former official of the Victoria School Board added *Whirlaway*'s chirpy little ditties.

Author's collection

Clive King, *Stig of the Dump*. Illustrated by Edward Ardizzone. London: Puffin Books, 1963. As with Morant, Kipling's *Puck of Pook's Hill*'s time-warp setting partly inspired the tale of Stig, the 'primitive and elemental' secret inhabitant of the sleepy Kentish village. Many young readers must have yearned to have adventures with such a free-spirited young caveman-pal.

Author's collection

time-travel fantasy – and his discussion of the Cambrian epoch teaches us all we ever need to know about trilobites! Apparently intended for school use, the carefully accurate illustrations by Jean Elder (an Australian illustrator of fairy books; see pp. 194–5) were bright and memorable. But *Whirlaway* was ahead of its time. Morant's book remains barely known, and we have been unable to trace any British reviews of it, and few in Australia. Sales there were limited, and the destruction of its London publishers' surviving stock in the Blitz prevented further exports to Australia. One Australian

Whirlaway enthusiast, the former MP Race Matthews, examined fragments of text for a further projected book by Morant, *The Ether Chariot*, which, he says, was 'to have done for astronomy what *Whirlaway* was intended to do for geology and palaeontology', but this was never completed. Morant's book is now very rare indeed.

Time travel is often used in fantasies for children. Another popular classic is *Stig of the Dump* by Clive King, published as a Puffin Original in 1963. King was a British Council officer who spent much of his time working in the Middle East, drawing on this for most of his novels, but *Stig* was based in the North Downs of Kent, where King grew up. In the plot, a young boy, Barney, staying with his grandparents on the South Downs, falls into a chalk pit, and stumbles over the shaggy-haired Stig, who seems to be a Stone Age boy. The boys have adventures together, but nobody else believes Stig to be real.

Brilliantly illustrated by Edward Ardizzone, *Stig of the Dump* became very widely read in Britain, and was broadcast on television by both ITV and the BBC. Although it has been translated into a few European languages and Japanese, *Stig* seemed too English in its approach to become more widely popular, and did not attract American library buyers. In Britain, one 21st-century teacher has described it as 'moving rapidly towards the dusty hell of the top shelf', so possibly teachers' rapid adoption of *Stig* for school use might have destroyed it as a book to be read by contemporary children for enjoyment. A great pity.

When Wolves Were Running

John Masefield became famous as a poet, but two magical stories of his became even better known than his verse.

To prevent his incessant reading, as a boy John Masefield (1878–1967) was sent by an unsympathetic guardian aunt to train as an officer on HMS *Conway* in the Merchant Navy; a very tough schooling. Masefield first became known for his poems about the sea, starting with his *Salt Water Ballads* (1902). By the time he was appointed Poet Laureate in 1930, he was the best-known poet to contemporary children – generations learned and relished his poems at school ('I must go down to the seas again, to the lonely sea and the sky / And all I ask is a tall ship and a star to steer her by', or 'Dirty British coaster with a salt-caked smoke stack /Butting through the Channel in the mad March days').

As well as his poetry, Masefield was a readable and vivid novelist, and some of those books written for children were particularly successful. His earlier children's books were adventure stories such as *Jim Davis* (1911), which owed quite a lot to Robert Louis Stevenson. In the 1920s, Masefield embarked on a series of adult novels about a young sailor and his experiences (half real, half dreamed) in Latin America, including *Sard Harker* (1924) and *ODTAA* (i.e., 'One Damn Thing After Another'; 1926). Seemingly Masefield's latent memories of his own childhood, mixed with the themes of these novels, led him to write two children's books, later described by the *New York Times* as 'the sort of book that grown-ups like to give a child for Christmas, and then enjoy reading themselves'.

In *The Midnight Folk* (1927) Masefield wrote about a young orphan boy, Kay Harker, and his magical experiences in games with talking

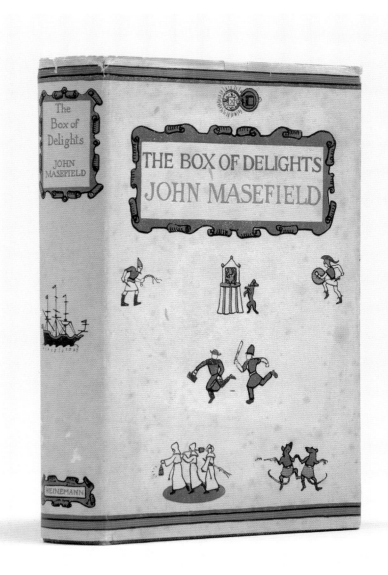

John Masefield, *The Box of Delights: Or, When the Wolves Were Running*. London: Heinemann, 1957. Illustrated by Judith Masefield (who had earlier illustrated some of her father's poems, which, as Poet Laureate, he presented to King George V). As well as its inception as a children's novel, it was adapted by the author as an opera libretto and recorded for radio and television. Its popularity was perhaps in part due to the realism which underlay the fantasy: the writer Alan Garner observed: 'Masefield showed children what others would not allow: that adults could be dangerous, that bullies did not always run when confronted ... and that happy endings were not automatic.'

Peter Harrington Rare Books, London

C. S. Lewis, *The Lion, the Witch and the Wardrobe*. Harmondsworth: Puffin Books, 1959. Pauline Baynes depicts Susan and Lucy garlanding the stern but benevolent (and Christ-like) Aslan, who safely guides them through Narnia. The extended religious metaphor in the book may be glaringly obvious to the adult reader, but for many children (like this author) the magical fantasy eclipsed any worthier subtext. The Puffins were the format in which most children read the books, and their full-colour wraparound covers are if anything more appealing than those of the first hardback edition by Geoffrey Bles (1950).

Author's collection

animals, and the dangers he faced from his governess, Sylvia Daisy Pouncer (who doubles as a witch). In the sequel, *The Box of Delights: Or, When the Wolves Were Running* (1935) Kay was older, coming home for Christmas from his public school. The story was again full of magic, and the characters once again included Sylvia Daisy Pouncer, now wife of the chief villain: was Masefield working out his feelings about his cruel aunt? Even though the *faux naïf* illustrations by Masefield's daughter Judith did little for the story, this elaborate, satirical whodunnit was immediately successful. Its shelf-life was extended further by its being broadcast as a serial on the radio by the BBC on its Children's Hour programme, first in 1943, and thereafter frequently repeated.

The Box of Delights was very important in the memories of many children. No doubt two Oxford scholars, Tolkien and C. S. Lewis, were equally aware of Masefield's book, and their own contributions to the field of the

development of fantasy novels for children were to be still more important. C. S. Lewis (1898–1963) wrote seven fantasy novels intended for children, which were published between 1950 and 1956. These were very serious in their intent, for Lewis was a committed Christian.

The Chronicles of Narnia, set in an imaginary land, where animals could speak and magic was all around, described the adventures of the children (evacuated to the countryside to avoid the Blitz during the Second World War) who found an entrance to Narnia hidden in a wardrobe in a spare bedroom, as described in *The Lion, the Witch and the Wardrobe* (1950). Some critics have been equivocal about the Christian message in the Narnia books, but there was no doubt about their popularity with readers. The pleasure for children was increased by the pictures by Pauline Baynes, an artist discovered and introduced to Lewis by Tolkien.

Scrapes and Slow Poison: Where William Brown Met the Famous Five

Two young authors of children's books started to write for George Newnes (a publisher of children's magazines and books) in the early 1920s, and changed the face of writing for children for ever.

'Rice Mould Pudding', published in Newnes's *Home Magazine* in February 1919, was the first 'William' story by Richmal Crompton (Richmal Crompton Lamburn, 1890–1969), a young Classics schoolteacher then working in Bromley, just outside London. The story was a great success, and was followed in 1922 by *Just William*, the first of many volumes about William Brown and his friends. Crompton thought of her William stories as potboilers, aimed originally at adult readers (she wrote nearly fifty volumes of adult fiction). Her books about William, however, were amazingly successful, popular with adults as well as children. By the Second World War they had inspired a film (*Just William*, 1940), a fan club and popular spin-off toys such as a toy theatre (with scripts by Crompton), sheet music and jigsaws illustrating episodes from Brown's adventures. By the time the last of her children's books was published in 1970, over 14 million copies of her William stories had been published, along with translations of the books in several languages.

The stories were enhanced by illustrations commissioned by Newnes from a Nottingham artist, Thomas Henry (Thomas Henry Fisher, 1879–1962). Newnes used Henry for a range of similar stories, including the 'Jane Turpin' stories by the Australian-born Evadne Price (1888–1985), which were published for many years from 1928 onwards. Jane Turpin was *always* getting into scrapes, and was often described as the female William, but her creator claimed,

Richmal Crompton, *Just William*. London: George Newnes, 1922. Dust jacket illustrated by Thomas Henry. The back jacket carries further adverts for George Newnes's children's books. As well as illustrating another thirty-three of the books, Henry produced comical seaside postcards of the saucy Donald McGill type – and their robust, cheeky style can be seen in the *William* illustrations.

Courtesy Lez McLair

remarkably, that she had never heard of William Brown.

Another new author published by Newnes (and others) in the early 1920s, Enid Blyton (1897–1968) was a fresh phenomenon in children's writing. Like Crompton she was a teacher working in the London area, with an enormous appetite for writing, yet Blyton had little in common otherwise with the author of the William stories. Blyton's early writing was for children's annuals and magazines, particularly for the influential *Teachers' World,* which she skilfully used as a vehicle to develop her long-term contact with children, as well as teachers. The journal was owned by Evans Brothers, London, who later published many of Blyton's books in the 1940s and 1950s, beginning with *Rainy Day Stories,* 1942.

Blyton's first book, *Child Whispers* (1922), was illustrated by her friend Phyllis Chase, but Blyton soon dropped her in favour of other artists, particularly Eileen Soper, who illustrated about fifty Blyton books (including all the *Famous Five* volumes); and the Dutch cartoonist Harmsen Van der Beek (who was, later on, to create *Noddy*'s distinctive look in 1952).

Blyton became a one-woman writing factory, and a very profitable one. By 1923, she was already earning £230 a year from her writing, and overall she wrote nearly 800 children's books, published in nearly ninety different languages, which by the time of her death had sold more than 600 million copies. This is remarkable for a writer who never won any awards and was disliked and even feared by reviewers, librarians and the BBC, who thought her books were not good influences for children ('slow poison' as the respected critic Margery Fisher once described them).

Nonetheless, children seem still to adore *Noddy, The Famous Five,* the *Naughtiest Girl at School* and the many other series created by this prolific author. The copyrights in her books were sold for £14.6 million in 1995 to publishers who thought they were an excellent investment.

Publishers still reissue her titles, silently altering her words when they think their changes make them more acceptable in modern children's books. Parents still buy them, and there is a flourishing Enid Blyton Society on the web.

ABOVE
Enid Blyton, *Child Whispers.* London: J. Saville & Co., 1922. Not many these days will be familiar with this early work by the most famous of authors of children's detective stories. This collection of twenty-eight poems, with its front cover illustrated by Phyllis Chase, was one of her best-known poetry books. Titles like 'A Fairy Necklace', 'The Jolly Wind' and 'The Naughty Gnome' bring to mind the tone of her later *Noddy* books.

The British Library

RIGHT
Examples of early *William* merchandising: a wartime *Just William* children's theatre, illustrated by Thomas Henry, and a *Just William* fan club badge, c.1940.

Courtesy Lez McLair

Northern Lights and Lives

Swedish children's books developed quite late, and were often
very different from those of the English-speaking countries.

Having only minor involvement in colonisation, the Scandinavian countries were different from most others in Western Europe. Only Sweden, with its long history of non-involvement, was able to remain out of the conflict in both world wars, and its neutrality made for differences in its culture. It was really only at the end of the 19th century, with the plays of Strindberg, that Swedish literature gained world recognition. For school use, Selma Lagerlöf (1858–1940), who in 1909 received the Nobel Prize for Literature, wrote a geography **reader**, commissioned by the Swedish National Teachers Association. This was her *Nils Holgerssons underbara resa genom Sverige* (*The Wonderful Adventures of Nils*), published in 1906, which told the story of a boy bewitched by a farm sprite, a *tonte,* which made Nils very small. The boy then travels around Sweden on the backs of wild geese, and incidentally (like the readers of the book) learns a lot about the geography of the country.

It was an attractive idea, and Lagerlöf's book became deservedly popular in Sweden and throughout Scandinavia. It continued to be used as a schoolbook for many years and was reprinted in translation in many countries – but strangely it never became very popular in Britain, where publishers and readers have often been unreceptive to books written in minor languages. (Its eventual translation into English, and the illustrations, both came from the United States.)

The British were much more welcoming fifty years later to what was probably the best-known Swedish book of all time, but even though *Pippi Långstrump* was published

Astrid Lindgren, *Pippi Långstrump* (*Pippi Longstocking*). Stockholm, Rabén & Sjögren, 1945. Cover illustration by Ingrid Vang Nyman. Lindgren's Pippi is something like a female Popeye, blessed with super strength, and a highly original mind that confounds traditional gender expectations. 'DO YOU SUFFER FROM FRECKLES?' she is asked, and she, her face covered with them, stoutly replies 'No ... I don't suffer from them. I like them. Good morning!' *Pippi* was a surprise, a cheerful and no doubt energising read for wartime girl readers weary of tales of docile princesses and school stories.

Courtesy Rabén & Sjögren, Stockholm

Selma Lagerlöf, *Nils Holgerssons underbara resa genom Sverige.* (*The Wonderful Adventures of Nils.*) Stockholm: A. Bonnier, 1906, 1907. Published in two parts, and written as a school reader, the story of Nils and his travels on his goose explored nature, wildlife and folklore.

Courtesy Blackwell's Rare Books, Oxford

in Stockholm in 1945, it took nine years before Oxford University Press published an English edition, possibly because there were doubts about the book's message. *Pippi Longstocking* by Astrid Lindgren (1907–2002) was the story of an exceptionally strong, wayward, feisty and disruptive girl, originally told by the author as a get-well story to her daughter when she was ill and absent from school. One suspects elements of Lindgren's memories of her own adolescence in her stories about Pippi.

Fashions change, and having been formerly a very traditional conservative society, by the 1940s Sweden was moving towards liberal values and was responsive to feminist views. In the wartime period, traditional authors and parents would have been horrified by Lindgren's disruptive, disobedient heroine – but children loved the stories, and many teachers and librarians became equally positive about the *Pippi* books. Lindgren's books were a great commercial success, and sold so well that in 1976 she claimed in a satirical story that, because of anomalies in the Swedish tax system, she was being charged tax of 102% of her income: changes in the Swedish tax system (and indeed the political party in power) followed!

Having sold nearly 150 million copies of the *Pippi* books and seen their publication into nearly a hundred languages, Lindgren became far more than just an author; she became a national institution. After her death in 2003 the Swedish government established the Astrid Lindgren Memorial Award, effectively the same as the Nobel Prize, which was to be awarded to authors, illustrators, oral storytellers and promoters of reading. In the long term, this ALMA award may prove as important and influential worldwide as the Nobel Prize.

The Fourth Dimension

Always present in children's literature, fantasies about time and space travel developed in the 19th century, gaining popularity particularly after the Second World War.

Many books about children's literature discuss the books by George MacDonald, the friend of Lewis Carroll who advised him to seek publication for *Alice in Wonderland*. Though little read today, MacDonald's *At the Back of the North Wind* (1871) inspired many later writers, including C. S. Lewis and J. R. R. Tolkien, and among them was the American Madeleine L'Engle (1918–2007).

As with adventure stories, the no-man's-land between fantasy for adolescents and that intended for adult readers is often very ill-defined. Questioning whether such authors of classic early science fiction as Isaac Asimov or Ray Bradbury (or even Jonathan Swift) aimed their books deliberately at adults is really to miss the point, because young readers quickly took possession of these books. In the 1950s, when science fiction was starting to be taken seriously in the literary world, and with the example of the successful short-story magazine *Galaxy Science Fiction* in front of them, many writers attempted the form.

Authors' intentions are important. As Madeleine L'Engle proclaimed, 'You have to write the book that wants to be written – and if the book will be too difficult for grown-ups, then you write it for children.' L'Engle's idea for *A Wrinkle in Time* (1963) was found 'difficult', and there were many rejections from publishers before it was accepted for publication – possibly because this ingenious time-travel story had, like C. S. Lewis's Narnia books, a strong religious element. This interplay between storytelling and proselytising was also present in the works of Tolkien and C.S. Lewis (see p. 213).

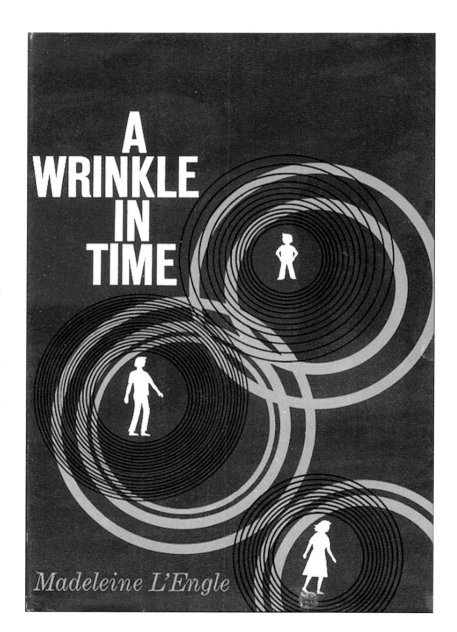

Madeleine L'Engle, *A Wrinkle in Time*. New York: Farrar, Straus & Giroux, 1963. Cover design by Ellen Raskin. L'Engle believed the many rejections she received for the manuscript arose from its unusual combination of its heroine and subject: a female protagonist in a science-fiction book.
Courtesy of Aleph-Bet Books, Pound Ridge, N.Y.

'With head, hands, wings, or feet, [Lucifer] pursues his way ...' (Book II, line 949): from Milton's *Paradise Lost*. Illustrated by Gustave Doré. Edited by R. Vaughan. London: Cassell, Petter and Galpin [1866]. Rejected in some quarters for what was seen as its occultism, both UK and American titles of Philip Pullman's *His Dark Materials* and *The Golden Compass* are drawn from Books II and VII of *Paradise Lost*: 'Unless th' Almighty Maker them ordain / His dark materials to create more Worlds, / Into this wilde Abyss the warie fiend / Stood on the brink of Hell and look'd a while, / Pondering his Voyage.'

Author's collection

Engle's book was described in many ways: as science fiction, as a **Bildungsroman** or coming-of-age novel, as a story of family life, or as a response to the Cold War. Some critics saw it as a feminist tract or even a work of Satanism(!) L'Engle's book produced strong reactions. But *A Wrinkle in Time* became a great favourite among adolescent readers, and is still one of the bestselling American children's books.

The English writer Philip Pullman (b. 1946) received almost as many adverse reviews as L'Engle for his award-winning trilogy *His Dark Materials* (1995–2000; published in America as *The Golden Compass*). It was in part a retelling of Milton's epic poem *Paradise Lost*, in another of its guises, a coming-of-age tale of two children wandering through a series of parallel universes. Pullman's books received a lot of adverse comment from American Roman Catholics in particular. In Britain, the charge that the books are anti-religion has been much more muted. As one critic commented, 'It's difficult to imagine adolescent novels any more openly subversive.' Pullman's *His Dark Materials*, widely read by adults as well as adolescents, seems to have been found by book groups to be another 'difficult' book, so much so that a special reader's guide has been produced to help readers to grapple with Pullman's concepts.

In other media, simplicity seems paramount. Hollywood made a (very successful) film version of the first book in Pullman's *Dark Materials* trilogy, tweaking and recasting Pullman's darkest messages, with the result that the book's religious meaning was almost totally obscured. As one cynical critic put it, 'the studio opted to kidnap the book's body and leave behind its soul'.

CHAPTER 10

The War Years and Beyond

After the end of the First World War, book publishing for children in Britain showed few immediate changes.

A few new publishers showed interest in good publishing for children, sometimes looking back to older works, such as the stories by the 19th-century French author Charles Nodier (like *The Luck of the Bean-Rows*, and *The Woodcutter's Dog*, both 1921), which were translated into English and published by Daniel O'Connor with fine illustrations by Claud Lovat Fraser. Francis Meynell, at his newly-founded Nonesuch Press, experimented with Bernard and Elinor Darwin's *Tale of Mr Tootleoo* and an attractive version of Perrault's *Histories or Tales of Past Times Told by Mother Goose with Morals* (both 1925) just as, much later, in the 1960s Meynell published finely printed editions of children's classics in the Nonesuch Cygnets series.

These were unusual in the interwar years, however, and in wartime many printers and publishers, such as Wills & Hepworth in Loughborough, reinvigorated publishing

Children searching for books among the ruins of their school in Coventry after a German air raid, 10 April 1941. The elder author remembers prep school lessons in the gloom and discomforts of an air-raid shelter.

Photograph by Paul Popper. Popperfoto/Getty Images

Eric Fitch Daglish, *How to See Plants*. The Children's Nature Series, Book II. London: J. M. Dent, 1932. This beautifully illustrated nature book, containing numerous engravings, was typical of a pre-war style, but perhaps a little dry for the modern children at whom it was aimed, and never achieved a huge commercial success for the publisher.

Author's collection

programmes they had established earlier (see pp. 226–7). There were many new and innovative publishing firms, such as Boriswood, Jonathan Cape, Victor Gollancz or Faber & Faber, producing well-designed and interesting books for adults, but such efforts in juvenile publishing were rare. Yet there were exceptions: Jonathan Cape with its twelve-volume *Swallows and Amazons* series by Arthur Ransome, running from 1930 into the war years and beyond, set the tone for a whole generation of young readers; in 1939 Faber published the ever-popular *Old Possum's Book of Practical Cats* by T. S. Eliot, then editor there himself: these texts are still full of life.

The staunchly left-wing Victor Gollancz was another innovative publisher, remembered now more for the publications of the Left Book Club (which he founded in 1935), with their brilliantly designed jackets conceived by the typographer Stanley Morison, than for his cheap editions which foreshadowed the books published as Pelicans or Penguin Specials by Allen Lane in the late 1930s. Perhaps inspired by G. D. H. Cole's *Intelligent Man's Guide Through World Chaos*, which he published in 1932, Gollancz commissioned from Naomi Mitchison (1897–1999) a book of essays for children by leading liberal thinkers. This well-intentioned volume, *An Outline for Boys and Girls and their Parents* (also 1932) was attacked by many at the time for its modernist views, and is now largely forgotten. Most parents, it seems, did not want challenges of this sort. We are inclined to agree with Susan Hill, who wrote about issue-led books: 'You name it, there is a novel for children about it. But all children are anxious, adult life contains much that is ugly and unhappy, unpleasant or downright bad. Why introduce them to that too early through books, which can be such a force for enjoyment?'

Though at the time it was by no means obvious, the most significant change in

British publishing in the 1930s came from the production of cheap, high-quality paper-bound books, or paperbacks, often named collectively as Penguins after the series started by Allen Lane in 1935. In the 1920s Ernest Benn experimented (and failed) with cheap paper-bound novels. The Continental series of paperback books in English, published by Tauchnitz in Leipzig and later by Albatross Editions (run by J. Holroyd-Reece from Paris), were well known in Britain. Lane closely copied the Albatross style with his Penguins; his success with these sixpenny books was in getting the reluctant book trade (printers and booksellers) to accept that there would be an appetite amongst the public for *good* paperbacks – it took an initial order for 63,000 copies from Woolworths to show that his project was viable (just as the Ladybird series's success was in part due to offering the books to a wider audience, through cheaper outlets). But buyers liked 'Penguins', and they became very popular. Lane, advised by William Emrys Williams, was soon able to add the non-fiction 'Pelican Books' to the firm's list, and in 1937 Allen Lane issued the first of their 'Penguin Specials', which they produced in a timely response to the general public's worries about the coming Second World War.

There were many people concerned with children's publishing who had worries about the quality of non-fiction for children, including Dent. In 1932–4, J. M. Dent published some attractive volumes in the Children's Nature Series, illustrated with wood-engravings by Eric Fitch Daglish, but these were all black and white and the books relatively expensive, so they weren't the success they might have been. At Oxford University Press, the post-war appointment in 1956 of Mabel George to head the children's publishing department saw rapid improvement in the quality of text and illustrations in its books for young readers.

In the 1930s, a few people familiar with the cheap **lithographed** books being published in Soviet Russia and in France urged the production of similar books in Britain, most notably the artist and political activist Pearl Binder (see pp. 232–3). The book designer Noel Carrington (1895–1989), then in charge of book publishing at Country Life, became one of the most important figures in the development of British children's publishing. At Country Life, he commissioned the *Orlando* books from Kathleen Hale (see p. 143), *High Street* (1938) from the architectural historian J. M. Richards, with illustrations by Eric Ravilious, and Mervyn Peake's piratically dark comic novel for children, *Captain Slaughterboard Drops Anchor* (1939), illustrated by himself.

In a happy moment in February 1938, at a meeting of the Double Crown Club, Carrington buttonholed Allen Lane, telling Lane about the lithographed books the Soviets were producing and his idea for a cheap, paperback series of well-illustrated children's non-fiction. Lane accepted the suggestion, on condition that the books could sell at sixpence like the Penguins, and be planned in print runs of at least 20,000 copies. Carrington was confident this could be done, using the facilities of the printers W. S. Cowell at Ipswich. One of Lane's great virtues as a publisher was that he allowed his series editors considerable freedom. But by the time the contract was agreed, the Second World War had started. Carrington wrote: 'Evacuated children are going to need books more than ever … Let us plan to get out half a dozen as soon as we can.'

Carrington's plans called for oblong books of thirty-two pages, with cover and inside pages printed together, in a very effective formula which allowed for colour to be printed on one side of the paper and black and white on the other side, printed lithographically by Cowells. The choice of

illustrators was crucial, and Carrington could call on a range of brilliant artists to produce the series now well known as Puffin Picture Books (see pp. 234–5). The first few Puffins published in 1940 were frankly patriotic (*War in the Air*, *War at Sea*, *Great Deeds of the War*), but included others advocated by Carrington like Arnrid Johnston's *Animals of the Countryside* (1941). S. R. Badmin's *Trees in Britain* (1943) was so successful that it was made required reading at agricultural colleges. As Carrington recalled in 1957,

The series … would arouse, [and] satisfy, the child's awakening interest in its surround-ings: natural phenomena in the first place, then human activities such as the theatre, machines, and travel. I felt that colour was essential, and that artists could for various reasons be more successful in books of this nature than the camera.

Carrington's plan proved enormously successful. As well as the Puffin Picture Books, Allen Lane and Carrington organised the production of 'Baby Puffins' (stories for

Tom Gentleman, *Brae Farm*. London: Transatlantic Arts, 1945. Rather in the new 'Puffin style', the handwritten text and bright lithographs in this story of a peacefully situated Highland farm must have offered urban children a cheerful break from the gloom of shuttered and sandbagged wartime Britain.

By permission of David Gentleman

the very young), 'Puffin Cut-Out Books' (so useful in those days when toys were scarce) and Porpoise Books, a hard-bound, more expensive and less profitable series edited by Grace Allen Hogarth, an American editor who had worked with the illustrator Edward Ardizzone on his first *Tim* books.

Carrington's Puffin Picture Books were followed soon by the very successful series of Puffin Story Books under the editorship of Eleanor Graham until her retirement in 1961, when the role was taken on by Kaye Webb. These editors shared the same ideals about the importance of literary quality with a growing group of children's librarians, such as Eileen Colwell. Noting the need for a range of books for children from different social backgrounds, and providing young readers with fresh insights into the realities of life outside Britain, these stories were as valuable educationally as Pelicans or Penguin Specials were to an adult audience. Despite never publishing Enid Blyton or W. E. Johns, between them Graham and Webb produced a huge range of titles, including many new books as well as established classics. It is hard to imagine any British household of the post-war years without some of their little volumes. Despite the success of Carrington's Puffins, they were not the end of his adventures with children's publishing. He also published books often similar in production and content under such imprints as Pilot Press or Transatlantic Arts. After 1945, many of these were printed by W. R. Royle & Sons, a firm which began printing greetings cards and other books created after the firm, stock and premises of Raphael Tuck was destroyed in the Blitz.

It is remarkable that so many good books for children were published in the war years. The total number of titles published in Britain in 1937 was 17,137, but by 1943 the number had dropped to 6,705 books. Children's books and schoolbooks formed 20% of the total published (at a conservative estimate): from 3,427 in 1937 to 1,341 titles in 1943. Raids by the Luftwaffe in Britain destroyed more than an estimated 20 million books, including the total stock of the main wholesale company Simpkin Marshall. Many people employed in papermaking, printing and bookbinding were called away on war duties, so many firms had to call men back from retirement, who worked hard to keep the machines functioning without replacement parts. Paper was rationed, printers eventually receiving only 37.5% of that used in 1937 – a policy which meant that such firms as Penguin and Wills & Hepworth (who had always had a high paper usage owing to their high print runs) were still relatively well provided for, whereas some other publishers of costlier, smaller edition books now found themselves starved of supplies. Rationing of paper continued until 1949, and new post-war publishers received an allocation of only ten tons per year, enough for only *small* editions of five books, which obliged some, like Charles Ede of the Folio Society (established in 1947), to haggle for extra paper from Continental suppliers.

The '**Book Production War Economy Agreement**' of 1942 between the Ministry of Supply and the Publishers Association had codes governing the manufacturing of books, covering such aspects as print size, words per page, and so on. Though the agreement was voluntary, publishers who didn't join in had their paper ration cut. Much of the paper was needed for material published by the Ministry of Foods, and, undoubtedly, some of its publications were significant for children as well as adults, such as the booklets in the 'Kitchen Front Broadcasts' series written by Charles Hill, the Minister of Health.

One effect of the war was to make supplying New Zealand and Australian and other overseas bookshops with British titles extremely difficult. Though this contributed strongly to the dearth of books 'down under', it also encouraged indigenous publishing. In Britain, the demand for books grew, despite the limitations placed on wartime publishing. Whether the effects of these constraints were good or bad is debatable: Susan Hill has commented,

how rare and exotic a thing was a brand-new book to a child born during the war, and learning to read and to love books and stories in the 1940s and early 1950s. Books came printed on poor, thin almost transparent paper, and bore a horrid official stamp that they conformed to Government War Standards, and they were not easy to come by.

Yet war standards often led to better book design. The thin paper and well-planned typography of Jonathan Cape's new editions of Arthur Ransome's books (for example), are much to be preferred to the children's books produced in the mid-1930s, which were often printed on thick, blotting-paper-like paper, with an over-abundance of blank pages. (Adopting the wartime adage of 'Make do and Mend', the passing down or swapping of books undoubtedly preserved copies of older books which would have been made available to new child readers.)

Books *were* short in supply, with a marked log-jam in the production of new ones. Wartime planning led, in time, to improved children's public library services, but in the 1940s children's books were produced by many publishers now long forgotten, such as the Gulliver Book Company of Lower Chelston in Devon. During the war years, with few other luxuries available, some publishers saw the opportunity to find new markets, and to target books at young adults as well as children (see pp. 131 and 231). The intended audience was of little importance, however, if the books were used by adults,

like the 1942 Penguin Special on *Aircraft Recognition*, or the 'Achievement Books' issued by the Pilot Press, an illustrated wartime series celebrating such national efforts as *Achievement in Feeding Britain* and *Achievement in British Aircraft*.

Some important books from the war years, such as the *Père Castor* volumes, translated by Rose Fyleman and published by Allen & Unwin in the 1940s, and T. H. White's small masterpiece, *Mistress Masham's Repose* (1943), did not then receive the attention they deserved. Books for children were of lower priority than the provision of suitable reading for serving forces abroad. The development of a military library system was part of the work of the Education Corps, and Penguins provided many of the 'armed services editions' distributed to troops. (In occupied France, the *Wehrmacht* similarly provided their forces with special editions prepared by the Insel-Bucherei.)

As well as providing entertaining reading matter at a time of social deprivation, children's (and adults') books could serve a more insidious function. In Nazi Germany, Goebbels's propaganda machine turned its attention to children, using the Grimm folk tales as one vehicle (see pp. 236–7) to promote their ideology. 'Every fairy tale is politically alignable without raping the poetry within,' declared Hubert Schonger, the producer of several Nazi film adaptations of fairy tales, but Goebbels told him to go gently: 'Children will see through propaganda quicker than their parents ever could.' The propaganda in wartime and post-war books published by a freer (but still supervised) press in Allied countries might have been less overt, but nonetheless they served to reinforce national and patriotic values.

Between the wars, there was little evidence of German influence on British publishing, apart from on the design of British paperbacks, after Hitler had come to power

Charles Hill, *Wartime Food for Growing Children*. Pamphlets from the Ministry of Foods, published alongside its 'Kitchen Front Broadcasts'. HMSO: 1942. Though the booklets were not aimed at children, youngsters would clearly have benefited from the advice, which advised mothers on how to stretch the family rations (and exhorted fathers not to take too large a share themselves of the 'building' foods). Other booklets, such as the 1945 leaflet on foraging, *Hedgerow Harvest*, might have had both adult and child readers in mind.

Courtesy of Manchester Libraries and Archives

in 1933 (see pp. 228–9). There were many instances of Germans and Austrians who left what had been their home countries after 1933, such as H. J. Kaeser, who moved to Sweden. English editions of the children's books written by the German-Jewish H. A. Rey, illustrated by his wife Margret Rey, started to appear in 1938–9 when the Reys lived in Paris, but their series of books about a mischievous monkey, Curious George, was published before they fled France for New York, and the books did not really become known in Britain until the end of the Second World War. The monkey's fame in America was great enough to result in a paper-doll version by Kathy Allert, published by Dover in 1982.

The fall of France to Germany in 1940 also led to French authors of children's books having their work published in the United States instead. The delightful picture books by 'Françoise' (Françoise Seignobosc), who also emigrated there in 1937, seem now to have dropped out of fashion, but Antoine de Saint-Exupéry's *Little Prince* (see p. 229) is still very popular (though perhaps less universally admired in Britain).

Though many children's books largely ignored the fact that the Second World War was in progress, its pattern sometimes showed up very strongly in the work of author-artists. As one of the best known, Edward Ardizzone (1900–1979) was already well known by the time he became an official war artist, and the first of his own *Tim* stories, *Little Tim and the Brave Sea Captain,* was published by Oxford University Press in 1936. For *Tim All Alone* (1956; see p. 238), Ardizzone was awarded the Library Association's inaugural Kate Greenaway Medal – for by then he had become the best known and perhaps the public's favourite of British book illustrators. Among the many titles he illustrated was a 1974 edition of Graham Greene's (1946) foray into children's

books, *The Little Train* (and its sequels), and four of the very underrated (and perhaps forgotten?) books by the Sweden-based, German-Jewish feminist Hildegard Johanna Kaeser, whose *Mimff* stories were published in English by OUP from 1939 to 1960.

Almost as popular in America were the illustrations by Garth Williams (1912–96) for delighted readers of Laura Ingalls Wilder's *Little House* series, as well as E. B. White's *Stuart Little* (1945), and *Charlotte's Web* (1952), which latter title was as immediately successful in Britain as it was in America.

One of the children's authors who was notably affected by the Second World War was Roald Dahl (1916–90). Dahl was working in Tanganyika for the oil company Shell at the start of the war, and enrolled in the RAF in Kenya. He crash-landed in the Libyan desert, and was eventually invalided out. He turned his hand to writing after narrating stories of his time in the RAF to C. S. Forester. These horrific and fantastic tales for the *New Yorker*, later published in book form as *Someone Like You* (1953), were immediately popular. Like the short-story writer Hector Hugh Munro (1870–1916), better known as 'Saki', Dahl 'tiptoed along the tightrope between the macabre and the comic'. Dahl's writing took him later into writing for children, and he is now probably best known for *Charlie and the Chocolate Factory* (1964), one of the most successful children's books of the 20th century. Dahl's books have been often illustrated by Quentin Blake, who really inherited Ardizzone's mantle as Britain's best-loved illustrator (see pp. 238–9). Blake's masterfully light and comical touch serves to alleviate some of the underlying black savagery and cruelty discernible in Dahl's work, which worries some adult readers. Susan Hill's reservations about issue-based children's novels could well be applied to Dahl's writing. But children love his work.

Accidental Success in Publishing

Many children's publishers hoped to issue cheap, uniform and inexpensive series which would almost sell themselves. One obscure provincial printer found a way to do it well.

Just as publishers seek titles to provide a steady income, so printing firms often look for work to keep their staff and plant busy during otherwise slack periods. In 1873 in the small Leicestershire manufacturing town of Loughborough a flourishing local bookseller, Henry Wills, added printing and bookbinding to his existing trades. He was later joined by William Hepworth, and the firm, as Wills & Hepworth, was in operation from 1906. It was a substantial firm, employing 150 employees (a third of them women), and producing many elementary and Sunday school books for the Society for Promoting Christian Knowledge (SPCK).

Some SPCK books produced before the war were the models for two books produced at Loughborough under the Ladybird Books imprint and deposited at the British Museum in August 1914: *Tiny Tots Travels* and *Hans Andersen's Fairy Tales*. Neither were outstanding in terms of their content (the *Fairy Tales* was an amateurish translation), and they were far inferior to Grant Richards's Dumpy Books (see pp. 172–3), but the format Wills & Hepworth had devised worked well. The books were profusely illustrated, often by well-known artists. Using standard paper sizes, printed in black on one side and colour on the reverse (of one or more sheets folded to make a gathering of sixteen pages), and then sewn and bound in paper laid over boards, Ladybirds were always in this style. It suited the needs of the printing plant well. Over the next twenty-five years, Wills & Hepworth tried a variety of styles: thick, bulky volumes, annuals, so-called 'untearable

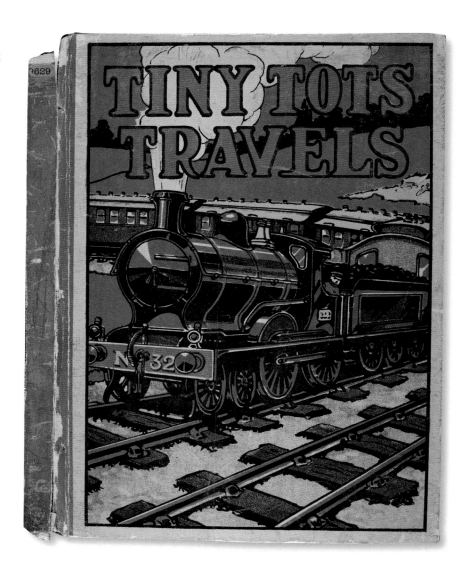

M. Burbridge, *Tiny Tots Travels*. Loughborough: Wills & Hepworth, 1914. This, with *Hans Andersen's Fairy Tales*, was the first of the books published in the Ladybird series, though this early Ladybird appears chunkier than the those which were published later, with their instantly recognisable format. The Ladybird imprint and logo were registered for copyright the following year, though the series didn't begin in earnest until 1940.
The British Library

books' (on thick paper) – all aimed at a rather undiscerning market, but none as successful as their Ladybird Books.

With in-house printing and binding, and adequate paper supplies, Wills & Hepworth's production of Ladybirds continued apace from 1940. The first was an oddity: *Bunnikin's Picnic Party* (1940) by Angusine MacGregor, who had illustrated numerous 'bunny' books for Blackie, such as Jessie Pope's *Bobbitty Flop* and *Flip and Fuzzy* (both 1911). In 1940, MacGregor's work was old-fashioned, but buyers seemed to like it; similar books, often heavily revised versions of fairy tales, were reprinted well into the 1950s.

Wills & Hepworth's rather odd, random choice of books to publish then suddenly changed. Ladybird's Traveller, or commercial agent, Douglas Keen (1913–2008), re-joining the firm after his RAF service, saw an unfulfilled demand in schools and the book trade. He was confident that Wills & Hepworth should move upmarket to issue well-written, well-illustrated non-fiction books. Keen was aware of the earlier Puffin Picture Books introduced by Noel Carrington. After some persuasion, in 1945 Wills & Hepworth published *In Green Pastures*, the first of six serious non-fiction Ladybirds written by 'Uncle Mac of the B.B.C.', Derek

McCulloch, the producer of *Children's Hour*.

Keen now started commissioning respected writers such as L. du Garde Peach, and equally eminent artists, for natural history books for use in schools. His policy paid off: translations into many African and Asian languages allowed Wills & Hepworth to sell well in the colonies, while their Key Word Reading Scheme series (started in 1964), and others, introduced books to almost every schoolchild in Britain. There were mistakes, such as the Ladybirds set in the **Initial Teaching Alphabet** (a failed experiment that educationalists urged upon some schools and publishers in the 1960s), but they were rare.

All empires come to an end. In 1973 Wills & Hepworth sold their very successful but highly specialised firm to Pearson, and Keen retired. The Ladybirds series drifted along, without any particular focus, until the Loughborough-based business closed in the 1990s, and the brand was transferred by Pearson to Penguin. Penguin Books' changes, shown by the recent choices of titles published under the Ladybird imprint, have been controversial, and sadly the future of the series seems unsettled. Keen's work was described as 'a great legacy to British kids', and his Ladybird books are enthusiastically collected by nostalgic former readers today.

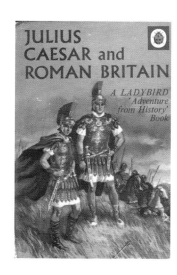
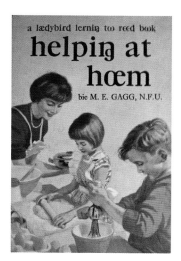

Views from the Continent

Apart from *Struwwelpeter*'s Hoffmann and the brothers Grimm, the British adopted few German children's writers. Erich Kästner was one exception.

The British publishing world employed many printers and artists from Germany, and German publishers, like Raphael Tuck and Ernest Nister, formed a distinct group of children's book manufacturers. But surprisingly, in Victorian times they produced relatively few translations of German children's books, even from popular authors such as Clementine Helm. Despite the enormous success in Germany of Wilhelm Busch's *Max und Moritz* (1865) – which inspired the American comic strip, *The Katzenjammer Kids* – it resulted in only one British edition.

The First World War prompted some remarkable pacifist writing (for adults), including Erich Maria Remarque's *Im Westen nichts Neues* (*All Quiet on the Western Front*, 1929) which was popular in Britain. The contemporaneous *Emil und die Detektive* (*Emil and the Detectives*) by Erich Kästner (1899–1974), was one of the first children's books to include believable inner-city children as its characters, who spoke a credible vernacular. Joseph Goebbels disliked Kästner's work intensely, and had many of them destroyed, like Remarque's books, as 'contrary to the German spirit' in the Nazi book burnings of May 1933 (proclaiming 'I consign to the flames the writings of Heinrich Mann, Ernst Gläser, Erich Kästner'), though *Emil and the Detectives* itself was never proscribed by the German censors. Presumably, as a children's book, it was regarded as insignificant.

The placing of the illustrations in English editions of *Emil* suggest that the translators and the publishers failed to fully understand Kästner's jokes, but it did not matter: in Britain, *Emil* was adopted enthusiastically.

Erich Kästner, *Emil und die Detektive. Ein Roman für Kinder*. Berlin: Williams & Co., 1931 [1929]. The original German edition was illustrated by the anti-fascist German-Jewish cartoonist Walter Trier (1890–1951), well known, following his move to London in 1936, for his covers of the magazine *Lilliput* (for adults). He illustrated many of Kästner's books.
Private collection

Wilhelm Busch, *Max und Moritz: Eine Bubengeschichte in sieben Streichen* (*Max and Moritz: A Story of Seven Boyish Pranks*). Munich: Verlag von Braun und Schneider, 1906. Though now less well known to English-speaking readers than Saint-Exupéry's whimsical *Little Prince*, Busch's darkly comic tale of the mischievous boys, here stealing a chicken from the Widow's house, was influential.

Private collection

Schnupdiwup! Da wird nach oben
Schon ein Huhn herauf gehoben;

Dramatised, set to music, and 'retold' or otherwise adapted for educational use, Kästner's work has been widely read.

The same is hardly true of a French near contemporary, written by André Maurois: *Patapoufs et Filifers* (1930). Maurois was well known and liked in Britain, but his brilliantly amusing, anti-war fantasy for children did not appear here in English until 1941. As *Fattypuffs and Thinifers* it slowly became

recognised as a minor classic, but is apparently little read today.

By contrast, the story *Le Petit Prince* (*The Little Prince*) has been described (particularly in the United States) as the most important French children's book of the Second World War. Antoine, Comte de Saint-Exupéry (1900–1944) was already famous for the books about his flights as a pilot in West Africa and Argentina. After Hitler's defeat of France in 1940, Saint-Exupéry lived in New York and worked to persuade America to join the war against Hitler. There, he wrote *Le Petit Prince*, which was published in both French and English in New York in 1943. He had rejoined the Free French Air Force in 1942, but was shot down on a mission over the Mediterranean in July 1944. As a doomed, aristocratic hero, Saint-Exupéry was very chic, and became a literary sensation in America. The story of *Le Petit Prince*, superficially about the meeting of a crashed airman with a boy from a remote asteroid, contained many musings about freedom and responsibility.

Saint-Exupéry's book may be read on several levels, and has many possible meanings. Brian Alderson has commented that with it 'existential angst enters children's literature'; noting that it has been described as 'an absurd, not to say perverse, piece of whimsy'. Nonetheless, Saint-Exupéry's writing attracted many readers, and his own brilliant pen-and-wash illustrations (now preserved in the Pierpont Morgan Library in New York) worked well with the text of his extraordinary book, written in unhappy times.

Wartime Gift Books – for Children or Adults?

In the difficult years for the book trade during the Second World War, some publishers issued unusual and ambitious small-sized books in short print runs, which included books for children as well.

Many publishing companies have issued cheap books in uniform dress, for adults as well as children. These have ranged from Marshall and Harris's miniature books at the start of the 19th century (see pp. 118–19), to Routledge and Warne's Toy Book series of the 1860s, to the ultra-cheap Books for the Bairns series published by the writer and spiritualist W. T. Stead from 1896, and Dent's Everyman's Library (from 1906 onwards). Like other publishers in the difficult days of the late 1930s, the literary firm Chatto & Windus perceived a demand among consumers for short books, and so created a new series which it marketed as 'Zodiac Books'. This was a series of small 'gift' books in striking bindings influenced in part, perhaps, by the Curwen Press. Many of its titles reflected the firm's partners' interests, with selections of Cavalier poetry and the like, but other titles also revealed the strong influence of the firm's jacket designer, Enid Marx.

Marx (1902–98) was an extraordinarily versatile artist: in 1944 she was awarded the title of Royal Designer for Industry (RDI), and was well known for her writing on popular, traditional folk arts, for her illustrations, plus her designs for furnishing fabrics and for the London Underground, and for many applied crafts. Well aware of the attractive Soviet children's books which were to inspire the production of Puffin Picture Books, and of Kathleen Hale's *Orlando* books (see p. 143), Marx wrote and designed several little books for children for other publishers as well as the one she was chiefly employed by, including, for Oxford University Press,

Enid Marx, *A Book of Nursery Rhymes*. Zodiac Books series. London: Chatto and Windus, 1939. In a letter, the firm described Marx as 'the model artist, the doyenne of designers', and clearly they had a successful partnership.

Author's collection

Les Cris de Paris. Zodiac Books series. London: Chatto and Windus, undated. As well as Marx and Peake, Zodiac published a range of books for children and adults. This, produced just after the war, was like an earlier 'book of trades', featuring sellers of muffins, parasols or mackerel. It was no doubt intended for adults, but its brightly coloured cuts would have appealed to children too.

Author's collection

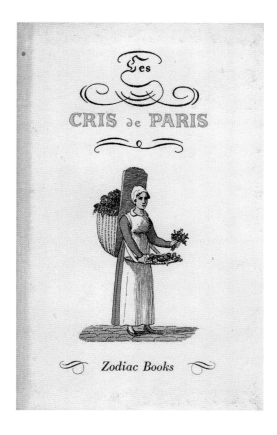

her delightfully light-hearted *Bulgy the Barrage Balloon* (1941), several for Faber & Faber, an early Puffin Picture Book (*A Book of Rigmaroles; or, Jingle Rhymes*, 1945), and for Chatto & Windus, *Nelson: The Kite of the King's Navy*, 1942. The latter was very much like her book about barrage balloons and one suspects Chatto & Windus took it on reluctantly. Chatto's Zodiac Books series ran from 1937–55 (with a four-year hiatus during the war) and for this Marx illustrated *A Book of Nursery Rhymes*, in 1939.

A rather unusual choice for the Zodiac Books series was Lewis Carroll's *The Hunting of the Snark* (1941), which the unusually gifted Mervyn Peake (1911–68) illustrated, though he is said to have been paid only £5 for his efforts. Peake studied the technique of many illustrators as a basis for his own, later commenting that in illustrating books it was necessary 'to subordinate myself totally to the book, and slide into another man's soul'. Whatever Peake saw in Lewis Carroll's soul, his Zodiac Book had the same haunting, dark, gothic (and often rather frightening) style which was present in the later books he illustrated after the Second World War. Peake's very individual manner was to be found in his writing for his *Gormenghast* novels written between 1946 and 1959: they are all about children, and often very amusing, but emphatically *not* written for a juvenile audience.

Despite having published some good, interesting books, Chatto & Windus's success with its Zodiac Books was very muted. Clearly, there were production problems in the early war years, and tensions with illustrators of some of the volumes; but other publishers shared such difficulties too. It is possible that booksellers and buyers, sensing Chatto's mixed objectives, never developed much brand recognition or loyalty to the sputtering series; a great pity, because some of the Zodiac Books were among the best produced in Britain at the time.

'Out with Mysticism and Fantasy of Children's Books!'

The striking appearance of Russian children's books in the 1920s eventually persuaded British publishers to copy them – Puffin Picture Books was one of the first imprints to absorb the style.

Attempts to make young Russians into good Soviets was part of Revolutionary business after 1917. The active interest taken in education by Bolshevik leaders was important, and the role played by Lenin's wife Nadezhda (Nadya) Krupskaya (1869–1939) influenced Russian policy on libraries and publishing under Stalin until her death. Krupskaya's part was significant, but the brilliance and dynamism

of Russian children's books in the 1920s had begun much earlier, in about 1910, when the graphic works of Muscovite avant-garde artists, influenced by the Italian Futurist artist Marinetti who had visited the city in 1914 (just prior to the Revolution), set out to give 'a slap to the face of public taste'. This was echoed by Soviet artists Galina and Olga Chichagova in 1925 in their two-part poster showing traditional (and Tsarist) tales being

Pearl Binder, *Misha Learns English*. A Puffin Picture Book. Harmondsworth: Penguin Books, [1942]. Binder's pro-Soviet text carefully avoided the fact that Misha's mother would have been forced to send her son to a crèche. Her charming illustrations were 'drawn direct to the plate by the author' and printed by Sanders Phillips and Co. Ltd at the Baynard Press.

Private collection. By permission of Pearl Binder's children.

ousted in favour of a purposeful Soviet youth, busy under the direction of Lenin: 'Out with mysticism and fantasy of children's books!' the sisters declared. 'Work, battle, technology, nature – the new reality of childhood.'

The production of books by artists such as Vladimir Mayakovsky and David Burlyuk, students expelled from the Moscow Art School for their political activities, was startling. One fellow student at Moscow Art School was Feodor Rojankovsky, who fought on the White side in the Russian Revolution. As a constant emigré from his homeland, 'Rojan', as he was known, very effectively re-invented himself: in France, as an illustrator for Flammarion's *Père Castor* stories of the 1930s, and, after the fall of France, in New York, where he became a popular and successful illustrator for the American publishing firm Golden Books.

All Soviet children's books were didactic, and many were little more than crude propaganda, rather like the later books published during the Cultural Revolution in China of the 1970s. But many of the better Soviet books of the 1920s and 1930s worked brilliantly as books for children. The frequent employment of an oblong format, printed by **lithography** with simple, striking colour images, and a marked deployment of photomontage made the books memorable, and modish (see pp. 20–21). The publishers and editors included Samuil Marshak (1887–1964), perhaps the most prolific and popular children's writer in the USSR, and his older brother Ilya Marshak (1896–1953), who illustrated many complex scientific texts for a young audience under the pseudonym of 'M. Ilin'.

Very little of this work was widely known in the West, though Russian emigré artists in Poland, German, Czechoslovakia and France drew heavily upon it. In Britain, any direct Soviet influence on children's books was virtually non-existent: one of the most successful of all Russian children's books was Korney Chukovsky's *Crocodile* (1917), but when republished by Elkin Mathews in London in 1932, with the original illustrations by 'Re-Mi' (Aleksei Remizov), it received little notice. Soviet sympathisers, having visited the USSR, brought back samples from their travels, but it was to be a long time and required the development of paperback publishing in the UK before the Russian style became widely acceptable to British publishers, and was adopted by them (see p. 143).

One of those with left-leaning sympathies was the artist and writer Pearl Binder. The daughter of Jacob Binderevski, a Jewish jobbing tailor who had emigrated from Russia in the 1890s, and an Anglo-Jewish mother, Pearl moved from Manchester to the East End of London in the 1920s and made it her home, producing some wonderful lithographs of its cramped and lively back streets. She was also involved in television broadcasting for children in its earliest days in 1937. Binder travelled to Russia and was much taken with the children's books there, reporting on them for Noel Carrington's magazine *Design for Today* in January 1934, drawing attention to writers such as Marshak and Chukovsky, and artists like Edward Krimmer, Charushki and Lebedev. For Carrington, this exposure had a marked impact on the design of his Puffin Picture Books, including Binder's own *Misha Learns English* (1942), and, more widely, the look of wartime children's books in Britain.

Children's Books Take Flight

Changes foreshadowed in children's books in Britain culminated in Noel Carrington's conception of Puffin Picture Books during the Second World War.

Discontents about the quality and content of children's publishing were often expressed between the First and Second World Wars. These ranged from doubts about quality expressed in reviews in the (right-wing) *Spectator* to attacks from the left via George Orwell and others complaining about its heavily entrenched middle-class values. But there was no doubt that juvenile publishing was less healthy than it had been at the beginning of the century, when competition from Germany had provided attractive and well-printed alternatives to the books produced at home.

The changes came largely by chance: by 1935 the publication of Penguins was just getting under way, coinciding with changes in the marketing of cheap books, the adoption of new ideas about book illustration and improvements in the use of photolithography. 'One of the lessons,' wrote the artist, writer and traveller Pearl Binder about Soviet books in her article for *Design for Today* in 1934, 'we might take to heart is the USSR policy that only the very best is good enough for the future men and women of the world.' Binder (1904–90) was notable not only for her knowledge of Russian art; she was also one of the founders of the Artists' International

James Gardner, of Carlton Studio, London, *War in the Air*. A Puffin Picture Book [no. 3]. Harmondsworth: Penguin Books, [1940]. The earliest Puffin Picture Books were deliberately somewhat jingoistic, but the effective use of the coloured lithographs for illustration attracted children, and the series became very popular.

Private collection

John Dumayne, *Woodworking for Children*. Written and illustrated by J. Dumayne. A Puffin Picture Book [no. 57]. West Drayton; New York: Penguin Books, [1945]. Many Puffins were cheerful, light-hearted books, but some of the instructional volumes were deliberately understated and matter-of-fact. This one demonstrates the clear layout and effective design of books in the 'How to' series. They were easy for children to follow and more appealing than many earlier books in this category.

Author's collection

Association. Her writing for the Design and Industries Association (DIA), founded in 1915, was also significant: the DIA worked hard to bring British design forward from the William Morris/Arts-and-Crafts movement to a more modernist approach. Another key figure in the DIA was Noel Carrington, then working for Country Life Publications, owned by Newnes. At Country Life, Carrington published Kathleen Hale's *Orlando* (see p. 143) and also Eric Ravilious's *High Street* (1939), both innovative children's books displaying fine lithographic illustrations.

Having persuaded Allen Lane (of Penguin) to back his ideas for some children's picture books which would be similar in style to the earlier Soviet publications, Carrington engaged a wide range of authors and artists for the Puffin Picture Books series. The first were consciously patriotic propaganda efforts, with *War at Sea*, *War in the Air* and *War on Land* published in December 1940, but

Carrington's ideas for the series called for other books too, such as *Animals of the Countryside* (1941) or *Woodworking for Children* (1945), which were deliberately educational, and succeeded because of the quality of their illustrations and the very effective use of colour.

Some Puffins were intended to open children's minds to thinking about the post-war period (in such books as *About a Motor Car*, 1946, or *Village and Town*, 1947), and in addition, there were many story books, like Pearl Binder's *Misha Learns English* (1942; see p. 232), or Kathleen Hale's *Orlando* books. These slim, paper-covered books were widely read (often to pieces) by children. But from 1941 onwards, when Eleanor Graham became editor of the new series of Puffin Story Books for Penguin, more and more children gravitated from the picture books of their early days to reading the cheap and comprehensive collection built up by Puffin in its Story Books series. At first limited to reprinting children's books first issued by other publishers, in time Puffin moved to publishing original titles, such as *Stig of the Dump* (see p. 211). Because of the small allowance of paper issued to Penguin Books for their Puffin Picture Books series during the war, Carrington turned to using other publishers more and more to issue his brilliantly designed and written picture books. Whether for Penguin or other publishers, Carrington's work as an editor and designer was important for children of the war years because of the books he commissioned. His innovative design and thoughtful production influenced later publishers such as Dorling Kindersley to produce educational books which were equally imaginative and exciting, as well as thoroughly covering their subjects.

No Fairy Tale: Propaganda and the Children's Book

It can be argued that the whole of children's literature, pretty much, is an attempt to steer children's beliefs in one direction or another. But publishers, and those they work for, have not been above using children's books to further the ideologies of their chosen political regimes.

The seemingly innocent coming-of-age story of *Bambi* (p. 137) was banned by the Nazis for its 'pro-Semitic' propaganda. The book had been enjoyed, together with Johanna Spyri's *Heidi*, by Hitler's private secretary and bunker-wife, Eva Braun. While the dreaded 'He' of the *Bambi* cannot be a reference (however apt) to Hitler himself – the book pre-dates his rise to power by several years – its author Felix Salten *was* an active Zionist, and his book deals with themes of persecution and assimilation undoubtedly reflective of the Jewish experience in Germany and elsewhere in Western Europe at the time.

Salten, a great hiker and lover of the outdoors, retained an acute sense of nature's reality as red in tooth and claw, an aspect of his book which was sidestepped by Walt Disney in his sentimental film adaptation of it. Even so, Disney's animation, relocated to the eastern American woodlands, and intensely anti-hunting, showed the destructive and blundering hunters as

Karl Hobrecker (after Grimm), *Rotkäppchen* (*Little Red Riding Hood*). Alte deutsche Volksmärchen series, issue 2. Illustrations by Hildegard Mössel. Winterhilfswerk des Deutschen Volkes (WHW), *c.*1940–42. Button Book. Many folk tales revolve around the solitude (though not the joy) that *Waldeinsamkeit* or 'wood-lonesomeness' inspires. *Hansel and Gretel*, *Little Red Riding Hood* and *Sleeping Beauty* all concern innocent adventurers set upon or imprisoned in secluded hovels or castles, in or surrounded by the deep, dark woods. To the indoctrinated child Red Riding Hood's persecutor might have had associations other than mere animal danger, spelled out much more clearly in other anti-Semitic propaganda.

Author's collection

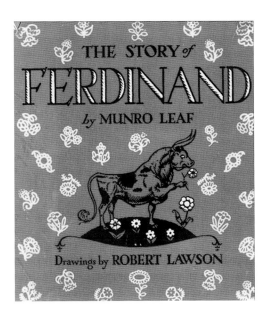

enough of a threat to the innocent animals' life as to elicit strong objections from the American Rifle Association.

The German love of nature is well known – it is a culture which after all has a word for the quiet reflective joy that comes from beeing alone in the woods: *Waldeinsamkeit*. The concept goes hand in hand with their rich folklore, which the National Socialists misused to foster a false sense of continuity with Hitler's distorted vision of *Der Volk* ('the People') as a heroic 'master race'.

One instance of this was the republishing of Grimms' fairy tales in the form of 'button books' by the German publishing house Winterhilfswerk, or HWK. Often awarded to Aryan children for dutiful service, these small booklets with loops on them were designed to be worn from the button of one's coat or *Hitlerjugend* ('Hitler Youth') uniform, to show a good moral example to others. More explicit forms of propaganda aimed at children were contained in picture books like *The Poisonous Mushroom* (1938), issued by the prominent Nazi publisher Julius Streicher, which depicted the Jew as a scourge on society.

In the Soviet Union, colourful books with a modernist edge like the Yiddish-language *Di Potsht* by Samuil Marshak (*The Post*; Odessa, 1934), proclaimed the might of Soviet power (see pp. 232–3). In the United States, the 1940s saw the rise of superheroes to preserve and protect 'American' values in magazines like *Captain America* and *Captain Marvel*. In China, Mao's Little Red infants eagerly absorbed pro-regime adventure stories like Xu Guangyao's *Xiao bing Zhang Ga* (*Little Soldier Zhang Ga*; Beijing, 1962). This was not new – the use of children's books to instil cultural and political ideals dates back to the 1644 *Childes First Tutor* and beyond (see pp. 54–5) – but modern mass production and distribution enables greater reach than ever.

Governments fearful of retaining their hold on power may, like the Nazis, censor books they regard as undermining their own aims. *The Story of Ferdinand*, by American author Munro Leaf, is one such, which came under attack by authorities around the world. Released in 1936, shortly before the outbreak of the Spanish Civil War, this simple story of a peace-loving bull was regarded in Spain as pacifist anti-Franco propaganda and banned (though in other quarters it was seen as *pro*-Franco). In America, after a slow start, *Ferdinand* became popular with children and adults, and by December 1938 had knocked *Gone with the Wind* off the bestseller list, but it was viewed variously as anarchist *and* fascist, or the bull character as latently homosexual or even a manic depressive. Hitler banned it as 'degenerate democratic propaganda'. In 1946, as a part of the American work of reconstruction in occupied Germany, *Ferdinand* was translated and some 30,000 newsprint copies distributed freely to German children by Jella Lepman, a German–Jewish woman then working for the US Army Re-Education Program for Women and Youth, and who was later important in the founding of IBBY, the International Board on Books for Young People.

An Incomparable Illustrator

At a time when there were many gifted illustrators of children's books in Britain, one illustrator's work stood out. Edward Ardizzone remains much loved, and stylistically influential, today.

"*What is the use of a book,*" thought Alice, "*without pictures or conversations?*" So much of the pleasure for children comes from illustrations by artists in sympathy with their authors. The selection of the 'right' artist is sometimes made by an author, but often by the publisher or the book designer. Writers often praised the wood-engravers of the 1860s and later illustrators who, like Beatrix Potter towards the end of the 19th century, seized on the technical advantages of the new photo-mechanical methods.

There was another equally splendid period for book illustration during the 1940s and 1950s, when Puffin Picture Books and other publishers exploited coloured **lithography** to augment the processes used for letterpress printing. Many gifted artists made the children's books of this period very attractive, at a time when they were the main vehicle for book illustration. (Apart from firms like the Folio Society, established after the war, or the *Radio Times*, there was a limited number of publications for adults which required illustration.) Artists such as Lynton Lamb (1907–77), Faith Jaques (1923–97), Helen Oxenbury (b. 1938), the Hungarian Victor Ambrus (b. 1935) and the Pole Jan Pieńkowski (b. 1936) enriched British publishing in the way that the Russian illustrator 'Rojan' had strengthened both French and British pre-war juvenile literature with his pictures for the *Père Castor* books. Often in subtle ways, such

Tim's parents were at the garden gate when they arrived.
Captain McFee and the boatman were there, too.

You can imagine how pleased Tim was to see his father and mother and his old friends again.
The captain told Tim's parents all about

Edward Ardizzone, *Little Tim and the Brave Sea Captain*. Oxford University Press, 1936. For more than half a century, children have loved the charmingly illustrated adventures of 'Little Tim'.

Author's collection

Eleanor Farjeon, *The Little Book Room*. Illustrated by Edward Ardizzone. Oxford University Press, 1955. A happy partnership of author and illustrator, Ardizzone illustrated this with 36 line drawings, and he and Farjeon both felt they were the best he had ever done.

Author's collection

artists increased public awareness and approval of children's literature; for example, with the menu cards Lamb designed in the early 1950s for the Orient Steam Navigation Company, using Edward Lear's work.

Head and shoulders above these talented illustrators was Edward Ardizzone (1900–1979), an artist in the tradition of Thomas Rowlandson. Ardizzone was a foreigner (his father was French–Italian, and Ardizzone was born in Tonkin), but he grew up in Suffolk, becoming totally British in outlook. In 1926, a gift of £500 from his father encouraged him to set up as a professional artist, and his first book commission, from Peter Davies, was to illustrate Sheridan Le Fanu's macabre *In a Glass Darkly* (1929).

Rather as Kathleen Hale wrote her first *Orlando* book for her children (see p. 143),

Ardizzone's first children's book was written for his own child. *Little Tim and the Brave Sea Captain* was sent by Oxford University Press to New York for first publication there in 1936, where Grace Allen Hogarth (the book's editor) made the unusual decision to have the text hand-lettered, rather than use printing type, but nonetheless produced a charming, oversized book. The pictures were based on the artist's childhood memories of the docks at Ipswich.

During the Second World War, Ardizzone served as an official war artist in France, North Africa and Italy (and much of his work is now held in the Imperial War Museum, London). But he had not forgotten his *Little Tim* stories, and over the years produced several more: *Tim All Alone* (1956) received the first Kate Greenaway Award from the Library Association, and *Tim's Last Voyage* brought the series to an end in 1972.

Meanwhile, Ardizzone was busy illustrating other books. Some were established favourites, like Bunyan's *Pilgrim's Progress* (Faber, 1947) and Walter de la Mare's *Peacock Pie* (Faber, 1946), but also such books as Clive King's *Stig of the Dump* (see p. 211) and Eleanor Farjeon's *Little Book Room* (1955, awarded the Carnegie Medal by the Library Association and the Hans Christian Andersen Medal by IBBY). Books illustrated by Ardizzone almost always had an extra appeal, and it seemed that publishers, libraries and readers could not have enough of his work.

Almost a century after the first publication of Ardizzone's drawings, readers of all ages are still drawn to the books illustrated by him, sometimes irrespective of their authors. His pictures serve to strengthen the text, an amazing asset to the publishers of his work.

A Disruptive Success?

Traditionally, buyers of children's books, whether parents, teachers or librarians, have been wary of children's enthusiasm for books which challenge received ideas. Roald Dahl's hugely popular books have done just that.

At frequent intervals, parents, educators and the press, concerned with the welfare of the young, have been overtaken by fits of moral panic. Sometimes these have been caused by religious fears about children's souls (see pp. 90–91), sometimes by anxiety that the young will be corrupted by revolutionary ideas (see pp. 116–17), but more often from the desire to shield the young from sex or violence (see pp. 206–7). Modern attempts at censorship may often involve merely excluding books from library shelves, but, more seriously, it may take the form of pressure upon publishers by worshippers of political correctness to change this or that. One example is the recent (and worrying) instruction by one major and highly regarded academic publisher to remove all reference to pork or sausages in its children's books, to avoid offence to readers whose religion prohibits the consumption of such products. But can children not understand that others live by different rules? It is important that in children's education, and in their reading matter, cultural pluralism is fostered to encourage open-mindedness and respect for differing views. Censorship and revisionism is the opposite of this.

One *Guardian* writer, writing about novels for adolescents serving their fascination with Nazi history, claimed 'when the politics of hatred are worryingly on the rise, more fiction like this, asking uncomfortable questions, can only be a good thing for [young adults]'. Or is it? Susan Hill asserted that 'realism comes home soon enough, and many children have too much anguish to

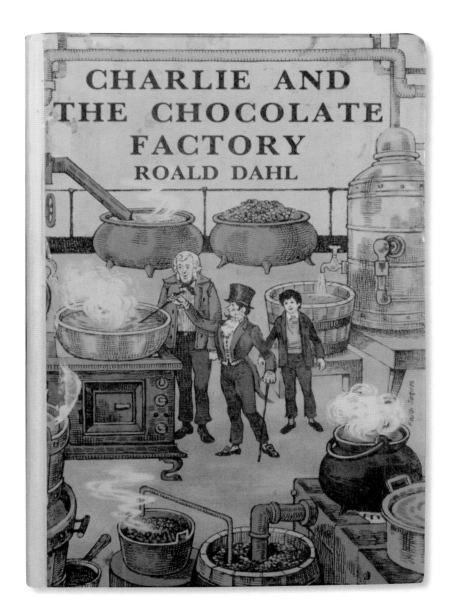

Roald Dahl, *Charlie and the Chocolate Factory*. Illustrations by Faith Jaques. London: George Allen & Unwin, 1967. Joseph Schindelman was the original illustrator of the cover of Dahl's book when it was published in the United States by Alfred Knopf. Jaques illustrated the first British edition, and others followed; one wonders if Dahl or the publishers found her pictures too tame for the darker aspects of the text.
Rooke Books, Bath

Roald Dahl, *Revolting Rhymes*. London: Jonathan Cape, 1982. As William Golding's *Lord of the Flies* attested, children have dark instincts and delight in the 'nasty' from the safety of their bed-covers – and parents do not always approve. Quentin Blake has become *the* Dahl illustrator, his success perhaps in part because he tones Dahl down a fraction, rendering the stories as more comically mischievous than wicked, softening the author's acid edge.

Author's collection

cope with in their everyday lives as it is. Their books can be one corner of life that remains untainted by the troubles brought upon their heads by unthinking, unloving adults.'

Should we seek exposure, or protection? The writer Roald Dahl (1916–90) moved into writing for children after he had made his reputation with his disturbing stories for adults. At Repton School, Dahl claimed to have been bullied and ferociously beaten (by masters), but fellow pupils at the school have remembered Dahl as a bully himself and a hater of authority. Whatever the cause, his stories for adults often have a sadistic tinge, and the child characters, often disruptive or disobedient, usually meet with a nasty fate.

Dahl's 1964 *Charlie and the Chocolate Factory* was described by the critic John Rowe Townsend as 'fantasy of an almost literally nauseating kind', and similar adverse criticisms have been levelled at other books, such as the novel *Matilda* (1988) and his 1982 collection of 'alternative' fairy stories, *Revolting Rhymes*. Another reviewer observes that Dahl's method was 'to pick on human weaknesses and vices, such as gluttony, bossiness, or untidiness' and then invite his young readers to rejoice in the sticky ends of characters with such unappealing traits. Sarah Trimmer or Charlotte M. Yonge would have been horrified by the nihilist tone of Dahl's work.

Publishers and Hollywood, however, sensed that Dahl would be a winner, and children's enthusiasm for his books have confirmed that the entertainment industry was right. Children adore them, and the print run for the first edition of *Charlie and the Chocolate Factory* was 2 million copies, while Dahl's books overall have sold well over 40 million copies. Dahl is hardly 'politically correct'. The fact that Aldi in Australia banned the sale of *Revolting Rhymes* (interestingly, for use of the word 'slut', rather than the traditionally violent and disturbing content of the fairy tales themselves) did no harm at all to Dahl's popularity. Will he still be read and enjoyed by children after a century has passed?

CHAPTER 11

Growing Up Fast: Comics, TV and New Media

By Victorian times, specialist publishers had recognised that, provided they attracted the right attention, children's books could be profitable products.

We use the world 'product' deliberately, for it was around this time that authors and publishers began to see themselves as part of a mass-production business, filling a need in the same way that other entrepreneurs moved into large-scale manufacturing of foodstuffs, clothing or other items, which would generate a much greater income through selling large quantities at modest individual returns than by selling fewer items at much higher prices.

By the middle of the 19th century, plenty of people like the travel publishers George Bradshaw and Thomas Cook recognised how much money could be made from producing guidebooks for adults. Newspaper proprietors at the start of the 20th century were also very much aware of this, but Sir C. Arthur Pearson (1866–1921), the founder of the *Daily Express* and owner of the *Evening Standard,* was interested in many things beyond improving his market share or the making of profit. In 1892, Pearson established the Fresh Air Fund, a charity for sending children from city slums on annual trips to the countryside, and he was also instrumental in providing funds to start Robert Baden-Powell's newly established Boy Scout movement. It was natural, then, that it was Pearson who published *Scouting for Boys,* one of the most

successful publications of the century, and indeed of all time (see pp. 248–9). Heavily influenced by similar movements in America, Lord Baden-Powell's movement was itself influential worldwide, not least in totalitarian countries.

Noting both the value of comic strips to attract readers, and the demand for annuals (often given as Christmas presents) in pre-1914 Britain, newspaper proprietors made extensive use of them in their attempts to dominate the market. Whether *Pip, Squeak and Wilfred,* or *Teddy Tail* was better than

Johann Mettenleiter, *A pupil receiving a book at a public prize-giving, at the end of a school year.* Hand-coloured copper engraving, *c.*1810.

INTERFOTO collection /Alamy Stock Photo

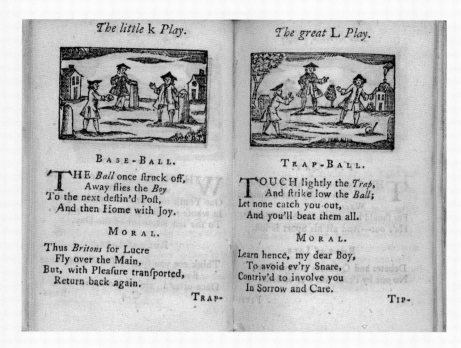

The little k Play.

BASE-BALL.

THE *Ball* once ſtruck off,
 Away flies the *Boy*
To the next deſtin'd Poſt,
 And then Home with Joy.

MORAL.

Thus *Britons* for Lucre
 Fly over the Main,
But, with Pleaſure tranſported,
 Return back again.

TRAP-

The great L Play.

TRAP-BALL.

TOUCH lightly the *Trap*,
 And ſtrike low the *Ball*;
Let none catch you out,
 And you'll beat them all.

MORAL.

Learn hence, my dear Boy,
 To avoid ev'ry Snare,
Contriv'd to involve you
 In Sorrow and Care.

TIP-

A Little Pretty Pocket-Book ... London: Printed for Newbery and Carnan ... at St Paul's Church Yard, 1770 [first, 1744]. Later reprinted by Isaiah Thomas in Worcester, Massachusetts, this small volume of verse is interesting in so many ways. 'To entertain Little Master Tommy, and Pretty Miss Polly,' the book came with a ball (for a boy) or a pincushion (for a girl) – an early example of tie-in merchandising and of the global reach of the market for popular books. The engraving above illustrates the origins of baseball: it precedes the formal establishment of the rules of rugby and soccer by some sixty years, but reflects the rough-and-tumble aspects of those games in their infancy.

The British Library

Rupert Bear (see pp. 250–51), was once debated by their readers with the same fervour that boys supported the Roundheads and despised the Cavaliers (or vice versa). Probably the quality of the writing and illustration in these annuals differed very little except in the minds of their young readers; in any case, for the price, by a generous relative, of around half a crown (or 2s.6d, a somewhat larger sum than it might appear today), children received gifts which they treasured and turned back to read again and again. These annuals of the 1930s, so popular at the time, have a continuing market value and are steadily collected by elderly readers, who enjoyed them as children, and by younger generations coming to them anew.

Annuals such as *Rupert Bear* helped middle-class children to establish the protocols for their own lives. There were rules for correct behaviour which covered most aspects of life, and in Victorian times British society was particularly active in codifying them. The Marylebone Cricket Club, or MCC (for example), formulated rules for the game of cricket which was played by many boys at

the end of the 18th century. In later generations, in the rapidly expanding public schools the rules for football and other games, notably association football ('soccer') and rugby ('rugger'), were also codified – for rugger, some thirty-seven first rules, set by three senior schoolboys in 1845, were followed by the 'Cambridge Rules' set for soccer in 1848. Guidebooks such as Wisden's *Cricketer's Almanack* (first published in 1864 and still published annually) are devoured by cricket enthusiasts of all ages. Though the rules of the game hardly became everyday reading for the young, the growing popularity of such games meant they appeared with increasing frequency in stories for both boys and girls, and books by such writers as Angela Brazil or Anthony Buckeridge were very widely read.

Changes in governance in the Victorian era greatly increased funding for schools of all kinds. Not only grammar, preparatory and public schools, but also Sunday schools and those described as 'church schools' were assisted by government funding after 1833, and particularly the non-denominational state- or council-run 'board schools', created after the passing of the Education Act of 1870. The growth in publishing directed at schools took several forms: the repackaging of books which would be used as school prizes was one. Many books produced by such publishers as the Religious Tract Society were read enthusiastically – or dutifully – by their recipients.

It is interesting to note that, in cases when the winners of a school prize were given a choice of prize book, the girls would as often choose books considered to be written for boys as those supposedly for their own gender, and nearly always different books from those selected by their elders. One 1888 survey showed that many girls' books only sold well because these were purchased by parents, and indeed, as Jonathan Rose has pointed out:

when London elementary schoolchildren of both sexes selected school prizes in 1910, the only 'girls' book' high on the list was *Little Women* (1,625 choices), along with *Robinson Crusoe* (2,283), *David Copperfield* (1,114), *Ivanhoe* (1,096), and *Westward Ho!* (1,136).

Giving books as prizes to 'good' or high-achieving young scholars or churchgoers became commonplace in Victorian times; awarding prizes to the authors for the books themselves is a 20th-century phenomenon. For children's authors, the first significant award, in the United States, was the **Newbery Medal** (named for the 18th-century London publisher John Newbery), which was initially funded by Frederic Melcher, the editor of *Publisher's Weekly*, and administered by the American Library Association. It was first awarded in 1923. The ALA deliberately selected as its first recipient a serious informational book, Hendrik Van Loon's *Story of Mankind* (pp. 252–3), the success of which helped to establish the ALA's role in presenting the award, and also alerted publishers to an area of potentially profitable publishing, and (of course) improved sales of the book itself. Van Loon's book nowadays looks quaintly old-fashioned, but (as soon afterwards the Soviet publishers and Carrington's Puffin Picture Books showed) the market for such good, clearly written and skilfully illustrated books was very large. The quality of informational books is now much higher than was common before the Second World War.

The poorest children had no books and little access to libraries or literature. All they usually encountered were the **readers** prepared for class use or the lurid penny printings that circulated on street corners. As Matthew Arnold observed in his *General Report* of 1860, the readers were by no means the best books available for children (see

pp. 96–7); he described the cheapest readers as being as low in quality as they were in price, using extracts from authors 'of the second and third order' who were offering 'dry scientific expositions' and texts that were 'feeble, incorrect and colourless'. Even worse (so *The Times* alleged in 1882), teachers were being bribed to select particular textbooks to propose to their school board members. Once publishing for schools became profitable, petty corruption was inevitable.

Firms wanting to get into juvenile publishing started in several ways. The publishers of **penny dreadfuls** and **dime novels** exploited all the possibilities of increasing sales – there is a very enlightening account of this, based on personal knowledge, in Anthony Trollope's short story 'The Spotted Dog' (which was originally published in *Saint Paul's Magazine* in 1870). As better magazines established themselves and came to replace the cheaper comics in popularity, with the production of *The Boy's Own Paper*, *Chatterbox* and the like, publishers increasingly made their annual volumes more attractive in their literary content, illustrations and binding. The antiquarian bookseller and historian Percy Muir argues that the boys' magazines of the 1860s and 1870s show that young readers were no longer prepared to confine their reading to the books chosen by their parents. The continuing popularity of the annuals for later generations too is asserted by Arthur Marshall, who in his account, *Whimpering in the Rhododendrons: The Splendours and Miseries of the English Preparatory School* (1982), notes that 'the basic literary diet consisted of the colossal annuals *Chums* and the *Boy's Own Paper*', and adds that, once in the school, 'these volumes became public property ... avidly read by anyone who picked [them] up' (see pp. 168–9).

Possibly the demand for annuals declined in the 1940s, and in any case the paper

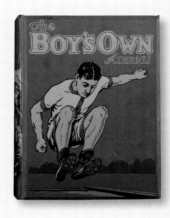

Arthur Lincoln Haydon (ed.), *The Boy's Own Annual* (vol. 42). London: 'Boy's Own Paper' Office, 1920. The paper was published weekly (and after November 1913, monthly) from autumn to summer, following the school year. From 1879 onwards, the year's issues were bound together as annuals. Increasingly, after the First World War, these moved away from an elaborately decorated and gilt-enhanced style, to one with heartier colour blocks and bold typefaces. The annuals still featured 'action' scenes, often of Indian chieftains whooping it up on horseback, but also more everyday sporting figures to whom boy readers could more realistically relate.

Rooke Books, Bath

shortages during the Second World War meant that many were forced to cease publication. One great asset was that wartime conditions ended the use of 'featherweight' paper, commonly used in cheaper annuals. It was no doubt due to the depressed condition of British juvenile publishing in the 1930s that British publishers overlooked the Belgian and French *bandes dessinées* (or BDs), so different in style from the comics of Britain and America. But after the end of the war, when publishing on the Continent was starting to revive, the strip cartoons and picture books by Hergé (Georges Remi, 1907–83) tempted English writers to bring *Tintin* across the Channel. Some British adults were almost as taken aback when they initially encountered these books in translation as they had been when they first saw Disney's cartoons: as with the films featuring Mickey Mouse (or the later Disney productions) grown-ups often deplored what they saw as the books' superficial vulgarity, just as they disliked the way their favourite literary characters were distorted or over-simplified by the Disney Studios.

The *Tintin* books were often vulgar, but in a way that British readers responded well to. *King Ottokar's Sceptre* and the other *Tintin* tales were imaginative, informative and witty: they seemed to carry aspects of the Gallic approach to life that the British found very appealing. Admittedly, some of the earlier *Tintin* volumes expressed a (then widely held) mild racism which would be found unacceptable today. Hergé was seldom at any time a politically correct cartoonist; that he was not was part of his charm. (He was of course not alone in this. In his 1940 essay on 'Boys' Weeklies', George Orwell famously categorised the xenophobia of the children's strip cartoon stories, identifying seven common racial stereotypes – 'Frenchman: Excitable. Wears beard, gesticulates wildly', 'Spaniard, Mexican etc. Sinister, treacherous',

and so forth. Hergé succumbed to such lazy generalisations as much as anyone.)

A later competitor to Hergé's *Tintin* books, first published in 1959, was *Astérix le Gaulois* (*Asterix the Gaul*) by René Goscinny and Albert Uderzo (see pp. 256–7). The enormous popularity of their works made these the bestselling of all French books. Goscinny and Uderzo deliberately used modern French stereotypes for the different peoples (the Goths are all militarists, the Helvetians obsessed with time-keeping and cleaning, the Britons all like warm beer and tasteless food that they swamp in mint sauce, and so on), but the comical element in this seems only to make the stories even more attractive. The popularity of the stories led to a rash of translations into the major European languages but, remarkably, into a huge range of minor regional languages too – Alsatian and Breton in France, Frisian and Limburgish in the Netherlands, and Mirandese in Portugal among them. Was the success of these translated editions into regional and provincial tongues reflecting widespread disenchantment with official imposition of a standardised and centralised languages which chafed on their localised cultural traditions?

The Japanese **manga**, production of which increased greatly after the end of the Second World War, have a link with American comics and the French/Belgian *bandes dessinées*, and also with the underworld culture, which caused worries about obscenity in the 1950s. Just as in previous generations, when some people disapproved of the new science fiction novels, teachers and librarians today see a value in graphic novels to encourage reluctant readers. *Tintin*, *Asterix* and *Astro Boy* have all been successful with all sorts of readers, keen as well as reluctant ones, and the advocates of graphic novels make large claims for them. Whether publishers of these have equal success lying ahead of them seems highly uncertain – one wonders at the graphic-novel treatment of Marx's *Communist Manifesto* by the Canadian Red Quill Press, for instance, or the treatment of the Jack the Ripper murders in the magazine comic strip *From Hell* (1989–96, published in one volume in 1999), itself with its own cult following. What is certain is that some publishers have recognised that there is a demand for sex in adolescent reading, in the way that the publishers of the novels featuring Hank Janson did (but at one time this impulse might have been more innocently served by children sniggering over 'The Lady of Shalott', or stolen copies of *Lady Chatterley's Lover*). Contemporary **bowdlerisers** would have a very difficult task.

Featuring these characters in cartoons and graphic novels was by no means the only way their creators earned their livings: the life of a character outside the comic or book could be very remunerative. The production of merchandise associated with much-loved books' characters, such as stuffed-toy Rupert Bears, or posters and T-shirts featuring illustrations from the *Tintin* books, is a major part of children's publishing today. This had quite early origins, however, with Newbery and Harris's 18th-century publishing firm, or possibly before. Many successful series, like J. K. Rowling's *Harry Potter* novels, became almost industries in themselves. The Moomin characters created by the Finnish writer Tove Jansson originally appeared in cartoon strips, but the books she wrote about them, starting with *Moomin and the Great Flood* in 1945, were the foundation of her worldwide fame – and the production of Moomin memorabilia has become ever more profitable, especially in Japan, where teenagers and adults lap up what seems to the West to be 'for children' (see pp. 254–5).

New media has had an enormous effect on children's awareness of 'literature'. The crude early Disney films about Mickey Mouse attracted many, and the Disney Studio's later

film versions of the stories of *Pinocchio* (1940) and *Bambi* (1942), among others, have become regarded by some as 'the' versions, with their authors' original written tales forgotten. The same may be true of some of the BBC's early programmes broadcast on *The Children's Hour*: though the first volumes of S. G. Hulme Beaman's *Toytown* stories were published in the 1920s, it was the radio broadcasts which stuck in people's memories. Television, and the clever use of stop-motion animation in such TV series as *Noggin the Nog* or the French *Magic Roundabout*, created a demand, and this was augmented by the reinterpretation of the stories in print, so children could read them all over again.

Books like these, based on television or radio programmes, were by no means the only interesting, attractive publications being issued in the mid-20th century to compete with the older favourites. If there is a difference now from then, it is that the more commercially successful children's authors (and their publishers) have begun to think of the books they create as spanning over a whole range of media, and the next step is for the authors to create themselves as 'personalities' (by appearing at book signings

A BBC cameraman demonstrating stop-motion animation for *Muffin the Mule*, shown walking up a carrot stalk, 1949. Created by a Punch-and-Judy puppeteer, the puppet show was broadcast – for those lucky children with access to a television – on British television from 1946–57 (and revived as a cartoon in 2005). Muffin's popularity ensured that books about him were published and his character attracted merchandising spin-offs, including toys and lampshades. Muffin's exploits were even published in book form in the USSR in 1958.

William Sumits/The LIFE Picture Collection/Getty Images

Storytime Hangout: The Three Billy Goats Gruff. Penguin Digital/Google+, 2013. Readers of these stories can share the experience with members of their family online, wherever they may be in the world, an idea which evokes the cosy world of shared storytelling around the hearth of a previous age.

Courtesy of Bartle Bogle Hegarty/Penguin Books Ltd

and popular events and also by writing blogs or contributing to social media), and also for the publishers to devise readily marketable products. Some authors may be dragged unwillingly into areas such as merchandising of their created characters, and public appearances. Others accept the financial rewards it offers. It is interesting to look at the websites of highly successful authors – such as J. K. Rowling, Philip Pullman or Michael Morpurgo – to see how they present themselves there.

The creator of the *Harry Potter* books is of course exceptional. Rowling's success with *Harry Potter and the Philosopher's Stone* (1997) and the later volumes in her series of fantasy novels came as a great surprise to many. From being a poor, solitary writer receiving welfare benefits, and advised by her publisher to find a day job since she had little chance of making money from writing (she received a dozen rejections before her first *Harry Potter* manuscript was accepted), Rowling has turned out to be a breaker of many records, selling more than 450 million copies of the *Harry Potter* books, and becoming perhaps the richest children's writer of all time. Rowling's books have become equally popular with adult readers. Unlike some other famous writers and artists, Rowling strengthened her position as a creator enormously by ensuring that she had control over film-making and other spin-offs from her writing (through her own company, Pottermore). It shows the same shrewd

business head displayed a couple of centuries earlier by John Newbery or Dorothy Kilner. Many also admire Rowling for giving much of her wealth to charitable causes.

The possibilities for other ambitious young writers today are very tempting, and the ease of self-publishing makes the opportunities even greater, though prudent publishers may still advise these new authors to 'get a day job'. Many toddlers today are raised looking at tablets and mobiles (just as many 1970s and 1980s parents began to use the television as a babysitting tool) and developments in programming and animation aid many who seek to produce interactive children's 'books' to capture this very young market. Penguin has produced an online app with Google for *The Billy Goats Gruff*. The success or failure of this form of literature remains to be seen, and there are already grave concerns about damage to children's vision, and sleep patterns, from continual exposure to electronic screens. Many other successful writers and illustrators, staying much closer to traditional ideas of what a book for young children should be, have found their own new ways to create memorable, magical stories. Maurice Sendak is one such (see pp. 196–7), whose appeal is undiminished in our electronic age, and Eric Carle, whose *Very Hungry Caterpillar* continues to have a very long life (see pp. 260–61), is another. Both Sendak and Carle have given generously to libraries and museums in the United States, just as Judith Kerr has deposited her records with Seven Stories, the National Centre for Children's Books in Newcastle upon Tyne. With institutions like these, and the seemingly limitless digital material being added to the internet, the resources for people writing histories of children's books (and for the children reading the books) are much fuller now than those which were available before the Second World War.

A Long Jamboree

Scouting originally meant 'military reconnaissance', but its meaning was to be transformed by the efforts of Lieutenant General Robert Baden-Powell, a.k.a. 'BP'.

The modern Scouting movement started with the work of a man seemingly modelled on a character from Kipling. Lieut. Gen. Robert Baden-Powell (1857–1941), known as 'BP', was a professional soldier whose work was in mapping and reconnaissance in Afghanistan in the 1880s, but his professional activities allowed him to become a sportsman: his book on *Pig Sticking and Hog Hunting* (1889) became a popular guide.

BP's life's work might have taken the same course as that of many ambitious officers serving in India during the late 19th century, most of whom were keen to take part in 'the great game' of intelligence-seeking between Britain and Russian. Baden-Powell certainly did his share of this, and in the early 1890s undertook what the *Oxford Dictionary of National Biography* describes as 'a number of gentlemanly espionage trips' in the eastern Mediterranean area. But as fortune would have it, BP's profession took him to South Africa, and during the second Boer War (1899–1902) he became famous for his successful protection of Mafeking (in the Cape Colony) from invading Boers. 'Mafeking Night' on 18 May 1900 became famous for the way London crowds had taken to the streets to celebrate the relief of BP's garrison. At Mafeking, Baden-Powell had devised a considerable number of ingenious ways of hoodwinking the Boer besiegers, and his use of boys as messengers was particularly successful. His interest in training for boys had developed earlier on, at the time when he realised his 1899 military manual *Aids to Scouting* (1899) was already being used by

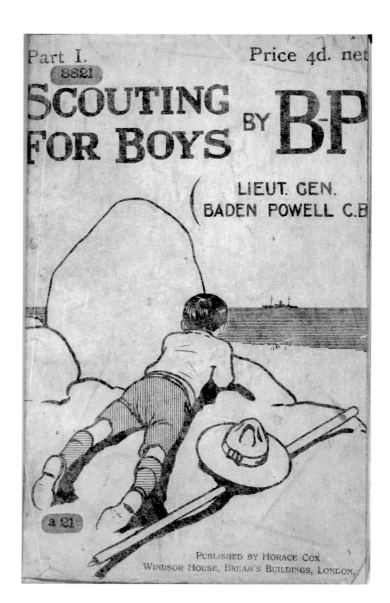

Lieut. Gen. Baden-Powell, *Scouting for Boys by BP. A Handbook for Instruction in Good Citizenship*. Windsor: Horace Cox, 1908. The manual's cover illustrations by the popular engraver John Hassall showed Scouts in their rangers' gear with hats and walking sticks, tracing tracks, watching for ships, at the helm of the boat, or up a mountain: 'in action' they became the heroes of the adventure stories they loved.

The British Library

Photographer unknown, Bain News Service, *Wyndygoul Council & War Dance*, c.1905. Ernest Thompson Seton's 'Woodcraft Indians' perform a war dance at the campground on Seton's Wyndygoul estate at Cos Cob, Greenwich, in Connecticut. Seton himself stands beside Standing Rock, banging a Native American-style drum. The first Woodcraft tribe was established here by Seton (reportedly he created the group from some young vandals who had been on his estate, instead of prosecuting them).

Library of Congress Prints and Photographs Division Washington D.C., LC-B22- 322-10 [P&P]

such groups as the Young Men's Christian Association and the Boys' Brigade.

In developing his work on scouting as a good activity for boys, BP was much influenced by the American Ernest Thompson Seton (1860–1946), who had developed the Woodcraft Indians group in 1902 (and this was reflected in BP's choice of topics for inclusion in his *Scouting for Boys*). Seton's role in setting up the Boy Scouts of America in 1910 was to be of great significance to BP.

Another man who was interested in providing boys with a sound, wholesome, interesting and rewarding path through life was the newspaper owner C. Arthur Pearson, who published Baden-Powell's *Scouting for Boys* in fortnightly parts during 1918. BP's simple and sincere text was well pitched to its audience, and boys (and girls too, in fact)

were very ready to pay heed to policies laid out by a man who was already regarded as a hero. BP's text echoed what were regarded as the quintessential virtues of a late-Victorian imperialist soldier (and some would say it also showed the downside of imperialism). BP's original text for *Scouting for Boys* has been subjected to severe criticism because of its reflection of the middle-class attitudes of a century ago, but the scouting movement of the 21st century has moved on.

The manual became such a success worldwide that the Scout movement today has 28 million active members, including the younger boys known as Cubs (or properly, 'Wolf Cubs', named after Kipling's *Jungle Books* hero), who were incorporated into the movement in 1916. BP's sister Agnes, and later on his wife, Olave Baden-Powell (1889–1977), recognised the movement's popularity with girls and organised sister organisations: the Girl Guides (from 1910 onwards; Olave became its Chief Guide in 1918) and (for the younger girls), the Brownies (from 1914). It has been estimated that since the first publication of BP's manual, there have been well over eighty different language editions published worldwide, with sales estimated at 100 to 150 million copies – and considering that the Scouting movement was closely controlled in Soviet Russia and in Nazi Germany, the popularity and influence of it was amazing. Through the continuing work of the Scoutmasters and 'Brown Owls' who run local groups, or the larger organisation which organises the occasional International Jamboree, the Scouts and Girl Guides movements still seem full of life.

A Very Long-Lived Bear

Intense competition between London newspaper proprietors at the end of the First World War led to some long-lived cartoon characters, who had a life beyond their comic-strips. The longest survivor of all was 'Rupert Bear'.

It's hard today to remember how bitter was the rivalry between popular newspapers at the time when print was the main medium, and radio and film were just emerging. Comic strips were one way to attract regular readers, so the *Daily Mail* included its 'Teddy Tail' from 1915 onwards, from 1919 the *Daily Mirror* had 'Pip, Squeak and Wilfred', the *Daily Herald* 'Bobby Bear' and in the children's comic *The Rainbow* (published by the Amalgamated Press) there was the bear-like 'Tiger Tim' – who had begun life in 1904 as leader of the Bruin Boys in the *Daily Mail*. Lord Beaverbrook (Max Aitken) was then endeavouring to make his *Daily Express* into the most successful mass-circulation paper in the world; to face the competition he instructed his editor to find and introduce an animal character to outdo those of his rivals. By chance, the wife of a sub-editor on the paper, Mary Tourtel (1874–1948), was experienced in animal drawing, and she was put forward to produce the pictures and text for 'The Adventures of a Little Lost Bear', a strip which first appeared in November 1920 and continues to appear in various media today.

In all these comic strips, as with the films created in the Disney Studios, the final work was the result of often quite sophisticated and commercially minded collaborations in which authors, artists, press production staff and promoters worked hard to make their products profitable.

Mary Tourtel's character, Rupert Bear, was an upright bear – always dressed in checked trousers, a sweater and a scarf – essentially a well-dressed and solidly middle-class little

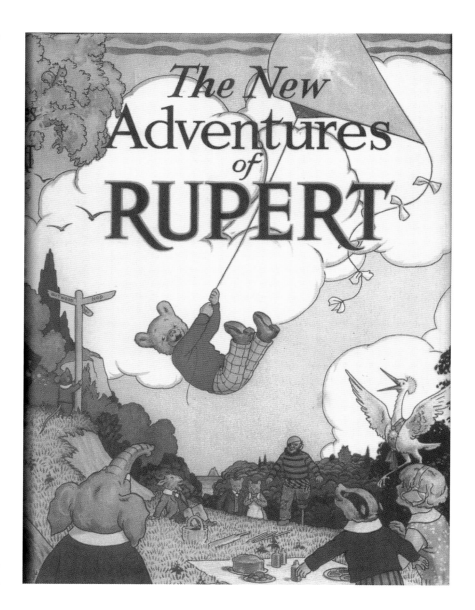

[Alfred Bestall], *The New Adventures of Rupert Bear*. London: Beaverbrook Newspapers, 1936. Despite the publication of previous spin-off books, this was the very first *Rupert* annual issued by the *Daily Express*, created by Bestall, who did not sign his *Rupert* work out of respect for Tourtel until after her death in 1948. It was so popular that production continued throughout the Second World War, on 'war economy' paper. The lively dust jacket shows Rupert swinging from a kite. This book was produced in facsimile in 1985, giving rise to similar facsimile editions, although six of the original annuals have not been reprinted owing to concerns about their content.

Followers of Rupert © Rupertbear.co.uk

boy with a bear's head, who lived with his parents in the fictional English village of Nutwood and who had (intermittent) wholesome adventures. Tourtel provided the pictures and the (rather lumpy) verse texts until 1935, when she retired and the responsibility passed to another freelance artist, Alfred Bestall (1892–1986), who had worked for *Punch.* Though formerly he had concentrated on illustration only, Bestall's *Rupert Bear* stories were quite as captivating as the earlier ones, and he initiated the publication of the first of the *Rupert Bear* annuals in 1936. Later, responsibility for the *Rupert* stories passed to other authors and illustrators and, as a profitable venture, has yet shown no signs of coming to an end. A website called 'The Followers of Rupert Bear', a range of soft toys, china mugs and other memorabilia (rather similar to the offerings available to Beatrix Potter enthusiasts), and a healthy collectors' market in which old annuals command high prices all indicate that Mary Tourtel's cartoon strip for the *Daily Express* still has a lot of life in it.

The *Rupert Bear* annuals, first published in 1936 at half a crown, were an ideal (and then rather generous) choice for a Christmas gift from an uncle or aunt. Contemporary *Rupert* annuals are still issued by different publishers who have acquired the franchise, and they reportedly still sell well (and at much higher prices) in numbers of over 50,000 copies a year. The demand for these has declined somewhat from the early days of the *Daily Mirror*'s reported sales of 100,000 copies for the 1923 *Pip, Squeak and Wilfred Annual,* but they still form an important part of children's reading which has scarcely figured in the stock bought for public libraries and have seldom been considered in histories or critical works on children's literature. That was never true of the *Paddington Bear* stories written by Michael Bond from 1959 onwards, nor of the *Winnie-the Pooh* books (see pp. 140–41) but both have attracted similar merchandising opportunities, for soft toys, tea-towels and other memorabilia created for and bought by adults as well as children. Soft, cuddly and cute for children, it seems animals, and particularly bears, also have something of the whiff of the honey-pot about them for publishers.

How It All Began, and How It Works

In the 1920s the Dutch-American journalist Hendrik Van Loon wrote and illustrated *The Story of Mankind* for his young sons. It was a great success with many readers.

By 1900 there were many books intended to help parents answer difficult questions, and in Britain Arthur Mee's *The Children's Encyclopaedia* became widely read (see pp. 92–3). It may even have helped to inspire Hendrik Van Loon (1882–1944), a Dutch immigrant in America. Van Loon studied first at Cornell, and then moved to Munich to work for a doctorate: he seemed to be set on the path for an academic life and was a popular lecturer. His first books, based on his research into Dutch history at Munich, were described as books written by someone who enjoyed history, but academics and reviewers condemned him for his sweeping statements and minor inaccuracies. His talents were as a populariser, rather than as a scholar.

The Story of Mankind was commissioned from Van Loon following his appreciative review of H. G. Wells's popular *Outline of History* (1919–20), and his own book, written for children, was in turn well received by educationalists and librarians. Anne Carroll Moore, then Superintendent of the Children's Library at the New York Public Library, and powerful in library affairs, was very enthusiastic about it when it was published by Boni & Liveright in New York in 1921: 'the most invigorating and, I venture to predict, the most influential children's book for many years to come'. It was partly through Moore's work at the American Library Association that Van Loon's book was chosen for the ALA's first Newbery Medal in 1922.

The Story of Mankind was then issued in London by Harrap. Like the Americans, British readers liked the many quirky

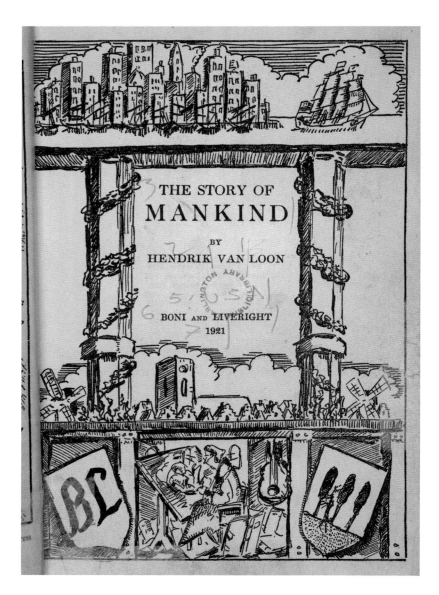

Hendrik Van Loon, *The Story of Mankind*. New York: Boni & Liveright, 1921. Though he had no formal training in art, Van Loon was as prolific an illustrator as writer, commenting on this volume that 'he prefers to make his own maps and sketches because he knows exactly what he wants to say and cannot possibly explain this meaning to his more proficient brethren in the field of art'. He recommended drawing for schoolchildren as an aid to driving new knowledge home.

The British Library

A STREET THROUGH TIME

A 12,000-YEAR WALK THROUGH HISTORY

ILLUSTRATED BY **STEVE NOON**

Steve Noon, *A Street Through Time*. DK Children, 2012. This book is typical of the illustration-led, cheerful and often noisy design of the DK style, for their books are crammed with information, detail and timelines.

Courtesy of Dorling Kindersley

illustrations by the author, who believed that the combination of pictures and text was the best way to convey information to young readers. Van Loon's books remained popular for generations, and though some of his other books, such as his *Story of the Bible* (1923) were attacked, most, like *The Story of Inventions: Man the Miracle Maker* (1934), were well received and sold numerous copies.

Revised editions of *The Story of Mankind* appeared for many years, prepared by Van Loon's sons, but gradually dropped out of favour when his writing style, once found engaging and attractive, began to seem mannered and old-fashioned. Van Loon regarded himself as too progressive for his era, but times change: some of his views about race and religion are now found unacceptable by modern readers and, in the West, his work is now largely ignored, in much the same way as Mee's *The Children's Encyclopaedia*.

Even the best expository books tend to have shorter shelf-lives than others described as classics, and in time are replaced by more modern-seeming works. Like some of the Soviet picture books, or the Puffin Picture Book titles selected by Noel Carrington (see pp. 232–5), the work of Van Loon and others led to the production of a huge range of informational books for children. Many such books are produced nowadays by large sophisticated firms. Dorling Kindersley is one, which started as a small privately owned book-packaging partnership in 1974, producing a *First Aid Manual* for the Red Cross and St John's Ambulance, but soon it started publishing its own books. It established a distinctive visual style of its own for its factual books for both children and adults, using glossy white space and numerous integrated illustrations. The high quality of these, in such titles as their *Big Book of Dinosaurs* (1994) or their *Children's Illustrated Bible* (2000) is remarkable and led to a demand for more of such books. 'DK' is now an important part of a global book publishing empire, publishing in sixty-two languages worldwide. The enormously profitable stake of the Kindersley share in the firm when it was sold to Pearson in 2000 (for over £300 million) is testament to the huge commercial value of children's publishing today.

Almost Anything But a Book – Comics, Television and New Animations

Many children's favourite characters have first appeared in comic strips or in the newer media, and quickly become products of the entertainment industry too.

Many people, young and old, fondly remember their favourite characters on radio or television programmes they absorbed as children. Some of these characters were first introduced in small books or cartoon strips in newspapers; others were originally created for radio programmes or (like the BBC's 1946 *Muffin the Mule*) television animations, and then produced in book form as an alternative format. Once sufficiently well known, many spin-off products might be produced from the original character, from soft toys and colouring books, jigsaws, decorated plates or mugs, to interactive media and gift cards – all created by those with franchises.

One of the earliest and most popular of British subjects to be used in this way was *Toytown*, created by S. G. Hulme Beaman (1887–1932) and broadcast on the BBC *Children's Hour* from 1929 until the author's death. It was frequently repeated on radio over the years, with the character of Larry the Lamb ('I'm only a little l-a-a-a-m-b') being particularly memorable. After *The Children's Hour* ceased in 1964, *Toytown* was transferred to Thames Television Channel as a stop-motion marionette show.

To some extent the fame of this superb series was eclipsed by Enid Blyton's *Noddy in Toyland* series, published between 1949 and 1963, which was presented on television soon after the first books appeared. For those who dislike Blyton's work (and many do), *Noddy* encapsulates its worst features, but this has not reduced her popularity one whit – particularly, it seems, in France, where the

Tove Jansson, *Småtrollen och den stora översvämningen* (*The Moomins and the Great Flood*). Helsinki: Söderström & Co., 1945. In this first in the series of book, the strange, white beasts Moominmamma and Moomintroll find their way through an otherworldy forest to Moomin Valley in search of Moominpappa.

© Moomin Characters™

illustrations by her Dutch artist Harmsen van Beek are still much admired. (Sales of over 70 million copies of her books indicate that Blyton was finely tuned to her market.)

There have been many other ingenious stories for younger children published first in book form or as television series, such as Reverend Wilbert Awdrey's *Thomas the Tank Engine* books, or Smallfilms' *Noggin the Nog* (1959–65) and *The Clangers* (first run 1969–72), both clever series written and devised by Oliver Postgate and Peter Firmin. The television series (and sets of books) acquired a sort of cult status and were distinctly different from the type of films marketed by Disney. The same is equally true of two hilarious French television programmes, *The Magic Roundabout* (*Le Manège enchanté*, 1963–71) and the series featuring a hand-puppet, *Hector's House* (*La Maison de Toutou*; 1965–70), which are both remarkable in that the storylines and text in the French and English versions are totally different. With many of these types of programmes, television success ensured that publication in alternative formats, as books or toy spin-offs. would soon follow.

From Finland, Tove Jansson (1914–2001) brought a more Nordic approach to her creations. In Scandinavian mythology, trolls are imps or dwarfs who inhabit caves or subterranean dwellings; sometimes benign, but more often mischievous. Jansson picked up the idea from an uncle who warned her that if pilfering food she would feel a '*Mumintrollet*' breathing cold air on her neck. Her innocent, hippo-like Moomintrolls started to appear in newspapers and magazines in the 1940s, and the first book about them, *Småtrollen och den stora översvämningen* (*The Moomins and the Great Flood*) appeared in Swedish in 1945. Jansson's next *Moomin* books in 1946 and 1948 built her reputation in Scandinavia. In Britain, the Moomins became known through a cartoon strip in the London *Evening News* (1959–76). In an unusual family arrangement, the cartoons for the last few years were drawn and written by Tove Jansson's brother Lars. Moomins are particularly popular in Japan, partly due to a TV series by Fuji TV Zuiyo Enterprises which started there in 1969, and the Japanese have been very active in producing Moomin memorabilia. In the United States – perhaps because Jansson refused to sell the franchises to Disney – her charming little trolls are less well known.

Comical Adventures

In the past, British children learned about Gaul from Caesar's *Gallic Wars*. *Asterix* was a rather different source of information.

Penny dreadfuls and comics in Britain and the United States attracted young readers in a different way from the Japanese **manga** or *bandes dessinées* of Belgium and France. Of the latter, one of the earliest and best known, Hergé's *Adventures of Tintin*, first appeared in a right-wing magazine (*Le Petit Vingtième*) published in Brussels in 1929. Hergé's amusing pictures and sometimes erudite stories for an older readership carried words in balloons, a technique copied from American comics of the early 20th century. *Tintin* books entertained Belgian and French children for over twenty years before Methuen's first English translation of *King Ottokar's Sceptre* appeared in 1958.

Translating the text within speech bubbles in picture books may seem simple, but in the case of *Tintin* it was not. The translators, Michael Turner and Leslie Lonsdale-Cooper, had to adapt the implicitly coarse expletives (never actual swearing) of the character Captain Haddock, and provide suitable spoonerisms for the two detectives, Thomson and Thompson (in the original, Dupond et Dupont) – and then fit the translated text into the existing speech bubbles. Captain Haddock's oaths, in translation – 'bashi-bazouks' or 'blue blistering barnacles' – were seized on with delight by many British children for their own use. The popularity of the books saw attempts to turn them into films, first in a stop-motion puppet animation, *The Crab with the Golden Claws* (1947) and later on with action films, such as *Tintin and the Golden Fleece* (1961), its original script written not by Hergé, but André Barret and Rémo Forlani.

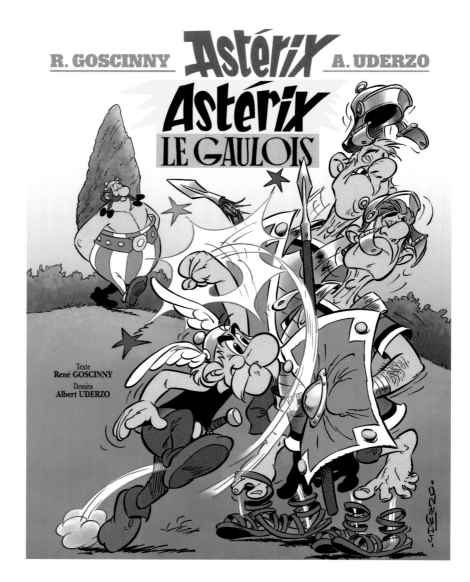

René Goscinny and Albert Uderzo, *Astérix le Gaulois*. Paris: Editions Hachette, 1999. First published by Pilote in 1959. Uniquely among the *Asterix* titles, the plate on p. 35 of this first French album is one redrawn by Marcel Uderzo, who helped his illustrator brother with the colouring, as the original had been lost. It is the only one not drawn by Albert.

In 1959 a French rival to Hergé's books appeared in the form of *Asterix le Gaulois,* a cartoon about the cunning Gaul, 'Asterix', and his friend, the jovial 'Obelix', who lived at the time when most of France was controlled by the Romans under Julius Caesar. It was an instant success with readers of the Franco-Belgian magazine *Pilote* in 1959, but even so, the publisher of the first book decided to produce only 6,000 copies. Within fifty years, over 325 million copies of the Asterix books were sold around the world (by 2009, there were some thirty-four titles), making the co-creators René Goscinny and Albert Uderzo France's bestselling authors abroad. Goscinny died in 1977, but after the writer's death, the artist Uderzo continued to write and draw illustrations for more books in the *Asterix* series before selling the rights to Hachette.

The *Asterix* books represent an unexpected bubbling-up of French patriotism. The Parc Astérix, a very successful theme park near Paris, rivals Disneyland Paris. French enterprise has brought many spin-offs from the stories, with foodstuffs and board and video games (and other developments which would have astounded Julius Caesar).

In Japan, in the 18th century, the strong market for *kibyōshi* (picture books) increased enormously after Japan was opened to the West. One children's magazine issued there was *Shōnen Sekai* (*The Youth's World*),

published from 1895 to 1914. It had many imitators, and the years after the Second World War saw the development, heavily influenced by Disney, of manga. This was by no means limited to Japanese readers: Osama Tezuka's *Astro Boy* (*Mighty Atom*), published by Kobunsha from 1952 until 1968, became almost as successful in Europe as *Mickey Mouse, Tintin* or *Asterix.*

Though the genre of graphic novels, *bandes dessinèes* (BDs) and manga attracts artists and writers of all abilities (some very skilled), educationalists worry about their literary quality, for child and teenage readers. One downside to the enormous commercial success of graphic novels is the explicit violent and sexual material the medium also attracts, in part because the laws around animation have been less strict than for photographic material. Many French supermarkets display BDs with violent or pornographic covers in the guise of sexualised (and often disturbingly juvenile) 'action heroes/heroines', and there have been successful prosecutions for pornography in manga in both Japan and the United States. It remains to be seen whether the concern that first arose around American comics of the 1950s (see pp. 206–7) will be more strongly asserted in relation to some modern graphic novels.

Coming to Terms with the War

The First World War was long largely ignored in children's literature, but Michael Morpurgo's *War Horse* changed all that.

Michael Morpurgo (b. 1943) grew up, often lonely and unhappy, as a pupil at boarding schools in the years immediately after the Second World War. After obtaining a degree at King's College London, and spending an apparently unsuccessful time at the military academy at Sandhurst, Morpurgo became a primary-school teacher; his time spent teaching coloured his writing. Much influenced by his friend, the poet Ted Hughes, he became heavily involved in composing poems and stories at about the same time that he and his wife started the charity 'Farms for City Children', which aimed to give town children some experience of the countryside.

Morpurgo's award-winning children's book *War Horse*, published in 1982 by Kaye & Ward, is perhaps now more famous for its stage version (2007) and film by Steven Spielberg (2011). A bold attempt to depict the First World War through the experience of a horse commissioned for military service, Morpurgo's tale has much appeal. Sentimental in the way of that other famous horse story, *Black Beauty* (see pp. 166–7), *War Horse* proved very popular with British children, and also their parents and teachers, who perhaps saw it as a useful introduction to discussion about war, and hoped that the humanity underlying its message would instil in their pupils desirable traits.

Morpurgo, who had grown up enjoying *Peter and the Wolf* and *Beauty and the Beast* on stage, and had seen several of his previous books adapted for stage and screen, was unconvinced that his epic war tale would

The National Theatre's stage production of Michael Morpurgo's *War Horse*, 2017. Inspired by conversations with First World War veterans in a tiny Devon village pub, Morpurgo tried to give a non-partisan account of the war from the perspective of an unfortunate farm horse, who is purchased and trained by the British, captured and used by Germans, and who spends the winter on a French farm.

Brinkhoff/Moegenburg/The National Theatre

Judith Kerr, *The Tiger Who Came to Tea*, c.1968. Original artwork by Kerr for the book first published by Collins. Kerr's witty and charming illustrations capture the beautiful beast with an exotic elegance reminiscent of Babar – but nonetheless he remains a tiger, with an ever-present undercurrent of danger. Like *War Horse*, Kerr's book has recently been adapted successfully for the stage.

Courtesy of Seven Stories, The National Centre for Children's Books

interest in the First World War will continue or if *War Horse* will survive as well as Anna Sewell's book.

With a background very different from that of Morpurgo, Judith Kerr (b. 1923) was just nine years old when her German–Jewish family fled Nazi Germany, eventually arriving in Britain in 1936. (Her father, an eminent intellectual and theatre critic, was on the Nazi wanted list, and his books were burned.) Judith Kerr grew up in London during the Blitz, then worked for the Red Cross, and subsequently became naturalised as a British citizen. She had always wanted to be an artist, and trained at the Central School for Arts and Crafts in London. Like Kathleen Hale (see p. 143), Kerr wrote stories about a cat character to entertain her children. Kerr's *Mog* stories were published by Collins (from 1970 to 2002), and much liked by children, who relished Mog's habits. (One later volume, *Mog's Christmas Calamity*, was produced in 2015 for the Save the Children Fund.)

Preceding the nineteen popular *Mog* stories, Kerr had written and beautifully illustrated a charming tale, *The Tiger Who Came to Tea* (1968). In it, a huge tiger mysteriously invites himself to tea with an eight-year-old girl and her mother, eats everything, drinks up all the milk and beer in the fridge, followed by all the water from the taps, and then leaves. Given Kerr's own experiences, some have speculated about a hidden – or subconscious – message about the Nazi threat (described in Kerr's 1971 account, *When Hitler Stole Pink Rabbit*), but the millions of copies sold show that Judith Kerr understood thoroughly how to create books to please children, and her books are likely to be read for many years to come.

work in the theatre. He himself had laboured unsuccessfully for five years over a screenplay of it. But it was eventually made, by the scriptwriter Nick Stafford, and though one reviewer commented that he had 'taken a book that was written for children, and tried to give it the expressive weight of a play for adults', adding that the plot 'can't stand the strain', the drama nonetheless proved immensely popular with audiences. The play was enhanced, no doubt, by the ingenious and effective use of life-size puppets of the horses, created by the South African Handspring Puppet Company. Spielberg's film, described as 'technically superb and unabashedly old-fashioned', was likewise much liked and very profitable.

Morpurgo's sincere attempts to make the world a better place come through very clearly from his own website as well as his books, but it remains to be seen whether our current

Hungry for More: Caterpillars, Board Books and Interactive Gruffs

As John Locke anticipated, children learn best through interaction with their subjects. Eric Carle's very hungry caterpillar is one perennially popular example of how this can be done.

John Locke's revolutionary ideas on education profoundly influenced publishing for children, and were early exemplified in the books of John Newbery. Regarding the infant's mind as a clean slate (*tabula rasa*) to be filled through experience and education (rather than to have outside information heaped upon it), Locke held that children best develop their thinking by using their full sensory perception: to explore an object, an idea and the world around them in different ways, including through play. This idea of *interaction* in learning has remained fundamental during the following three centuries, and underpins much modern publishing for children.

Eric Carle's *The Very Hungry Caterpillar*, published in 1969 in Cleveland by the World

Publishing Company, is an exceptionally popular and effective example of using interaction for learning. The New York-born illustrator and designer trained at the Akademie der bildenden Künste (Academy of Fine Arts) in Stuttgart, before turning his hand to children's books. He found great success with this simple tale (aimed at very young children), which followed the week-long life cycle of a caterpillar, from his first day as an egg on a leaf, to his last, when he emerges from his chrysalis a fat and beautiful butterfly.

Through seven days he traverses voraciously, on Monday chomping one apple, on Tuesday, two pears, on Wednesday three plums, and so forth, culminating in a weekend feast of excess:

Eric Carle, *The Very Hungry Caterpillar*. New York: Philomel Books, 1994. Double page from the first board-book edition. In a fortieth-anniversary edition (by which time his book had sold over 29 million copies in forty-seven languages) Carle explained how initially, idly punching holes in a stack of paper, he had envisaged a bookworm. 'Willi the Worm' was born, soon to be replaced with a green worm, and then the caterpillar of today.

Courtesy Eric Carle Studio

He started to look for some food.

On Monday he ate through one apple. But he was still hungry.

Tom Potts was fooling with a gun
(Such follies should not be),
When—bang! the pesky thing went off
Most unexpectedly!

Tom didn't know 'twas loaded, and
It scared him 'most to death—
He tumbled flat upon the floor
And fairly gasped for breath.

The bullet smashed a fine French clock
(The clock had just struck three),
Then made a hole clean through the wall,
As you can plainly see.

Peter Newell, *The Hole Book*. New York: Harper & Brothers, 1908. Tom Potts fools with a gun, and his accidental bullet whistles clean through many scenes of turn-of-the-century American society.

The British Library

On Saturday he ate through one piece of chocolate cake, one ice-cream cone, one pickle, one slice of Swiss cheese, one slice of salami, one lollipop, one piece of cherry pie, one sausage, one cupcake, and one slice of watermelon.

After this he feels a little bit poorly. Carle's book effectively instils the concepts of numbers, days of the week, nature study, the realisation that our beginnings may never know our endings (and why it's a bad idea to overeat) in one fell swoop. The choice of medium for these lessons is particularly striking: the author created his vibrant illustrations in collage. Each page size corresponds to the amount of food consumed, thus on the first day, Monday (with one apple) the page is the smallest, on Friday (five oranges), it is the largest. Each page has a hole where it has been 'chewed' through – inviting explorative fingers to appear the other side like wriggling caterpillars for the child's delight.

Though the most famous, Carle's book was not the first to feature such perforations: in Peter Newell's 1908 pictorial verse-story *The Hole Book*, young Tom Potts accidentally discharges a bullet which proceeds to whistle through hats, cats, hives and bagpipes before coming at last to lodge in Mis' Newlywed's rather stout cake:

And this was lucky for Tom Potts,
The boy who fired the shot –
It might have gone clean round the world,
And killed him on the spot.

A voracious demand from publishers for digital formats targeted at an ever-younger audience has resulted in the pairing by Penguin Digital (a branch of Penguin Books) with Google+ in *Storytime Hangout: The Three Billy Goats Gruff*. This onscreen application brings a traditional tale to our 'selfie'-hungry age, allowing young readers digitally to insert their own faces into the storyline (something, for previous generations, which only imagination could achieve). Despite such innovations, current sales in printed books remain surprisingly strong. But what is more remarkable is the market for children's board books, which in 2013–14 (according to a global survey conducted by the American publishing giant Nielsen in January 2015) outstripped all other publishing formats, growing by an astonishing 22% worldwide. Carle's *The Very Hungry Caterpillar*, published in board-book form in 1994, no doubt added to this success. It goes to show that the old favourites die hard.

Records of a Lost Age: Children's Books as Historical Artefacts

Almost every children's book which has survived for more than a hundred years has things about it which make it interesting.

In deciding on our '100 books', we looked at many more than those selected. Our last, *The Girl's Own Book*, was initially rejected as 'unimportant' in itself, yet a subsequent 'forensic' examination uncovered many surprising aspects hidden from a cursory glance. It suggests a way of thinking about a book's significance that may, in our digital age, be easily overlooked.

This thick duodecimo volume had all its edges gilt – a touch of luxury rare in children's books, suggesting an upmarket production. Though battered and faded, the publisher's binding in olive cloth, stamped in black and gold, must have been very handsome when new. Its publisher's imprint: Griffith, Farran & Co., readers will recognise from the Japanese stories printed on crêpe paper (see p. 182). As successors to both Newbery and Harris, to be published by them was a mark of quality.

The five hundred-plus pages are printed apparently from **stereotype** or **electrotype** plates, many with wood-engraved illustrations, and tipped-in **lithographic** plates (many are by the Dalziels, among the best Victorian commercial illustrators). In these, the girls have shoulder-length hair and mid-calf dresses, in similar fashion to Tenniel's illustrations for *Alice* (1865). The undated title page (not naming the author) states that this is a 'new edition, considerably enlarged by Mrs L. Valentine and others'. It bears the imprint of John & Robert Maxwell, publishers of Shoe Lane, Fleet Street and St Bride Street, Ludgate Circus. Only the half-title indicates

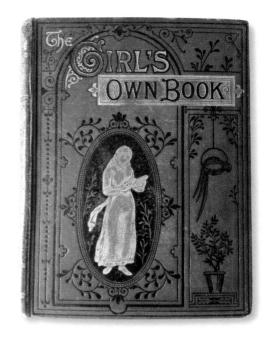

L. Valentine, *The Girl's Own Book of Amusements, Studies, and Employments. New edition considerably enlarged & modernised by Mrs. L. Valentine and others.* London: John and Robert Maxwell, Publishers, (*c*.1869?). First published in Boston in 1831, this edition repeats information in the earlier edition. Stereotyping meant publishers could easily and cheaply reprint new editions, and sometimes such stereo plates were bought in. The rather pre-Raphaelite figure in its almost ecclesiastical arch has echoes of the then very popular Holman Hunt.

Collection Dawn Cave

the book's authorship: 'By L. M. Child.'

'L. M. Child' was Lydia Maria Child (1802–80), a famous New England emancipationist, and author of the very popular *American Frugal Housewife* (1829), and *The Mother's Book* and *The* [Little] *Girl's Book* (both 1831). Mrs Child may have been inspired to write her book for girls by seeing the earlier English *Boy's Own Book* (1829) by William Clarke, which was more interesting than its pompous subtitle suggested – '*a complete encyclopedia of all the diversions, athletic, scientific, and recreative, of boyhood and youth*'. Revised editions continued to be published throughout the 19th century.

American and British publishers in the 1830s had no qualms about appropriating each other's books, and just as the Boston and New York publishers reprinted Clarke, so

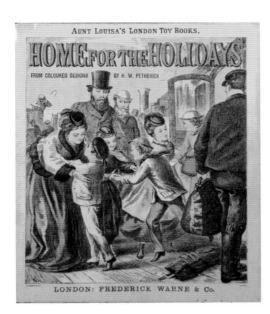

AUNT LOUISA'S LONDON TOY BOOKS.
HOME FOR THE HOLIDAYS
FROM COLOURED DESIGNS BY H. W. PETHERICK
LONDON: FREDERICK WARNE & Co.

the rather unscrupulous Thomas Tegg, who produced many spurious 'Peter Parley' books (see p. 105) in London, decided to reprint Mrs Child's books.

Clarke's book (still readable today) covered activities traditionally for boys, such as 'goff or sandy-ball' [golf], cricket, swimming or fencing, as well as indoor pursuits including 'scientific recreations' and keeping pets. Mrs Child's had dancing, callisthenics, embroidery and and other indoor pursuits, quizzes and charades among them. She wished to turn her readers into 'young ladies', not tomboys. Later British and American editions developed in different and separate ways, and some were edited by 'Clara de Chatelain' – a French emigrée in England who translated many children's books for Tegg and others.

Our edition, however, was enlarged by quite another woman, 'L. Valentine', who also worked with Tegg. Laura Valentine (1814–99; née Laura Jewry, pen-names Mrs. S. Valentine and Aunt Louisa;), was one of the many underpaid and disregarded Victorian women working in children's publishing. As 'Aunt Louisa' she acquired a modest fame (but little financial reward) for her series of **toy books** published by Frederick Warne, and the McLoughlin Brothers.

Child's *Girl's Own Book* is difficult to track down through publishers' records or bibliographies. (Nineteenth-century legal deposit libraries were not interested in children's books; nor were publishers obliged to deposit second or subsequent printings. In consequence, British records are patchy.) A similar copy in the Victoria & Albert Museum, speculatively dated [187–?], states that it was sold by William Tegg, Pancras Lane, Cheapside, though it has a different binding. Tegg retired from publishing in 1890. It may be that Griffith, Farran & Co. then bought up the unbound sheets from Tegg, and reissued them in a new, fancier binding. Although then nearly sixty years old, the book would have been received by a girl of the 1890s as a very attractive gift.

Even in the most *unattractive* children's books there is often a story to be unwoven. Searching for more information about *The Girl's Own Book* exposes many facets of Victorian life. (One thinks back also to *Who Killed Cock Robin*, p. 19, the cloth book carefully restitched by some devoted parent or sister, and the glimpse into a hidden domestic life that conveys.) It is almost always worthwhile trying to learn more about a book, its physical volume, its author or publisher. Much can be found out about previous owners, too: who received it as a school prize, who read (or hated) it. *The Girl's Own Book* is not especially important, but its survival as an artefact contributes to our knowledge of the books for children which were received by our great grandparents.

BIBLIOGRAPHY

It would be possible to fill many pages with references to books and articles about Beatrix Potter, Lewis Carroll and many other children's authors mentioned or discussed in this book. We have deliberately omitted many on individual authors, illustrators or publishing firms. Online sources like Wikipedia or the *Oxford Dictionary of National Biography* often give useful information, as do the online services of libraries and museums with special collections of children's books in Britain, such as: the British Library (e.g. http://www.bl.uk/playtimes); the National Library of Scotland (http://www.nls.uk/collections/rare-books/collections/childrens-books); the Opie Collection in the Bodleian Library (http://libguides.bodleian.ox.ac.uk/c.php?g=423106&p=2889093); and the Victoria & Albert Museum (http://www.vam.ac.uk/content/articles/n/national-art-library-childrens-literature-collections/). We have found particularly helpful the resources of Reading University (https://www.reading.ac.uk/special-collections/collections/sc-childrens.aspx) and Seven Stories (http://www.sevenstories.org.uk/collection).

For descriptions of old books (and many facsimiles) the Hockliffe Project based at De Montfort University (http://hockliffe.dmu.ac.uk/HPall_catalog.html) is a useful source. The work of the Children's Book History Society (http://www.cbhs.org.uk/) and the Imaginative Book Illustration Society (http://bookillustration.org/index.html) are also important sources.

In Canada, the Osborne Collection in Toronto (http://www.torontopubliclibrary.ca/osborne/) is of great importance. Many of the great libraries in the United States have substantial and important collections of children's books, and their websites provide a wealth of information and reproductions from their books; collections formed of books from the UK as well as the US. We have made particular use of the American Antiquarian Society (http://www.americanantiquarian.org/children.htm), Library of Congress Children's Literature Center (http://www.loc.gov/rr/child/) and indeed their main website, the Baldwin Library at the University of Florida (http://cms.uflib.ufl.edu/baldwin/Index.aspx), the Cotsen Children's Library at Princeton (http://www.princeton.edu/cotsen/), the Children's Literature Research Collections at the University of Minnesota (https://www.lib.umn.edu/clrc) and the DeGrummond Collection at the University of Southern Mississippi (http://www.lib.usm.edu/degrummond). The online 'Looking Glass for the Mind' exhibition at the University of Washington (http://content.lib.washington.edu/exhibits/looking-glass/intro.html) is especially useful for schoolbooks.

Many other national and research libraries have important collections, and often digitised versions which can be seen online: for example, the National Library of Australia has the elusive *Whirlaway* (see p. 210) (http://nla.gov.au/nla.obj-75565571/view?partId=nla.obj-75565661#page/no/mode/1up).

The websites devoted to individual authors or artists are of variable quality, but many provide enthusiastic and well-informed introductions to their work. For comics and graphic novels there are many specialist collections in research libraries, and Comic Books Lambiek in Amsterdam (https://www.lambiek.net/home.html) provides an introduction to this complex field. In addition, the many enthusiastic collectors and dealers of children's books, either generally or more specialist, such as, in Spain, Ana Maria Ortega's site devoted to pop-up books (http://emopalencia.com/desplegables.htm), have been particularly helpful.

Among many other books and articles we have found these very helpful:

Alderson, Brian. *Sing a Song For Sixpence: the English Picture Book Tradition.* Cambridge: Cambridge University Press, 1986

Alderson, Brian & Felix de Mariz Oyens. *Be Merry and Wise: Origins of Children's Book Publishing in England, 1650–1850.* New Castle: Oak Knoll Press, 2006

Avery, Gillian. *Behold the Child: American Children and Their Books, 1621–1922.* London: Bodley Head, 1994

Avery, Gillian & Julia Briggs, eds. *Children and their Books; a Celebration of the Work of Iona and Peter Opie.* Oxford: Clarendon Press, 1989

Baines, Phil. *Puffin by Design, 70 Years of Imagination 1940–2010.* London: Allen Lane, 2010

Briggs, Julia, Dennis Butts & M. O. Grenby. *Popular Children's Literature in England.* Aldershot: Ashgate, 2008

Bromer, Anne & Julian Edison: *Miniature Books: 4,000 Years of Tiny Treasures.* New York: Harry N. Abrams, 2007

Carpenter, Humphrey & Mari Pritchard. *The Oxford Companion to Children's Literature.* Oxford: Oxford University Press, 1984

Cott, Jonathan & Maurice Sendak. *Victorian Color Picture Books.* New York: Stonehill, 1984

Darton, F. J. Harvey. *Children's Books in England: Five Centuries of Social Life.* 3rd edition revised by Brian Alderson. Cambridge: Cambridge University Press, 1982

Edwards, Owen Dudley. *British Children's Fiction in the Second World War.* Edinburgh: Edinburgh University Press, 2007

Felmingham, Michael. *The Illustrated Gift Book 1880–1930.* London, Scolar Press, 1988; [Aldershot] Wildwood House, 1989

Fergus, Jan. *Provincial Readers in Eighteenth Century England.* Oxford: Oxford University Press, 2006

Field, Hannah. *Novelty Value: the Child Reader and the Victorian Material Book.* Minneapolis: University of Minnesota Press, 2018

Gathorne-Hardy, Jonathan. *The Rise and Fall of the British Nanny.* London: Hodder & Stoughton, 1972

Grenby, M. O. *The Child Reader, 1700–1840.* Cambridge: Cambridge University Press, 2011.

Haining, Peter. *Movable Books: An Illustrated History.* London: New English Library, 1979

Hellman, Ben. *Fairy Tales and True Stories: the History of Russian Literature for Children and Young People (1574–2010).* Leiden: Brill, 2013

Hilton, Mary, Morag Styles & Victor Watson, eds. *Opening The Nursery Door; Reading, Writing and Childhood 1600–1900.* Abingdon: Routledge, 1997.

Holman, Valerie. *Print for Victory: Book Publishing in Britain 1939–1945.* London: The British Library, 2008

Hunt, Peter, ed. *Children's Literature: an Illustrated History.* Oxford: Oxford University Press, 1995

Hurlimann, Bettina. *Three Centuries of Children's Books in Europe.* Oxford: Oxford University Press, 1968

Immel, Andrea & Michael Witmore, eds. *Childhood and Children's Books in Early Modern Europe, 1550–1800.* New York: Routledge, 2006

Jackson, Mary V. *Engines of Instruction, Mischief and Magic; Children's Literature in England from its Beginning to 1839.* Aldershot: Scholar Press, 1980

Johnson, Lorraine & Brian Alderson. *The Ladybird Story: Children's Books for Everyone.* London: British Library, 2014

Kramer, Samuel Noah. *History Begins at Sumer: Thirty-nine Firsts in Man's Recorded History.* Philadelphia, University of Pennsylvania Press: 1956 (3rd revised edition, 1988)

Kümmerling-Meibauer, Bettina, ed. *Emergent Literacy: Children's Books from 0 to 3.* Amsterdam: John Benjamins Publishing Company, 2011

Lerer, Seth. *Children's Literature: A Reader's History, from Aesop to Harry Potter.* Chicago: University of Chicago Press, 2009

Maxwell, Richard. *The Victorian Illustrated Book.* Charlottesville: University of Virginia Press, 2002

Neuberg, Victor E. *The Penny Histories: A Study of Chapbooks for Young Readers Over Two Centuries.* London: Oxford University Press, 1968

Opie, Iona & Peter Opie. *A Nursery Companion.* Oxford: Oxford University Press, 1980

Peakman, Julie. *Mighty Lewd Books: the Development of Pornography in Eighteenth-Century England.* Basingstoke: Palgrave Macmillan, 2003

Pelachaud, Gaëlle. *Livres animés, du papier au numériqu*e. Paris: L'Harmattan, 2010

Perrin, Noel. *Dr. Bowdler's Legacy; a History of Expurgated Books in England and America.* Boston: David R. Godine, 1992

Quayle, Eric. *The Collector's Book of Children's Books.* London: Studio-Vista, 1971

Reynolds, Kimberley. *Left Out: The Forgotten Tradition of Radical Publishing for Children in Britain 1910–1949.*

Oxford: Oxford University Press, 2016

Rose, Jonathan. *The Intellectual Life of the British Working Classes.* London & New Haven: Yale Nota Bene, 2002

Rothenstein, Julian & Budashevskaya, Olga. *Inside the Rainbow: Russian Children's Literature 1920–35: Beautiful Books, Terrible Times.* London: Redstone Press, 2013

Springhall, John. *Youth, Popular Culture and Moral Panics: Penny Gaffs to Gangsta-Rap, 1830–1996.* Basingstoke: Macmillan, 1998

Spufford, Margaret. *Small Books and Pleasant Histories: Popular Fiction and its Readership in Seventeenth-Century England.* Cambridge: Cambridge University Press, 1981

Steiner, Evgeny. *Stories for Little Comrades: Revolutionary Artists and the Making of Early Soviet Children's Books.* Seattle: University of Washington Press, 1999

Te Heesen, Anke. *The World in a Box, The Story of an Eighteenth-Century Picture Encyclopedia.* Chicago: University of Chicago Press, 1997

Warner, Marina. *Once Upon a Time; a Short History of Fairy Tale.* Oxford: Oxford University Press, 2014

Watson, Victor, ed. *The Cambridge Guide to Children's Books in English.* Cambridge: Cambridge University Press, 2001

White, Colin. *The World of the Nursery.* New York: E. P. Dutton, Inc., 1984

Zipes, Jack. *The Irresistible Fairy Tale: The Cultural and Social History of a Genre.* Princeton: Princeton University Press, 2013

GLOSSARY

abecedary/ium//ies/ia (*also* **alphabetary**): letters of the alphabet, usually printed in sequential order, and used as practice exercises: *A was an Apple pie, B bit it, C cut it*, and so forth.

azbuka: a Cyrillic alphabet derived from Greek, used for writing Slavic languages, which lends its name to the alphabet books made popular by Leo Tolstoy.

bandes dessinées (**BDs**) : French or Belgian graphic novels or comic strips, such as *Tintin* or *Asterix*; often called 'le Neuvième Art' ('the new art'). See also manga.

battledores: varnished cards on which was printed the A.B.C., the Lord's Prayer, and a few short syllables, employed as a substitute for the hornbook. Possibly first invented by Salisbury bookseller Benjamin Collins about 1750 and widely used until about 1860.

Bildungsroman: a German term widely used in Britain and America to describe coming-of-age novels.

Book Production War Economy Agreement: A voluntary code governing book production, covering print size, words per page, blank pages etc., brought in by the Ministry of Supply and the Publishers Association in 1942. Paper rationing in Britain continued until 1949.

bowdlerise : named for Thomas Bowdler, who expurgated *The Family Shakespeare* (1807), omitting words or phrases 'which cannot with propriety be read aloud in a family'. Often used today for reasons of 'political correctness'.

broadsidea: publications printed on one side of a single sheet of paper: often containing ballads and other street literature.

chapbooks: small paper-covered booklets, often illustrated with crude woodcuts, and commonly in circulation in the 17th to 19th centuries; sold for a penny on streets, and at markets and fairs by travelling hawkers or 'chapmen' (i.e. tradesmen).

chirimen-bon (ちりめん本): known in the West as 'crêpe-paper' books, books made by crinkling *washi* (i.e., Japanese paper) pre-printed with text and wood-block illustrations, before binding it, in the Japanese fashion, into pages. Popular in the Meiji period (1868–1912).

chromolithography: process of printing coloured illustrations using lithographic stones to print the various colours; very popular for children's books from about 1840.

conduct/courtesy books: books attempting to educate the reader on social norms, often emphasising the woman's role in the 'cult of domesticity' that flourished in the Victorian era. 'Conduct book' is often used interchangeably with 'courtesy book', which (in mediaeval times) were intended to teach the ruling classes how to behave and administer their roles.

die-cut: a process of cutting shapes in paper using a metal tool or die, used on a press like a letter press.

dime novels: cheap, sensational novels published for a dime (10 cents) in the 19th century in the United States. The term is often used pejoratively, classed with 'shilling shockers' or 'penny dreadfuls' as undesirable reading.

Dutch gilt: decorated paper, for covers or endpapers, made by printing, stamping or embossing a gilt and coloured pattern on paper; popular in the 18th century. Also called 'Brocade'. Despite its name, 'Dutch gilt' was not made in the Netherlands but came from Augsburg in Germany, or Italy.

electrotypes: printing surfaces made by electroforming a thin shell of copper which exactly replicates the original, and is then backed to make a printing surface. Invented by the early Victorians, and used extensively to take copies from wood-engraved illustrations (e.g. Tenniel's *Alice in Wonderland*) it provided a very durable printing surface for multiple reprinting.

emblem books: books with allegorical illustrations, with accompanying explanatory text, particularly popular in Europe during the 16th and 17th centuries.

haptic: relating to the sense of touch, e.g. embossed texts or illustrations in books for the blind, or other tactile formats such as 'touchy-feely' books.

hornbooks: teaching aids, usually in the form of a paddle or flat wooden tablet (rarely, ivory or precious metal) with a handle, with a piece of vellum or paper showing the alphabet (or numerals and/or the Lord's Prayer) covered by a thin sheet of translucent horn for protection. Confusingly, sometimes known as a battledore.

Initial Teaching Alphabet (ITA): a misconceived idea, introduced by Sir James Pitman in the early 1960s, intended to be a practical simplified writing system to teach English-speaking children to read more easily than could be done with traditional spelling. The idea spread to Australia and the US, but its use in Britain was discontinued in the late 1970s.

intaglio: a printing process in which the image is incised into a surface (usually copper) and the incised line or sunken area holds the ink. Prints are made by passing an inked plate in contact with paper through a rolling press.

lithography: a planographic printing process invented by Alois Senefelder in the 1790s, in which marks are made in an oil- or wax-based medium onto a smooth limestone (later, polymer-surfaced aluminium) plate. When brushed with water, the marks reject the water; when the stone is inked, the stone receives ink only in the marked areas. Important in the mid-19th century and often used for coloured illustrations.

manga/manhua: Japanese (manga) and Chinese (manhua) comic strip books, comparable with the French *bandes dessinées* (BDs); since the Second World War, very popular with readers of all ages.

Newbery Medal: named for the 18th-century London publisher of children's books John Newbery, a well-respected award made since 1921 by the (US) Association for Library Service to Children for the most distinguished contribution to American literature for children.

penny dreadfuls: cheap, sensational books published in Britain in the 19th century, usually priced at a penny, 1d.

pourquoi **stories:** from French, 'why'. Aetiological legends or fictional narratives explaining why something exists. Many legends of indigenous peoples take this form, e.g. in Native American, Pacific Island and African cultures, to explain how (for example) fire, the moon or winter, came to be.

primers: small introductory books on any subject; often elementary schoolbooks, for teaching children to read, as a first means of instruction. May also refer to prayer books or devotional manuals for the use of lay people.

problem novels: used in recent times to denote fiction for young people, including books on such subjects as drug addiction or sexual problems.

rag books: books from the 19th or 20th centuries made for young children, which were printed on fabric, or on paper mounted on fabric. Modern touchy-feely books are derived from these.

readers: compilations or anthologies of writings on a particular subject (or by a particular author), often used as school textbooks or reading exercises; for many poorer children, often their only access to reading matter.

shaped books: books generally intended for young children, with pages die-cut to form the shape of a figure or an object (e.g. an animal or tractor). Collectors, and of course children, like them; most librarians find shelving them difficult.

stereotype: a process developed in the 18th century for making durable metal printing plates by taking a mould from pages of composed type or wood-engravings in papier-mâché, and then casting a copy from it.

subscription lists: lists of people who ordered (and often paid) in advance of publication, often printed within the books concerned.

subscription publishing: a form of marketing that blossomed in post-Civil War America, when thousands of sales agents (many veterans and war widows) canvassed small-town households armed with a prospectus and sample book, offering, for cash on delivery, bespoke publishing and binding for every price range. Mark Twain's major titles were all first sold this way. It found new currency in the present age with the advent of desktop 'print on demand' publishing.

touchy-feely books: novelty books for very young children, usually of fabric, often with a loop to attach to a cot, and with different textures and colours to keep babies amused. Sometimes called 'soft' books.

toy books: cheaper series of coloured picture-books for young children, often in paper covers, with the emphasis on pictures rather than text.

type founding: from the time printing was invented by Gutenberg (15th century) most books were printed from type cast in type-foundries. The designs of the letters varied from one country to another and changed over time; in Britain and America in the 18th century, books were printed from old-face roman types, typically from typefaces designed by William Caslon; in the 19th century, modern-face romans came into use, and sans-serif faces were also used. A fount of type includes characters for every upper- and lower-case letter from A–Z in both roman and *italic*, plus numerals and punctuation marks. Typefounders also cast (and printers used) gothic types ('Old English' for Britain and the Netherlands, 'rotunda' for the Latin countries). German-speaking countries (and Scandinavia) used the German gothic called Fraktur to print books in those languages, but used roman (and *italic*) for books in Latin, French or other languages. Type production was mechanised from the 1840s.

ukiyo-e: meaning 'Pictures of the Floating World'; images of Japanese everyday life and folkloric scenes, produced in the Edo period (1615–1868), famously by Hokusai. *Ukiyo-e* began as simple black-and-white prints from a single block, occasionally hand-coloured. Later, elaborate coloured wood-blocks (known as *nishiki-e* or 'brocade pictures') became popular.

vocabulary: a list of common words used in a particular language, often compiled in a specialised book, particularly to aid with learning a language (or dialect).

Wimmelbook **(***Wimmelbuch/ Wimmelbilderbuch***):** from the German *wimmeln*, meaning 'to teem' (or 'swarm') and *Bilderbuch*, 'picture book'. Wordless, usually large-format picture-books containing illustrations of highly detailed and busy panoramic scenes. The 'teeming' compositional device is found in much Northern European art, such as that of Pieter Bruegel. *Wimmelbuch* give the emergent reader a cognitive challenge different from merely recognising an object; instead they have to locate it within a background of visual 'noise'. Ali Migutsch's *Rundherum in meiner Stadt* (1968) is one example. Martin Handford's well-known *Where's Wally?* puzzlebook is another.

ACKNOWLEDGEMENTS

The debt owed to others by the authors in researching and putting together this book is enormous. As so often, the list is too long to thank everyone individually; so we offer a general but heartfelt thanks to all who have helped in the making of this book. In particular special mention must be made of Dawn Cave, a former children's librarian whose wide knowledge of the subject and diligence in reading (and correcting) our texts has been invaluable, quite apart from her role as wife and mother in introducing us to so many children's books. The wider family – all keen readers – have also been helpfully ready with their opinions on 'our' 100 Books; we have enjoyed the heated discussions. (Seeing how attached others are to the books of their own childhoods has in itself been revealing.) Our newest addition, Hannah, became a delightful focus for our thinking about the future of children's reading.

Outside of the home – where so many children's reading starts – are the friends, colleagues, librarians and scholars who have expanded our knowledge of children's books.

In particular we would like to thank the many private book dealers and collectors, such as Aleph-Bet Books, N.Y., Gary Haines, Peter Harrington, Ana Maria Ortega and Álvaro Guttiérrez, PBA Galleries, San Francisco, and Rooke Books; the staff of institutional libraries such as Rebecca Howdeshell (Bridwell Library, Southern Methodist University), Keiichi Ishibashi (Tokyo Printing Museum); Isabel Planton (Lilly Library, Indiana), Sue Miller (CICE Dublin), Carol Okroj (Nottingham City Libraries), Farzana Whitfield and Erich Kesse (SOAS, London), Judith Wright (Archivist, Boots UK), and the staff of Rutland County Library, who have so generously contributed their expertise and images for our book. Other readers, scholars and collectors have been particularly helpful: Jayne Amat, *Dato'* Anwar Faisul, Simon Cauchi, Simone Charles, Richard Davies, Hannah Field, Graham Furniss, John Hare, Susan Judah, Race Matthews, Barry Moser, Elethia Rackham, John Randle and Nicola Wilson have all made our work more pleasurable.

At the British Library, we would like to thank Robert Davies, Jon Crabb and Sally Nicholls within the Publishing Department, designer Briony Hartley, also copyeditor Louisa Watson and editor Carolyn Jones; the staff of the Reading Rooms and Imaging Services (for an enormous number of items to be photographed). Thanks to all; the mistakes, as ever, are our own.

Additional Picture Credits

All works illustrated are reproduced by kind permission of their owners. Unless otherwise specified, images are © The British Library Board. Every attempt has been made to trace copyright holders and we apologise for any unwitting omissions. Specific additional acknowledgements are as follows:

© Alamy: pp. 82 (Heritage Image Partnership Ltd); 83 left; 125, 242 (INTERFOTO collection/ Alamy Stock Photo)

Andrea Davis Kronlund/National Library of Sweden: p. 63

BBH Labs/ Penguin Digital /Penguin Books Ltd: p. 247

Bodleian Library, University of Oxford: pp. 55, 105

Collection Ana Maria Ortega; photo © Álvaro Guttiérrez: pp. 51, 64–5, 68–9

Courtesy of Lorna Macphee: p.143

General Research Division, The New York Public Library, Astor, Lenox and Tilden Foundations: p. 83 right

© Getty Images: pp. 24 (Gene Lester/Archive Photos); 28 (Werner Forman/Universal Images Group); 49 (Carl de Souza/AFP); 196 (Drew Angerer/Getty Images News); 220 (Popperfoto/ Getty Images); 246 (William Sumits/The LIFE Picture Collection)

Great Ormond Street Hospital Children's Charity (GOSHCC): p.176

Heidelberg University Library (Creative Commons licence CC-BY-SA 3.0): p.77

The J. Paul Getty Museum, Los Angeles (open access): p. 71

© Museum of London, p.57 right

Royal Collection Trust © HM Queen Elizabeth II 2017; Illustrated by Queen Victoria; Doll animations by Felix Petruška; Designed by Duška Karanov; Project Manager Debbie Bibo: p. 50

Sangster's Book Stores Limited, Kingston (Ja.): p. 47 left

© 2017 Scala, Florence/ Photo The Morgan Library & Museum: pp. 126, 133

SOAS University of London. Photo Erich Kesse: p. 66

Special Collections, University of Virginia, Charlottesville, VA: pp. 170–71

Wellcome Images, London (Creative Commons Attribution only licence CC BY 4.0): p.113 right

Yale Center for British Art, Paul Mellon Collection (open access): pp. 70, 85 right

Copyrights

Edward Ardizzone artwork from *The Little Book Room* by Eleanor Farjeon (OUP, 1963), *Little Tim and the Brave Sea Captain* © Edward Ardizzone (OUP, 1936); and *Stig of the Dump* by Clive King (Puffin Books, 1963). Permission granted by the Ardizzone Estate: pp. 211, 238, 239

ASTERIX®- OBELIX® / © 2017 LES EDITIONS ALBERT RENE / GOSCINNY – UDERZO: p. 256

Pauline Baynes – THE LION, THE WITCH AND THE WARDROBE by C.S. Lewis copyright © C.S. Lewis Pte. Ltd, 1950. Illustration by Pauline Baynes © copyright CS Lewis Pte Ltd, 1950. Reprinted by permission: p. 213

Pearl Binder by permission of Pearl Binder's children: p.2 32

Quentin Blake © by kind permission of United Agents on behalf of Quentin Blake: p. 241

Nandalal Bose by permission of Visva-Bharati: p. 66

Eric Carle *The Very Hungry Caterpillar* by Eric Carle. Copyright ©1969 and 1987 by Eric Carle. All rights reserved. Used with Permission: p. 260

John Dumayne. *Woodworking for Children*. Puffin Picture Books, no. 57 (1945) © Penguin Books Ltd: p. 235

Jean Elder by permission of the artist's estate: p. 210

James Gardner, *The War in the Air*. Puffin Picture Books, no. 3 (1940) © Penguin Books Ltd: p. 234

May Gibbs © The Northcott Society and the Cerebral Palsy Alliance, 2017: p.194

Duncan Grant © Estate of Duncan Grant. All rights reserved, DACS 2017: p. 38

Kathleen Hale by kind permission of Michael Parkin Fine Art: p. 143

Reginald Heade by kind permission of Telos Publishing: p. 207

Faith Jaques © the estate of the artist: p. 240

Tove Jansson ©Moomin Characters™: p. 254–55

Susan Judah by kind permission of the artist: p. 46

Judith Kerr © Copyright Kerr-Kneale Productions Limited: p. 259

Joan Kiddell-Munroe by kind permission of Oxford University Press: p.147

Dorothy Kunhardt © Courtesy of The Meserve-Kunhardt Foundation: p. 22

Ladybird Books: *Tiny Tots Travels*, Courtesy Ladybird Books Ltd; *Julius Caesar and Roman Britain*, © Ladybird Books Ltd, 1959; *Helping at Home. (Ladybird 1966 ITA edition)* © Ladybird Books Ltd, 1966, *The Computer. Ladybird Book How It Works Series* (654) © Ladybird Books Ltd, 1972: pp. 226–27

Enid Marx © the Enid Marx Estate, by kind permission: p. 230

Barry Moser by kind permission of the artist: p. 163

William Nicholson © Desmond Banks: p. 138

Kay Nielsen, with the agreement of Hodder & Stoughton Limited: p.181

Pixie O'Harris © reproduced by permission: p. 195

Ellen Raskin © the Estate of Ellen Raskin, the author and publishers: p. 218

Gwen Raverat © Estate of Gwen Raverat. All rights reserved, DACS 2017: p. 43

Joan G. Robinson © 1953 by Joan G. Robinson reproduced by kind permission of Deborah Sheppard c/o Caroline Sheldon Literary Agency Ltd: p. 145

E. H. Shepard line illustrations copyright © E. H. Shepard. Reproduced with permission of Curtis Brown Group Ltd on behalf of the Shepard Trust: pp. 140–41

Edward Steichen © The Estate of Edward Steichen / ARS, NY and DACS, London 2017: p. 20

Margaret Tempest © The Society of Authors as the Literary Representative of the Alison Uttley Literary Property Trust, and the Estate of Margaret Tempest, p. 139

Walter Trier © by permission of the artist's estate: p. 228

Ingrid Vang Nyman © by kind permission of Rabén & Sjögren, Stockholm: p. 216

Jack B Yeats © Estate of Jack B Yeats. All rights reserved, DACS 2017: p. 40

INDEX